George Birkbeck Hill

Footsteps of Dr. Johnson

George Birkbeck Hill

Footsteps of Dr. Johnson

ISBN/EAN: 9783743342231

Manufactured in Europe, USA, Canada, Australia, Japa

Cover: Foto ©ninafisch / pixelio.de

Manufactured and distributed by brebook publishing software (www.brebook.com)

George Birkbeck Hill

Footsteps of Dr. Johnson

FOOTSTEPS OF DR. JOHNSON

> "'Tis pleasant through the loop-holes of retreat
> To peep at such a world."

Footsteps of Dr. Johnson

(SCOTLAND)

BY

GEORGE BIRKBECK HILL, D.C.L.

PEMBROKE COLLEGE, OXFORD

WITH ILLUSTRATIONS BY LANCELOT SPEED

LONDON:
SAMPSON LOW, MARSTON, SEARLE & RIVINGTON
(LIMITED)
St. Dunstan's House, Fetter Lane
1890.

CHISWICK PRESS:—C. WHITTINGHAM AND CO., TOOKS COURT,
CHANCERY LANE, LONDON.

TO

The Prior and Members

OF

The Johnson Club,

(MOST CLUBABLE OF MEN)

IN MEMORY OF

PLEASANT EVENINGS SPENT WITH THEM IN

FLEET STREET, LICHFIELD, AND OXFORD,

This Work is Dedicated.

PREFACE.

T the beginning of last year, at the request of Messrs. Sampson Low and Co., I began to prepare a work in which, under the title of *Footsteps of Dr. Johnson*, I was to describe the various places that he had either inhabited or visited. It was to be copiously illustrated with views. I had made considerable progress with my task when I saw that its extent required that it should be divided into two separate works. Scotland in itself afforded ample materials for at least a single volume. In this opinion I was confirmed by my friend Mr. Lancelot Speed, the artist who was to prepare the illustrations. My publishers yielded to our advice and allowed us to confine ourselves entirely to that country. The materials which I had got together for England and Wales I have put on one side, in the hope that the present venture will prove sufficiently successful to encourage author, artist, and publishers alike to follow it up with a companion work.

Of Johnson's journey through Scotland we have three different accounts, his *Letters to Mrs. Thrale*, his *Journey to the Western Islands*, and Boswell's *Journal of a Tour to the Hebrides*. In writing his *Journey* he may have had before him the letters which he had written on the spot. Many interesting circumstances, however, which he mentioned in them he omitted in his formal narrative. Boswell's *Journal*, though published ten years after Johnson's work, was written first; and it was not only written, but it was published before the publication of the *Letters*. His single account, therefore, and Johnson's two accounts are independent narratives. It would have been easy to weave all three together into one work, and to have done nothing more. It went, however, against the grain with me to make a mixture of that sort. The plan which I have pursued has been much more laborious; but it will, I trust, commend itself both to "the gentle reader"—who is, I take it, a somewhat indolent reader—and also to the student of the manners and customs of a past age. Of all history there was no part which Johnson held equal in value to the history of manners. With this judgment my own taste leads me to agree. I take far greater interest in the daily life, the briars and roses of the working-day world as it was known to our forefathers, than in all the conquests of Chatham and of Clive. I have made, therefore, the attempt to bring before my readers the Scotland which Johnson saw, the Scotland which he had expressly come to study. "The wild objects" which he said he wished to see I have not neglected, but here I trust chiefly to Mr. Speed's art. "The peculiar manners" which interested him far more than natural objects have been my special study. Even before I took the present work in hand I had examined them somewhat closely; but last summer, on my return from Scotland, in a quiet recess of the Bodleian Library, I carried my inquiries a good deal farther. In covering so large an extent of ground and in such a mass of details it is idle to hope that no error has been made. I can honestly say that I have done my best to be accurate.

The country which Johnson traversed is famous for other footsteps besides his. I have called in the earlier and later travellers to add interest to the scene, and I have thrown in anecdotes with a liberal hand. "I love anecdotes," he said. To Boswell's descriptions of the men with whom he associated I have often been able to add a great deal from memoirs and other books to which that writer had not access; I have gathered some few traditions of the *Sassenach mohr*, the big Englishman, which still linger in the Highlands and the Hebrides.

The tour in which I followed his course I was forced to divide into two parts. Beginning at Inverness I went first through the Western Highlands and the Hebrides, and so southwards through Glasgow to Auchinleck, Boswell's home in Ayrshire. Later on I visited Edinburgh and its neighbourhood, and completed my task by going northwards to Inverness. I mention this to guard against any apparent inaccuracy in dates which might be discovered in my narrative. I cannot pretend to have seen every place which Johnson saw; but those spots which I passed by are few in number. In the former part of my trip I was fortunate enough to have Mr. Speed for my companion; but over the latter part of the ground we had, to my regret, to travel at different times. Like Boswell he had done much "to counteract the inconveniences of travel."

I have the pleasant duty of expressing my acknowledgments for the kindness with which I was received and for the assistance which was given me in my inquiries. Most of all am I indebted to the Rev. Roderick Macleod, of Macleod, Vicar of Bolney, who, by the numerous introductions with which he honoured me, greatly facilitated my progress in the Isle of Skye. To his father Macleod of Macleod, and his aunt, Miss Macleod of Macleod, I am under great obligations. My thanks are due also to the Duke of Argyle; the Earl of Cawdor; the Earl of Erroll; Sir Charles Dalrymple, of New Hailes; Captain Burnett, of Monboddo House; Mr. Macleane of Lochbuie; Mr. John Lorne Stewart, Laird of Coll; Mr. J. Maitland Anderson, Librarian of the University of St. Andrews; Mr. G. J. Campbell, of Inverness; Mr. P. M. Cran, the City Chamberlain, and Mr. William Gordon, the Town Clerk of Aberdeen; Mr. Lachlan Mackintosh, of Old Lodge, Elgin; Dr. Paterson, of Clifton Bank, St. Andrews; Professor Stephenson, of the University of Aberdeen; Mr. A. E. Stewart, of Raasay; and to my friend Mr. G. J. Burch, B.A., Librarian of the Institution of Civil Engineers, for some time the Compiler of the Subject Catalogue in the Bodleian Library.

To my friend, General Cadell, C.B., of Cockenzie House, I owe the sketches of the ruins of Ballencrieff, and of a group of ash-trees which were said to have been planted on Johnson's suggestion.

Both at Inverary Castle and at Dunvegan Castle I was allowed to have photographs taken not only of the rooms, but also of the interesting portraits of the former owners who had been Johnson's hosts.

To the Rev. Alexander Matheson, minister of Glenshiel, who came many miles over the mountains to help me with his knowledge as a local antiquary, I am, alas! too late in bringing my acknowledgments It was with great regret that early in the spring I learnt of the sudden death of this amiable man.

I have once more the pleasure of giving my thanks to Mr. G. K. Fortescue, Superintendent of the Reading Room of the British Museum, who does so much to lighten the labours of the student.

Should any of my readers be able to add to the traditions of Johnson which I have collected, or to throw light on any of the questions which I have investigated I trust that they will honour me with their communications. Hope comes to all, and a second edition of these *Footsteps* is within the range of possibility. In it their kindness shall meet with proper acknowledgment.

G. B. H.

OXFORD; *July 4th, 1890.*

TITLES OF MOST OF THE WORKS QUOTED IN THIS BOOK.

The date in each case shows, not the year of the original publication, but of the edition to which I have referred.

An Act for Abolishing the Heveditable Jurisdictions. 1747.
An Act to Amend the Disarming Act of the 19 Geo. II., made in the 21 Geo. II. Edinburgh, 1748.
Annual Register.
Armstrong, Mostyn J. *An Actual Survey of the great Post-Roads between London and Edinburgh.* 2nd ed. 1783.
Arnot, Hugo. *History of Edinburgh.* Edinburgh. 1st ed. 1779; 2nd ed. 1788.

Beattie, James. *Essays on Poetry and Music.* 3rd ed. London, 1779. *Scotticisms.* Edinburgh, 1787. *Life,* by Sir William Forbes. London, 1824.
Berkeley, George Monck. *Poems.* London, 1797.
Boswell, Sir Alexander. *Songs chiefly in the Scottish Dialect.* Edinburgh, 1803. (Published anonymously.)
Boswell, James. *Life of Johnson and Journal of a Tour to the Hebrides,* ed. by J. W. Croker, 1 vol., 8vo, 1848; and by G. B. Hill, 6 vols., Oxford, 1887. *Journal of a Tour to the Hebrides,* ed. by R. Carruthers. *Letters to the Rev. W. J. Temple.* London, 1857. *Boswelliana,* ed. by Charles Rogers. London, 1874. *Correspondence with the Hon. Andrew Erskine,* ed. by G. B. Hill. London, 1879.
Buchanan, J. L. *Travels in the Western Highlands from 1782 to 1790.*

Camden, William. *Description of Scotland.* Edinburgh, 1695.
Carlyle, Rev. Dr. Alexander, *Autobiography.* Edinburgh, 1860.
Carlyle, Thomas. *Early Letters,* ed. by C. E. Norton. 2 vols. London, 1886. *Reminiscences,* ed. by J. A. Froude. London, 1881.
Castellated and Domestic Architecture of Scotland, by David Macgibbon and Thomas Ross. 3 vols. Edinburgh, 1887-9.
Chalmers, George. *Life of Thomas Ruddiman.* London and Edinburgh, 1794.
Chambers, Robert. *Traditions of Edinburgh.* London and Edinburgh, 2 vols., 1825; 1 vol., 1869. *History of the Rebellion in Scotland,* 1745. 2 vols. Constable's *Miscellany,* 1827.

TITLES OF WORKS QUOTED

Cockburn, Lord. *Life of Lord Jeffrey.* 2 vols. Edinburgh, 1852. *Memorials of His Time.* 1 vol. 1856.
Court and City Register for 1769. London.
Cox, G. V. *Recollections of Oxford.* London, 1868.
Creech, William. *Letters respecting the Trade, Manners, &c., of Edinburgh.* (Published anonymously.) Edinburgh, 1793.
Croker, John Wilson. *Correspondence and Diaries,* ed. by L. J. Jennings. London, 1884.

D'Arblay, Mme. *Diary.* 7 vols. London, 1842. *Memoirs of Dr. Burney.* 3 vols. London, 1832.
Defoe, Daniel. *Tour through the whole Island of Great Britain by a Gentleman.* Vol. 3. London, 1727.
Douglas, Francis. *A General Description of the East Coast of Scotland.* Paisley, 1782.
Dunbar, E. D. *Social Life in Former Days.* 2 vols. Edinburgh, 1865-6.

Edinburgh Chronicle, or Universal Intelligencer for 1759-60.
Edinburgh. *The City Cleaned and Country Improven.* Edinburgh, 1760.
Edinburgh Directory for 1773-4, by Peter Williamson. Reprint, William Brown. Edinburgh, 1889.
Edinburgh. *History and Statutes of the Royal Infirmary of Edinburgh,* 1749. *Regulations for the Workhouse.* Edinburgh, 1750. For the History of Edinburgh, see ARNOT, and for *Letters from Edinburgh,* see TOPHAM.
Eldon, *Life of Lord Chancellor.* By Horace Twiss. 2 vols. 1846.
Essay upon Feudal Holdings, Superiorities, and Hereditary Jurisdictions in Scotland. London, 1747.
Excursion to the Lakes in Westmoreland and Cumberland in 1773. London, 1774.

Forster, John. *Life of Oliver Goldsmith.* 2 vols. London, 1871.
Garnett, T. M. D. *Observations on a Tour through the Highlands, &c.* 2 vols. London, 1800.
Garrick, David. *Private Correspondence.* 2 vols. London, 1831.
Gentleman's Magazine.
Gibbon, Edward. *Miscellaneous Works.* 5 vols. London, 1814.
Gilpin, William. *Observations relative chiefly to Picturesque Beauty made in the year 1776.* London, 1789.
Grant, Sir Alexander. *The Story of the University of Edinburgh.* 2 vols. London, 1884.
Gray, Thomas. *Works,* ed. by the Rev. J. Mitford. 5 vols. London, 1858.
Grierson, James. *Delineations of St. Andrews.* Edinburgh, 1807.

Henderson, Andrew. *The Edinburgh History of the late Rebellion of 1745-6.* 4th ed. London, 1752. *Considerations on the Scots Militia,* 1761.
Hervey, John, Lord. *Memoirs.* 2 vols. London.
Home, John. *Works.* 3 vols. Edinburgh, 1822.
Howard, John. *State of the Prisons in England and Wales.* Warrington, 1777.
Hughes, Michael. *A Plain Narrative of the late Rebellion by Michael Hughes, A Volunteer from the City of London.* London, 1747.
Hume, David. *History of England,* 8 vols. London, 1773. *Letters to William Strahan,* ed. by G. B. Hill. Oxford, 1888. *Life,* by J. H. Burton. 2 vols. Edinburgh, 1846.

Irving, Joseph. *The Book of Dumbartonshire.* 3 vols. Edinburgh, 1879.

Johnson, Samuel. *Letters.* Published by H. L. Piozzi. 2 vols. London, 1788. *Works.* 11 vols. Oxford, 1825.

TITLES OF WORKS QUOTED.

Journey through Part of England and Scotland with the Army. By a Volunteer. 1747.

Kames, Lord. *Life and Writings.* 2 vols. Edinburgh, 1807. *Sketches of the History of Man.* 3 vols. Edinburgh, 1807.

Knox, John. *A Tour through the Highlands, &c., in 1786.* London, 1787.

Letters from a Gentleman in the North of Scotland. 2 vols. London, 1754.
Letters on Iceland, &c., by Uno von Troill, D.D. London, 3rd ed., 1783.
London and its Environs. 6 vols. London, 1761.

Macaulay, Thomas Babington (Lord Macaulay). *Miscellaneous Writings and Speeches.* London, 1871. *Life,* by Sir George Trevelyan. 2 vols. London, 1877.
Mackintosh, Sir James. *Memoirs of his Life.* 2 vols. London, 1836.
Macky, J. *A Journey through Scotland.* London, 1723.
Malmesbury, First Earl of. *Letters.* 4 vols. London, 1844.
Marchmont Papers. London, 1831.
Martin, M. *A Description of the Western Islands.* 2nd ed. 1716.
M'Nicol, Rev. Donald. *Remarks on Dr. Johnson's Journey to the Hebrides.* Glasgow, 1817.
Modern Scottish Minstrel. Edited by C. Rogers. 1870.
Monboddo, Lord, (James Burnet). *Ancient Metaphysics.* 6 vols. Edinburgh, 1779-99. *Origin and Progress of Languages.* 6 vols. Edinburgh, 1773-92.

Pennant, Thomas. *Tour in Scotland,* London, 1772. *Voyage to the Hebrides.* London, 1774-76.
Paterson, Daniel. *British Itinerary.* 2 vols. London, 1800.
Present State of Scotland. London, 1738.

Quarterly Review, No. 71. Article on John Home, by Sir Walter Scott.

Ray, James. *A Compleat History of the Rebellion.* Bristol, 1752.
Rogers, Samuel, *Early Life of,* by P. W. Clayden. London, 1887.
Ruskin, John. *Lectures on Architecture and Painting.* London, 1854.

Sacheverell, William. *An Account of the Isle of Man.* London, 1702.
Saint-Fond, Faujas B. *Voyage en Angleterre, en Ecosse, et aux Iles Hebrides.* 2 vols. Paris, 1797.
Scotland and Scotsmen in the Eighteenth Century, from the MSS. of John Ramsay of Ochtertyre. By A. Allardyce. 2 vols. Edinburgh and London, 1888.
Scots Magazine. Edinburgh.
Scott, Sir Walter. *Novels.* 41 vols. Edinburgh, 1860. *Life,* by J. G. Lockhart. 10 vols. Edinburgh, 1839.
Scottish Minstrel. Edited by the Rev. C. Rogers. Edinburgh, 1870.
Scottish Notes and Queries. Aberdeen, 1888.
Selwyn, George, and his Contemporaries. 4 vols. London, 1882.
Smith, Adam. *Wealth of Nations.* 3 vols. London, 1811.
Smollett, Tobias. *History of England.* 5 vols. London, 1800. *Humphry Clinker.* 3 vols. 4th ed. London, 1792.
Speeches, &c., in the Douglas Cause, by a Barrister-at-Law. London, 1767.
St. Andrews. As it was and as it is. 3rd ed. 1838.
Stockdale, Rev. Percival. *Memoirs.* London, 1809.
Storer, J. and H. S. *Views in Edinburgh.* Edinburgh, 1820.
Survey of the Province of Moray. Aberdeen, 1798.
Swift, Jonathan. *Works.* 24 vols. London, 1803.

TITLES OF WORKS QUOTED.

Thicknesse, Philip. *Observations on the Customs of the French Nation.* London, 1766.

Topham, Edward. *Letters from Edinburgh.* London, 1776 (Published anonymously.)

Walpole, Horace. *Memoirs of the Reign of George II.* 3 vols. London, 1846 ; *Journal of the Reign of King George III.* 2 vols. London, 1859. *Memoirs of the Reign of King George III.* 4 vols. London, 1845. *Letters.* 9 vols. London, 1861-6.

Wesley, John. *Journals.* 4 vols. London, 1830.

Wolfe, Major-General James. *Life,* by Robert Wright. London, 1864.

Wordsworth, William. *Works.* 6 vols. London, 1857.

LIST OF FULL PAGE ILLUSTRATIONS AND MAP.

PORTRAIT OF DR. JOHNSON, AFTER REYNOLDS	frontispiece
STAFFA	facing page 24
LOCH NESS	,, ,, 28
INCH KEITH	,, ,, 84
MONTROSE	,, ,, 104
FINDLATER	,, ,, 130
THE FIDDLER'S WALK, CAWDOR	,, ,, 142
FOYERS	,, ,, 150
THE MORISTON RIVER	,, ,, 152
MAM RATTACHAN	,, ,, 164
BERNERA BARRACKS, GLENELG	,, ,, 166
CORRICHATACHIN, NEAR BROADFORD, SKYE	,, ,, 168
RAASAY CASTLE	,, ,, 172
DUNVEGAN CASTLE	,, ,, 184
ISLAND ISA	,, ,, 200
THE CUCHULLIN HILLS, FROM THE CAVE ON WIA ISLAND, SKYE	,, ,, 204
McLEOD'S MAIDENS, SKYE	,, ,, 206
SLIGACHAN, THE CUCHULLIN HILLS, SKYE	,, ,, 210
COLL ISLAND	,, ,, 216
SANDILAND	,, ,, 224
LOCHBUY	,, ,, 232
BEN CRUACHAN, FROM THE HILL ABOVE OBAN	,, ,, 244
TREES AT BALLENCRIEFF, PLANTED AT DR. JOHNSON'S SUGGESTION	,, ,, 300
FACSIMILE LETTER	,, ,, 308
ROUTE MAP OF SCOTLAND	,, ,, 318

LIST OF TEXT ILLUSTRATIONS.

	PAGE
Dr. Johnson's Bedroom, Dunvegan	1
Mam Rattachan	3
Sound of Ulva	5
Glencroe	13
Armidale	23
Loch Ness, near Foyers	27
Loch Lomond	31
The Tolbooth	55
Hume's House	57
White Horse Close	70
James's Court	73
The Old Library	84
St. Leonard's College	89
St. Andrews	93
West Door, St. Andrews	96
Golf at St. Andrews	98
St. Mary's College Library	101
Leuchars	103
View on the Tay	104
Aberbrothick	106
On the Way to Montrose	108
Gardenston Arms	109
Monboddo	114
King's College, Aberdeen	121
Marischal College	122
Ellon	124
Slains Castle	126
The Bullers of Buchan	128
Elgin	131
Elgin Cathedral	133
Fores	134
Cawdor	136
Penance-Ring, Cawdor Church	137
Drawbridge, Cawdor Castle	138
Cawdor Castle	139

LIST OF ILLUSTRATIONS.

xvii

	PAGE
VAULT, CAWDOR CASTLE	140
TAPESTRY CHAMBER, CAWDOR CASTLE	141
DUNGARDIE, A VITRIFIED FORT NEAR FOYERS	148
LOCH NESS	149
MAP OF FOYERS	150
INVERMORISTON	152
THE RUINS OF THE HOUSE AT ANOCH	153
THATCHED HOUSE	154
CLUNIE	157
EILAN DONAN	158
GLEN SHIEL BATTLE-FIELD	159
FAOCHAG	160
SKYE, FROM GLENELG	166
THE SOUND OF SLATE	167
CORRICHATACHIN	170
RAASAY	175
DUN CAN	178
PORTREE HARBOUR	180
KINGSBURGH	181
THE FERRY TO KINGSBURGH	184
RORIE MORE'S NURSE	186
WATERGATE, DUNVEGAN	192
DINING ROOM, DUNVEGAN	193
PORTRAIT OF SARAH, LADY MACLEOD, BY RAEBURN	194
RORIE MORE'S HORN	195
" " ARMOUR	196
MACLEOD'S TABLES	197
TERRACE, DUNVEGAN	199
HERONRY	200
SACRAMENT SUNDAY	201
A CROFTER'S HUT IN SKYE	203
TALISKER HEAD AND ORCESAY	204
LANDING PLACE, TALISKER	207
VIEW OF TALISKER	208
ON THE ROAD TO SCONSER	212
SAILING PAST THE ISLE OF RUM	213
ARDNAMURCHAN POINT	214
COL	215
COL: THE LAIRD'S HOUSE	216
COLVAY	217
LOCH NA KEAL	219
INCHKENNETH CHAPEL	223
MACKINNON'S CAVE	225
MULL	227
RUINS IN IONA	231
CARSAIG ARCHES: MULL	232
KERRERA ISLAND	243
DUNOLLY CASTLE, OBAN	244
INVERARY CASTLE	246

	PAGE
Elizabeth Gunning	247
Johnson's Host	248
The Avenue of Beeches	249
The Hall, Inverary Castle	250
The Old Dining Room	251
Tapestry Bedroom	252
"Rest, and be Thankful"	254
Milestones on the Tarbet Road	255
Rosedew	256
Inch Galbraith	257
Yew Tree Island	258
Cameron	260
Smollett's Pillar	261
Dunbarton	262
Dundonald Castle	267
Old Auchans	269
Dining Room at Old Auchans	270
Auchinleck	273
New Hailes	291
Library, New Hailes	295
Ballencrieff	301
Hawthornden	305

INTRODUCTION.

 A TRAVELLER who passed through the Hebrides in the year 1786 recorded that in many houses he was given the room to sleep in which had been occupied by Dr. Johnson.[1] Twenty-eight years later, when Sir Walter Scott with some of his friends landed in Skye, it was found on inquiry that the first thought which had come into each man's mind was of Johnson's Latin Ode to Mrs. Thrale.[2] The Highlanders at Dunvegan, Scott goes on to say, saw about Johnson there was something worthy of respect, "they could not tell what, and long spoke of him as the *Sassenach mohr*, or big Englishman."[3] He still lives among them, mainly, no doubt, by his own and Boswell's books, but partly also by tradition. Very few of the houses remain where he visited. Nevertheless, in

DR. JOHNSON'S BEDROOM, DUNVEGAN.

two of these in the Hebrides, and in one in the Lowlands, I was shown his bedroom. Proud, indeed, would the old man have been

---

[1] John Knox's *Tour through the Highlands*, pp. 77, 132.
[2] Croker's *Boswell*, p. 514.
[3] Croker's *Correspondence*, ii. 325; Croker's *Boswell*, p. 499.

could he have foreseen that an Englishman who followed on his steps one hundred and sixteen years later would be shown at New Hailes, at Rasay, and at Dunvegan, "Dr. Johnson's Chamber." At Rasay is preserved his walking-stick—not the famous "piece of timber" which was destined for some museum, but was stolen or lost in Mull, but one which he had occasionally used. In his bedroom an engraving of him hangs on the wall. The china tea-set out of which he had drunk is preserved by a descendant of the laird who was his host. At Dunvegan his portrait is set up in a post of honour in the noble drawing-room of the famous old castle, and his autograph letter to Macleod of Macleod rests among the ancient memorials of that still more ancient family. That it is endorsed "Dr. Johnston's Letter" may be twisted into a compliment. So popular was he that his very name was "Scottified."

In many places I found traditions of him still remaining—some, no doubt, true; others false. But whether false or true, by their vitality they show the deep mark which the man made as he passed along. In Glenmorison there are countryfolk who profess to know by the report of their forefathers the "clear rivulet" in "the narrow valley, not very flowery but sufficiently verdant," where Johnson reposed on "a bank such as a writer of romance might have delighted to feign, and first conceived the thought of the narration" of his tour.[1] In a farmhouse on Loch Duich, just below the mountain which exhausted his patience and good-humour, and nearly exhausted his strength, I was told of the speech which he made as he reached the top of the pass. "He turned as he was beginning the descent, and said to the mountain, 'Good-bye, Ma'am Rattachan, I hope never to see your face again.'"[2] From Rasay a friendly correspondent wrote to tell me how the great man had climbed up Dun Can, the highest mountain in the island, and had danced on the top. I have pointed out that it was Boswell and not Johnson who performed this feat, but the tradition, doubtless, will linger on. At Dunvegan Miss Macleod of Macleod, who remembers her grandmother, Johnson's hostess, and her aunts, "the four daughters, who knew all the arts of southern elegance, and all the modes of English economy,"[3] has preserved some traditions more worthy of trust.

---

[1] Johnson's *Works*, ix. 36.
[2] Johnson calls this mountain "Ratiken;" Boswell, "the Rattakin." It is known as Mam-Rattachan. *Mam* signifies *a mountain pass or chasm*. See Blackie's *Etymological Geography* (ed. 1875), p. 112.
[3] Johnson's *Works*, ix. 63.

"One day," she said, "he had scolded the maid for not getting good peats, and had gone out in the rain to the stack to fetch in some himself.[1] He caught a bad cold. Lady Macleod went up to his room to see how he was, and found him in bed, with his wig turned inside out, and the wrong end foremost, serving the purpose of 'a cap by night,' like the stocking of Goldsmith's *Author*. On her return to the drawing-room, she said, 'I have often seen very plain people, but anything as ugly as Dr. Johnson, with his wig thus stuck on, I never have seen.'[2] She was (her granddaughter added) greatly pleased with his talk, for she had seen enough of the world to enjoy it; but her daughters, who were still quite girls, disliked him much, and called him a bear."

At the inn at Broadford, sitting in the entrance-hall, I fell into talk with an elderly man, a retired exciseman, who lived close by. He, too, had his traditions of the *Sassenach mohr*. His father had known

MAM RATCAHAN.

---

[1] "The peats at Dunvegan, which were damp, Dr. Johnson called 'a sullen fuel.' Here a Scottish phrase was singularly applied to him. One of the company having remarked that he had gone out on a stormy evening, and brought in a supply of peats from the stack, old Mr. M'Sweyn said, 'that was *main souser*.'"—Boswell's *Johnson*, v. 303.

[2] See Boswell's *Johnson*, v. 214, for Boswell's account.

an old lady, blind of one eye, who was fond of telling how in her childhood, at the time of Johnson's visit, she had been watching the dancing in that famous farmhouse of Corrichatachin, where Boswell got so drunk one night over the punch, and so penitent the next morning over a severe headache and the Epistle for the Twentieth Sunday after Trinity.¹ A large brass button on the coat-tail of one of the dancers had struck her in her eye as he whirled round and had so injured it that she lost the sight. My informant had a story also to tell of the learned minister, the Rev. Donald Macqueen, who accompanied Johnson in part of his tour. "A crofter seeing the two men pass, asked the minister who was his companion. Macqueen replied, 'The man who made the English language.' 'Then he had very little to do,' rejoined the crofter; meaning, according to the Gaelic idiom, that he might have been much better employed." My friendly exciseman had known also an old lady who remembered Johnson coming to her father's house in Mull. According to a custom once very common in the Highlands, though even in those days passing fast away, she had been sent for three or four years to a shepherd's hut to be fostered. It was shortly after her return home that Johnson's visit was paid. He did not hide his displeasure at the roughness which still clung to her. She had not forgotten, moreover, how he found fault with the large candles, rudely made of pieces of old cloth twisted round and dipped in tallow.² My acquaintance ended his talk by saying: "If Dr. Johnson had returned to Scotland after publishing his book, he would have got a crack on his skull."

At Craignure, in the Isle of Mull, the landlord of the little inn had his story to tell of the untimely death of young Maclean of Col, that "amiable man," who, while the pages of Johnson's *Journey to the Western Islands* "were preparing to attest his virtues, perished in the passage between Ulva and Inch-Kenneth."³ My host's great-grandmother, a Macquarrie of Ulva, on the night when the boat was upset, had been watching the cattle near the fatal shore. An old woman who was to have been her companion had failed her, so that she was alone. She saw nothing, and heard no cries. "A

---

¹ Boswell's *Johnson*, v. 258.
² My informant placed the scene of this story at the house of a Captain or Colonel Campbell in Mull. There was a Mr. Campbell, one of the Duke of Argyle's tacksmen, or chief tenants, in that island, who furnished Boswell and Johnson with horses; but it is not mentioned that they went to his house—they certainly did not pass a night there. See Boswell's *Johnson*, v. 332, 340.
³ Johnson's *Works*, ix. 142.

half-witted person," my informant added, in a serious voice, "had warned one of the party not to go; but his warning was not heeded, and the man lost his life."

At Lochbuie two traditions, I found, had been preserved in the family of the laird, the great-grandson of that Maclean of Lochbuie whom Boswell had heard described as "a great roaring braggadocio," but found only "a bluff, comely, noisy old gentleman. He bawled out to Johnson (as Boswell tells us), 'Are you of the John-

SOUND OF ULVA.

stons of Glencroe or of Ardnamurchan?' Dr. Johnson gave him a significant look, but made no answer."[1] The report has come down in the family that Johnson replied that he was neither one nor the other. Whereupon Lochbuie cried out, "Damn it, Sir, then you must be a bastard." There can, I fear, be no doubt that this rejoinder belongs to those *excellens impromptus à loisir* in which Rousseau excelled[2]—that *esprit de l'escalier*, as the French describe it. If the laird, like Addison, could draw for a thousand pounds, he had, I suspect, but nine pence in ready money.[3] For had this repartee been made at the time, and not been merely an after-invention, Boswell most certainly would not have let it pass unre-

---

[1] Boswell's *Johnson*, v. 341.   [2] See *Les Confessions*, liv. iii.
[3] Boswell's *Johnson*, ii. 256.

corded. The second tradition is scarcely more trustworthy. Johnson at the tea-table, I was told, helped himself to sugar with his fingers, whereupon Lady Lochbuie at once had the basin emptied, and fresh sugar brought in. He said nothing at the time, but when he had finished his tea he flung down the cup, exclaiming that if he had polluted one he had also polluted the other. A lady of the family of Lochbuie, whose memory goes back ninety years, in recounting this story when I was in Scotland, added, "But I do not know whether it was true." That it was not true I have little doubt. In the first place, we have again Boswell's silence; in the second place, to the minor decencies of life Johnson was by no means inattentive. At Paris he was on the point of refusing a cup of coffee because the footman had put in the sugar with his fingers; and at Edinburgh, in a passion, he threw a glass of lemonade out of the window because it had been sweetened in the same manner by the waiter. In one of his letters to Mrs. Thrale he expressed his displeasure in Skye at the very practice with which he is charged a few weeks later in Mull. Describing his visit to the house of Sir Alexander Macdonald, he wrote : " The lady had not the common decencies of her tea-table : we picked up our sugar with our fingers." [1]

It is strange that while in Mull, that "most dolorous country," that "gloom of desolation," as Johnson described it, these stories of him are preserved, the boatman who took me across the narrow passage between it and Inch-Kenneth had no traditional knowledge of his host, Sir Allan Maclean, and of his retirement in that little island. To the forefathers of the men of Mull the head of the Macleans would have been an object of reverence and even of fear, and Johnson only a passing wonder. " I would cut my bones for him," said one of his clan, speaking of Sir Allan in Boswell's hearing.[2] But of the Highland chief who lived among them no remembrance remains, while the *Sassenach mohr*, who spent but a few days in the island-home of the Macleans, is still almost "a household word."

I was indeed surprised to find through the Highlands and the Hebrides how much he still remained in men's thoughts. On Loch Lomond, the boatman who rowed me to the islands on which he had landed, a man of reading and intelligence, said that though he had

[1] *Piozzi Letters*, i. 138.   [2] Boswell's *Johnson*, v. 337.

himself read Johnson's *Journey*, yet "Scotchmen still feel too sore to like reading him." Whatever soreness still lingers is, I have little doubt, much more due to his sarcasms recorded by Boswell than to any passages in his own narrative. But it is surprising that Scotchmen cannot more generally join in a hearty laugh at his humorous sallies, though they are at their own expense. That the Scotch of a hundred years and more ago were over-sensitive is not astonishing. At that time in most respects they were still far behind England. It was England that they were striving to follow in their arts, their commerce, and their agriculture. It was the English accent that they were striving to catch, and the English style in which they laboured to write. It was to the judgment of Englishmen that their authors, no small or inglorious band, anxiously appealed. That they should be sensitive to criticism beyond even the Americans of our day was not unnatural. For in the poverty of their soil, and the rudiments of their manufactures and trade, they found none of that boastful comfort which supports the citizen of the United States, even when he is most solicitous of English approbation. But at the present day, when they are in most respects abreast of Englishmen, and in some even ahead, they should disprove the charge that is brought against them of wanting humour by showing that they can enjoy a hearty laugh, even though it goes against them. Johnson's ill-humour did not go deep, and, no doubt, was often laughed away. Of that rancour which disgraced Hume his nature was wholly incapable. He wished no ill to Scotland as Hume wished ill to England.[1] "He returned from it," writes Boswell, " in great good-humour, with his prejudices much lessened, and with very grateful feelings of the hospitality with which he was treated."[2]

Not all Scotch critics were hostile towards him. The *Scots Magazine*, which last century was to Edinburgh what the *Gentleman's Magazine* was to London, always spoke of him with great respect. Writing of him early in the year in which he visited Scotland, it says:

"Dr. Johnson has long possessed a splendid reputation in the republic of letters, and it was honestly acquired. He is said to affect a singularity in his manners and to contemn the social rules which are established in the intercourse of civil life. If this extravagance is affected, it is a fault; if it has been acquired by the habitudes

---
[1] See *Letters of David Hume to William Strahan*, pp. 96, 114, 132.
[2] Boswell's *Johnson*, v. 20.

of his temper and his mistakes, it scarcely merits censure. We allow to the man who can soar so high above the multitude to descend sometimes beneath them."[1]

In the two reviews of his *Journey* in the same magazine, there is not one word of censure; neither when Boswell, eleven years later, brought out his account of the tour, had they any fault to find. In the character which they drew of Johnson on his death they leave unnoticed his attacks on Scotland. They are even generous in their praise. Speaking of his pension they say: "It would have been a national disgrace if such talents, distinguished by such writings, had met with no other recompense than the empty consciousness of fame."[2] There were also men of eminence in Scotland who at once acknowledged the merits of the book. "I love the benevolence of the author," said Lord Hailes.[3] The "virtuous and candid Dempster," the "patriotic Knox," Tytler, the historian, "a Scot, if ever a Scot there were," had each his word of high praise.[4] Sir Walter Scott, writing many years later, said: "I am far from being of the number of those angry Scotsmen who imputed to Johnson's national prejudices all or a great part of the report he has given of our country. I remember the Highlands ten or twelve years later, and no one can conceive of how much that could have been easily remedied travellers had to complain."[5]

These men, nevertheless, formed a small minority. The outcry that was raised against Johnson was at once loud and bitter. To attacks for many a long year he had been used, but yet this time he was startled. "He expressed his wonder at the extreme jealousy of the Scotch, and their resentment at having their country described as it really was."[6] Boswell mentions "the brutal reflections thrown out against him," and "the rancour with which he was assailed by numbers of shallow irritable North Britons."[7] How quickly the storm gathered and burst is shown in a letter written by an Englishman from Edinburgh a few days after the book was published:

"Edinburgh, Jan. 24, 1775. Dr. Johnson's *Tour* has just made its appearance here, and has put the country into a flame. Everybody finds some reason to be affronted. A thousand people who know not a single creature in the Western Isles interest themselves in their cause, and are offended at the accounts that are given of them. Newspapers, magazines, pamphlets, all teem with abuse of the Doctor.

---

[1] *Scot. Magazine*, 1773, p. 135.
[2] *Ib.* 1784, p. 685.
[3] Boswell's *Johnson*, v. 406.
[4] *Ib.* ii. 305-6.
[5] Croker's *Correspondence*, ii. 34.
[6] Boswell's *Johnson*, ii. 306.
[7] *Ib.* ii. 303-5.

He was received with the most flattering marks of civility by everyone. He was looked upon as a kind of miracle, and almost carried about for a show. Those who were in his company were silent the moment he spoke, lest they should interrupt him, and lose any of the good things he was going to say. He repaid all their attention to him with ill-breeding, and when in the company of the ablest men in this country, who are certainly his superiors in point of abilities, his whole design was to show them how contemptibly he thought of them. Had the Scotch been more acquainted with Dr. Johnson's private character they would have expected nothing better. A man of illiberal manners and surly disposition, who all his life long had been at enmity with the Scotch, takes a sudden resolution of travelling amongst them; not, according to his own account, 'to find a people of liberal and refined education, but to see wild men and wild manners.'"¹

The "patriotic Knox," as Boswell calls him, the author of *A Tour through the Highlands and Hebride Isles in* 1786, a man freer from prejudices than the common run, and one who readily acknowledged the merits of Johnson's book, bears equal witness to the wrath of his countrymen.

"Dr. Johnson (he writes) set out under incurable impressions of a national prejudice, a religious prejudice, and a literary jealousy. From a writer of such abilities and such prejudices the natives of Scotland had reason to expect a shower of arrows without mercy, and it was possibly from this prepossession that they were ready to fall upon him as one man the moment that his book appeared. Their minds were charged with sentiments of indignity, resentment and revenge, which they did not fail to discharge upon his head in whole platoons from every quarter."²

To us, who know Johnson better than we know any other author who has ever lived, the charge of literary jealousy seems ridiculous. But Knox lived before Boswell's *Life* was published. Scotland, in which learning and even literature had slumbered for nearly a century, had started up from her long sleep, and was bent on turning the Auld Reekie into the Modern Athens. All her geese were swans, though of swans she had at this season a fair flock. "Edinburgh is a hotbed of genius," wrote Smollett, shortly before Johnson's visit, and as a proof of it he instanced among "authors of the first distinction," Wallace, Blair, Wilkie, and Ferguson. Hume still earlier had proclaimed that at last there was

---

¹ *Letters from Edinburgh*, 1774-5, London, 1776, published without a name, but written by Captain Edward Topham, pp. 137-140. Arnot, in his *History of Edinburgh*, p. 384, after ridiculing Topham's statement, that golf is played on the top of Arthur' Seat, continues : " These letters are written with spirit and impartiality. But the facts and criticisms contained in them are for the most part equally ill-founded. Yet so candid is the author amidst his errors, that it is hard to say whether he is more erroneous when he speaks in praise or censure of the Scottish nation." It is possible and perhaps probable that he has exaggerated the ill-will against Johnson. The passage which he puts in quotation marks is not in the *Journey*.

Knox's *Tour*, p. lxvii.

"a hope of seeing good tragedies in the English language," for Johnny Home had written his *Douglas*. Wilkie of the *Epigoniad*, the great historian held, was to be the Homer, and Blacklock the Pindar, of Scotland.[1] But it was in Ossian Macpherson that the hopes of the country had at one time soared highest. By Dr. Blair, the Edinburgh Professor of Rhetoric, he had been ranked with Homer and Virgil.[2] The national pride, the honour of Scotland, was concerned, and the meanest motive was attributed to the man who had ventured to pronounce his poems an impudent forgery. Macpherson was a dangerous enemy. Against "the menaces of a ruffian" a thick cudgel might avail; but the secret arts of a literary forger were not so easily baffled. His position was one of great power, for from the Court he received a pension at first of £600 a year, and afterwards of £800, "to supervise the newspapers. He inserted what lies he pleased, and prevented whatever he disapproved of being printed."[3] It was from this tainted source that no doubt sprang many of "the miserable cavillings against the *Journey* in newspapers, magazines, and other fugitive pieces."[4] These, as Boswell tells us, "only furnished Johnson with sport." Nevertheless, though they did not trouble his mind, they marred the fame of his book, and prejudiced not only the immediate, but even the traditional judgment of Scotland. Enough dirt was thrown, and some of it did stick and sticks still. Lies were sent wandering through the land, and some of them have not even yet found their everlasting rest. One disgusting story, not unworthy of the inventive genius of Ossian himself, is still a solace to Scots of the baser sort. That it is a lie can be plainly proved, for it rests on a supposed constant suspicion in Johnson of the food provided for him. Now we know from his own writings that only twice in his tour had he "found any reason to complain of a Scottish table."[5] Moreover, in his letters to Mrs. Thrale and in Boswell's *Journal*, we can follow his course with great accuracy and minuteness. Had there been any foundation for this lie it must be found on the road between Inverness and the seashore. Now we know what meals he had at each station. Even in the miserable inn at Glenelg, where his accommodation was at its worst, if he had chosen he could have had mutton chops and freshly-killed poultry.

[1] Burton's *Life of Hume*, ii. 31.   [2] Boswell's *Johnson*, i. 396.
[3] Walpole's *Journal of the Reign of George III*, (ed. 1859), ii. 17, 483.
[4] Boswell's *Johnson*, ii. 307.   [5] Johnson's *Works*, ix. 19.

Finding both too tough, he supped on a lemon and a piece of bread.

The attacks of the angry critics, published as they were in fugitive pieces, might have been forgotten had they not been revived three or four years later in "a scurrilous volume," as Boswell justly describes it, "larger than Johnson's own, filled with malignant abuse under a name real or fictitious of some low man in an obscure corner of Scotland, though supposed to be the work of another Scotchman, who has found means to make himself well known both in Scotland and England."[1] The "low man" was the Rev. Donald M'Nicol, and the "obscure corner" that long and pleasant island of Lismore which the steamers skirt every summer day as they pass with their load of tourists between Oban and the entrance of the Caledonian Canal. M'Nicol's predecessor in the manse was the Rev. John Macaulay, whose famous grandson, Lord Macaulay, was to rebuke those "foolish and ignorant Scotchmen, who moved to anger by a little unpalatable truth which was mingled with much eulogy in the *Journey to the Western Islands*, assailed him whom they chose to consider as the enemy of their country with libels much more dishonourable to their country than anything that he had ever said or written."[2] When Johnson was shown M'Nicol's book he said: "This fellow must be a blockhead. They don't know how to go about their abuse. Who will read a five shilling book against me? No, Sir, if they had wit, they should have kept pelting me with pamphlets." The book, however, seems to have been widely read, and in the year 1817 was reprinted at Glasgow in a fine large type. A Scotch gentleman recently told me that he fears that to many of his countrymen Johnson's tour is only known through M'Nicol's attack.

It was Macpherson at whom Boswell aimed a blow when he wrote of the "other Scotchman whose work it was supposed to be." If Ossian had no hand in it himself, it was certainly written by someone fired with all his hatred of the man who had branded him as a forger. Johnson is described as "a man of some reputation for letters, whose master-passion was hatred of Scotland. When the *Poems of Ossian* were published, and became the delight and admiration of the learned over all Europe, his cynical disposition instantly took the alarm."[3] It was from this time that "we may

---

[1] Boswell's *Johnson*, ii. 308.
[2] Macaulay, *Miscellaneous Writings*, &c. Ibid., ii. 263-7.
1871, p. 390.
[3] *Remarks on Dr. Johnson's Journey to the*

date the origin of his intended tour to Scotland." It was from malice that he started so late in the year—a malice, by the way, which nearly brought him to a watery grave. "It was not beauties he went to find out in Scotland, but defects; and for the northern situation of the Hebrides the advanced time of the year suited his purpose best."¹ Johnson, with a discretion which other travellers in like circumstances would do well to imitate, had passed over Edinburgh with the remark that it is "a city too well known to admit description." This wise reticence is twisted into a proof of malevolence. So, too, is the brevity with which he mentions Dundee. "We stopped awhile at Dundee," he recorded, "where I remember nothing remarkable."² Surely this is a very innocent sentence. Even Boswell, whose record was generally far fuller, dismisses this place with three words. "We saw Dundee," he says.³ But M'Nicol at once discovered the miserable jealousy of the Englishman. "He passes very rapidly through the town of Dundee, for fear, I suppose, of being obliged to take notice of its increasing trade."⁴ How delicately Johnson treated this town in his published narrative is shown by his description of it in his private letter to Mrs. Thrale. To her he had written: "We came to Dundee, a dirty despicable town."⁵ Much as M'Nicol belaboured Johnson, he could not refrain from claiming him as of Scotch origin. "We are much deceived by fame," he wrote, "if a very near ancestor of his, who was a native of that country, did not find to his cost that a tree was not quite such a rarity in his days."⁶ This mysterious hero of the gallows was no doubt no Johnson at all, but a Johnston—of Ardnamurchan, probably, or of Glencoe.⁷

M'Nicol is ingenious in his treatment of the great Ossian controversy. "The poems," he says, "must be the production either of Ossian or Mr. Macpherson. Dr. Johnson does not vouchsafe to tell us who else was the author, and consequently the national claim remains perfectly entire. The moment Mr. Macpherson ceases to be admitted as a translator, he instantly acquires a title to the original."⁸ Granted that he was a ruffian who had tried by menaces to hinder the detection of a cheat. What of that? He was a great original ruffian, and his cheat was a work of great

---

¹ *Remarks on Dr. Johnson's Journey to the Hebrides,* p. 270.
² Johnson's *Works,* ix. 8.
³ Boswell's *Johnson,* v. 71.
⁴ *M'Nicol,* p. 287.

⁵ *Piozzi Letters,* i. 114.
⁶ *M'Nicol,* p. 273.
⁷ See *ante,* p. 5.
⁸ *M'Nicol,* p. 266.

original genius. So that Caledonia, if she had one forger the more, had not one poet the less. She made up in genius what she lost in character. But this Dr. Johnson failed to see, being, poor man, "naturally pompous and vain, and ridiculously ambitious of an exclusive reputation in letters." It must have been this same pom-

GLENCOE.

posity, vanity, and ambition which led him to say of these poems : "Sir, a man might write such stuff for ever, if he would *abandon* his mind to it."[1]

That Johnson's narrative should have roused resentment is not surprising. Even his friend Beattie, "much as he loved and revered him," yet found in it "some asperities that seem to be the effect of national prejudice."[2] That "this true-born Englishman," as Boswell delights to call him, should have given a wholly unpre-

---

[1] Boswell's *Johnson*, iv. 183. [2] *Ib.* ii. 435, n. 1, and Forbes's *Life of Beattie*, p. 218.

judiced account of any country not his own was an impossibility. As regards Scotland, the position which he took certainly admitted of justification. "When I find," he said, "a Scotchman to whom an Englishman is as a Scotchman, that Scotchman shall be as an Englishman to me."[1] Boswell, and perhaps Boswell alone, exactly answered this requirement, and the two men were fast friends. For many other Scotchmen, indeed, he had strong feelings of regard, and even of friendship—for Andrew Millar the bookseller, for William Strahan the printer, for Blair, Beattie, John Campbell, Hailes, and Robertson, among authors, and for his poor assistants in the great work of his Dictionary, who all came from across the Tweed. There was no want of individual affection, no John Bull disinclination that had to be overcome in the case of each fresh acquaintance which he made. His "was a prejudice of the head and not of the heart."[2] He held that the Scotch, with that clannishness which is found in almost equal strength in the outlying parts of the whole island, in Cornwall and in Cumberland, achieved for themselves in England "a success which rather exceeded the due proportion of their real merit."[3] Jesting with a friend from Ireland, who feared "he might treat the people of that country more unfavourably than he had done the Scotch," he answered, "Sir, you have no reason to be afraid of me. The Irish are not in a conspiracy to cheat the world by false representations of the merits of their countrymen. No, Sir: the Irish are a *fair people;*—they never speak well of one another."[4] To Boswell he began a letter, not meant, of course, for the public eye, by saying: "Knowing as you do the disposition of your countrymen to tell lies in favour of each other."[5] When he came to write his *Journey*, he was led neither by timidity nor false delicacy to conceal what he thought. He attacks that "national combination so invidious that their friends cannot defend it," which is one of the means whereby Scotchmen "find, or make their way to employment, riches, and distinction."[6] He upbraids that "vigilance of jealousy which never goes to sleep,"[7] which sometimes led them to cross the borders of boastfulness and pass into falsehood, when Caledonia was their subject and Englishmen their audience. "A Scotchman," he writes, "must be a very sturdy moralist who does not love Scotland better than truth; he will always love it better than inquiry."[8] Even in his talk when among Scotchmen

[1] Boswell's *Johnson*, ii. 306. [3] *I*. ii. 301. *Ib.* ii. 296. [7] *Work*, ix. 158.
[2] *Ib.* v. 20. *Ib.* ii. 307. *Ib.* p. 154. *Ib.* p. 116.

he was inclined "to expatiate rather too strongly upon the benefits derived to their country from the Union." "'We have taught you,' said he, 'and we'll do the same in time to all barbarous nations, to the Cherokees, and at last to the Ouran-Outangs,' laughing with as much glee as if Monboddo had been present. BOSWELL. 'We had wine before the Union.' JOHNSON. 'No, Sir; you had some weak stuff, the refuse of France, which would not make you drunk.' BOSWELL. 'I assure you, Sir, there was a great deal of drunkenness.' JOHNSON. 'No, Sir; there were people who died of dropsies, which they contracted in trying to get drunk.'"

Such pleasantry as this could hardly have given offence to any one into whose skull a jest could penetrate by any operation short of a surgical one. But it was a very different matter when the spoken jest passed into a serious expression of opinion in print. All the theoretic philosophy of which Scotland justly boasts was hardly sufficient to support with patience such a passage as the following: "Till the Union made the Scots acquainted with English manners the culture of their lands was unskilful, and their domestic life unformed; their tables were coarse as the feasts of Esquimaux, and their houses filthy as the cottages of Hottentots." His attacks on the Highlanders would have been read with patience, if not with pleasure, in Lowland circles. "His account of the Isles," wrote Beattie, "is, I dare say, very just. I never was there." These were not the "asperities" of which that amiable poet complained. Yet they were asperities which might have provoked an incensed Highlander to give the author "a crack on his skull," had he looked not to the general tenour of the narrative, but to a few rough passages scattered up and down. M'Nicol would surely have roused the anger of his countrymen to a fiercer heat had he forborne to falsify Johnson's words, and strung together instead a row of his sarcastic sayings. The offensive passages are not indeed numerous, but out of such a collection as the following irritation enough might have been provided: "the genuine improvidence of savages;" "a muddy mixture of pride and ignorance;" "the chiefs gradually degenerating from patriarchal rulers to rapacious landlords;"¹ "the animating rabble"² by which of old a chief was attended; "the rude speech of a barbarous people:"³ "the laxity of their conversation, by which the inquirer, by a kind of intellectual retrogradation, knows less as he hears more;"⁴ "the Caledonian bigotry" which helps "an inaccurate auditor" to believe in the genuineness of Ossian.⁵

To the sarcasms which had their foundation in Johnson's dislike of Presbyterianism Lowlanders and Highlanders were equally exposed. On Knox and "the ruffians of reformation"⁶ he has no mercy. It is true that he maintains that "we read with as little emotion the violence of Knox and his followers as the irruptions of Alaric and the Goths."⁷ But how deeply he was moved Boswell shows, where he describes him among the ruins of the once glorious magnificence of St. Andrews. "I happened to ask where John Knox was buried. Dr. Johnson burst out, 'I hope in the high-way. I have been looking at his reformations.'"⁸ The sight of the ruined houses of prayer in Skye drew from him the assertion that "the malignant influence of Calvinism has blasted ceremony and decency together."⁹ In another passage he describes the ancient "epidemical enthusiasm compounded of sullen scrupulousness and warlike ferocity, which, in a people whom idleness resigned to their own thoughts, was long transmitted in its full strength from the old to the young."¹⁰ Even for this inveterate ill a cure had at length been found. "By trade and intercourse with England it is visibly abating."

By the passages in which he described the bareness of the eastern coast the most irritation was caused. The very hedges were of stone, and not a tree was to be seen that was not younger than himself. "A tree might be a show in Scotland as a horse in Venice."¹¹ For this he was handled as roughly as Joseph's brethren. He was little better than a spy who had come to see the nakedness of the land. The Scotchmen of that day could not know, as we know now, that "he treated Scotland no worse than he did even his best friends, whose characters he used to give as they appeared to him both in light and shade. 'He was fond of discri-

---

¹ *Works*, ix. 86.   ² *Ib.*
³ *Ib.* p. 112.   ⁴ *Ib.* p. 47.
⁵ *Ib.* p. 115.
⁶ *Ib.* p. 5. Johnson, it should be remarked, does not write "the ruffians of the Reformation." He uses the word as South does, when he speaks of "those times which had reformed so many churches to the ground" (South's *Sermons*, ed. 1823, i. 173). No man upheld the Reformed Church of England more strongly than South.
⁷ *Works*, ix. 6.
⁸ Boswell's *Johnson*, v. 61.
⁹ *Works*, ix. 61.   ¹⁰ *Ib.* p. 4.
¹¹ *Ib.* p. 7.

mination,' said Sir Joshua Reynolds, 'which he could not show without pointing out the bad as well as the good in every character.'"[1] If in his narrative he has not spared the shade, every fair-minded reader must allow that he has not been sparing of the light. John Wesley, who had often travelled over the same ground as far as Inverness, on May 18, 1776, recorded in his Journal at Aberdeen: "I read over Dr. Johnson's *Tour to the Western Isles*. It is a very curious book, wrote with admirable sense, and, I think, great fidelity; although in some respects he is thought to bear hard on the nation, which I am satisfied he never intended."[2]

That Johnson was not careless of the good opinion of the Scotch is shown by his eagerness to learn what Boswell had to tell him about the book. "Let me know as fast as you read it how you like it; and let me know if any mistake is committed, or anything important left out."[3] A week later he wrote: "I long to hear how you like the book; it is, I think, much liked here." The modesty of the closing passage of his narrative should have done something towards disarming criticism. "Having passed my time almost wholly in cities, I may have been surprised by modes of life and appearances of nature that are familiar to men of wider survey and more varied conversation. Novelty and ignorance must always be reciprocal, and I cannot but be conscious that my thoughts on national manners are the thoughts of one who has seen but little."[4] The compliment which he paid to the society of the capital must surely have won some hearts. "I passed some days in Edinburgh," he wrote, "with men of learning whose names want no advancement from my commemoration, or with women of elegance, which perhaps disclaims a pedant's praise."[5] He never lets slip an opportunity of gracefully acknowledging civilities and acts of kindness, or of celebrating worth and learning. As he closed his book, so he had opened it with a well-turned compliment. It was, he said, Boswell's "acuteness and gaiety of conversation and civility of manners which induced him to undertake the journey."[6] He praises the kindness with which he was gratified by the professors of St. Andrews, and "the elegance of lettered hospitality" with which he was entertained.[7] At Aberdeen the same grateful heart

---

[1] Boswell's *Johnson*, ii. 306.
[2] Wesley's *Journal*, iv. 74. He repeats this statement five years later (*Ib*. p. 297).
[3] Boswell's *Johnson*, ii. 269.
[4] *Ibid.*, ix. 164.
[5] *Ib*. p. 1.
[6] *Ib*. p. 159.
[7] *Ib*. p. 5.

is seen. Among the professors he found one whom he had known twenty years earlier in London. "Such unexpected renewals of acquaintance may be numbered among the most pleasing incidents of life. The knowledge of one professor soon procured me the notice of the rest, and I did not want any token of regard."[1] He had the freedom

> Johnson. ✗ *Abredoniæ vigesimo tertio die mensis Augusti 1773 in{sup}to{/sup} Magistratuum Domo Vir Generosus ac Doctrina Clarus Samuel Johnson L.L.D. receptus et admissus fuit in numerum et fratrum Gildæ præfatæ Burgi de Aberdeen in demissimi affectus et amoris ac minime observantiæ tesseram Quibus licet Magistratus illum Amplectuntur.*[2]

of the city conferred upon him. In acknowledging the honour he compliments the town at the expense of England, by mentioning a circumstance which, he says, "I am afraid I should not have had to say of any city south of the Tweed; I found no petty officer bowing for a fee."[3] With Lord Monboddo he was never on friendly terms. "I knew that they did not love each other," writes Boswell, with a studied softness of expression. Yet Johnson in his narrative praises "the magnetism of his conversation."[4] With Lord Auchinleck he had that violent altercation which the unfortunate piety of the son forbade the biographer to exhibit for the entertainment of the public. Nevertheless, he only mentions his antagonist to compliment him.[5] If he attacked Presbyterianism, yet to the Presbyterian ministers in the Hebrides he was unsparing of his praise. He celebrates their learning, which was the more admirable as they were men "who had no motive to study but generous curiosity or desire of usefulness."[6] However much he differed from "the learned Mr. Macqueen" about Ossian, yet he admits that "his knowledge and politeness give him a title equally to kindness and respect."[7] With

---

[1] *Works*, p. 11. [3] See Appendix. *Ib.* pp. 30, 159. *Ib.* p. 102.
[2] *Works*, p. 14. [4] *Ib.* p. 10. [7] *Ib.* p. 54.

the aged minister of Col he had a wrangle over Bayle, and Clarke, and Leibnitz. "Had he been softer with this venerable old man," writes Boswell, "we might have had more conversation."¹ This rebuke Johnson read in Boswell's manuscript. The amends which he makes is surely ample. He describes the minister's "look of venerable dignity, excelling what I remember in any other man. I lost some of his goodwill by treating a heretical writer with more regard than in his opinion a heretic could deserve. I honoured his orthodoxy, and did not much censure his asperity. A man who has settled his opinions does not love to have the tranquillity of his conviction disturbed; and at seventy-seven it is time to be in earnest."²

The people he praises no less than their ministers. "Civility," he says, "seems part of the national character of Highlanders. Every chieftain is a monarch, and politeness, the natural product of royal government, is diffused from the Laird through the whole clan."³ He describes the daughter of the man who kept the hut in Glenmorison, where he passed a night. "Her conversation like her appearance was gentle and pleasing. We knew that the girls of the Highlanders are all gentlewomen, and treated her with great respect, which she received as customary and due."⁴ He praises the general hospitality. "Wherever there is a house the stranger finds a welcome. If his good fortune brings him to the residence of a gentleman he will be glad of a storm to prolong his stay."⁵ How graceful is the compliment which he pays to Macleod of Rasay! "Rasay has little that can detain a traveller except the Laird and his family; but their power wants no auxiliaries. Such a seat of hospitality amidst the winds and waters fills the imagination with a delightful contrariety of images. Without is the rough ocean and the rocky land, the beating billows and the howling storm; within is plenty and elegance, beauty and gaiety, the song and the dance. In Rasay if I could have found a Ulysses I had fancied a Pharacia."⁶ To the other branch of the Macleods he is no less complimentary. "At Dunvegan I had tasted lotus," he wrote, "and was in danger of forgetting that I was ever to depart."⁷ He met Flora Macdonald, and does not let the occasion pass to pay her a high compliment. "Hers is a name that will be mentioned in history, and, if courage and fidelity be virtues, mentioned with

¹ Boswell's *Johnson*, v. 288.   ⁴ *Ib.* p. 32.   ⁵ *Ib.* pp. 94, 97.
² *Works*, ix. 118.   ³ *Ib.* p. 25.   ⁶ *Ib.* p. 62.   ⁷ *Ib.* p. 97.

honour."[1] In fact, he rarely introduces in his narrative any living person but in way of compliment or acknowledgment. "He speaks ill of nobody but Ossian," said Lord Mansfield, Scotchman though he was.[2] "There has been of late," he once said, "a strange turn in travellers to be displeased."[3] There was no such turn in him. From the beginning to the end of his narrative there is not a single grumble. In Mull last summer I had the pleasure of meeting an old general, a Highlander, who had seen a great deal of rough service in the East Indies. Someone in the company let drop an unfavourable remark on Johnson. "I lately read his *Journey*," the general replied, "and when I thought of his age, his weak health, and the rudeness of the accommodation in those old days, I was astonished at finding that he never complained." In his food he had a relish for what was nice and delicate. Yet he records that "he only twice found any reason to complain of a Scottish table. He that shall complain of his fare in the Hebrides has improved his delicacy more than his manhood."[4] "If an epicure," he says in another passage, "could remove by a wish in quest of sensual gratifications, wherever he had supped he would breakfast in Scotland."[5] Boswell, we read, "was made uneasy and almost fretful" by their bad accommodation in the miserable inn at Glenelg. "Dr. Johnson was calm. I said he was so from vanity. JOHNSON. 'No, Sir, it is from philosophy.'"[6] The same philosophy accompanied him not only through his journey, but through his letters and his narrative. Nearly five weeks after he had left Edinburgh he wrote to Mrs. Thrale: "The hill Rattiken and the inn at Glenelg were the only things of which we or travellers yet more delicate could find any pretensions to complain."[7] Yet he was by no means free from bodily troubles, as his letters show. He was "miserably deaf," he wrote at one time, and was still suffering from the remains of inflammation in the eye, he wrote at another time. His nerves seemed to be growing weaker. The climate, he thought, "perhaps not within his degree of healthy latitude."[8] The climate, indeed, had been at its worst. In all September he had only one day and a half of fair weather, and in October perhaps not more.[9] Kept indoors as he was by the rain, he often suffered under the additional discomfort of bad accommo-

---

[1] *Works*, p. 63.
[2] Boswell's *Johnson*, ii. 318.
[3] *Ib*. iii. 236.
[4] *Works*, ix. 19. 51.
[5] *Ib.* p. 52.
[6] Boswell's *Johnson*, v. 146.
[7] *Piozzi Letters*, i. 137.
[8] *Ib.* pp. 127, 165.
[9] *Ib.* p. 182.

dation. Two nights he passed in wretched huts; one in a barn; two in the miserable cabin of a small trading-ship; one in a room where the floor was mire. Even in some of the better houses he had not always a chamber to himself at night, while in the daytime privacy and quiet were not to be enjoyed. At Corrichatachin, where he twice made a stay, "we had," writes Boswell, "no rooms that we could command; for the good people had no notion that a man could have any occasion but for a mere sleeping place; so, during the day, the bed-chambers were common to all the house. Servants eat in Dr. Johnson's, and mine was a kind of general rendezvous of all under the roof, children and dogs not excepted."[1]

He not only passes over in silence the weariness and discomforts of his tour, but he understates the risks which he ran. On that dark and stormy October night, when the frail vessel in which he had embarked was driven far out of its course to Col, he was in great danger. "'Thank God, we are safe!' cried the young Laird, as at last they spied the harbour of Lochiern."[2] This scene of peril, of which Boswell gives a spirited description, is dismissed by Johnson in his letter to Mrs. Thrale in a few words: "A violent gust, which Bos. had a great mind to call a tempest, forced us into Col, an obscure island."[3] In his narrative, if he makes a little more of it, he does so, it seems, only for the sake of paying a compliment to the seamanship of Maclean of Col.[4] It was this stormy night, especially, that was in Sir Walter Scott's mind when he described "the whole expedition as being highly perilous, considering the season of the year, the precarious chance of getting seaworthy boats, and the ignorance of the Hebrideans, who are very careless and unskilful sailors."[5]

If votive offerings have been made to the God of storms by those who have escaped the perils of the deep, surely some tall column might well be raised on the entrance to Lochiern by the gratitude of the readers of the immortal *Life*. Had the ship been overwhelmed, not only the hero, but his biographer, would have perished. One more great man would have been added to the sad long list of those of whom the poet sang:

> "Omnes illacrimabiles
> Urgentur, ignotoque longa
> Nocte, carent quia vate sacro.'

---

[1] Boswell's *Johnson*, v. 262.   [2] *Ib.* v. 283.   [4] *Works*, ix. 117.
[3] *Piozzi Letters*, i. 167.   [5] Boswell's *Johnson*, v. 283, n. 1.

"In endless night they sleep unwept, unknown,
No bard had they to make all time their own."

By the men of Johnson's time the journey was looked upon as one of real adventure. When Boswell visited Voltaire at Ferney, and mentioned their design of taking this tour, "he looked at him as if he had talked of going to the North Pole, and said, 'You do not insist on my accompanying you?' 'No, Sir.' 'Then I am very willing you should go.'"[2] Dr. Percy, of the *Reliques*, wrote from Alnwick Castle that a gentleman who had lately returned from the Hebrides, had told him that the two travellers were detained prisoners in Skye, their return having been intercepted by the torrents. "Sir Alexander Macdonald and his lady," Percy adds, "at whose house our friend Johnson is a captive, had made their escape before the floods cut off their retreat; so that possibly we may not see our friend till next summer releases him."[3] A Glasgow newspaper gave much the same report, but attributed his delay to the danger of crossing in the late autumn "such a stormy surge in a small boat."[4] On the Island of Col they were indeed storm-bound for eleven days. "On the travellers' return to Edinburgh," writes Boswell, "everybody had accosted us with some studied compliment. Dr. Johnson said, 'I am really ashamed of the congratulations which we receive. We are addressed as if we had made a voyage to Nova Zembla, and suffered five persecutions in Japan.'"[5] Dr. Robertson "had advanced to him repeating a line of Virgil, which I forget," Boswell adds. "I suppose either,

or
Post varios casus, per tot discrimina rerum;

— — multum ille et terris jactatus et alto.

Johnson afterwards remarked that to see a man come up with a formal air and a Latin line, when we had no fatigue and no danger, was provoking." Of exaggeration he had always a strong hatred, and would not allow it in his own case any more than in another's. He had undergone great fatigue, and he had been in real danger, but of both he made light. It was in high spirits that he returned home after his tour of a hundred days. "I came home last night," he wrote to Boswell, "and am ready to begin a new journey."[8]

---

[1] Francis': Horace, *Odes*, IV. ix. 26.
[2] Boswell's *Johnson*, v. 14.
[3] From the original, in the possession of Mr. W. R. Smith, of Greatham Moss, West Liss.
[4] Boswell's *Johnson*, v. 344.

"Through various hazards and events we move." Dryden, *Æneid*, i. 204.
"Long labour both by sea and land he bore." *Ib.* i. 3.
Boswell's *Johnson*, ii. 268.

JOHNSON'S DELIGHT IN HIS TOUR.

He had fulfilled his long-cherished wish, and no wonder his spirits were high. His father, the old Lichfield bookseller, had put into his hands when he was very young Martin's *Description of the Western Islands*, and had thus roused his youthful fancy.[1] His longing to visit the wild scenes of which he had read in his childhood would in all likelihood have remained ungratified, had it not been for Boswell. He had known that lively young gentleman but a very few weeks, when, over supper "in a private room at the Turk's Head Coffee-house in the Strand," he promised to accompany him to the Hebrides.[2] Ten years elapsed before the promise was fulfilled. "I cannot but laugh," he said at Armidale in Skye, "to think of myself roving among the Hebrides at sixty. I

ARMIDALE.

wonder where I shall rove at four-score."[4] To Mrs. Thrale soon after his birthday he wrote: "You remember the Doge of Genoa, who being asked what struck him most at the French Court, answered, 'Myself.' I cannot think many things here more likely to affect the fancy, than to see Johnson ending his sixty-fourth year in the wilderness of the Hebrides."[5] "Little did I once think," he wrote another day, "of seeing this region of obscurity, and little did you once expect a salutation from this verge of European life. I have now the pleasure of going where nobody goes, and seeing what nobody sees."[6] So close to this verge did Mrs. Thrale suppose he was, that she thought that he was in sight of Iceland.[7] She and his friends of the Mitre or the Literary Club would have been astonished could they have

[1] Boswell's *Johnson*, i. 450.   [3] *Ib.*   [5] *Piozzi Letters*, i. 158.   [7] *Ib.* i. 120.
[2] He was sixty-four.   [6] *Ib.* i. 188.
[4] Boswell's *Johnson*, v. 278.

seen him that night in Col when "he strutted about the room with a broad-sword and target," and that other night when Boswell "put a large blue bonnet on the top of his bushy grey wig."[1]

The motives which led him on his adventurous journey were not those which every summer and autumn bring travellers in swarms, not only from England, but from the mainland of Europe, from across the wide Atlantic, from India, from Southern Africa, from Australia and New Zealand to these Highlands of poetry and romance. "I got," he said, "an acquisition of more ideas by my tour than by anything that I remember. I saw quite a different system of life."[2] It was life, not scenery, which he went to study. On his return to the south of Scotland he was asked "how he liked the Highlands. The question seemed to irritate him, for he answered, 'How, Sir, can you ask me what obliges me to speak unfavourably of a country where I have been hospitably entertained? Who *can* like the Highlands? I like the inhabitants very well.'"[3] The love of wild scenery was in truth only beginning as his life was drawing to its close. "It is but of late," wrote Pennant in 1772, "that the North Britons became sensible of the beauties of their country; but their search is at present amply rewarded. Very lately a cataract of uncommon height was discovered on the Bruar."[4] Fifteen years later Burns, in his *Humble Petition of Bruar Water*, shows that the discovery had been followed up:

> "Here haply too at vernal dawn
> Some musing Bard may stray,
> And eye the smoking dewy lawn
> And misty mountain grey."

But in the year 1773 Johnson could say without much, if indeed any exaggeration, that "to the southern inhabitants of Scotland the state of the mountains and the islands is equally unknown with that of Borneo and Sumatra; of both they have only heard a little and guess the rest."[5] Staffa had been just discovered by Sir Joseph Banks. It seems almost passing belief, but yet it is strictly true, that Staffa —Staffa, as one of the wonders of creation —was unknown till the eve of Johnson's visit to the Hebrides. The neighbouring islanders of course had seen it, but had seen it without curiosity or emotion. They were like the impassive

---

[1] Boswell's *Johnson*, v. 324.
[2] *Ib.* iv. 199.
[3] *Ib.* v. 377.
[4] *Tour in Scotland* (ed. 1776), ii. 59. The Bruar is near Blair-Athole.
[5] Johnson's *Works*, ix. 84.

Frenchman who lived in Paris throughout the whole of the Reign
of Terror, and did not notice that anything remarkable went on.
It was on August 12, 1772, a day which should for ever be famous
in the annals of discovery, that Banks coming to anchor in the
Sound of Mull, "was asked ashore" by Mr. Macleane of Drumnen. At his house he met with one Mr. Leach, an English
gentleman, who told him that at the distance of about nine leagues
lay an island, unvisited even by the Highlanders, with pillars on it
like those of the Giant's Causeway.[1]

No yachtsman as yet threaded his way through the almost
countless islets of our western seas; the only sails as yet reflected
on the unruffled surface of the land-locked firths were the fisher's
and the trader's. For the sea as yet love was neither felt nor
affected. There was no gladness in its dark-blue waters. Fifteen
years were to pass before Byron was born—the first of our poets,
it has been said, who sang the delights of sailing. A ship was still
"a jail, with the chance of being drowned."[2] No Southerner went
to the Highlands to hunt, or shoot, or fish. No one sought there a
purer air. It was after Johnson's tour that an English writer urged
the citizens of Edinburgh to plant trees in the neighbourhood of
their town because "the increase of vegetation would purify the
air, and dispel those putrid and noxious vapours which are
frequently wafted from the Highlands."[3] It was on an early day
of August, in a finer season than had been known for years, that
Wolfe, the hero of Quebec, complained that neither temperance
nor exercise could preserve him in any tolerable health in the un-
friendly climate of Loch Lomond.[4] Of all the changes which have
come over our country, perhaps none was more unforeseen than the
growth of this passion for the Highlands and the Hebrides. Could
Johnson have learnt from some one gifted with prophetic power
that there were passages in his narrative which would move the
men of the coming century to scoff, it was not his references to
scenery which would have roused his suspicion. I have heard a
Scotchman laugh uproariously over his description of a mountain
as "a considerable protuberance." He did not know however
where the passage came, and he admitted that, absurd as it
was, it was not quite so ridiculous when taken with the context.

---

[1] Troil' *Letters on Iceland* (3rd ed.), p. 288. There is a notice of the discovery in the *Gentleman's Magazine* for 1772, p. 545, and in the *Annual Register* for the same year, i. 139.

[2] Boswell's *Johnson*, i. 348.

[3] Topham's *Letters from Edinburgh*, p. 233.

[4] He was stationed there with his regiment. Wright's *Life of General Wolfe*, p. 271.

"Another mountain," said Boswell, "I called immense. 'No,' replied Johnson, 'it is no more than a considerable protuberance.'"[1] It was his hatred of exaggeration and love of accurate language which provoked the correction—the same hatred and the same love which led him at college to check his comrades if they called a thing "prodigious."[2] But to us, nursed as we have been and our fathers before us in a romantic school, the language of Johnson and of his contemporaries about the wild scenes of nature never fails to rouse our astonishment and our mirth. Were they to come back to earth, I do not know but that at our extravagancies of admiration and style, our affectations in the tawdry art of "word-painting," and at our preference of barren mountains to the meadow-lands, and corn-fields, and woods, and orchards, and quiet streams of southern England, their strong and manly common sense might not fairly raise a still heartier laugh.

The ordinary reader is apt to attribute to an insensibility to beauty in Johnson what, to a great extent, was common to most of the men of his time. It is true that for the beauties of nature, whether wild or tame, his perception was by no means quick. Nevertheless, we find his indifference to barren scenery largely shared in by men of poetic temperament. Even Gray, who looked with a poet's eye on the crags and cliffs and torrents by which his path wound along as he went up to the Grande Chartreuse, yet, early in September, when the heather would be all in bloom, writes of crossing in Perthshire "a wide and dismal heath fit for an assembly of witches."[3] Wherever he wandered he loved to find the traces of men. It was not desolation, but the earth as the beautiful home of man that moved him and his fellows. *Mentem mortalia tangunt*. He found the Apennines not so horrid as the Alps, because not only the valleys but even the mountains themselves were many of them cultivated within a little of their very tops.[4] The fifth Earl of Carlisle, a poet though not a Gray, in August, 1768, hurried faster even than the post across the Tyrol from Verona to Mannheim, "because there was nothing but rest that was worth stopping one moment for." The sameness of the scenery was wearisome to his lordship, "large rocky mountains, covered with fir-trees; a rapid river in the valley; the road made like a shelf on the side of the hill." He rejoiced when he took his

---

[1] Boswell's *Johnson*, v. 141. [2] *I*. iii. 303. [3] Gray's *Works*, iv. 57. [4] *Ib*. ii. 78.

leave of the Alps, and came upon "fields very well cultivated, valleys with rich verdure, and little woods which almost persuaded him he was in England."[1]

There is a passage in Camden's description of Argyleshire in which we find feelings expressed which for the next two centuries were very generally entertained. "Along the shore," he writes, "the country is more unpleasant in sight, what with rocks and what with blackish barren mountains."[2] One hundred and fifty years after this was written, an Englishman, describing in 1740 the beautiful road which runs along the south-eastern shore of Loch Ness, calls the rugged mountains "those hideous productions of nature."[3] He pictures to himself the terror which would come upon the Southerner who "should be brought blindfold into some narrow rocky hollow, inclosed with these horrid prospects,

LOCH NESS, NEAR FOYERS.

and there should have his bandage taken off. He would be ready to die with fear, as thinking it impossible he should ever get out to return to his native country."[4] This account was very likely read by Johnson, for it was published in London only nineteen years before he made his tour. In the narrative of a Volunteer in the Duke of Cumberland's army, we find the same gloom cast by

[1] *George Selwyn and his Contemporaries*, ii. 319.
[2] Camden's *Description of Scotland* (ed. 1695), p. 137.
[3] *Letters from a Gentleman in the North of Scotland*, ii. 330.
[4] *Ib.* p. 13.

mountain scenery on the spirits of Englishmen. The soldiers who were encamped near Loch Ness fell sick daily in their minds as well as in their bodies from nothing but the sadness produced by the sight of the black barren mountains covered with snow, with streams of water rolling down them. To divert their melancholy, which threatened to develop even into hypochondriacal madness, races were held. It was with great joy that the volunteer at last "turned his back upon these hideous mountains and the noisy ding of the great falls of waters."[1]

Even the dales of Cumberland struck strangers with awe. Six months before Wordsworth was born, Gray wandered up Borrowdale to the point where now the long train of tourist-laden coaches day after day in summer turns to the right towards Honister Pass and Buttermere. "All farther access," he wrote, "is here barred to prying mortals, only there is a little path winding over the Fells, and for some weeks in the year passable to the Dale's-men; but the mountains know well that these innocent people will not reveal the mysteries of their ancient kingdom, the reign of Chaos and Old Night."[2]

A few days after Johnson had arrived in Scotland, Mason, the poet, visited Keswick. Many of the woods which had charmed his friend Gray had been since cut down, and a dry season had reduced the cascade to scanty rills. "With the frightful and surprising only," he wrote, "I cannot be pleased."[3] He and his companion climbed to the summit of Skiddaw, where, just as if they were on the top of the Matterhorn, they found that "respiration seemed to be performed with a kind of asthmatic oppression."[4] To John Wesley, a traveller such as few men have ever been, wild scenery was no more pleasing than to the man who wandered for the first time. Those "horrid mountains" he twice calls the fine ranges of hills in the North Riding of Yorkshire, whose waters feed the Swale and the Tees, though it was in summer-time that he was travelling.[5] To Pennant Glencroe was "the seat of melancholy."[6] Beattie, Burns's "sweet harmonious Beattie," finds the same sadness in the mountains:

"The Highlands of Scotland" (he writes) "are a picturesque, but in general a melancholy country. Long tracts of mountainous desert, covered with dark heath,

---

[1] James Ray's *History of the Rebellion of 1747* (ed. 1752), pp. 365, 383.
[2] Gray's *Works*, iv. 150.
[3] Walpole *Letters*, v. 501.
[4] *An Excursion to the Lakes*, p. 157.
[5] Wesley's *Journal*, iii. 336, 465.
[6] *Tour in Scotland*, i. 222.

THE MELANCHOLY HIGHLANDS.

and often obscured by misty weather; narrow valleys, thinly inhabited and bounded by precipices resounding with the fall of torrents; a soil so rugged, and a climate so dreary, as in many parts to admit neither the amusements of pasturage nor the labours of agriculture; the mournful dashing of waves along the friths and lakes that intersect the country; the portentous noises which every change of the wind, and every increase and diminution of the waters, is apt to raise in a lonely region full of echoes, and rocks, and caverns; the grotesque and ghastly appearance of such a landscape by the light of the moon:—objects like these diffuse a gloom over the fancy which may be compatible enough with occasional and social merriment, but cannot fail to tincture the thoughts of a native in the hour of silence and solitude."[1]

The French writer, Faujas de Saint Fond, who visited the Highlands about the year 1780, was touched with the same unromantic gloom. When on his way from the barren mountains of the north he reached the fertile southern shore of Loch Tay, and caught the first glimpse of the change to happier climes, his soul experienced as sweet a joy as is given by the first breath of spring. He had escaped from a land where winter seemed eternally to reign, where all was wild, and barren, and sad.[2] Even Macleod of Macleod, the proprietor of nine inhabited isles and of islands uninhabited almost beyond number, who held four times as much land as the Duke of Bedford, even that "mighty monarch," as Johnson called him,[3] looked upon life in his castle at Dunvegan as "confinement in a remote corner of the world," and upon the Western Islands as "dreary regions."[4] Slight, then, must have been the shock which Johnson gave even to the poets among his fellows, when on "a delightful day" in April, he set Fleet Street with its "cheerful scene" above Tempé, and far above Mull.[5] To the men of his time rocks would have "towered in horrid nakedness,"[6] and "wandering in Skye" would have seemed "a toilsome drudgery."[7] Nature there would have looked "naked," and these poverty-stricken regions "malignant."[8] Few would have been "the allurements of these islands," for "desolation and penury" would have given as "little pleasure" to them as it did to him.[9] In Glencroe they would have found "a black and dreary region,"[10] and in Mull "a gloomy desolation."[11] Everywhere "they would have been repelled by the wide extent of hopeless sterility,"[12] and everywhere fatigued by the

---

[1] Beattie's *Essay on Poetry and Music*, p. 169.
[2] *Voy. en Auvergne*, etc., p. 201. *Piozzi Letters*, i. 154, and Boswell's *Johnson*, v. 231.
[4] Croker's *Boswell* (ed. 1835), iv. 227.
[5] Boswell's *Johnson*, iii. 302.
Johnson's *Works*, ix. 28.
Piozzi Letters, i. 138.
Works, ix. 75, 153.
[9] p. 153.
[10] p. 150.
[11] ib. p. 156.
[12] ib. p. 35.

want of "variety in universal barrenness."[1] In the midst of such scenes, as the autumn day was darkening to its close, they would have allowed that, "when there is a guide whose conduct may be trusted, a mind not naturally too much disposed to fear, may preserve some degree of cheerfulness; but what," they would have asked, "must be the solicitude of him who should be wandering among the crags and hollows benighted, ignorant, and alone?"[2] Upon the islets on Loch Lomond they would have longed "to employ all the arts of embellishment," so that these little spots should no longer "court the gazer at a distance, but disgust him at his approach, when he finds instead of soft lawns and shady thickets nothing more than uncultivated ruggedness."[3] Everywhere they would have regretted the want of the arts and civilization and refinements of modern life.

Had Johnson been treated more kindly by the weather, doubtless the gloom of the landscape would have been less reflected upon his pages. Fifty-eight days of rain to three days of clear skies would have been sufficient to depress even the wildest worshipper of rude nature. In the eleven days in which he was kept prisoner by storms in Col, he had "no succession of sunshine to rain, or of calms to tempests; wind and rain were the only weather."[4] When the sun did shine he lets us catch a little of its cheerful light. His first day's Highland journey took him along the shore of Loch Ness in weather that was bright, though not hot. "The way was very pleasant; on the left were high and steep rocks, shaded with birch, and covered with fern or heath. On the right the limpid waters of Loch Ness were beating their bank, and waving their surface by a gentle undulation."[5] The morrow was equally fine. How prettily he has described his rest in the valley on the bank, where he first thought of writing the story of his tour, "with a clear rivulet streaming at his feet. The day was calm, the air was soft, and all was rudeness, silence and solitude."[6] Very different would have been the tale which he told had he travelled in the days of fast and commodious steamboats, good roads and carriages, comfortable inns, post-offices, telegraphs, and shops. He would not have seen a different system of life, or got an acquisition of ideas, but he might have found patience, and even promptings for descriptions of the beauties of rugged nature. "In an age when every London

[1] *Piozzi Letters*, i. 135.   [4] *Piozzi Letters*, i. 169.
[2] *Works*, ix. 73.   [3] *Ib.* p. 156.   [5] *Works*, ix. 25.   [6] *Ib.* p. 36.

citizen makes Loch Lomond his wash-pot, and throws his shoe over Ben Nevis,"[1] the old man may easily be mocked for his indifference to scenery. But the elderly traveller of our times, who whirled along "in a well-appointed four-horse coach," indicates the beauties of nature to his companions, and utters exclamations of delight, as from time to time he takes his cigar from his lips, might have felt as little enthusiasm as Johnson, had he had, like him, to cross Skye and Mull on horseback, by paths so narrow that each rider had to go singly, and so craggy that constant care was required.

LOCH LOMOND.

The scenery in which he took most delight was the park-lands of southern and midland England.

> "Where lawns extend that scorn Arcadian pride,
> And brighter streams than fam'd Hydaspes glide.
> There all around the gentlest breezes stray,
> There gentle music melts on every spray;
> Creation's mildest charms are there combin'd,
> Extremes are only in the master's mind."[2]

"Sweet Auburn" would have been dearer to him than all the wilds of the Highlands. But Auburn scenery he did not find even in the Lowlands. Had Goldsmith passed his life in Ayrshire or even in "pleasant Teviotdale," the *Deserted Village* would never have been written. Burns had never seen an Auburn, nor even that simpler rural beauty which was so dear to Wordsworth. No "lovely cottage in the guardian nook" had "stirred him deeply." He knew nothing of the sacredness of

---

[1] Lockhart's *Life of Scott*, iii. 239. [2] Goldsmith's *Traveller*, l. 319.

"The roses to the porch which they entwine."[1]

In Scotland was seen the reverse of the picture in which Goldsmith had painted Italy.

"In florid beauty groves and fields appear,
Man seems the only growth that dwindles here."[2]

In Scotland man was nourished to the most stubborn strength of character, but beauty was the growth that dwindled. In the hard struggle for bare living, and in the gloom of a religion which gave strength but crushed loveliness, no man thought of adorning his home as if it had been his bride. Wordsworth compared the manses in Scotland with the parsonages, even the poor parsonages in England, and said that neither they nor their gardens and grounds had the same "attractive appearance."[3] The English country-house, with its lawns, its gardens, and its groves, which adds such a singular charm to our landscape, had not its counterpart on the other side of the border. Elderly men could still recall the day when the approach to the laird's dwelling led past the stable and the cow-house, when the dunghill was heaped up close to the hall-door, and when, instead of lawns and beds of flowers, all around grew a plentiful crop of nettles, docks, and hemlocks.[4] Some improvement had been already made. A taste had happily begun for "neat houses and ornamental fields," and to the hopeful patriot there was "the pleasing prospect that Scotland might in a century or sooner compare with England, not indeed in magnificence of country-seats, but in sweetness and variety of concordant parts."[5] Even at that time it supplied England with its best gardeners,[6] and nevertheless it was a country singularly bare of gardens. "Pray, now, are you ever able to bring the *sloe* to perfection?" asked Johnson of Boswell.[7] So far was nature from being adorned that she had been everywhere stripped naked. Woods had been cut down, not even had groups of trees been spared, no solitary oak or elm with its grateful shade stood in the middle of the field or in the hedge-row; hedge-rows there were none. The pleasantness of the prospect had been everywhere sacrificed to the productiveness of the field. The beautiful English

---

[1] Wordsworth's *Works*, ii. 284.
[2] *The Traveller*, l. 125.
[3] Wordsworth's *Works*, iv. 99.
[4] *Scotland and Scotchmen in the Eighteenth Century*, ii. 99.

[5] Kames' *Sketches of the History of Man*, i. 274.
[6] Boswell's *Johnson*, ii. 77. The superiority of the gardeners was most likely due to the superiority of the education of the poorer classes.
[7] *Ib.* ii. 78.

landscape was gone. "The striking characteristic in the views of Scotland," said an observant traveller, "is a poverty of landscape from a want of objects, particularly of wood. Park scenery is little known. The lawn, the clump, and the winding walk are rarely found."[1] As he crossed the border he might have said with Johnson: "It is only seeing a worse England. It is seeing the flower gradually fade away to the naked stalk."[2] "Every part of the country," wrote Goldsmith from Edinburgh in his student days, "presents the same dismal landscape. No grove nor brook lend their music to cheer the stranger, or make the inhabitants forget their poverty."[3] There was none of "the bloomy flush of life." The whole country was open, and resembled one vast common with a few scattered improvements.[4] Along the western road from Longworth to Dumfries it exhibited "a picture of dreary solitude, of smoky hovels, naked, ill-cultivated fields, lean cattle and a dejected people, without manufactures, trade or shipping."[5]

The eastern coast, along which Johnson travelled, was singularly bare of trees. He had not, he said, passed five on the road fit for the carpenter." The first forest trees of full growth which he saw were in the north of Aberdeenshire.[7] "This is a day of novelties," he said on the morrow. "I have seen old trees in Scotland, and I have heard the English clergy treated with disrespect."[8] Topham, while attacking his *Journey to the Western Isles*, yet admitted that it was only in the parks of a few noblemen that oaks were found fifty years old.[9] Lord Jeffrey maintained so late as 1833 that within a circle of twenty miles from Watford there was more old timber than in all Scotland.[10] Burns, in his *Humble Petition of Bruar Water to the Duke of Athole*, testifies to the want of trees:—

> "Would then my noble master please
> To grant my highest wishes,
> He'll shade my banks wi' tow'ring trees,
> And bonnie spreading bushes."

There were, of course, noble trees scattered throughout the country. Gray describes "the four chestnuts of vast bulk and height in Lord

---

[1] W. Gilpin's *Observations relative to Picturesque Beauty* in the year 1776, i. 117, 123, 141.
[2] Boswell's *Johnson*, iii. 248.
[3] Forster's *Life of Goldsmith*, i. 433.
[4] *Gentleman's Magazine*, 1754, p. 119.

Knox's *Tour through the Highlands of Scotland*, p. 5.
Piozzi Letters, i. 120. [7] *Work*, ix. 17
Boswell's *Johnson*, v. 120.
Letters from Edinburgh, p. 230.
[10] Cockburn's *Life of Lord Jeffrey*, i. 348.

Breadalbane's park," and Pennant, "the venerable oaks, the vast chestnuts, the ash trees, and others of ancient growth, that gave solemnity to the scene at Finlarig Castle." A love of planting, which began about the time of the Union, was gradually extending. Defoe noticed the young groves round the gentlemen's houses in the Lothians, and foretold, that in a few years Scotland would not need to send to Norway for timber and deal. The reviewer of Pennant's *Tour* in the *Scots Magazine* for January, 1772, rejoiced to find that the spirit of planting was so generally diffused, and looked forward to the advantages arising from it, which would be enjoyed by posterity. Sir Walter Scott defended Johnson against the abuse which had unjustly been cast on him. The east coast, if the young plantations were excepted, was as destitute of wood as he had described it. Nay, to his sarcasms he greatly ascribed that love of planting which had almost become a passion. It was not for nothing, then, that Johnson had joked over the loss of his walking-stick in Mull, and had refused to believe that any man in that island who had got it would part with it. "Consider, Sir, the value of such a piece of timber there."

The modern traveller who, as he passes through the Lothians or Aberdeenshire, looks with admiration on farming in its perfection, would learn with astonishment how backward Scotch agriculture was little more than one hundred years ago. While in England men of high rank and strong minds were ambitious of shining in the characters of farmers, in Scotland it was looked upon as a pursuit far beneath the attention of a gentleman. Neither by the learned had it been made a study. There were those who attributed this general backwardness to the soil and climate; but it was due, said Lord Kames, "to the indolence of the landholders, the obstinate indocility of the peasantry, and the stupid attachment of both classes to ancient habits and practices." The liberal intercourse between the two countries, which was an unexpected result of the Rebellion of 1745, greatly quickened the rate of improvement.

"Before that time the people of Northumberland and the Merse, who spoke dialects of the same language, and were only separated by a river, had little more

---

[1] Gray's *Works*, iv. 59.
[2] Pennant's *Tour in Scotland*, ii. 21.
[3] Defoe's *Tour through Great Britain*; Account of Scotland, iii. 15.
[4] *Scots Magazine*, 1772, p. 25.
[5] Croker's *Boswell* (8vo. ed.), p. 285.
[6] Croker's *Correspondence*, ii. 34.
[7] Boswell's *Johnson*, v. 310.
[8] Topham's *Letters from Edinburgh*, p. 366.
[9] Tytler's *Life of Lord Kames*, i. 112.

BACKWARDNESS OF FARMING.

intercourse than those of Kent and Normandy. After the Rebellion a number of noblemen and gentlemen amused themselves with farming in the English style. The late Lord Eglinton spared no expense in getting English servants. He showed his countrymen what might be done by high cultivation. Mr. Drummond, of Blair, sent over one of his ploughmen to learn drill husbandry, and the culture of turnips from Lord Eglinton's English servants. The very next year he raised a field of turnips, which were the first in the country. And they were as neatly dressed as any in Hertfordshire. A single horse ploughing the drills astonished the country people, who, till then, had never seen fewer than four yoked. About the year 1771 our tenants were well-disposed to the culture of turnips. They begin to have an idea of property in winter as well as in summer; nor is it any longer thought bad neighbourhood to drive off cattle that are trespassing upon their winter crops."

The young Laird of Col, just before Johnson's visit, had gone to Hertfordshire to study farming, and had brought back "the culture of turnips. His intention is to provide food for his cattle in the winter. This innovation was considered by Mr. Macsweyn as the idle project of a young head heated with English fancies; but he has now found that turnips will grow, and that hungry sheep and cows will really eat them." Yet progress was not so rapid but that Adam Smith held that a better system could only be introduced "by a long course of frugality and industry; half a century or a century more perhaps must pass away before the old system which is wearing out gradually can be completely abolished."

The cultivation of vegetables for the table and of fruits was also taking a start, though much remained to be done. When Johnson was informed at Aberdeen that Cromwell's soldiers had taught the Scotch to raise cabbages, he remarked, that "in the passage through villages it seems to him that surveys their gardens, that when they had not cabbage they had nothing." Pennant, however, the year before, in riding from Arbroath to Montrose, had passed by "extensive fields of potatoes—a novelty till within the last twenty years." It was not till Johnson had travelled beyond Elgin that he saw houses with fruit trees about them. "The improvements of the Scotch," he remarks, "are for immediate profit; they do not yet think it quite worth their while to plant what will not produce something to be eaten or sold in a very little time." The Scotch historian of Edinburgh complained that "the apples which were brought to market from the neighbourhood were unfit for the table." "Good apples are not to be seen," wrote Topham in his *Letters*

---

[1] *Scotland and Scotchmen of the Eighteenth Century*, ii. 212, 227, 228, 231, 272, 277.
[2] Johnson's *Works*, ix. 128.
[3] *Wealth of Nations*, i. 309.
[4] *Pencil Letters*, i. 116.
[5] Pennant's *Tour in Scotland*, ii. 158.
[6] *Pencil Letters*, i. 121.
[7] Arnot's *History of Edinburgh*, p. 347.

from Edinburgh. "It was," he said, "owing to the little variety of fruit that the inhabitants set anything on their tables after dinner that has the appearance of it, and I have often observed at the houses of principal people a plate of small turnips introduced in the dessert, and eaten with avidity."[1] Smollett indirectly alludes to this reflection on his native country when, in his *Humphry Clinker*, he says that "turnips make their appearance, not as dessert, but by way of *hors d'œuvres*, or whets."[2] Even in the present day, the English traveller far too often looks in vain for the orchards and the fruit tree with its branches trained over the house-wall. Yet great progress has been made. In Morayshire, in the present day, peaches and apricots are seen ripening on the garden walls. In the year 1852 an Elgin gardener carried off the first prize of the London Horticultural Society for ten varieties of the finest new dessert pears.[3] If Scotland can do such great things as this, surely justification is found for the reproaches cast by Johnson on Scottish ignorance and negligence.

So closely have the two countries in late years been drawn together by the wonderful facilities of intercourse afforded by modern inventions, that it is scarcely possible for us to understand the feelings of our adventurous forefathers as they crossed the Borders. At the first step they seemed to be in a foreign country. "The first town we come to," wrote Defoe, "is as perfectly Scots as if you were one hundred miles north of Edinburgh; nor is there the least appearance of anything English either in customs, habits, usages of the people, or in their way of living, eating, dress, or behaviour."[4] "The English," Smollett complained, "knew as little of Scotland as of Japan."[5] There is no reason to think that he was guilty of extravagance, when in his *Humphry Clinker* he makes Miss Tabitha Bramble, the sister of the Gloucestershire squire, imagine that "she could not go to Scotland but by sea."[6] It is amazing to how late a day ignorance almost as gross as this came down. It was in the year in which George II. came to the throne that Defoe, in his preface to his *Tour through Great Britain* wrote:—"Scotland has been supposed by some to be so contemptible a place as that it would not bear a description."[7] Eleven years

---

[1] *Letters from Edinburgh*, p. 229.
[2] *Humphry Clinker*, ii. 233.
[3] E. D. Dunbar's *Social Life*, ii. 147.
[4] Defoe's *Tour through Great Britain: Account of Scotland*, vol. iii. p. 6.
[5] *Humphry Clinker*, ii. 212.
[6] *Ib.*
[7] Defoe's *Tour through Great Britain*, vol. iii. p. vii.

later, in 1738, we find it described much as if it were some lately discovered island in the South Seas.

"The people in general," we read, "are naturally inclined to civility, especially to strangers. They are divided into Highlanders who call themselves the antient Scots, and into Lowlanders who are a mixture of antient Scots, Picts, Britons, French, English, Danes, Germans, Hungarians, and others. Buchanan describes the customs of the Highlanders graphically thus :— 'In their diet, apparel, and household furniture they follow the parsimony of the antients; they provide their diet by fishing and hunting, and boil their flesh in the paunch or skin of a beast; while they hunt they eat it raw, after having squeezed out the blood.' . . . The Western Islands (the author goes on to add) lie in the Deucaledonian Sea. . . . The natives of Mull when the season is moist take a large dose of aqua-vitæ for a corrective, and chew a piece of charmel root when they intend to be merry to prevent drunkenness. The natives of Skye have a peculiar way of curing the distempers they are incident to by simples of their own product, in which they are successful to a miracle.'"[1]

Into so strange and wild a country it required a stout heart to enter. A volunteer with the English army at the time of the Rebellion of 1745 wrote from Berwick:—"Now we are going into Scotland, but with heavy hearts. They tell us here what terrible living we shall have there, which I soon after found too true."[2] How few were the Englishmen who crossed the Tweed even so late as 1772 is shown by the hope expressed in the *Scots Magazine* for that year, that the publication of Pennant's *Tour* would excite others to follow in his steps.[3] Two years later Topham wrote from Edinburgh that "the common people were astonished to find himself and his companion become stationary in their town for a whole winter. . . . 'What were we come for?' was the first question. 'They presumed to study physic.' 'No.' 'To study law?' 'No.' 'Then it must be divinity.' 'No.' 'Very odd,' they said, 'that we should come to Edinburgh without one of these reasons.'"[4] How ignorant the English were of Scotland is shown by the publication of *Humphry Clinker*. The ordinary reader, as he laughs over the pages of this most humorous of stories, never suspects that the author in writing it had any political object in view. Yet there is not a little truth in Horace Walpole's bitter assertion that it is "a party novel, written by the profligate hireling Smollett, to vindicate the Scots, and cry down juries."[5] It was not so much a party as a patriotic novel. Lord Bute's brief tenure

---

[1] *The Present State of Scotland*, pp. 39, 42, 112, 114, 119.
[2] *A Journey through part of England and Scotland with the Army. By a Volunteer*, p. 53.
[3] *Scots Magazine*, 1772, p. 24.
[4] *Letters from Edinburgh*, p. 40.
[5] *Memoirs of the Reign of George III.*, iv. 328.

of ignoble office as Prime Minister and King's Friend, the mischief which he had done to the whole country, and the favour which he had shown to his North Britons, a few years earlier had raised a storm against the Scotch which had not yet subsided. "All the windows of all the inns northwards," wrote Smollett, "are scrawled with doggrel rhymes in abuse of the Scotch nation."[1] With great art he takes that fine old humorist, Matthew Bramble, from his squire's house in Gloucestershire on a tour to the southern part of Scotland, and makes him and his family send to their various correspondents lively and pleasant descriptions of all that they saw. At the very time that he was writing his *Humphry Clinker* a child was born in one of the narrow Wynds of Edinburgh who was to take up the work which he had begun, and as the mighty Wizard of the North, as if by an enchanter's wand, to lift up the mist which had long hung over the land which he loved so well, and to throw over Highlands and Lowlands alike the beauty of romance and the kindliness of feeling which springs from the associations given by poetry and fiction.

While the English as yet knew little of Scotland, the Scotch were not equally ignorant of England. From the days of the Union they had pressed southwards in the pursuit of wealth, of fame, and of position. Their migration was such that it afforded some foundation for Johnson's saying that "the noblest prospect which a Scotchman ever sees is the high road that leads him to England."[2] England was swiftly moving along the road to Empire, sometimes with silent foot, sometimes with the tramp of war. In America and in the East Indies her boundaries were year by year pushed farther and farther on. Her agriculture, her manufactures, her trade and her commerce were advancing by leaps and bounds. There was a great stir of life and energy. Into such a world the young Scotchmen entered with no slight advantages. In their common schools everywhere an education was given such as in England was only to be had in a few highly favoured spots. In their universities even the neediest scholar had a share. The hard fare, the coarse clothing, and the poor lodgings with which their students were contented, could be provided by the labours of the vacation. In their homes they had been trained in

---

[1] *Humphry Clinker*, ii. 176. See my edition of *Letters of David Hume to William Strahan*, pp. 56-64, for the violence of feeling between the English and Scotch at this time.

[2] Boswell's *Johnson*, i. 425.

habits of thrift. They entered upon the widely extending battle
of life like highly trained soldiers, and they gained additional force
by acting together. If they came up "in droves," it was not one
another that they butted. They exhibited when in a strange land
that "national combination" which Johnson found "so invidious,"
but which brought them to "employment, riches, and distinction."[1]
Their thrift, and an eagerness to push on which sometimes amounted
to servility, provoked many a gibe; but if ever they found time
and inclination to turn from Johnny Home to Shakespeare they
might have replied in the words of Ferdinand:

> "Some kinds of baseness
> Are nobly undergone, and most poor matters
> Point to rich ends."

On the advantages of the Union to Scotland Johnson was not
easily tired of haranguing. Of the advantages to England he said
nothing probably because he saw nothing. Yet it would not be
easy to tell on which side the balance lay. Before the Union, he
maintained, "the Scotch had hardly any trade, any money, or any
elegance."[2] In his *Journey to the Western Islands* he tells the
Scotch that "they must be for ever content to owe to the English
that elegance and culture which, if they had been vigilant and
active, perhaps the English might have owed to them."[3]

Smollett, who in national prejudice did not yield even to him, has
strongly upheld the opposite opinion. In his *History* he describes
Lord Belhaven's speech against the Union in the last parliament
which sat in Scotland—a speech "so pathetic that it drew tears
from the audience. It is," he adds, "at this day looked upon as a
prophecy by great part of the Scottish nation."[4] The towns on
the Firth of Forth, he maintained, through the loss of the trade
with France, had been falling to decay ever since the two countries
were united.[5] In these views he was not supported by the two
great writers who were his countrymen and his contemporaries.
It was chiefly to the Union that Adam Smith attributed the great
improvements in agriculture which had been made in the eighteenth
century.[6] It was to the Union that Hume attributed the blessing
"of a government perfectly regular, and exempt from all violence
and injustice."[7] Many years later Thomas Carlyle, in whom

---

[1] *Works*, ix. 158.
[2] Boswell's *Johnson*, v. 248.
[3] *Works*, ix. 24.
[4] Smollett's *History of England*, ii. 99.
[5] *Humphry Clinker*, iii. 7.
[6] *Wealth of Nations*, i. 398.
[7] Hume's *History of England*, vii. 438.

glowed the *perfervidum ingenium Scotorum* as it has glowed in few, owned that "the Union was one of Scotland's chief blessings," though it was due to Wallace and to men like him "that it was not the chief curse."[1]

It must never be forgotten that in this Union England was no less blessed than Scotland; that if she gave wealth to Scotland, Scotland nobly repaid the gift in men. In the sixteenth and seventeenth centuries the English stock had been quickened and strengthened and ennobled by fugitives seeking refuge on her shores from the persecutions of priests and kings, which passed over the coward and the base, and fell only on the brave and the upright. To the Fleming and the Huguenot was now added the Scot. In philosophy, in history, in law, in science, in poetry, in romance, in the arts of life, in trade, in government, in war, in the spread of our dominions, in the consolidation of our Empire, glorious has been the part which Scotland has played. Her poet's prayer has been answered, and in "bright succession" have been raised men to adorn and guard not only herself but the country which belongs to Englishmen and Scotchmen alike. Little of this was seen, still less foreseen by Johnson. The change which was going on in Scotland was rapid and conspicuous; the change which she was working outside her borders was slow, and as yet almost imperceptible. What was seen raised not admiration, but jealousy of the vigorous race which was everywhere so rapidly "making its way to employment, riches, and distinction." That Johnson should exult in the good which Scotland had derived from England through the Union was natural. Scarcely less natural that he should point out how much remained to be done before the Scotch attained the English level, not only in the comforts and refinements, but even in the decencies of life. One great peculiarity in their civilization struck him deeply. "They had attained the liberal without the manual arts, and excelled in ornamental knowledge while they wanted the conveniences of common life."[2] Even the peasantry were able to dispute with wonderful sagacity upon the articles of their faith, though they were content to live in huts which had not a single chimney to carry off the smoke.[3] Wesley, each time that he crossed the Borders, found a far harder task awaiting him than when he was upbraiding, denouncing, and exhorting an English

---

[1] *Past and Present* (ed. 1858), p. 80.   [2] *Works*, ix. 23.
[3] *Humphry Clinker*, iii. 83.

congregation. To the Scotch, cradled as they had been in the Shorter Catechism, and trained as they were from their youth up in theology, his preaching, like Paul's to the Greeks, was too often foolishness. He spoke to a people, as he complained, "who heard much, knew everything, and felt nothing."[1] Though "you use the most cutting words still they *hear*, but *feel* no more than the seats they sit upon."[2] Nowhere did he speak more roughly than in Scotland. No one there was offended at plain dealing. "In this respect they were a pattern to all mankind." But yet "they hear and hear, and are just what they were before."[3] He was fresh from the Kelso people and was preaching to a meeting in Northumberland when he wrote: "Oh! what a difference is there between these living stones, and the dead unfeeling multitudes in Scotland."[4] "The misfortune of a Scotch congregation," he recorded on another occasion, "is they know everything; so they learn nothing."[5]

With their disputations learning the meagreness of their fare and the squalor of their dwellings but ill contrasted. "Dirty living," said Smollett, "is the great and general reproach of the commonalty of this kingdom."[6] While Scotland sent forth into the world year after year swarms of young men trained in thrift, well stored with knowledge, and full of energy and determination, the common people bore an ill-repute for industry. They were underfed, and under-feeding produced indolent work. "Flesh-meat they seldom or never tasted; nor any kind of strong liquor except two-penny at times of uncommon festivity."[7] "Ale," wrote Lord Kames, "makes no part of the maintenance of those in Scotland who live by the sweat of their brow. Water is their only drink."[8] Adam Smith admitted that both in bodily strength and personal appearance they were below the English standard. "They neither work so well, nor look so well."[9] Wolfe, when he returned to England from Scotland in 1753, said that he had not crossed the Border a mile when he saw the difference that was produced upon the face of the country by labour and industry. "The English are clean and laborious, and the Scotch excessively dirty and lazy."[10]

This dirtiness would offend an Englishman more than a man of

---

[1] Wesley's *Journal*, iv. 13.
[2] *Ib.* p. 272. [3] *I.* iv. 229.
[4] *I.* ii. 412.
[5] *Ib.* iii. 179.
[6] *Humphry Clinker*, iii. 44.
[7] *Ib.* iii. 85.
[8] Kames's *Sketches of the History of Man*, ii. 336.
[9] *Wealth of Nations*, i. 222.
[10] Wright's *Life of Wolfe*, p. 276.

any other nation, for "high and low, rich and poor, they were remarkable for cleanness all the world over."[1] Matthew Bramble, in Smollett's *Humphry Clinker*, notices the same change. "The boors of Northumberland," he wrote, "are lusty fellows, fresh-complexioned, cleanly and well-clothed ; but the labourers in Scotland are generally lank, lean, hard featured, sallow, soiled and shabby. The cattle are much in the same style with their drivers, meagre, stunted, and ill-equipt."[2] Topham, in his *Letters from Edinburgh*, asserts the misery, but denies the idleness. Temperance and labour were, he says, in the extreme ; nevertheless, on all sides were seen, "haggard looks, meagre complexions, and bodies weakened by fatigue and worn down by the inclemency of the seasons." Neither were the poor of the capital any better off. Their wretchedness and poverty exceeded, he thought, what was to be found anywhere else in the whole world. But though as a nation the Scotch were very poor, yet they were very honest.[3] A traveller through the country in 1766 goes so far as to maintain that the common people in outward appearance would not at first be taken to be of the human species. Though their indigence was extreme, yet they would rather suffer poverty than labour. Their nastiness was greater than could be reported. Happily their rudeness was beginning to wear off, and in the trading towns where the knowledge of the use of money was making them eager enough to acquire it, they were already pretty well civilized and industrious.[4] Wages were miserably low. The Scotch labourer received little more than half what was paid to the Englishman ; yet grain was dearer in Scotland than in England.[5] The historian of Edinburgh thus sums the general condition of the labouring poor :—

"The common people have no ideas of the comforts of life. The labourers and low mechanics live in a very wretched style. Their houses are the receptacles of nastiness, where the spider may in peace weave his web from generation to generation. A garden, where nothing is to be seen but a few plants of coleworts or potatoes, amidst an innumerable quantity of weeds, surrounds his house. A bit of flesh will not be within his door twice a year. He abhors industry, and has no relish for the comforts arising from it."

Lord Elibank's famous reply to Johnson's definition of *oats* had

[1] Kames's *Sketches of the History of Man*, i. 265.
[2] *Humphry Clinker*, ii. 213.
[3] *Letters from Edinburgh*, pp. 270, 361.
[4] *Gentleman's Magazine*, 1766, p. 209.
[5] *Wealth of Nations*, i. 100. See also Arnot's *History of Edinburgh*, p. 557, and Knox's *Tour*, p. cxviii.
Arnot's *History of Edinburgh* (ed. 1779), p. 353.

every merit but a foundation of fact. "Oats," wrote Johnson, "a grain which in England is generally given to horses, but in Scotland supports the people." "Very true," replied his lordship, "and where will you find such men and such horses?"[1]

The natural result of this general poverty was seen in the number of beggars who thronged the streets and roads. Scotland was neither blessed with a good poor-law nor cursed with a bad one. The relief of want was left altogether to charity. In Edinburgh Johnson thought that the proportion of beggars was not less than in London. "In the smaller places it was far greater than in English towns of the same extent." The mendicants were not, however, of the order of sturdy vagabonds. They were neither importunate nor clamorous. "They solicit silently, or very modestly."[2] Smollett went so far as to maintain in his *Humphry Clinker*, which was published only two years before Johnson's visit, that "there was not a beggar to be seen within the precincts of Edinburgh."[3] For some years, indeed, the streets had been free of them, for a charity workhouse had been erected, to which they were all committed. But the magistrates had grown careless, and the evil had broken out afresh. "The streets are crowded with begging poor," wrote one writer. "We see the whole stairs, streets, and public walks swarming with beggars every day," wrote another.[4]

The general neglect of the decencies of life was due chiefly to poverty, but partly, no doubt, to that violent outburst against all that is beautiful and graceful which accompanied the Reformation in Scotland. A nation which, as a protest against popery, "thought dirt and cobwebs essential to the house of God," was not likely in their homes to hold that cleanliness was next to godliness. The same coarseness of living had been found in all classes, though it was beginning to yield before English influence. Dr. Alexander Carlyle, in the year 1742, notices as a sign of increasing refinement, that at the tavern in Haddington, where the Presbytery dined, knives and forks were provided for the table. A few years earlier each guest had brought his own. There was, however, only one glass, which went round with the bottle.[6] The same custom had prevailed in Edinburgh when Lord Kames was

---

[1] Boswell's *Johnson*, i. 244, n. 8.
[2] Johnson's *Works*, ix. 9.
[3] *Humphry Clinker* (ed. 1792), iii. 5.
[4] *Scots Magazine*, 1772, p. 636, and 1773, p. 393. *Humphry Clinker*, iii. 5.
[6] Dr. Alexander Carlyle's *Autobiography*, p. 64.

a young man. French wine was placed on the table, he said, in a small tin vessel, which held about an English pint. A single drinking-glass served a company the whole evening, and the first persons who called for a new glass with every new pint were accused of luxury.[1] Boswell could remember the time when a carving knife was looked upon as a novelty. One of his friends was rated by his father, " a gentleman of ancient family and good literature, for introducing such a foppish superfluity." In the previous generation whatever food was eaten with a spoon, such as soup, milk, or pudding, used to be taken by every person dipping his spoon into the common dish.[2] When an old laird was complimented on the accomplishments which his son had brought home from his travels, " he answered that he knew nothing he had learnt but to cast a sark (change a shirt) every day, and to sup his kail twice."[3] Of the food that was served up, there was not much greater variety than of the dishes in which it was served. When Wesley first visited Scotland, even at a nobleman's table, he had only one kind of meat, and no vegetables whatever. By the year 1788, however, vegetables were, he recorded, as plentiful as in England.[4] The butter in these early days made in country houses, " would have turned stomachs the least squeamish." But by the introduction of tea a great improvement had been made. Bread and butter was taken with it, and a demand arose for butter that was sweet and clean. Wheaten bread, too, began to be generally eaten. So great a delicacy had it been, that the sixpenny loaf and the sugar used to be kept "locked up in the lady's press."[5] In the Highlands, at all events, there was a great variety as well as abundance of food. The following was the breakfast which in Argyleshire was set before the travellers in *Humphry Clinker:*—

"One kit of boiled eggs; a second full of butter; a third full of cream; an entire cheese made of goat's milk; a large earthen pot full of honey; the best part of a ham; a cold venison pasty; a bushel of oatmeal made in thin cakes and bannocks, with a small wheaten loaf in the middle for the strangers; a large stone bottle full of whisky, another of brandy, and a kilderkin of ale. There was a ladle chained to the cream kit, with curious wooden bickers to be filled from this

---

[1] Kames's *Sketches of the History of Man* (ed. 1807), i. 507.
[2] *London Magazine* for 1778, p. 198.
[3] *Scotland and Scotsmen in the Eighteenth Century*, ii. 64. George Drummond of Blair, of whom this story is told, did not succeed to his estate till 1739 (*ib.* p. 112), so that this rude

mode of eating came down nearly to the date of Johnson's visit, even in the houses of gentlemen. In the houses of "the substantial tenants" it continued till much later (*ib.* p. 64).

[4] Wesley's *Journal*, iv. 418.
[5] *Scotland and Scotsmen in the Eighteenth Century*, ii. 70, 71, 251.

reservoir. The spirits were drunk out of a silver quaff, and the ale out of horn. Finally a large roll of tobacco was presented by way of desert, and every individual took a comfortable quid, to prevent the bad effects of the morning air."

Knox, in his *Tour through the Highlands*, gives a still vaster bill of fare. The houses of the country gentlemen were for the most part small. "It was only on festivals or upon ceremonious occasions, that the dining-room was used. People lived mostly in the family bed-chamber, where friends and neighbours were received without scruple. Many an easy, comfortable meal," writes Ramsay, of Ochtertyre, "had I made in that way." It was to this custom that the Scotch had of turning a bed room into an eating-room that an English traveller refers, when he says that the Edinburgh taverns are the worst in the world, for "you sup underground in a bed-chamber." Even at the modern houses there was generally a total absence of an accommodation such as would not at the present day be tolerated in a labourer's cottage by a sanitary inspector in any district in England.

The state of the capital was far worse even than the state of the country. It was one of the last places in the world on which would have been bestowed that favourite and almost exalted epithet of praise — *neat*. The houses, indeed, were solidly built, and the rooms of the well-to-do people were comfortable and clean, and often spacious. "Nothing could form a stronger contrast than the difference between the outside and the inside of the door." Within all was decency and propriety, without was a filthy staircase leading down into a filthy street. Every story was a complete house, occupied by a separate family. The steep and dark staircase was common to all, and was kept clean by none. It was put to the basest uses. The gentry did not commonly occupy the lowest stories or the highest. The following is the list of the inhabitants of a good house in the High Street:

"First door upstairs, Mr. Stirling, fishmonger.
"Second door, Mrs. Urquhart, who kept a lodging house of good repute.
"Third flat, the Dowager Countess of Balcarras.
"Fourth flat, Mrs. Buchan, of Kelly.

INTRODUCTION

"Fifth flat, the Misses Elliots, milliners.
"Garret, a great variety of tailors and other tradesmen.

There were no water pipes, there were no drain pipes, there were no cess-pools, and there were no covered sewers in the streets. At a fixed hour of the night all the impurities were carried down the common staircase in tubs, and emptied into the street as into a common sewer, or else, in defiance of the law, cast out of the window. "Throwing over the window" was the delicate phrase in which this vile practice was veiled. It was "an obstinate disease which had withstood all the labour of the Magistrates, Acts of Council, Dean of Guild Courts for stencheling,[2] tirlesing,[3] and locking up windows, fines, imprisonments, and banishing the city."[4] The servants were willing to serve for lower wages in houses where this practice was winked at. It gave rise to numerous quarrels which caused constables more trouble than any other part of their duty.[5] According to the account given by the English maid in *Humphry Clinker*, when "the throwing over" began, "they called *gardy loo* to the passengers, which signifies *Lord have mercy upon you.*"[6] A young English traveller, who, the first night of his arrival in Edinburgh, was enjoying his supper, as he tells us, and good bottle of claret with a merry company in a tavern, heard, as the clock was striking ten, the beat of the city drum, the signal for the scavenging to begin. The company at once began to fumigate the room by lighting pieces of paper and throwing them on the table. Tobacco smoking, it is clear, could not have been in fashion. As his way to his lodgings lay through one of the wynds he was provided "with a guide who went before him, crying out all the way, *Hud your Haunde.*"[7] The city scavengers cleansed the streets as fast as they could, and by opening reservoirs which were placed at intervals washed the pavement clean.[8]

To this intolerable nuisance the inhabitants generally seemed

---

[1] *Reekiana*, by Robert Chambers, p. 227: "The house was situated at the head of Dickson's Close, a few doors below Niddry Street." I have found all these names, except Sterling's, in the recent interesting reprint of the *Edinburgh Directory* for 1773-4, published by William Brown, Edinburgh, 1889.

[2] "Stenchel. An iron bar for a window." Jamieson's *Scottish Dictionary*.

[3] *Tirlesing* is not given by Jamieson.

[4] *The City Cleaned and Country Improven*. Edinburgh, 1760, p. 5.

[5] *The City Cleaned and Country Improven*, pp. 6, 8.

[6] *Humphry Clinker*, ii. 227. *Gardy loo* is a corruption of *gardez l'eau*, a cry which, like so many other Scotch customs and words, bears witness to the close connection which of old existed between Scotland and France.

[7] Burt's *Letters from a Gentleman*, &c., i. 21.

[8] Topham's *Letters from Edinburgh*, p. 152.

insensible, and were too apt to imagine the disgust of strangers as little better than affectation.¹ Yet it was not affectation which led John Wesley, in May, 1761, to make the following entry in his Journal:—

> "The situation of the city on a hill shelving down on both sides, as well as to the east, with the stately castle upon a craggy rock on the west, is inexpressibly fine. And the main street so broad and finely paved, with the lofty houses on either hand (many of them seven or eight stories high) is far beyond any in Great Britain. But how can it be suffered that all manner of filth should still be thrown, even into this street, continually? Where are the Magistracy, the Gentry, the Nobility of the Land? Have they no concern for the honour of their nation? How long shall the capital city of Scotland, yea and the chief street of it, stink worse than a common sewer?"²

Ten years earlier he had described the town as dirtier even than Cologne. According to Wolfe, it was not till after Christmas, when the company had come into it from the country, that it was "in all its perfection of dirt and gaiety."³ Gray called it "that most picturesque (at a distance) and nastiest (when near) of all capital cities."⁴ "Pray for me till I see you," he added, "for I dread Edinburgh and the ——."⁵ To add to the insalubrity, the windows would not readily open. In Scotland they neither opened wide on hinges, nor were drawn up and down by weights and pulleys. For the most part the lower sash only could be raised; and when lifted, it was propped open by a stick or by a pin thrust into a hole.⁶ "What cannot be done without some uncommon trouble or particular expedient will not often be done at all. The incommodiousness of the Scotch windows keeps them very closely shut."⁷ From this closeness Johnson suffered not a little, for he loved fresh air, "and on the coldest day or night would set open a window and stand before it," as Boswell knew to his cost.⁸ Topham, who sided with his Scotch friends against Johnson, scoffed at these observations on window-frames and pulleys. "Men of the world," he wrote, "would not have descended to such remarks. A petty and frivolous detail of trifling circumstances are [*sic*] the certain signs of ignorance or inexperience."⁹ Johnson, in introducing the subject, had guarded himself against such reflections. "These diminutive observations," he said, "seem to take away something

---

¹ *Humphry Clinker*, ii. 221.
² Wesley's *Journal*, iii. 54.
³ Wright's *Life of General Wolfe*, p. 147.
⁴ Gray's *Works*, iv. 52.
⁵ *Ib.* p. 61.

⁶ This arrangement is still not uncommon in country places.
⁷ Johnson's *Works*, ix. 18.
⁸ Boswell's *Johnson*, v. 300.
Letters from Edinburgh, p. 141.

from the dignity of writing. But it must be remembered that the true state of every nation is the state of common life."[1] This indifference to pure air no doubt spread death far and wide. In Sir Walter Scott's family we see an instance of the unwholesomeness of the Old Town. His six elder brothers and sisters, who were all born in the College Wynd, died young. It was only by sending him to breathe country air that he was reared. His father's younger children were born in one of the new squares, and they for the most part were healthy.[2]

From one burthen that weighed heavily in England the guests in most houses in Scotland were free. It was the Scotch, who, as Boswell boasted, "had the honour of being the first to abolish the unhospitable, troublesome, and ungracious custom of giving vails to servants. 'Sir,' said Johnson, 'you abolished vails, because you were too poor to be able to give them.'"[3] How heavily they weighed on all but the rich is shown by an anecdote that I have read somewhere of a poor gentleman, who refused to dine with his kinsman, a nobleman of high rank, unless with the invitation a guinea were sent him to distribute among the expectant servants, who, with outstretched hands, always thronged the hall and blocked up the doorway as he left. "I paid ten shillings to my host's servants for my dinner and retired," is the record of a man who had received the honour of an invitation to the house of an English nobleman of high rank.[4] Even Queen Caroline had complained of "the pretty large expense" to which she had been put in the summer of 1735 in visiting her friends, not at their country houses, but in town. "That is your own fault (said the King), for my father, when he went to people's houses in town, never was fool enough to be giving away his money."[5] It was to the gentlemen of the county of Aberdeen that was due the merit of beginning this great reformation. About the year 1759 they resolved at a public meeting that vails should be abolished and wages increased.[6] Early in February, 1760, the Select Society of Edinburgh, following their lead, passed a resolution to which their President, the historian Robertson, seems to have lent the graces of his style. They declared that "this custom, being unknown to

---

[1] *Works*, ix. 18.
[2] Lockhart's *Life of Scott*, i. 108.
[3] Boswell's *Johnson*, ii. 78. Sheridan, in his *Life of Swift*, records an earlier abolition of vails in Ireland (Swift's *Works*, ii. 108).
[4] Thicknesse's *Observations on the Customs and Manners of the French*, 1766, p. 106.
[5] Lord Hervey's *Memoirs*, ii. 59.
[6] Arnot's *History of Edinburgh*, p. 376.

other nations and a reproach upon the manners and police of this country, has a manifest tendency to corrupt the hospitality and to destroy all intercourse between families. They resolved that from and after the term of Whitsuntide next every member of the Society would absolutely prohibit his own servants to take vails or drink-money, and that he would not offer it to the servants of any person who had agreed to this resolution."[1] Like resolutions followed from the Faculty of Advocates, the Society of Clerks to His Majesty's Signet, the Heritors of Mid-Lothian headed by the Earl of Lauderdale, the Grand Lodge of Freemasons, headed by the Earl of Leven, and the Honourable Company of Scots Hunters headed by the President, the Earl of Errol.[2] The same good change was attempted a few years later in England, but apparently without success. The footmen, night after night, raised a riot at Ranelagh Gardens, and mobbed and ill-treated some gentlemen who had been active in the attempt. "There was fighting with drawn swords for some hours; they broke one chariot all to pieces. The ladies go into fits, scream, run into the gardens, and do everything that is ridiculous."[3]

That "felicity" which England had in its taverns and inns was not equally enjoyed in Scotland. Certainly it was not in Edinburgh that was to be found "that throne of human felicity a tavern chair."[4] Yet in the Lowlands generally the fare in the inns was good and the accommodation clean. Along both the eastern and the western roads John Wesley was well pleased with the entertainment with which he met. "We had all things good, cheap, in great abundance, and remarkably well dressed."[5] In the *Gentleman's Magazine* for December, 1771, a curious list is given of the inns and innkeepers in Scotland. According to this account the fare generally was good, while everywhere was found "excellent clean linen both for bed and board." The traveller did well, however, who had his sheets *toasted* and his bed warmed, for the natives, used as they were to sleeping in their wet plaids, were careless about a damp bed. Goldsmith, on the other hand, spoke as ill of the Scotch inns as he did of the Scotch landscape. In them, he

---

[1] *Edinburgh Chronicle* for 1760, p. 495.
[2] *Ib.* pp. 503, 518, 583, 623. The Scots Hunters were, I suppose, the same as the Royal Hunters—a body of gentlemen volunteers who were raised at the time of the Rebellion of 1745, and served under General Oglethorpe.
[3] Walpole's *Memoirs of the Reign of George III.*, ii. 3, and *Letters of the First Earl of Malmesbury*, i. 108-9.
[4] Boswell's *Johnson*, ii. 452.
[5] Wesley's *Journal*, i. 228, 283.

says, "vile entertainment is served up, complained of, and sent down; up comes worse, and that also is changed, and every change makes our wretched cheer more unsavoury."[1] The scantiness of his purse, however, would have made him resort to the humblest houses, and probably his experience did not extend much outside of Edinburgh. Of the inns of that city, no one, whether native or stranger, had a good word to say. The accommodation that was provided, writes the historian of Edinburgh, "was little better than that of a waggoner or a carrier."[2] "The inns are mean buildings," he continues, "their apartments dirty and dismal; and if the waiters happen to be out of the way, a stranger will perhaps be shocked with the novelty of being shown into a room by a dirty sun-burnt wench without shoes or stockings. If he should desire furnished lodgings, he is probably conducted to the third or fourth floor, up dark and dirty stairs, and there shown into apartments meanly fitted up. The taverns in general are dirty and dismal as the inns; an idle profusion of victuals, collected without taste, and dressed without skill or cleanliness, is commonly served up. There are, however, exceptions, and a Scots tavern, if a good one, is the best of all taverns." Smollett, willing as he was to see the good side of everything in Scotland, yet represents the inn in Edinburgh at which Matthew Bramble alighted as being "so filthy and so disagreeable in every respect, that the old man began to fret."[4] Perhaps it was the same house which is described by Topham in the following lively passage in his *Letters*:[5]

"Nov. 15, 1774. There is no inn that is better than an alehouse, nor any accommodation that is decent or cleanly. On my first arrival my companion and myself, after the fatigue of a long day's journey, were landed at one of these stable-keepers (for they have modesty enough to give themselves no higher denomination) in a part of the town called the Pleasance. We were conducted by a poor devil of a girl, without shoes or stockings, and only a single linsey-wolsey petticoat, which just reached half-way to her ankles, into a room where about twenty Scotch drovers had been regaling themselves with whiskey and potatoes. You may guess our amazement when we were informed that this was the best inn in the metropolis, that we could have no beds, unless we had an inclination to sleep together, and in the same room with the company which a stage-coach had that moment discharged."

In the *Edinburgh Directory* for 1773-4, among the different

---

[1] *Present State of Polite Learning*, ch. xii.
[2] Arnot - *History of Edinburgh*, p. 658.
[3] *Ib.* pp. 352-4.
[4] *Humphry Clinker*, ii. 214.
[5] *Letters from Edinburgh*, p. 18.
 "The Pleasance consists of one mean street; through it lies the principal road to London."— Arnot's *History of Edinburgh*, p. 328.

trades, there is no entry under the heading of *inn-keepers*. There are *vintners*, who, I suppose, were also tavern-keepers, and *stablers*, who kept the inns. It was to this curious appellation that Topham referred when he said that the inn-keepers had the modesty to call themselves stable-keepers.

A few years after Johnson's visit a good hotel was at last opened in the New Town. The accommodation was elegant, but the charges extravagant.[1] The French traveller, Saint Fond, who stayed in it about the year 1780, said that the house was magnificent and adorned with columns, as his bill was with flourishes and vignettes. Half a sheet of note-paper was charged threepence, with sixpence added for the trouble of fetching it. He paid twice as much for everything as in the best inn on the road from London. In all his journeyings through England and Scotland he was only twice charged exorbitantly—at Dunn's Hotel in Edinburgh, and at the Bull's Head in Manchester.[2]

Johnson, coming from Berwick by the coast-road, entered Edinburgh by the Canongate. It was on a dusky night in August that, arm in arm with Boswell, he walked up the High Street. "Its breadth and the loftiness of the buildings on each side made," he acknowledged, "a noble appearance."[3] In the light of the day he does not seem to have been equally impressed. "Most of the buildings are very mean," he wrote to Mrs. Thrale; "and the whole town bears some resemblance to the old part of Birmingham."[4] In his Letters he does not touch on that appearance so unusual to Englishmen which, as we learn from his narrative, generally struck him in the ancient towns of Scotland.[5] Wesley's attention was caught by this same "peculiar oddness" and "air of antiquity." They were like no places that he had ever seen in England, Wales, or Ireland.[6] It was not, however, to Birmingham that that great traveller likened the famous High Street. There was nothing, he said, that could compare with it in Great Britain. Defoe's admiration had risen still higher. In his eyes it ranked as almost the largest, longest, and finest street in the world. Its solidity of stone he contrasted with the slightness of the houses in the South. Lofty though the buildings were, placed, too, on "the narrow ridge of a long ascending mountain," with storms often raging round them,

[1] Arnot's *History of Edinburgh*, p. 353.
[2] *Voyage en Angleterre*, &c., i. 200, 229; ii. 309.
[3] Boswell's *Johnson*, v. 23.
[4] *Piozzi Letters*, i. 109.
[5] *Ib.*, ii. 18.
[6] Wesley's *Journal*, ii. 228.

INTRODUCTION.

"there was no blowing of tiles about the streets to knock people on the heads as they passed; no stacks of chimneys and gable-ends of houses falling in to bury the inhabitants in their ruins, as was often found in London and other of our paper-built cities in England."[1] "The High Street is the stateliest street in the world," said another writer; "being broad enough for five coaches to drive up a-breast, while the houses are proportionately high."[2] According to Topham it surpassed "the famous street in Lisle, La Rue Royale."[3] "It would be undoubtedly one of the noblest streets in Europe," wrote Smollett, "if an ugly mass of mean buildings, called the Luckenbooths, had not thrust itself into the middle of the way."[4] Pennant had the same tale to tell. "As fine a street as most in Europe, was spoilt by the Luckenbooth Row and the Guard House."[5] Carlyle, when he came to Edinburgh as a boy-student, in the year 1809, had seen "the Luckenbooths, with their strange little ins and outs, and eager old women in miniature shops of combs, shoe-laces, and trifles."[6] One venerable monument had been wantonly removed, while so much that was mean and ugly was left to encumber the street. In 1756 those "dull destroyers," the magistrates, had pulled down "Dun-Edin's Cross."[7] From the bottom of the hill "by the very Palace door," up to the gates of the Castle the High Street, even so late as Johnson's time, was the home of men of rank, of wealth, and of learning. It did not bear that look of sullen neglect which chills the stranger who recalls its past glories. The craftsmen and the nobles, the poor clerks and the wealthy merchants, judges, shopkeepers, labourers, authors, physicians, and lawyers, lived all side by side, so that "the tide of existence" which swept up and down was as varied as it was full. The coldness of the grey stone of the tall houses was relieved by the fantastic devices in red or yellow or blue on a ground of black, by which each trader signified the commodities in which he dealt. As each story was a separate abode, there were often seen painted on the front of one tall house half-a-dozen different signs. Here was a quartern loaf over a full-trimmed periwig, and there a Cheshire cheese or a rich firkin of butter over stays and petticoats." To the north, scarcely broken as yet by the scattered buildings of the infant New Town,

---

[1] Defoe's *Tour through Great Britain; Account of Scotland* (ed. 1727), iii. 29, 30, 33.
[2] J. Mackie's *Journey through Scotland*, p. 65.
[3] *Letters from Edinburgh*, p. 8.
[4] *Humphry Clinker*, ii. 220.
[5] *Tour in Scotland*, i. 52.
[6] Carlyle's *Reminiscences*, ii. 5.
[7] See *Marmion*, note in the Appendix on Canto V., Stanza 25.
[8] *Letters from Edinburgh*, p. 28.

the outlook commanded that "incomparable prospect" which delighted Colonel Mannering, as he gazed from the window of Counsellor Pleydell's library on "the Frith of Forth with its islands; the embayment which is terminated by the Law of North Berwick, and the varied shores of Fife, indenting with a hilly outline the clear blue horizon."[1]

Every Sunday during the hours of service the streets were silent and solitary, as if a plague had laid waste the city. But in a moment the scene was changed. The multitude that poured forth from each church swept everything before it. The stranger who attempted to face it was driven from side to side by the advancing flood. The faithful were so intently meditating on the good things which they had just heard that they had no time to look before them. With their large prayer-books under their arms, their eyes fixed steadily on the ground, and wrapped up in their plaid cloaks, they went on regardless of everything that passed.[2]

Less than thirty years before Johnson, on that August night, "went up streets,"[3] the young Pretender, surrounded by his Highlanders, and preceded by his heralds and trumpeters, had marched from the Palace of his ancestors to the ancient Market Cross, and there had had his father proclaimed King by the title of James the Seventh of Scotland and Third of England. Down the same street in the following Spring his own standard, with its proud motto of *Tandem Triumphans*, and the banners of thirteen of his chief captains, in like manner preceded by heralds and trumpeters, had been borne on the shoulders of the common hangman and thirteen chimney-sweepers, to the same Cross, and there publicly burnt.[4] Here, too, was seen from time to time the sad and terrible procession, when, from the Tolbooth, some unhappy wretch was led forth to die in the Grass Market. As the clock struck the hour after noon, the City Guard knocked at the prison door. The convict at once came out, dressed in a waistcoat and breeches of white, bound with black ribands, and wearing a night-cap, also bound with black. His hands were tied behind him, and a rope was round his neck. On each side of him walked a clergyman, the hangman followed behind, muffled in a great coat, while all around, with their arms ready, marched the Town Guard. Every window in every floor of every house was crowded with spectators.¹ Happily the criminal law of Scotland was far less bloody than that which at this time disgraced England, and executions, except for murder, were rare.² There was also much less crime. While the streets and neighbourhood of London were beset by footpads and highwaymen, in Edinburgh a man might go about with the same security at midnight as at noonday. Street robberies were very rare, and a street murder was, it is said, a thing unknown. This general safety was due partly to the Town Guard, partly also to the Society of Cadies, or Cawdies, a fraternity of errand-runners. Each member had to find surety for good behaviour, and the whole body was answerable for the dishonesty of each. Their chief place of stand was at the top of the High Street, where some of them were found all the day and most of the night. They were said to be acquainted with every person and every place in Edinburgh. No stranger arrived but they knew of it at once. They acted as a kind of police, and were as useful as Sir John Fielding's thief-takers in London.⁴ In spite of these safeguards, in the autumn before Johnson's visit there was an outbreak of crime. A reward of one guinea each was offered for the arrest of forty persons who had been banished the city, and who were suspected of having returned.⁵ The worthy Magistrates, it should seem, were like Dogberry, and did not trouble themselves about a thief so long as he stole out of their company.

The Edinburgh Tolbooth and the other Scotch gaols were worse even than those cruel dens in which the miserable prisoners were confined in England. They had no court-yard where the fresh air of heaven might be breathed for some hours at least of every weary day. Not even to the unhappy debtor was any indulgence shown. That air was denied to him which was common to all. Even under a guard, said an expounder of the law, he had no right to the benefit of free air; "for every creditor has

---

¹ *Letters from Edinburgh*, pp. 58-62.
² According to Arnot, for many years preceding 1763, the average number of executions for the whole of Scotland was only three. There were four succeeding years in which the punishment of death was not once inflicted. By 1783, however, the English severity seems to have crept in, for in that year, in Edinburgh alone, in one week there were six criminals under sentence of death.—*History of Edinburgh*, p. 670.

³ The guard consisted of seventy-five private men.—*Ib.* p. 506.
⁴ Arnot's *History of Edinburgh*, pp. 502, 058, and *Letters from Edinburgh*, pp. 355-60. By the year 1783, says Arnot, in his second edition, p. 658, their number and their character had greatly sunk. See also *Humphry Clinker*, ii. 240.

Scots Magazine for 1772, p. 636.

an interest that his debtor be kept under close confinement, that by his *squalor carceris* he may be brought to the payment of his just debt."[1] He was to learn the fulness of the meaning of "the curse of a severe creditor who pronounces his debtor's doom, *To Rot in Gaol*."[2] At the present time even in Siberia there cannot, I believe, be found so cruel a den as that old Edinburgh Tolbooth, by whose gloomy walls Johnson passed on his way to Boswell's comfortable home close by, where Mrs. Boswell and tea were awaiting him. In one room were found by a writer who visited the prison three lads confined among "the refuse of a long succession of criminals." The straw which was their bed had been worn into bits two inches long. In a room on the floor above were two miserable boys not twelve years old. But the stench that assailed him as the door was opened so overpowered him that he fled. The accumulation of dirt which he saw in the rooms and on the staircases was

THE TOLBOOTH.

so great, that it set him speculating in vain on the length of time which must have been required to make it. The supply of the food and drink was the jailer's monopoly; whenever the poor wretches received a little money from friends outside, or from charity, they were not allowed the benefit of the market price. The choice of the debtor's prison was left to the caprice of his creditor, and that which was known to be the most loathsome was often selected.[3] The summer after Johnson's visit to Edinburgh

---

[1] John Erskine, quoted in Tytler's *Life of Lord Kames*, vol. i. app. x. p. 74, and in Arnot's *History of Edinburgh*, p. 299.

[2] Howard's *State of the Prisons*, p. 17.

[3] Arnot's *History of Edinburgh*, p. 300.

John Wesley, in one of the streets of that town, was suddenly arrested by a sheriff's officer on a warrant to commit him to the Tolbooth. Happily he was first taken to an adjoining building—some kind of spunging-house, it is probable—whence he sent word to his friends, and obtained bail. The charge brought against him was ridiculous, and in the end the prosecutor had heavy damages to pay.[1] Nevertheless, monstrous though the accusation was, had Wesley been not only a stranger and poor, but also friendless, it was in that miserable den that he would have been lodged. His deliverance might have been by gaol-fever.

Boswell himself, if we may trust the tradition, little more than four years before he welcomed Johnson, had run a risk of becoming acquainted with the inside of that prison. Scotland was all ablaze with the great Douglas cause. The succession to the large estates of the last Duke of Douglas was in dispute; so eagerly did men share in the shifting course of the long lawsuit, that it was scarcely safe to open the lips about it in mixed company. Boswell, with all the warmth of his eager nature, took the part of the heir whose legitimacy was disallowed by the casting vote of the President in the Court of Session. The case was carried on appeal to the House of Lords, and on Monday, February 27, 1769, the Scotch decision was reversed. A little before eight o'clock on Thursday evening the news reached Edinburgh by express. The city was at once illuminated, and the windows of the hostile judges were broken. Boswell, it is said, headed the mob. That his own father's house was among those which he and his followers attacked, as Sir Walter Scott had heard,[2] is very unlikely: Lord Auchinleck had voted in the minority, and so would have been in high favour with the rioters. A party of foot soldiers was marched into the city, a reward of fifty pounds was offered for the discovery of the offenders, and for some nights the streets were patrolled by two troops of dragoons.[3] "Boswell's good father," writes Ramsay of Ochtertyre, "entreated the President with tears in his eyes to put his son in the Tolbooth. Being brought before Sheriff Cockburn for examination, he was desired to tell all that happened that night in his own way. 'After,' said he, 'I had communicated the glorious news to my father, who received it very coolly, I went to

---

[1] Wesley's *Journal*, vol. iv. p. 17.
[2] Croker's *Boswell*, p. 387.
[3] *Scots Magazine* for 1769, p. 110; *The Speeches in the Douglas Cause* (most likely Boswell), p. 391; and Boswell's *Johnson*, ii. 230.

the Cross to see what was going on. There I overheard a group
of fellows forming their plan of operations. One of them asked
what sort of a man the sheriff was, and whether he was not to be
dreaded. 'No, no,' answered another; 'he is a puppy of the
President's making.' On hearing this exordium Mr. Cockburn
went off, leaving the culprit to himself."[1]

Among the sights which Johnson was shown at Edinburgh, the
New Town was not included. Yet some progress had been made
in laying out those streets,
"which in simplicity and
manliness of style and general breadth and bright-
ness of effect" were de-
stined to surpass anything
that has been attempted
in modern street archi-
tecture.[2] From Boswell's
windows, over the tops of
the stately elm-trees which
at that time ran in front of
James's Court and across
a deep and marshy hollow,
the rising houses could be
easily seen. Full in view
among the rest was the
new home Hume had
lately built for himself at
the top of a street which
was as yet unnamed, but

HUME'S HOUSE.

was soon, as St. David's, to commemorate in a jest the great
philosopher who was its first inhabitant. Had the change which
was so rapidly coming over Auld Reekie been understood in its
full extent, surely Johnson's attention would have been drawn to
it. Boswell only mentions the New Town to introduce the name
of "the ingenious architect" who planned it, Craig, the nephew
of the poet Thomson.[3] His mind, perhaps, was so set on
escaping from "the too narrow sphere of Scotland," and on re-

---

[1] Scotland and Scotsmen in the Eighteenth Century, vol. i. p. 173.
[2] Ruskin's Lectures on Architecture and Painting, p. 2.
[3] Boswell's Johnson, iii. 360, v. 68.

moving to London, that of Edinburgh and its fortunes he was careless. Yet, shrewd observer as he was of men and manners, he must have noticed how the tide of fashion had already begun to set from the Old Town, and was threatening to leave the ancient homes of the noble and the wealthy like so many wrecks behind. In many people there was a great reluctance to make a move. To some the old familiar life in a flat was dear, and the New Town was built after the English fashion, in what was known as "houses to themselves." "One old lady fancied she should be lost if she were to get into such an habitation; another feared being blown away in going over the New Bridge; while a third thought that these new fashions could come to nae gude."[1] Nevertheless, in spite of all these terrors, the change came very swiftly. So early as 1783, "a romping wife, or saleswoman of old furniture," occupied the house which not many years before had been Lord President Craigie's, while a chairman who had taken Lord Drummore's house had "lately left it for want of accommodation."[2] There were men of position, however, who, fashion or no fashion, clung to their old homes for many years later. Queensberry House, nearly at the foot of the Canongate, which in later years was turned into a Refuge for the Destitute, so late as 1803 was inhabited by the Lord Chief Baron Montgomery. Lord Cockburn remembered well the old judge's tall, well-dressed figure in the old style, and the brilliant company which gathered round him in that ancient but decayed quarter.[3]

It was full five years before Johnson's arrival that Dr. Robertson, pleading the cause of his poverty-stricken University, pointed out how the large buildings that were rising suddenly on all sides, the magnificent bridge that had been begun, and the new streets and squares all bore the marks of a country growing in arts and in industry.[4] It was in 1765 that the foundations were laid of the bridge which was to cross the valley that separates the Old and New Town. It was not till 1772 that "it was made passable."[5] In 1783 the huge mound was begun which now so conveniently joins the two hills. The earth of which it is formed was dug out in making the foundations of the new houses. Fifteen hundred cartloads on an average were thrown in daily for the space of three

---

[1] Letters from Edinburgh, p. 42.
[2] Arnot's History of Edinburgh, p. 633.
[3] Cockburn's Memorials of his Time, p. 185.
[4] Scots Magazine for 1768, p. 115.
[5] Arnot's History of Edinburgh, p. 314.

years.[1] The valley, which with its lawns, its slopes, its trim walks, its beds of flowers, and its trees, adds so much to the pleasantness and beauty of Edinburgh, was when Johnson looked down into it "a deep morass, one of the dirtiest puddles upon earth."[2] It was in its black mud that Hume one day stuck when he had slipped off the stepping-stones on the way to his new house. A fishwife, who was following after him, recognizing "the Deist," refused to help him unless he should recite first the Lord's Prayer and the Belief. This he at once did to her great wonder. His admiration for the New Town was unbounded. If the High Street was finer than anything of its kind in Europe the New Town, he maintained, exceeded anything in any part of the world.[4] "You would not wonder that I have abjured London for ever," he wrote to his friend, Strahan, in the year 1772, "if you saw my new house and situation in St. Andrew's Square." Adam Smith told Rogers the poet, who visited Edinburgh in 1789, that the Old Town had given Scotland a bad name, and that he was anxious to move with the rest."

The age which I am attempting to describe was looked upon by Lord Cockburn as "the last purely Scotch age that Scotland was destined to see. The whole country had not begun to be absorbed in the ocean of London." The distance between the two capitals as measured by time, fatigue, and money was little less than the distance in the present day between Liverpool and New York. Johnson, who travelled in post-chaises, and therefore in great comfort, was nine days on the road. "He purposed," he wrote, "not to loiter much by the way;" but he did not journey by night, and he indulged in two days' rest at Newcastle. Hume, three years later, travelling by easy stages on account of his failing health, took two days longer." Had Johnson gone by the public conveyance, the "Newcastle Fly" would have brought him in three days as far as that town at a charge of £3 6s. On the panels of the "Fly" was painted the motto, *Sat cito si sat bene*. Thence he would have continued his journey by the "Edinburgh Fly," which traversed the whole remaining distance in a single day in summer, and in a day and a half in winter. The charge for this was £1 11s. 6d. In these sums were not included the payments to the drivers and guards. The "Newcastle Fly" ran six times a week, starting from London an hour after midnight. The "Edinburgh Fly" ran only on Tuesdays, Thursdays, and Saturdays. A traveller then who lost no time on the road, leaving London at one o'clock on Sunday night, would in the summer-time reach Edinburgh by Thursday evening, and in the winter after mid-day on Friday.[1] Even the mail which was carried on horse-back, and went five times a week, took in good weather about 82 hours.[2] The news of the battle of Culloden, though it was forwarded by an express, was seven days all but two or three hours in reaching London.[3] There were men living in 1824 who recollected when the mail came down with only one single letter for Edinburgh.[4] By 1793 a great acceleration had been effected in the coach-service. It was possible, so the proud boast ran, to leave Edinburgh after morning service on Sunday, spend a whole day in London, and be back again by six o'clock on Saturday morning.[5] The weary traveller would have had to pass every night in the coach. By the year 1800 the journey was done from London to Edinburgh in fifty-eight hours, and from Edinburgh to London in sixty and a half.[6] But such annihilation of time and space, as no doubt this rapid rate of travelling was then called, was not dreamed of in Johnson's day. The capitals of England and Scotland still stood widely apart. It was wholly "a Scotch scene" which the English traveller saw, and "independent tastes and ideas and pursuits" caught his attention.[7] Nevertheless in one respect Edinburgh, as I have already said, felt strongly the influence of England. In its literature and its language it was laboriously forming itself on the English model. There had been a long period during which neither learning nor literature had shone in Scotland with any brightness of light. Since the days of the great classical scholars not a single famous author had been seen. There had been "farthing candles" from time to time, but no "northern lights."[8] The two countries were under the same

[1] Mostyn Armstrong's *Survey of the Post Roads*, [illegible] ed. 1783, p. [illegible]; and Twiss' *Life of Lord Eldon*, i. 34.

[2] It was three hours longer on the return journey from Edinburgh to London.—Arnot's *History of Edinburgh*, p. 336.

[3] *Gentleman's Magazine* for 1746, p. 226.

[4] *Ledgerwood* [illegible] ed. 1805, i. 77.

[5] W. Creech's *Letters to Sir John Sinclair*, p. 11.

[6] Paterson's *British Itinerary*, ii. 602.

[7] Cockburn's *Life of Jeffrey*, i. 157.

[8] Boswell's *Johnson*, v. 57, n. 3. See also ii. pp. 58, 62; Johnson's *Works*, ix. 157, and Tytler's *Life of Lord Kames*, i. 3.

sovereign, but there was no Age of Queen Anne north of the Tweed. There was indeed that general diffusion of learning which was conspicuously wanting in England. An English traveller noticed with surprise how rare it was to find "a man of any rank but the lowest who had not some tincture of learning. It was the pride and delight of every father to give his son a liberal education."[1] Nevertheless it had been "with their learning as with provisions in a besieged town, every man had a mouthful and no one a bellyful."[2] That there was a foundation for Johnson's pointed saying was many years later candidly admitted by Sir Walter Scott.[3] So great had been the dearth of literature that the printer's art had fallen into decay. About the year 1740 there were but four printing-houses in Edinburgh, which found scanty employment in producing school-books, law-papers, newspapers, sermons, and Bibles. By 1779 the number had risen from four to seven and twenty.[4] This rapid growth was by no means wholly due to an increase in Scotch authors. Edinburgh might have become "a hot-bed of genius," but such productiveness even in a hot-bed would have been unparalleled. The booksellers in late years, in defiance of the supposed law of copyright, had begun to reprint the works of standard English writers, and after a long litigation had been confirmed in what they were doing by a decision given in the House of Lords.[5]

The growth of literature in Scotland had taken a turn which was not unnatural. In the troubles of the seventeenth century the nation, while yet it was in its power, had neglected to refine its language. No great masters of style had risen. There had been no Sir William Temple "to give cadence to its prose."[6] The settled government and the freedom from tyranny which the country enjoyed on the fall of the Stuarts, the growth of material wealth which followed on the Union, the gradual diminution of bigotry and the scattering of darkness which was part of the general enlightenment of Europe had given birth to a love of modern literature. The old classical learning no longer sufficed. Having no literature of their own which satisfied their aspirations, the younger generation of men was forced to acquire the language of their

---

[1] *Gentleman's Magazine* for 1766, p. 167.
[2] Boswell's *Johnson*, ii. 363, n. 5.
[3] In the speech which he made in 1824 on the opening of the New Edinburgh Academy.—Lockhart's *Life of Scott*, vii. 271.
[4] Arnot's *History of Edinburgh*, p. 437.
[5] Boswell's *Johnson*, i. 437, n. 272, and Hume's *Letters to Strahan*, p. 275.
[6] Boswell's *Johnson*, iii. 257.

ancient rivals, brought as it had been by a long succession of illustrious authors to a high degree of perfection.¹ It was to the volumes of Addison that the Scotch student was henceforth to give his days and nights. To read English was an art soon acquired, but to write it, and still more to speak it correctly, demanded a long and laborious study. Very few, with all their perseverance, succeeded like Mallet in "clearing their tongues from their native pronunciation."² Even to understand the language when spoken was only got by practice. A young lady from the country, who was reproached with having seen on the Edinburgh stage some loose play, artlessly replied:—"Indeed they did nothing wrong that I saw; and as for what they said, it was high English, and I did not understand it."³ Dr. Beattie studied English from books like a dead language. To write it correctly cost him years of labour.⁴ "The conversation of the Edinburgh authors," said Topham, "showed that they wrote English as a foreign tongue," for their spoken language was so unlike their written.⁵ Some men were as careless of their accent as they were careful of their words. Hume's tone was always broad Scotch, but Scotch words he carefully avoided.⁶ Others indulged in two styles and two accents, one for familiar life, the other for the pulpit, the court of Session, or the professor's chair. In all this there was a great and a strange variety. Lord Kames, for instance, in his social hour spoke pure Scotch, though "with a tone not displeasing from its vulgarity;" on the Bench his language approached to English.⁷ His brother judge, Lord Auchinleck, on the other hand, clung to his mother tongue. He would not smooth or round his periods, or give up his broad Scotch, however vulgar it was accounted. The sturdy old fellow felt, no doubt, a contempt for that "compound of affectation and pomposity" which some of his countrymen spoke—a language which "no Englishman could understand."⁸ In their attempt to get rid of their accent they too often arrived at the young lady's *High English*, a mode of speaking far enough removed no doubt from the Scotch, but such as "made 'the fools who used it' truly ridiculous."⁹ There were others who were far more suc-

¹ *Scotland and Scotsmen in the Eighteenth Century*, i. 163.
² Johnson's *Works*, viii. 464.
³ *Scotland and Scotsmen, &c.*, ii. 63.
⁴ Forbes' *Life of Beattie*, p. 242.
⁵ *Letters from Edinburgh*, p. 55.
⁶ Hume's *Letters to Strahan*, p. 6. *Scotland and Scotsmen, &c.*, i. 211, ii. 544; and Tytler's *Life of Lord Kames*, ii. 240.
⁷ *Scotland and Scotsmen, &c.*, i. 167-170, ii. 543.
⁸ Boswell's *Johnson*, ii. 159. Lord Jeffrey was

cessful. "The conversation of the Scots," wrote Johnson, "grows every day less unpleasing to the English; their peculiarities wear fast away; their dialect is likely to become in half a century provincial and rustic, even to themselves. The great, the learned, the ambitious, and the vain, all cultivate the English phrase, and the English pronunciation; and in splendid companies Scotch is not much heard, except now and then from an old lady."[1] The old lady whom he chiefly had in his memory when he wrote this was probably the Duchess of Douglas. He had met her at Boswell's table. "She talks broad Scotch with a paralytick voice," he wrote to Mrs. Thrale, "and is scarce understood by her own countrymen."[2] Boswell himself, by the instruction of a player from Drury Lane, who had brought a company to Edinburgh, succeeded so well in clearing his tongue of his Scotch that Johnson complimented him by saying: "Sir, your pronunciation is not offensive."

In their pursuit of English literature the Scotch proved as successful as in everything else which they took in hand. Whatever ill-will may have existed between the two nations, there was no grudging admiration shown in England for their authors. In popularity few writers of their time surpassed Thomson, Smollett, Hume, Robertson, John Home, Macpherson, Hugh Blair, Beattie, and Boswell; neither had Robert Blair, Mallet, Kames, John Dalrymple, Henry Mackenzie, Monboddo, Adam Ferguson, and Watson, any reason to complain of neglect. If Adam Smith and Reid were not so popular as some of their contemporaries it was because they had written for the small class of thinkers; though the *Wealth of Nations*, which was published little more than two years after Johnson's visit, was by the end of the century to reach its ninth edition. "This, I believe, is the historical age, and this the historical nation," Hume wrote proudly from Edinburgh.[4] He boasted that "the copy-money" given him for his *History* " much exceeded anything formerly known in England." It made him " not only independent but opulent." Robertson for his *Charles V*. received £3,400, and £400 was to be added on the publication of the second edition.[5] Blair for a single volume of his *Sermons* was paid £600.[6]

Whatever ardour Scotchmen showed for English literature as

---

accused "of having lost the broad Scotch at Oxford, and of having gained only the narrow English." Cockburn's *Life of Jeffrey*, i. 46.
[1] *Works*, ix. 159.   [2] *Piozzi Letters*, i. 109.
[3] Boswell's *Johnson*, ii. 159.
[4] Hume's *Letters to Strahan*, p. 155.
[5] *Ib.* pp. xiv, 15.
[6] Boswell's *Johnson*, iii. 98.

men of letters, yet they never for one moment forgot their pride in their own country. In a famous club they had banded themselves together for the sake of doing away with a reproach which had been cast upon their nation. Just as down to the present time no Parliament has ventured to trust Ireland with a single regiment of volunteers, so Scotland one hundred years ago was not trusted with a militia. In the words of Burns,

"Her lost militia fired her bluid."[1]

In 1759 a Bill for establishing this force had been brought into Parliament, and though Pitt acquiesced in the measure, it was thrown out by "the young Whigs." Most Englishmen probably felt with Horace Walpole, when he rejoiced that "the disaffected in Scotland could not obtain this mode of having their arms restored."[2] Two or three years later the literary men in Edinburgh, affronted by this refusal, formed themselves into a league of patriots. The name of The Militia Club, which they had at first thought of adopting, was rejected as too directly offensive. With a happy allusion to the part which they were to play in stirring up the fire and spirit of the country, they decided on calling themselves "The Poker." Andrew Crosbie, the original of Mr. Counsellor Pleydell, was humorously elected Assassin, and David Hume was added as his Assessor, "without whose assent nothing should be done."[3] It was urged with great force that Scotland was as much exposed as England to plunder and invasion. Why, it was asked, was she refused a militia when one had been granted to Cumberland and Westmoreland, and Lancashire? Had not those countries contributed more adventurers to the forces of the Young Pretender than all the Lowlands? "Why put a sword in the hands of foreigners for wounding the Scottish nation and name? A name admired at home for fidelity, regaled [sic] in every clime for strictness of discipline, and dreaded for intrepidity."[4] In 1776 the Bill was a second time brought in, but was a second time rejected. "I am glad," said Johnson, "that the Parliament has had the spirit to throw it out."[5] By this time it was not timidity only which caused the rejection. The English were touched in their pockets. It was

---

[1] *The Author's Earnest Cry and Prayer.*
[2] Walpole's *Reign of George II.*, iii. 280.
[3] Dr. Alexander Carlyle's *Autobiography*, pp. 399, 419.
[4] Andrew Henderson's *Considerations on the Scots Militia* (ed. 1761), p. 26.
[5] Boswell's *Johnson*, iii. 1.

maintained that as Scotland contributed so little to the land-tax, so if she needed a militia she ought to bear the whole expense herself. "What enemy," asked Johnson scornfully, "would invade Scotland where there is nothing to be got?"[1] It was not till the year 1793, in the midst of the alarms of a war with France, that the force was at last established, and Scotland in one more respect placed on an equality with England.

In Edinburgh such a club as this, formed of all the eager active spirits in the place, could act with the greater vigour from the ease with which the members could meet. In whatever quarter of the town men lived, even if they had moved to the squares which had lately been built to the north and south, they were not much more widely separated than the residents in the Colleges of Oxford. The narrowness of the limits in which they were confined is shown by the small number of hackney-coaches which served their wants. In London, in 1761, there were eight hundred; by 1784 they had risen to a thousand.[2] In Edinburgh there were but nine; and even these, it was complained, were rarely to be seen on the stand after three o'clock in the afternoon. It was in sedan chairs that visits of ceremony were paid; the bearers were Highlanders, as in London they were generally Irishmen.[3] The dinner-hour was still so early that the meal of careless and cheerful hospitality was the supper. In 1763 fashionable people dined at two; twenty years later at four or even at five.[4] At the time of Johnson's visit three was probably the common hour. Dr. Carlyle describes the ease with which in his younger days a pleasant supper party was gathered together. "We dined where we best could, and by cadies[5] we assembled our friends to meet us in a tavern by nine o'clock; and a fine time it was when we could collect David Hume, Adam Smith, Adam Ferguson, Lord Elibank, and Drs. Blair and Jardine on an hour's warning."[6] Though the Scotch were "religious observers of hospitality,"[7] yet a stranger did not readily get invited to their favourite meal. "To be admitted to their suppers is a mark of their friendship. At them the restraints of ceremony are banished, and you see people really as they are." The Scotch ladies, it was noticed, at these cheerful but prolonged repasts drank more wine than an English woman

---

[1] Boswell's *Johnson*, n. 151. See also *Journal Right &c.* for 1776, i. 149.
[2] Busby's *Food* &c. ...
and Boswell's *Johnson*, ...
[3] Arnot's *History of Edinburgh*, ... 508.

[4] *Ib.* p. 662.
... a penny candle was obliged to carry a lantern to the remote ... part of the town.
[5] Carlyle's *Autobiography*, p. 275.
Gentleman's Magazine for 1766, p. 168.

could well bear, "but the climate required it."¹ The "patriotic Knox" describes the inhabitants of Edinburgh as being "not only courteous, obliging, open, and hospitable, but well-inclined to the bottle." It was not to the climate that he attributed this joyous devotion, but "to their social dispositions and the excellence of their wines."² Boswell has left us a description of a supper which he enjoyed at Hume's new house in St. Andrew's Square. He had Dr. Robertson and Lord Kames for his fellow-guests, and three sorts of ice-creams among the dishes. "What think you of the northern Epicurus style?" he asked. He complained, however, that he could recollect no conversation. "Our writers here are really not prompt on all occasions as those of London."³ He had been spoilt by the talk in the taverns of Fleet Street and the Turk's Head Club, and was discontented because he did not find in St. Andrew's Square a Johnson, a Burke, a Wilkes, and a Beauclerk.

Into Hume's pleasant house Johnson unhappily never entered.⁴ He even thought that his friend Dr. Adams, the Master of Pembroke College, had done wrong when he had met by invitation "that infidel writer" at dinner, and "had treated him with smooth civility."⁵ Yet a man who could yield to the temptation of the talk of Jack Wilkes had no right to stand aloof from David Hume. We should like to know what he would have thought of that philosopher's *soupe à la reine* made from a receipt which he had copied in his own neat hand, or of his "beef and cabbage (a charming dish) and old mutton and old claret, in which," he boasted, "no man excelled him." Perhaps, however, if Johnson could have been persuaded to taste the claret, old as it was, he would have shaken his head over it and called it "poor stuff." The sheep-head broth he would certainly have refused, though one Mr. Keith did speak of it for eight days after,⁷ and the Duke de Nivernois would have bound himself apprentice to Hume's lass to learn it.⁸ "The stye of that

---

¹ Topham's *Letters from Edinburgh*, p. 66.
² Knox's *Tour*, p. 9.
³ *Letters of Boswell to Temple*, p. 203.
⁴ This house for many years—not much less than seventy, I was told—has been occupied as a tailor's shop. By the kindness of the heads of the firm, Messrs. Lauder and Haydie, I was shown over the building. Though it has been a good deal altered for the purposes of business it is still substantially the same solid stone house which Hume in his prosperity built for the closing years of his life. The rooms are lofty, being about

fourteen feet high. The kitchen and the cellars were evidently contrived for a man who intended to feast with justice of his dinners and his wine. From the windows of every floor there must have been an uninterrupted view of the shores of Fife, across the Firth of Forth, and of the house in Kirkaldy, where Adam Smith was living.

⁵ Boswell's *Johnson*, ii. 441.
⁶ *Ib.* iii. 381.
⁷ *Eight day* is, I suppose, one of Hume's Gallicisms.
⁸ *Letters of Hume to Strahan*, p. 116.

fattest of Epicurus's hogs" he failed to visit. "You tell me," wrote the great Gibbon to a friend who was at Edinburgh just at the time of Johnson's arrival, "you tell me of a long list of Dukes, Lords, and Chieftains of renown to whom you are introduced; were I with you I should prefer one *David* to them all."[1] Boswell could easily have brought the two men together, intimate as he was with both. Early in his life he was able to boast that one of them had visited him in the forenoon and the other in the afternoon of the same day.[2] Hume's conversation perhaps was not after the fashion which Johnson liked. It certainly would not have come recommended to him by his broad Scotch accent. Nevertheless there was that about it which endeared it to his friends. For innocent mirth and agreeable raillery he was thought to be unmatched.[3] Adam Smith has celebrated his constant pleasantry. In his wit there was not the slightest tincture of malignity.[4] But Johnson would have nothing to do with him. In Boswell's house in James's Court, that Sunday he spent there in Dr. Robertson's company, he said "something much too rough both as to Mr. Hume's head and heart," which Boswell thought well to suppress. In the quiet stillness of that summer sabbath day in Edinburgh, the strong loud voice might almost have been carried across the narrow valley to St. Andrew's Square, and startled the philosopher in his retirement.

Neither did Johnson see Adam Smith, who in Hume's house had his room whenever he chose to occupy it. To meet a famous stranger he would, we may well believe, have willingly crossed the Firth from his house in Kirkaldy. But the two men had once met in London, and "we did not take to each other," said Johnson. Had he been more tolerant, and sought the society of these two great Scotchmen, he would have seen in Scotland the best which Scotland had to show. Even as it was, in his visit to the capital and the seats of the other universities, in his tour through Lowlands, Highlands and Isles, he saw perhaps as great a variety of men and manners as had been seen in that country by any Englishman up to his time.

---

[1] Gibbon's *Miscellaneous Works*, ii. 116.
[2] *Letters of Boswell to Temple*, p. 151.
[3] Dr. Carlyle's *Autobiography*, p. 276.
[4] Hume's *Letters to Strahan*, p. xl.

If we can trust the description of one of Hume's autograph letters (No. 1165) in Messrs. Puttick and Simpson's catalogue for July 30, 1886, Johnson was once Hume's guest. The compilers of auction catalogues, however, are not infallible authorities, and often make strange mistakes.

EDINBURGH (AUGUST 14–18). THE WHITE HORSE INN.

On Friday, August 6th, 1773, Dr. Johnson set off from London on his famous tour to the Western Islands of Scotland. His companion as far as Newcastle was Robert Chambers, Principal of New Inn Hall, Oxford, who had been lately appointed one of the new judges for India, and was going down to his native town to take leave of his family. The two friends travelled in a post-chaise. "Life has not many better things than this," said Johnson once when he was driven rapidly along in one with Boswell.[1] It was too costly a pleasure for him to indulge in often unless he could find a companion to share the expense. The charge for a chaise and pair of horses for two passengers from London to Edinburgh could scarcely have been kept under twenty-two pounds.[2] The weather was bright and hot.[3] At Newcastle Chambers's place in the chaise was taken by a fellow-townsman who was destined to go far beyond him in the career of the law—William Scott, afterwards Lord Stowell, the great judge of the High Court of Admiralty. The travellers entered Scotland by Berwick-on-Tweed, passing near to those nine wells which gave their name to the estate which had come down to David Hume's father through many generations. Very likely they dined at Dunbar, that "high and windy town," and thought, as they crossed the Brocksburn, how Cromwell's horse and foot charged across it in the mingled light of the harvest-moon and the early dawn on that September morning one hundred and twenty-three years before. Their next stage would bring them to Haddington, past the ruined Abbey where nearly a hundred years later that great Scotchman, Johnson's foremost champion, was often with a contrite and almost broken heart to seek his wife's grave in the desolate chancel. As they drove on they passed by the wide plain, shut in by the sea on one side and by a morass on the other, over which, only twenty-eight

---

[1] Boswell's *Johnson*, ii. 453.

[2] The charge for a chaise and pair was nine-pence a mile; in some districts more. There was a duty on each horse of one penny per mile. The driver expected a shilling or eighteen pence for each stage of ten or twelve miles, and always found good reasons for asking for more. The tolls paid at the turnpikes amounted to a considerable sum in a long journey. The duty was subsequently increased. See Mostyn Armstrong's *Actual Survey*, &c., p. 4, and Paterson's *British Itinerary*, vol. i. preface, p. vii.

[3] See the Table of Weather in the *Gentleman's Magazine* for 1774, p. 290.

years earlier, on another misty morning in September, the rude Highlanders had chased Cope's English Dragoons in shameful and headlong flight. Evening had overtaken the travellers by this time, so that they could not have seen "the one solitary thorn bush round which lay the greatest number of slain," or the grey tower of the church of Preston Pans, whence the afternoon before the battle, young Alexander Carlyle had looked down upon the two armies.[1] They passed Pinkie, where the Protector Somerset's soldiers had made such a savage massacre of the routed Scotch; and Carberry Hill, where Mary took her last farewell of Bothwell as she gave herself up to the Scottish lords. They passed, too, the serfs of Tranent and Preston Pans, "the colliers and salters who were in a state of slavery and bondage, bound to the collieries or salt-works for life."[2]

Entering Edinburgh by the road which goes near Holyrood House, and driving along the Canongate, they alighted at the entrance to White Horse Close, at the end of which stood the White Horse Inn. The sign, the crest of the house of Hanover, had probably been adopted on the accession of George I., and was a proof of loyalty to the reigning family. In London in the year 1761 there were forty-nine alleys, lanes and yards which were so called.[3] It was, however, said that the name had been given as a memorial of a white horse which, by winning a race on Leith Sands, had saved its master, the inn-keeper, from ruin.[4] According to the Scotch custom the inn was generally known not by its sign, but by the name of its landlord.[5] Thus Boswell calls this house Boyd's Inn. In the *Edinburgh Directory* for 1773-4 we find under the letter B, at the head of the *Stablers*, "Boyd, James, canongate head." In the present time, when an inn, however small, assumes the dignified title of *Hotel*, we may admire the modesty of these Edinburgh innkeepers, not one of whom pretended to be anything more than a stabler. In fact they scarcely deserved any higher name; their houses were on a level

with the inn at Rochester where the two carriers in Falstaff's time
passed so restless a night. A traveller who had stayed in this house
a year or two before Johnson's visit, described it as being "crowded
and confused. The master lives in the stable, the mistress is not
equal to the business. You must not expect breakfast before nine
o'clock, and you must think yourself happy if you do not find every

WHITE HORSE CLOSE.

room fresh mopped."[1] The date of 1683 inscribed upon the large
window above the outside steps,[2] showed that even in Johnson's
time it was an old house. For the whole of the eighteenth century
it was one of the chief starting places for the stage-coaches. It
sank later on into a carrier's inn, says Sir Walter Scott, "and has
since been held unworthy even of that occupation. It was a base
hovel."[3] Yet James Boyd, who kept it, retired with a fortune

---

[1] *Gentleman's Magazine* for 1771, p. 543.
[2] J. and H.'s Storer's *Descriptions of Edinburgh*. Dr. Chambers, in his *Traditions of Edinburgh*, p. 187, says that "the date is deficient in the decimal figure 16—3."
[3] Croker's *Boswell*, 8vo. ed. p. 270.

of several thousand pounds. That he possessed napery to the value of five hundred pounds is stated by Chambers to be a well-authenticated fact. " A large room in the house was the frequent scene of the marriages of runaway English couples. On one of the windows were scratched the words:

'Jeremiah and Sarah Bentham, 1768.'"[1]

It was from this miserable inn that Johnson, on August 14th, sent the following note to Boswell's house:

"Mr. Johnson sends his compliments to Mr. Boswell, being just arrived at Boyd's.

"Saturday night."

Boswell went to him directly, and learnt from Scott that "the Doctor had unluckily had a bad specimen of Scottish cleanliness. He then drank no fermented liquor. He asked to have his lemonade made sweeter; upon which the waiter, with his greasy fingers, lifted a lump of sugar, and put it into it. The Doctor, in indignation, threw it out of the window. Scott said he was afraid that he would have knocked the waiter down." Boswell at once carried off Johnson to his own house. Scott he left behind with the sincere regret that he had not also a room for him. Could the future eminence of the great judge have been foreseen, or had his "amiable manners" been generally known, surely some one would have been found eager to welcome him as a guest and rescue him from the Canongate Stabler. "He was one of the pleasantest men I ever knew," wrote Sir Walter Scott, fifty-five years later, when he met him at a dinner at Richmond Park, "looking very frail and even comatose."[2] He lived some while longer, and did not die till the memory of this jaunt, and of everything else had been lost in the forgetfulness in which his mind sank beneath the burthen of fourscore years and ten.[3] Let us hope that on his first visit to Edinburgh, like Matthew Bramble, "he got decent lodgings in the house of a widow gentlewoman."[4]

---

[1] Chambers's *Traditions of Edinburgh*, p. 194. Perhaps this was Jeremy Bentham's father, who two years earlier had married for the second time: what was his wife's Christian name I have not been able to ascertain. The son did not visit Edinburgh in 1768. Dr. Chambers gives on p. 318 a list of the great people living in the Canongate about the year 1769. According to it there were two dukes, sixteen earls, two countesses, seven barons, seven lords of session, thirteen baronets, and four commanders-in-chief. The *Edinburgh Directory* for 1773-4 contains, however, the names of only about a dozen peers and peeresses.

[2] Lockhart's *Life of Scott*, ix. 244.

[3] He died on January 28, 1836.

[4] *Humphry Clinker*, ii. 224. Lodging-house keepers are entered in the *Edinburgh Directory* as *Room-Setters* and *Boarders*. Some were both, others only *Room-Setters*.

The old inn still stands, a picturesque ruin and an interesting memorial of the discomfort of a long race of wandering strangers. No one here ever repeated with emotion, either great or small, Shenstone's lines:

> "Whoe'er has travelled life's dull round,
> Where'er his stages may have been,
> May sigh to think he still has found
> The warmest welcome at an inn."[1]

With a little care it could have been made a place where "a man might take his ease in his inn," for it stood aloof from the noise of the street, was well-built and was sufficiently roomy. An outside stone staircase, which after a few steps turned right and left, led up to the first floor, where doubtless, according to the common Scotch custom, the principal rooms were placed. With its turrets and its gables it must have looked pleasant enough to the young runaway couples as they hurried in from the Canongate, and passed the outside staircases and open galleries of the houses on each side of the Close, and so went up to the large room where many a name was scratched with a diamond ring on the pane. "And they are gone," gone like the lovers of St. Agnes' Eve.[2]

JAMES'S COURT.

"Boswell," wrote Johnson to Mrs. Thrale, "has very handsome and spacious rooms; level with the ground on one side of the house, and on the other four stories high." At this time he was living in James's Court, on the northern side of the Lawnmarket, having lately removed from Chessel's Buildings in the Canongate. It is not easy for the stranger who passes from the thronged street under the low archway into that quiet, but gloomy, and even shabby-looking court, to picture to himself the gay and lively company which once frequented it. Now ragged, bare-footed

---

[1] Johnson repeated these lines with great emotion at the excellent inn at Chapel-House, in Oxfordshire. Boswell's *Johnson*, ii. 452.

[2] Since writing the above I have learnt with great pleasure that this interesting but minor old building will not only be preserved, but preserved to good uses. It has been purchased by Dr. A. H. F. Barbour and his sister Mrs. Whyte, and by them presented to the Edinburgh Social Union. It will be put into a state of thorough repair, and let out to poor tenants on the plan followed by Miss Octavia Hill in London. I am informed that the two sides of the Close had been repaired by the Social Union before my visit, and that the pleasant outside staircases and open galleries which caught my eye were its work.

children are playing about; in some of the windows there are broken and patched panes of glass, while high above one's head, from the different storeys, are hanging out to dry garments of various sorts and hues, on a curious kind of framework, let down by a pulley and string, till it stands out square from the wall. Some of the houses are coloured with a yellow wash, in others the stones round the windows and at the corners are painted red. The uncoloured stone is a grey darkened by years of smoke. The lower windows are guarded by iron gratings. On the southern, or Lawnmarket side, a block of building juts out, and makes a division in the Court. This projection looks as ancient as any part, and was doubtless there in those old days when the place was inhabited by a select set of gentlemen, " who kept a clerk to record their names and proceedings, had a scavenger of their own, clubbed in many public measures, and had balls and assemblies among themselves."[1] It must have pleasantly recalled to Boswell the chambers

JAMES'S COURT

[1] Chambers's *Tradition of Edinburgh*, p. 68.

which had been lent him in the Temple that summer in which he first became acquainted with Johnson, for it, too, was a nest of lawyers. There were inhabiting it at this time thirteen advocates, among them Lord Elibank, seven Writers to the Signet and Clerks of Session, a Commissioner, and two first clerks of advocates. The other householders were only six in number: two physicians, one of whom was Sir John Pringle,[1] the President of the Royal Society of London, a teller in the Old Bank, a teacher of French, a dancing-mistress, and a gentlewoman. Pringle, who was Boswell's intimate friend, was one of "the three topics" which he begged Johnson to avoid at his father's house Presbyterianism and Whiggism being the other two. If any one of these subjects were introduced an altercation was certain to follow, for all three were as dear to Lord Auchinleck as they were distasteful to Johnson. Here Hume had lived till very lately in a house "which was very cheerful and even elegant, but was too small," he complained, "to display his great talents for cookery." Nevertheless it had been the one spot to which, when abroad, his heart untravelled had fondly turned. Even in the palace at Fontainebleau, while fresh from the flattery of the three young princes who were in turn to be kings of France, in this high tide of his fortune it was for "his easy-chair and his retreat in James's Court that twice or thrice a day" he longed. Here he had welcomed Benjamin Franklin, here Adam Smith had been his frequent guest, and here he had offered a shelter to Rousseau. In his absence from Edinburgh Dr. Blair had been his tenant, and here, no doubt, had written some of those sermons and lectures which were to attain so wide a popularity, and then to sink into as deep a neglect. The time once was when Blair's shrine would have drawn a crowd of pilgrims.

Hume and Boswell had for a short time been very near neighbours, as it was in the same block of buildings[2] that they lived. If the elder man had entertained the American patriot, Franklin, the younger had entertained the Corsican patriot, Pascal Paoli. He could boast, moreover, of the distinguished guests who thronged his house during Johnson's two visits, both at his first coming and

---

[1] Pringle seems to have kept on a house in Edinburgh though he was for the most part living at this time in London. See Hume's *Letters to Strahan*, p. 117.

[2] The Scotch called each set of rooms on every floor a *house*, and each block a *land*. Thus Hume had once lived in Jack's Land, in the Canongate. A *land* of thirteen stories, such as was shown to Johnson at the foot of the Post-house Stairs would contain twenty-six houses—two on every floor.

on his return from the Hebrides. Judges, and advocates who were destined one day to sit on the bench, the Deputy Commander-in-Chief, men and women of high birth, authors, divines, physicians, all came to see and hear the famous Englishman. We can picture to ourselves the sedan-chairs passing in under the low gateway, bearing the fine ladies and gentlemen who came to attend "the *levée* which he held from ten o'clock in the morning till one or two." The echo of the strong loud voice with the slow deliberate utterance still almost seems to sound in our ears as we wander about in this dreary spot. "I could not attend him," writes Boswell, "being obliged to be in the Court of Session; but my wife was so good as to devote the greater part of the morning to the endless task of pouring out tea for my friend and his visitors."

More than one caller, as he gazed on the huge frame, the scarred face, and the awkward strange movements of the man of whom they had heard so much, might have exclaimed with Lord Elibank, that "hardly anything seemed more improbable than to see Dr. Johnson in Scotland." What Edinburgh said and thought of him we should greatly like to know. But no letters recording his visit seem to be extant. Even the very house has disappeared. Time, which has spared everything else in this old Court, has not spared it. More than thirty years ago it was burnt to the ground. We should have liked to wander about the rooms, and wonder which was the bedchamber that Mrs. Boswell, "to show all respect to the Sage," so politely resigned to him; and where it was that Veronica, that precocious babe of four months, by wishing "to be held close to him, gave a proof from simple nature that his figure was not horrid." Where, we should have asked, was the dinner given him at which Mrs. Boswell did her best "to aid wisdom and wit by administering agreeable sensations to the palate"? Where, too, were the carpets spread on which he let the wax of the candles drop, by turning them with their heads downwards when they did not burn bright enough? In what closet did Boswell keep his books, whence on Sunday, with pious purpose, Johnson took down Ogden's Sermons, and retired with them to his own room? They did not, however, detain him long, and he soon rejoined the company. Which was the breakfast-room where Sir William Forbes introduced to him the blind scholar and poet, Dr. Blacklock? "Dear Dr. Blacklock, I am glad to see you," he said, with a most humane complacency. "I looked on him with reverence," he wrote to Mrs. Thrale. It has all utterly passed away; Forbes himself has been Sir Walter Scott's "lamented Forbes"[1] for more than fourscore years. All has passed away; not only the talk about Burke, and Garrick, and Hume, and Whitefield, and genius, and witchcraft, and the comparative difficulty of verse-making and dictionary making; but even the very walls which might have caught it in its echoes. Where this famous old house once stood now stands a modern bank, contrasting but ill in its more elaborate architecture with the severe, and even stern, simplicity of the ancient buildings. Nevertheless we are at no loss to picture to ourselves the home of Hume and Boswell. Their *land* occupied one half of the northern side of the Court; the other half, which no doubt corresponded with it in almost every respect, happily escaped the flames. It is so solidly built that if it is spared by the rage of fire and of modern improvement, it has little to fear from time. Its situation, looking down as it does with its northern front on the Mound, and the pleasant gardens in the valley below, has kept it from sinking in public estimation so much as most of the neighbouring buildings. It has indeed seen better days, but it has not lost all the outward signs of respectability; its panes are neither broken nor patched. The ground-floor, which was, we may assume, on the same plan as Boswell's house, is occupied by a book-binder,[2] who courteously showed me all over it. There were traces left in this busy workshop of past splendour, and I could see how handsome and spacious the rooms had once been. In the windows were deep recesses, where it must have been pleasant enough on a bright summer's day to sit in the cool shade and look out over the heads of the elm trees waving below, across the sparkling waters of the Forth, on the hills of Fife in the far distance. A stone staircase, furnished with iron gates, led down from the level of the Court to the street four storeys below, where the foundations of this lofty pile are laid in the rock. The staircase had its occupant, for at one of the windows a mat-maker was busy at his trade.*

There is no memorial to remind passers-by of the men who have made James's Court so famous. The stranger, as he climbs up the Lawnmarket to the Castle, is little likely to notice the obscure

---

[1] *Marmion*. Introduction to Canto is.
[2] Mr. Alexander Grieve. I find a bookbinder of the same name living in Bell's Wynd in 1773. *Edinburgh Directory for 1773-4*, Appendix, p. 5.

For my authorities for some of the statements in this note, see my *Letters of David Hume to William Strahan*, pp. 116-9.

archway through which so gay and bright and learned a company was ever passing to and fro. In the public gardens Allan Ramsay, John Wilson and Adam Black have each their statue. Viscount Melville's column lifts its head in St. Andrew's Square, far above David Hume's modest house, and in its inscription, in all probability, lies. The virtues and the glories of George IV. are lavishly commemorated. Even good Queen Charlotte is not suffered to be forgotten. In Chambers Street the name of the founder of *Chambers' Journal* is meant to live. On the finest site in all Edinburgh the insignificance of the fifth Duke of Buccleugh will struggle for immortality. We look in vain for the statue of David Hume, of Adam Smith, and of James Boswell. What street, what square, what bridge bear their names? Where does Edinburgh proudly boast to the stranger that she is the birth-place of the philosopher whose name is great in the history of the world, and of the biographer whose work has never been equalled? Where does she make it known that to her ancient city the author of the *Wealth of Nations* retired to spend the closing years of his life and to die? If no nobler monuments can be raised, surely some bronze tablet or graven stone might keep fresh the memory of the spot where Adam Smith had his chamber, where Benjamin Franklin came to visit David Hume, where Rousseau was offered a shelter, and where James Boswell's guests were Pascal Paoli and Samuel Johnson.

A STROLL THROUGH EDINBURGH.

It was in good company that Johnson, on the morning of Monday, August 16, "walked out to see some of the things which they had to show in Edinburgh," for he was under the guidance of the historian of Scotland. "I love Robertson," Johnson had said a few years earlier, "and I won't talk of his book." If Boswell had reported any part of this saying we may hope that it was only the first half, for he who neglects the author makes but a poor recompense by loving the man. At all events, Robertson was not troubled with diffidence, for at Holyrood "he fluently harangued" his companion on the scenes described in his History. No doubt he told many of those anecdotes for which Johnson that morning had declared his love as they breakfasted together, and took care not to attempt " to weave them into a system." As they passed into the Lawnmarket they had not before them that wide expanse which in the present day makes so noble an end to the High Street. The view was obstructed by the Weigh House, the Luckenbooths, the Tolbooth, and the Guard House.[1] At the Weigh House the boast, perhaps, was made that so great was the trade of the town that the public weighing-machine which was there kept brought in no less than a sum of £500 every year. At the Tolbooth and the Guard House, that "long low ugly building," which looked like "a black snail crawling up the High Street,"[2] something, perhaps, was said of the Porteous riots. But the real story of the Heart of Mid-Lothian could only have been told them by that little child of scarce two years in the College Wynd, how the wild mob on that September night, seven-and-thirty years before, burnt down the massive gate of the jail, and dragged their wretched prisoner by torchlight to the gallows, and how Jeanie Deans could not tell a lie even to save her sister from a shameful death. There was no one but this bright-eyed boy who could have even pointed out in the Luckenbooths the stall where poor Peter Peebles and Paul Plainstanes had for years carried on "that great line of business as mercers and linendrapers," which in the end led to a lawsuit that is famous all the world over. Having no one to tell them of all this they passed on through Parliament Close, "which new-fangled affectation has termed a square,"[3] to the Parliament House, which still showed "the grave grey hue that had been breathed over it by one hundred and fifty years," and which was still free from the disgrace of "bright freestone and contemptible decorations." The "sorrow and indignation," which the restorer's wanton changes aroused troubled a later generation.[4] Here it was that the Court of Session sat, the High Court of Justice of Scotland. It was in these August days empty of lawyers, for the Vacation had just begun ; but Johnson on his return saw it also in term time, and thought " the pleading too vehement and too much addressed to the passions of the judges. It was not the Areopagus," he said. Here Henry Erskine, the brother of the famous Chancellor, slipped a shilling into Boswell's hands, who had introduced

---

[1] See ante, p. 52.
[2] Heart of Mid-Lothian, ed. 1860, i. 247.
[3] Redgauntlet, ed. 1860, i. 253.
[4] Cockburn's Memorials, p. 106, and Heart of Mid-Lothian, ii. 117.

him to Johnson, saying that it was for the sight of his bear, and here Lord Auchinleck, seeing the great man enter, whispered to one of his brethren on the Bench that it was *Ursa Major*. In the Outer Hall had once sat the ancient Parliament of Scotland. Here it was that Lord Belhaven, at perhaps its last meeting, made that pathetic speech which drew tears from the audience. Here every day during term time there was a very Babel of a Court of Justice. Like Westminster Hall of old it was the tribunal of many judges, as well as the gathering ground of advocates, solicitors, suitors, witnesses, and idlers in general. Here it was that "the Macer shouted with all his well-remembered brazen strength of lungs: "Poor Peter Peebles *versus* Plainstanes, *per* Dumtoustie *et* Tough :

Maister Da-a-niel Dumtoustic." Here it was that a famous but portly wag of later days, "Peter" Robinson, seeing Scott with his tall conical white head passing through, called out to the briefless crowd about the fire-place, "Hush, boys, here comes old Peveril I see the Peak." Scott looked round and replied, "Ay, ay, my man, as weel Peveril o' the Peak ony day as Peter o' the Painch" (paunch).[1] Here Thomas Carlyle, a student of the University, not yet fourteen years old, on the afternoon of the November day on which he first saw Edinburgh, "was dragged in to a scene" which he never forgot :

"An immense hall, dimly lighted from the top of the walls, and perhaps with candles burning in it here and there, all in strange *chiaroscuro*, and filled with what I thought (exaggeratively) a thousand or two of human creatures, all astir in a boundless buzz of talk, and simmering about in every direction, some solitary, some in groups. By degrees I noticed that some were in wig and black gown, some not, but in common clothes, all well dressed ; that here and there on the sides of the hall, were little thrones with enclosures, and steps leading up, red-velvet figures sitting in said thrones, and the black-gowned eagerly speaking to them ; advocates pleading to judges as I easily understood. How they could be heard in such a grinding din was somewhat a mystery. Higher up on the walls, stuck there like swallows in their nests, sate other humbler figures. These I found were the sources of certain wildly plangent lamentable kinds of sounds or echoes which from time to time pierced the universal noise of feet and voices, and rose unintelligibly above it, as if in the bitterness of incurable woe. Criers of the Court, I gradually came to understand. And this was Themis in her 'Outer House,' such a scene of chaotic din and hurlyburly as I had never figured before."[2]

Here every year, on the evening of the King's birthday, there was a scene of loyal riot. At the cost of the city funds, some fifteen hundred guests, on the invitation of the magistrates, "roaring,

[1] Lockhart's *Scott*, vii. 126.   [2] *Reminiscences*, by Thomas Carlyle, ii. 5.

drinking, toasting, and quarrelling," drank the royal healths to a late hour of the night. "The wreck and the fumes of that hot and scandalous night" tainted the air of the Court for a whole week.¹ From the Hall our travellers passed into the Inner House, where the fifteen judges sat together as "a Court of Review." Like Carlyle, Johnson saw "great Law Lords this and that, great advocates, *alors célèbres*, as Thiers has it." There were Hailes, and Kames, and Monboddo on the Bench, and Henry Dundas, Solicitor General. The judges wore long robes of scarlet faced with white, but though their dignity was great, their salaries were small when compared with those paid to their brethren in Westminster Hall. The President had but £1,300 a year, and each of the fourteen Lords of Session but £700. Six of them, among whom was Boswell's father, received each £300 more as a Commissioner of Justiciary.² The room, or rather "den," in which they sat, "was so cased in venerable dirt that it was impossible to say whether it had ever been painted. Dismal though the hole was, the old fellows who had been bred there never looked so well anywhere else."³

In the same great pile of buildings as the Law Courts is the Advocates' Library, "of which Dr. Johnson took a cursory view." He, no doubt, "respectfully remembered" there its former librarian, Thomas Ruddiman, "that excellent man and eminent scholar," just as he remembered him a few days later at Laurencekirk, the scene of his labours as a schoolmaster. Perhaps a second time he "regretted that his farewell letter to the Faculty of Advocates when he resigned the office of their Librarian, was not, as it should have been, in Latin." According to Ruddiman's successor, David Hume, it was but "a petty office of forty or fifty guineas a year," yet "a genteel one" too. When that great writer came to write his letter of resignation, he used the curtest of English, and took care to express his contempt for the Curators. Two or three years earlier they had censured him for buying some French books, which they accounted "indecent and unworthy of a place in a learned library," and he had not forgiven them.⁴ It was in the *Laigh* (or Under) Parliament House beneath, in which at this time were deposited the records of Scotland, that Johnson, "rolling about in this old

---

¹ Cockburn's *Memorials*, p. 69.
² *Court and City Register for 1769*, p. 142.
³ From 1808 the judges began to sit in two separate chambers. Cockburn's *Memorials*, pp. 100, 244.
⁴ Hume's *Letters to Strahan*, p. xxvi.

magazine of antiquities," uttered those memorable words which have overcome the reluctance or the indolence of many an author: "A man may write at any time if he will set himself *doggedly* to it."

It was but a step from the Parliament House to the great church of St. Giles. Perhaps Johnson went round by the eastern end, and mourned over the fate which had befallen Dunedin's Cross less than twenty years before. A full century and more was to pass away before "the work of the Vandals" was undone, as far as it could be undone, by the pious affection of one of the greatest of Scotchmen.[1] Perhaps he turned to the west, and passed, little recking it, over the grave of John Knox. Even Boswell, Edinburgh-born though he was, did not know where the great Reformer lay buried, and a few days later asked where the spot was. "'I hope in the highway,' Dr. Johnson burst out." In the pavement of Parliament Close, a "way of common trade," a small stone inscribed "I. K. 1572," marks where he rests. St. Giles' was at this time "divided into four places of Presbyterian worship. 'Come,' said Johnson jocularly to Dr. Robertson, 'let me see what was once a church.'" Writing to Mrs. Thrale the next day he said: "I told Robertson I wished to see the cathedral because it had once been a church." Its "original magnificence," the loss of which Boswell justly lamented, has been partly restored by the lavish changes of late years. Nevertheless, the student of history may in his turn lament that in this restoration there has of necessity disappeared much that was interesting. "There was swept away, with as much indifference as if it had been of yesterday, that plain, square, galleried apartment," which, as the meeting-place of the General Assembly, "had beheld the best exertions of the best men in the Kingdom ever since the year 1640."[2] Jenny Geddes and her stool, moreover, are reluctant to answer the summons of the imagination in a scene which she herself would scarcely have recognized. Johnson went into only one of the four divisions, the New, or the High Church, as it was beginning to be called. Here Blair was preaching those sermons which passed through editions almost innumerable, and now can be bought in their calf binding for a few pence at almost any bookstall. The New Church was formed out of the ancient choir. In it were ranged the seats of the King, the judges, and the magistrates of the city. When Johnson saw it, "it was shamefully dirty. He said nothing at the

---

[1] Mr. Gladstone restored it in 1883.   [2] Cockburn's *Life of Lord Jeffrey*, i. 182.

time; but when he came to the great door of the Royal Infirmary, where upon a board was this inscription, 'Clean your feet,' he turned about slily and said, 'There is no occasion for putting this at the doors of your churches.'" Pennant also had noticed "the slovenly and indecent manner in which Presbytery kept the houses of God. In many parts of Scotland," he said, "our Lord seems still to be worshipped in a stable, and often in a very wretched one."[1] Nevertheless, it seemed likely that some improvement would soon be made, and that orthodoxy and dirt would not be held inseparable companions. In one or two highly favoured spots the broom and scrubbing-brush had, perhaps, already made their appearance; for according to Smollett "the good people of Edinburgh no longer thought dirt and cobwebs essential to the house of God."[2] It might still have been impossible "for the united rhetoric of mankind to prevail with Jack to make himself clean;"[3] yet example must at last have an effect. Scotchmen had travelled and had returned from their travels, and no doubt had brought back a certain love for decency and cleanliness even in churches. In one respect, it was noticed, they surpassed their neighbours. Their conduct during service was more becoming. "They did not make their bows and cringes in the middle of their very prayers as was done in England." They always waited till the sermon was over and the blessing given before they looked round and made their civilities to their friends and persons of distinction.[4]

I inquired in vain when I was in Edinburgh for the Post-house Stairs, down which Johnson on leaving St. Giles was taken to the Cowgate. Together with so much that was ancient they have long since disappeared. He was now at the foot of the highest building in the town. As he turned round and looked upwards he saw a house that rose above him thirteen storeys high, being built like James's Court on a steep slope. It has suffered the same fate as Boswell's house, having been destroyed by fire more than sixty years ago.[5] From the Cowgate Robertson led the way up the steep hill to the College of which he was the Principal. They passed through "that narrow dismal alley," the College Wynd, famous to all time as the birthplace of Sir Walter Scott. Johnson would

---

[1] *Tour in Scotland*, i. 233.
[2] *Humphry Clinker*, iii. 5.
[3] *The Tale of a Tub*, section xi.
[4] Defoe's *Tour through Great Britain*, 4. *... count of Scotland*, iii. 43, and Pennant's *Tour in Scotland*, ii. 240.
[5] Chambers, quoted in Croker's *Boswell*, p. 276.

have been pleased indeed could he have known how that bright young genius would one day delight in his poems, and how the last line of manuscript that he was to send to the press would be a quotation from the *Vanity of Human Wishes*.[1] "Hae miseriae nostrae," were the melancholy words which Robertson uttered as he showed his companion the mean buildings in which his illustrious University was lodged. Johnson, in the narrative of his tour, no doubt remembering what he saw both here and at St. Andrew's, grieved over a nation which, "while its merchants or its nobles are raising palaces suffers its universities to moulder into dust." Robertson, in an eloquent *Memorial*, had lately pleaded the cause of learning. The courts and buildings of the College were so mean, he said, that a stranger would mistake them for almshouses. Instead of a spacious quadrangle there were three paltry divisions, encompassed partly with a range of low and ever of ruinous houses, and partly with walls which threatened destruction to the passers-by. Boswell tells of one portion of the wall which, bulging out, was supposed, like "Bacon's mansion," to "tremble o'er the head" of every scholar, being destined to fall when a man of extraordinary learning should go under it. It had lately been taken down. "They were afraid it never would fall," said Johnson, glad of an opportunity to have a pleasant hit at Scottish learning. In spite of its poverty and the meanness of its buildings, such was the general reputation of the University, above all of the School of Medicine, that students flocked to it from all parts of Great Britain and Ireland, from the English settlements in North America and the West Indies, and even from distant countries in Europe. Their number at this time was not less than six or seven hundred; by 1789 it had risen to one thousand and ninety. The Principal did not allow himself to be soothed into negligence by this success. He grieved that "with a literary education should be connected in youth ideas of poverty, meanness, dirtiness, and darkness." The sum of money which he asked for was not large in a country whose wealth was so rapidly increasing. For £6,500 — not quite double the amount which he had been lately paid for his *History of Charles V.*—sixteen "teaching rooms" could be provided, while £8,500 more would supply everything else that was needed. Yet it was not till 1789 that the foundation stone was laid of the New

[1] Lockhart's *Scott*, iii. 269. The quotation no doubt was, "Superfluous lags the veteran on the stage;" the line with which Scott concluded the brief Appendix to *Castle Dangerous*.

College of Edinburgh. Happily Robertson was spared to play his part on that great day. Preceded by the Mace, with the Professor of Divinity on his right hand, and the Professor of Church History on his left, followed by the rest of his colleagues according to seniority, and by the students, each man wearing a sprig of green laurel in his hat, he headed the procession of the University.[1]

However mean were the buildings in general, with the library Johnson was much pleased. Fifty years earlier a traveller had noticed that " the books in it were cloistered with doors of wire which none could open but the keeper, more commodious than the multitude of chains used in the English libraries."[2] I was surprised to find that so late as 1723 the use of chains was generally continued in England. Yet about that time one of the Scotch exhibitioners at Balliol College reported that the knives and forks were chained to the tables in the Hall,[3] so that it was likely that at least as great care was taken with books of value. Johnson's attention does not seem to have been drawn to an inscription over one of the doors, which the French traveller, Saint-Fond, read with surprise—MUSIS ET CHRISTO. Had he noticed it, it would scarcely have failed to draw forth some remark.

THE OLD LIBRARY.

From the College the party went on to the Royal Infirmary. In the Bodleian Library I have found a copy of the *History and Statutes* of that institution printed in 1749. In it is given a table of the three kinds of diet which the patients were to have—" low, middle, and full." The only vegetable food allowed was oatmeal and barley-meal, rice and panado.[4] There was no tea, coffee, or cocoa. The only drink was ale, but in " low diet" it was not to be taken. It is to be hoped that the Infirmary was not under the

---

[1] *Scots Mag. Inv.*, 1768, p. 113; 1789, pp. 521-5.
[2] J. Mackay—*Journey thro' N. Scotland*, p. 69.
[3] *Scotland and Scotsmen in the Eighteenth Century*, ii. 307.
[4] See p. 52 of this pamphlet. *Panado* is defined by Johnson as *a food made by boiling bread in water*.

same severe ecclesiastical discipline as the workhouse. There the first failure to attend Divine worship was to be followed by the loss of the next meal, while for the second failure the culprit was " to be denied victuals for a whole day." [1]

The last sight which Johnson was shown in his " running about Edinburgh" was the Abbey of Holyrood House, "that deserted mansion of royalty," as Boswell calls it with a sigh. It was more the absence of a charwoman than of a king that was likely to rouse the regrets of an Englishman. "The stately rooms," wrote Wesley, "are dirty as stables." [2] Even the chapel was in a state of "miserable neglect." [3] It was in Holyrood that Robertson " fluently harangued " on the scenes of Scottish history. In the room in which David Rizzio was murdered " Johnson was overheard repeating in a kind of muttering tone, a line of the old ballad, *Johnny Armstrong's Last Good Night*:

> 'And ran him through the fair body.'"

The mood in which he was when he made so odd a quotation was perhaps no less natural than Burns's when he wrote :

> "With awe-struck thought and pitying tears,
> I view that noble, stately dome,
> Where Scotia's kings of other years
> Famed heroes, had their royal home." [4]

The Castle, that "rough, rude fortress," was not visited by Johnson till his return in November. He owned that it was " a great place ; " yet a few days after " he affected to despise it, when Lord Elibank was talking of it with the natural elation of a Scotchman. "It would," he said, " make a good prison in England." Perhaps there was not so much affectation as Boswell thought, for Johnson believed, he said, that the ruins of some one of the castles which the English built in Wales would supply materials for all those which he saw beyond the Tweed.[5]

INCH KEITH (AUGUST 18.)

On the morning of Wednesday, August 18th, the travellers, accompanied by Mr. Nairne, an advocate, set out on their northern

---

[1] *Regulations for the Workhouse of Edinburgh*, 1750, p. 30.
[2] *Wesley's Journal*, iv. 181.
[3] *Boswell's Johnson*, v. 382.
[4] *An Address to Edinburgh*.
[5] *Johnson's Works*, ix. 152.

tour. They were attended by Boswell's servant, Joseph Ritter, a Bohemian, "a fine stately fellow above six feet high, who had been over a great part of Europe, and spoke many languages. He was," adds Boswell, "the best servant I ever saw. Dr. Johnson gave him this character, 'Sir, he is a civil man, and a wise man.'" At Leith they took boat for Kinghorn on the other side of the Firth of Forth. In the passage Johnson observed the Island of Inch Keith, which, to his surprise, his companions had never visited, "though lying within their view, it had all their lives solicited their notice." He flattered his pride as "a true-born Englishman" by reflecting, had it been as near London as it was to Edinburgh, "with what emulation of price a few rocky acres would have been purchased." "I'd have this island," he said. "I'd build a house, make a good landing-place, have a garden and vines, and all sorts of trees. A rich man of a hospitable turn here would have many visitors from Edinburgh." By his wish they landed, putting in at a little bay on the north-west, the same "wild, stony little bay," no doubt, into which Thomas Carlyle and Edward Irving ran their boat one summer evening more than forty years later. "We found the island," writes Johnson, "a rock somewhat troublesome to climb, about a mile long and half a mile broad; in the middle were the ruins of an old fort, which had on one of the stones, 'Maria Re. 1564.' It had been only a blockhouse one storey high. The rock had some grass and many thistles, both cows and sheep were grazing. There was a spring of water. We pleased ourselves with being in a country all our own." The ruins have long since disappeared; with the stones a light-house was built. How our travellers were affected by the beautiful scenery that was all around, if indeed they were affected, we are not told. For natural beauties Boswell hoped to be able some day "to force a taste." In the description of visible objects he honestly owned he found a great difficulty. Johnson's descriptions of scenery are almost all of the artificial school. Both men were far too wise to affect raptures which they did not feel. Happily the view that the chance wanderer sometimes sees in that lonely island has been sketched for us by the hands of a master. Carlyle thus describes what he saw: "The scene in our little bay, as we were about proceeding to launch our boat, seemed to me the beautifullest I had ever beheld. Sun about setting just in face of us, behind Ben Lomond far away. Edinburgh with its towers; the great silver mirror of the Frith girt by such a framework of mountains; cities, rocks, and fields and wavy landscapes on all hands of us; and reaching right under foot, as I remember, came a broad pillar as of gold from the just sinking sun; burning axle, as it were, going down to the centre of the world."[1]

The weather was fine, so that our travellers had a pleasant crossing over "that great gulf" which Hume "regarded with horror and a kind of hydrophobia that kept him," he said, from visiting Adam Smith at Kirkaldy.[2] In *Humphry Clinker* Matthew Bramble had had so rough a passage, that when he was told that he had been saved "by the particular care of Providence," he replied, "Yes, but I am much of the honest Highlander's mind, after he had made such a passage as this. His friend told him he was much indebted to Providence. 'Certainly,' said Donald, 'but by my saul, mon, I'se ne'er trouble Providence again so long as the Brig of Stirling stands."[3]

THE DRIVE TO ST. ANDREWS (AUGUST 18).

At Kinghorn, "a mean town," which was said to consist chiefly of "horse-hirers and boatmen noted all Scotland over for their impudence and impositions,"[4] our travellers took a post-chaise for St. Andrews. A few years earlier Johnson would not have found there his favourite mode of conveyance. By the year 1758 post-chaises had only penetrated as far north as Durham.[5] He found the roads good, "neither rough nor dirty." The absence of toll-gates, "afforded a southern stranger a new kind of pleasure." He would not have rejoiced over this absence had he known that their want was supplied by the forced labour of the cottars. On these poor men was laid "an annual tax of six days' labour for repairing the roads."[6] Used as he was to the rapid succession of carriages and riders, and to the beautiful and varied scenery in the neighbourhood of London, he complained that in Scotland there was "little diversion for the traveller, who seldom sees himself either encountered or overtaken, and who has nothing to contemplate but grounds that have no visible boundaries, or are separated by walls of loose stone." There were few of the heavy waggons

---

[1] *Reminiscences*, i. 113.
[2] *Hume's Letters to Strahan*, p. 115.
[3] *Humphry Clinker*, ii. 249.
[4] Ray's *History of the Rebellion of 1745-6*, p. 284.
[5] Dr. A. Carlyle's *Autobiography*, p. 331.
[6] Lord Kames's *Sketches*, iii. 483.

which were seen on the roads in England. A small cart drawn by
one little horse was the carriage in common use. "A man seemed
to derive some degree of dignity and importance from the reputation of possessing a two-horse cart." Three miles beyond Kinghorn they drove through Kirkaldy, "a very long town, meanly
built," where Adam Smith perhaps at that very time was taking
his one amusement, "a long, solitary walk by the sea-side," smiling
and talking to himself and meditating his *Wealth of Nations*.¹
Here, too, Thomas Carlyle was to have "will and waygate" upon
all his friend Irving's books, and here "with greedy velocity" he
was to read the *Decline and Fall of the Roman Empire*, at the rate
of a volume a day. Along the beach he was to walk "in summer
twilights, a mile of the smoothest sand, with one long wave coming
on gently, steadily, and breaking in gradual explosion into harmless, melodious white at your hand all the way."² Of all the
scenery which Johnson saw, either here or on the rest of his drive,
his description is of the briefest. "The whole country," he wrote,
"is extended in uniform nakedness, except that in the road between
Kirkaldy and Cupar I passed for a few yards between two hedges."
Night, however, had come on before their journey was ended, for
they had lost time at Inch Keith. They could not, moreover,
have been driven at a fast pace, for between Kinghorn and St.
Andrews, a distance of nearly thirty miles, there was no change of
horses to be had.³ They crossed, perhaps without knowing it,
Magus Moor, where Archbishop Sharpe, "driving home from a
council day," was killed "by a party of furious men."⁴ In going
over this same moor many years later, Sir Walter Scott, being
moved, as he says, by the spirit to give a picture of the assassina-
tion, so told his tale that he "frightened away the night's sleep
of one of his fellow-travellers."⁵

St. Andrews (August 18-20).

Coming as they did through the darkness to St. Andrews, they
saw nothing of that "august appearance" which the seat of the
most ancient of the Scotch universities presented from afar. "It

---

¹ *Hume's Letters to Strahan*, p. 353, and Boswell's *Johnson*, iv. 24, n. 2.
² *Reminiscences*, i. 102-4.
³ Saint-Fond's *Voyage*, &c., ii. 253.
⁴ Burnet's *History of His Own Time*, ed. 1818, ii. 82. Balfour of Burley, the leader, is known to the readers of *Old Mortality*.
⁵ Lockhart's *Scott*, i. 72.

appears," said an early traveller, "much like Bruges in Flanders at a distance; its colleges and fine steeples making a goodly appearance."[1] They arrived late, after a dreary drive, but "found a good supper at Glass's Inn, and Dr. Johnson revived agreeably." Who was Glass and which was his inn I could not ascertain. The old Scotch custom of calling a house not after its sign but its landlord, renders identification difficult. Wherever it was they found it full; but "by the interposition of some invisible friend," to use Johnson's words, "lodgings were provided at the house of one of the professors." The invisible friend was a relation of that "most universal genius," Dr. Arbuthnot, whom Johnson once ranked first among the writers in Queen Anne's reign. Their host was Dr. Robert Watson, the author of the *History of Philip II. and Philip III. of Spain*, "an interesting, clear, well-arranged, and rather feeble-minded work," as Carlyle described it.[2] His house had formerly been part of St. Leonard's

ST. LEONARD'S COLLEGE.

College, but had been purchased by him at the time when that ancient institution, by being merged in St. Salvator's, lost its separate existence. A traveller who had visited St. Andrews about the year 1723 saw the old cells of the monks, two storeys high, on the southern side of the college. "On the west was a goodly pile of buildings, but all out of repair."[3] Wesley, who came to the town three years after Johnson, does not seem to have known how large a part of the old buildings had been converted into a private house, for he wrote that "what was left of St. Leonard's College was

---

[1] Macky's *Journey thro' Scotland*, p. 83.
[2] *Early Letters of Thomas Carlyle*, ed. 1886, i. 187.
[3] Macky's *Journey thro' Scotland*, p. 87.

only a heap of ruins."[1] Of the inside of the ancient chapel Johnson could not get a sight:

> "I was always, by some civil excuse, hindered from entering it. A decent attempt, as I was since told, has been made to convert it into a kind of green-house, by planting its area with shrubs. This new method of gardening is unsuccessful; the plants do not hitherto prosper. To what use it will next be put, I have no pleasure in conjecturing. It is something, that its present state is at least not ostentatiously displayed. Where there is yet shame, there may in time be virtue."

The virtue was somewhat slow in coming. Saint-Fond, who got a peep into the chapel, inferred that it was used for a winter store-house for the carrots and turnips which grew in the kitchen-garden that surrounded it. It has of late years been cleared of rubbish and restored to decency, which, perhaps, is all the restoration that is desirable. Some shrubs and overhanging trees have been allowed to throw a graceful veil over man's neglect. One strange sight the old monkish cells had witnessed earlier in the century. A man of liberal views had been elected Rector of the University. In his honour "the students made a bonfire at St. Leonard's Gate, into which they threw some of the Calvinistic systems which they were enjoined to read."[2] Not very many years before this innocent and even meritorious sacrifice was made, the terrible flames of religious persecution had blazed up in this city dedicated to piety and learning. It is possible that Johnson passed in the streets some aged man who in his childhood had seen a miserable woman burnt to death for witchcraft on the Witch Hill. So late as the seventh year of the present century a gentleman was living who had known a person who had witnessed this dreadful sight.[3]

In Dr. Watson's house the two travellers "found very comfortable and genteel accommodation." The host "wondered at Johnson's total inattention to established manners;" but he does not seem to have let his wonder be discovered by his guest. "I take great delight in him," said Johnson. How much delight Watson took in him we are not told. "He allowed him a very strong understanding;" and as well he might, for he heard some "good talk." It was at his breakfast-table that Johnson proudly pointed out how authors had at length shaken themselves free of patrons. "Learning," he said, "is a trade. We have done with patronage.

---

[1] Wesley's *Journal*, iv. 77.
[2] *Scotland and Scotsmen in the Eighteenth Century*, i. 268. The popular rector was Archibald Campbell, the victim of the Rev. Dr. Innes's literary fraud described in Boswell's *Johnson*, i. 360, and the father of "Lexiphanes." *Ib.* ii. 44.
[3] *St. Andrews As it was and as it is*, p. 161.

If learning cannot support a man, if he must sit with his hands across till somebody feeds him, it is as to him a bad thing." It was here, moreover, that he gave that amusing account of the change of manners in his lifetime. " I remember (said he) when all the *decent* people in Lichfield got drunk every night, and were not the worse thought of." That smoking had gone out seemed to him strange, for it was " a thing which requires so little exertion, and yet preserves the mind from total vacuity."

The exact spot where he was so comfortably lodged is doubtful. In the Hebrides some of the chambers in which he slept are still known. In a University, where the traditions of a scholar should surely linger long, the very house has been forgotten. It is believed, however, that Dr. Watson occupied that part of the ancient building which had once been Buchanan's residence. Some portion of that great scholar's study still remains, having outlived both time and change. Yet that Johnson should not have been informed of a fact which to him would have been so interesting, or that being informed he should not have mentioned it, is indeed surprising. His admiration for Buchanan's genius seems almost unbounded. If the city attracted him because it had once been archiepiscopal, so did the University, because in it Buchanan had once taught philosophy. "His name," he adds, "has as fair a claim to immortality as can be conferred by modern latinity, and perhaps a fairer than the instability of vernacular languages admits." Sir Walter Scott loved him almost as much as Johnson. " He was his favourite Latin poet as well as historian."[1]

Our travellers rose "much refreshed" from their fatigue, and to the enjoyment of a very fine day. They went forth to view the ruins not only of a cathedral, but almost of a city and a University. That it had once flourished as a city was shown by history: its ancient magnificence as the seat of a great archbishopric was witnessed by "the mournful memorials" which had escaped the hands of the devastator. Of its three Colleges only two were standing. It was " the skeleton of a venerable city," said Smollett.[2] Many years earlier a traveller, applying to it Lord Rochester's words, had described it as being "in its full perfection of decay." Pennant, who visited it only the year before Johnson, on entering the West Port, saw a well-built street, straight, and of a vast length and breadth, lying before him ; but it was so grass-grown, and so dreary

---

[1] Lockhart's *Life of Scott*, i. 175. [2] *Humphry Clinker*, ii. 206.

a solitude, that it seemed as if it had been laid waste by pestilence.¹ Another traveller, who came a little later, praised "the noble wide street," but lamented that most of the houses were "disfigured by what is termed a *fore-stair*—that is, an open staircase on the outside, carried in a zigzag manner across the front of the house." Before most of them was heaped up a huge dunghill.² A young English student fresh from Eton, the grandson of Bishop Berkeley, who entered the University about the year 1778, on seeing "this dreary deserted city, wept to think that he was to remain there three long years." So fond nevertheless did he become of the place that "he shed more tears at leaving than at entering."³ Saint-Fond saw grass growing in all the streets : " Tout y est triste, silencieux ; le peuple, y vivant dans l'ignorance des arts et du commerce, offre l'image de l'insouciance et de la langueur."⁴ I was told by an old inhabitant that not a single new house was built till after the year 1851, and that not long before that time sheep might be seen feeding in the grass-grown streets. Our travellers were touched by the general gloom. " It was," said Boswell, " somewhat dispiriting to see this ancient archiepiscopal city now sadly deserted." " One of its streets," wrote Johnson, " is now lost ; and in those that remain there is the silence and solitude of inactive indigence and gloomy depopulation." This loss of a street seems to have been imaginary. He was speaking, no doubt, of the road known under the name of *The Scores*, which runs in front of the Castle, and follows the line of the coast. But along its course neither pavements nor foundations have ever been discovered.⁵ Nevertheless the desolation was very great. Over one ruin, however, a good man might have justly exulted. In the archbishops' castle on the edge of the sea is shown the dreadful pit in which the unhappy prisoner, far below the level of the ground, spent his weary days in wretchedness and darkness, listening to the beating of the waves. Here ofttimes he waited for the hour to come when he should be raised by a rope to the surface, as if he were a bucket of water, and not a man, and dragged off to die before the people. Sometimes those poor eyes, grown weak by a darkness which was never broken, of a sudden had to face, not only the light of day, but

¹ *Tour in Scotland*, ii. 189. The population he estimated at about two thousand. *Ib.* p. 196.
² *Poems of G. M. Berkeley*, Preface. p. lxi.
³ *Ib.* p. lxii.

⁴ *Voyage en Auvergne*, &c. ii. 238.
⁵ My informant is Dr. John Paterson, of Clifton Bank, St. Andrews, to whose extensive knowledge as a local antiquary and most friendly assistance I am indebted.

the blaze of the torch which was to kindle the martyr's pile. Thinking on all this—on Patrick Hamilton, on Henry Forrest, on George Wishart, and on Walter Milne, who for their faith suffered death

ST. ANDREWS CASTLE.

ST. ANDREWS.

DOCKS.

by fire at St. Andrews—who does not rejoice that this dismal den was shattered to pieces, and that where once "an atheous priest" made the good tremble by his frown, now on the pleasant sward innocent children play about, and strangers from afar idly dream an hour away?

None of these thoughts came into the minds of the two travellers. They did not see this dreadful dungeon, for it was hidden beneath the rubbish of the ruined walls. The sight of it would, I hope, have moved Johnson to write otherwise than he did. Had he looked down into its gloomy depths, he would scarcely have said that "Cardinal Beaton was murdered by the ruffians of reformation." Never surely was a more righteous sentence executed than that whereby this murderer of George Wishart, in the very room where, lolling on his velvet cushion, he had looked forth on the martyr's sufferings, was himself put to death.

With far different feelings are we animated as we look at "the poor remains of the stately Cathedral." If we do not grieve for the rooks, nevertheless we mourn over the wild folly which struck down so glorious a rookery. Would that that fair sight still caught the sailor's eye which met John Knox's gaze when, "hanging tired over his oar in the French galley, he saw the white steeples of St. Andrews rising out of the sea in the mist of the summer morning!"[1] Desolate as is the scene of ruin now, it was far more desolate when Johnson saw it. The ground lay deep in rubbish. The few broken pillars which were left standing were almost hidden in the ruins heaped up around them. The Cathedral until very lately had been made a common quarry, "and every man had carried away the stones who fancied that he wanted them." Now all is trim. The levelled ground, the smooth lawn, the gravelled paths, the gently sloping banks, the trees and the shrubs, all bear witness to man's care for the venerable past, and to his reverence for the dead who still find their last resting-place by the side of their forefathers. The wantonness of the destruction, however, mocks at repair. The work was too thoroughly done by those fierce reformers, and by the quiet quarrymen of after ages. In all the cities of Scotland there were craftsmen, but it was in Glasgow alone that they rose to save their beloved Cathedral. Yet everywhere the people should have felt—to use Johnson's homely words—as, "wrapt up in contemplation," he surveyed these scenes—that "differing from a man in doctrine is no reason why you should pull his house about his ears." We may exclaim, as Wesley exclaimed at Aberbrothick, when he was told that the zealous reformers burnt the Abbey down, "God deliver us from reforming mobs!"[2]

In the ruined cloisters as our travellers paced up and down,

[1] Froude's *History of England*, ed. 1870, vi. 233.   [2] Wesley's *Journal*, iii. 397.

while the old walls gave "a solemn echo" to their steps and to Johnson's strong voice, he talked about retirement from the world. For such a discourse there could not easily have been found a more fitting scene.

"I never read of an hermit (he said) but in imagination I kiss his feet: never of a monastery, but I could fall on my knees and kiss the pavement. But I think putting young people there, who know nothing of life, nothing of retirement, is dangerous and wicked. It is a saying as old as Hesiod—

'ἔργα νέων, βουλαὶ δὲ μέσων, εὐχαὶ δὲ γερόντων.'[1]

That is a very noble line: not that young men should not pray, or old men not give counsel, but that every season of life has its proper duties. I have thought of retiring, and have talked of it to a friend; but I find my vocation is rather to active life."

Here, too, it was a different scene upon which he looked from that which meets our view. The gravestones which are now set against the walls of the cloisters were then buried beneath the rubbish of the cathedral. On the other side of this wall, in the grounds of the priory, were situated those "two vaults or cellars" where our travellers found a strange inmate.

"In one of them (writes Johnson) lives an old woman, who claims an hereditary residence in it, boasting that her husband was the sixth tenant of this gloomy mansion in a lineal descent, and claims by her marriage with this lord of the cavern an alliance with the Bruces. Mr. Boswell staid a while to interrogate her, because he understood her language; she told him that she and her cat lived together; that she had two sons somewhere, who might perhaps be dead; that when there were quality in the town notice was taken of her, and that now she was neglected, but did not trouble them. Her habitation contained all that she had; her turf for fire was laid in one place and her balls of coal dust in another, but her bed seemed to be clean. Boswell asked her if she never heard any noises, but she could tell him of nothing supernatural, though she often wandered in the night among the graves and ruins; only she had sometimes notice by dreams of the death of her relations."

I made as diligent an inquiry as I could after this kinswoman of the royal family of Scotland, but all in vain.

> "The glories of our blood and state
> Are shadows, not substantial things."

The memory has been preserved of "some cellar-looking places," but no tradition of human habitation has come down to our time.

"Dr. Johnson wanted to mount the steeples (writes Boswell), but it could not be done. One of them, which he was told was in danger, he wished not to be taken down; 'for (said he) it may fall on some of the posterity of John Knox; and no great matter.'"

[1] Translated by Boswell:
"Let youth in deeds, in counsel man engage;
Prayer is the proper duty of old age."

Among the posterity was to be born eight-and-twenty years later a little girl, destined to become famous as the wife of Thomas Carlyle.[1] What was the hindrance to the ascent of St. Rule's Tower I could not ascertain. The staircase, which is perfect, has in no part a modern appearance, but nevertheless, it is possible that some of the steps were missing. Saint-Fond, nevertheless, went up it not long after Johnson's visit. Sir Walter Scott, a few years before his death, visiting the ruins, wrote that he had not been strong enough to climb the tower.

WEST DOOR, ST. ANDREWS.

"When before did I remain sitting below when there was a steeple to be ascended? I sat down on a gravestone, and recollected the first visit I made to St. Andrews, now thirty-four years ago. What changes in my feelings and my fortunes have since then taken place!—some for the better, many for the worse. I remembered the name I then carved in runic characters on the turf beside the Castle Gate, and I asked why it should still agitate my heart."[2]

As we wander among these ancient ruins it is pleasant to think not only on the days when the cathedral stood in all its magnificence, and on those other days when the wild mob raved through it, but also on old Samuel Johnson, wrapped up in contemplation or preaching about retirement, and on Walter Scott resting on a

---

[1] Her descent from Knox is not fully established, though, says Carlyle, "there is really good likelihood of the genealogy." *Reminiscences by Thomas Carlyle*, ii. 103.

[2] Lockhart's *Life of Scott*, ix. 126.

gravestone and dreaming of his first love. We may pause, too, for one moment in the old chapel beneath the tower, at the spot where that good man and good antiquary Robert Chambers lies in everlasting rest. From the top of the tower I looked with pleasure on the long row of young trees planted along the main street. The reproach of bareness will not long hang over the town. Indeed, much had been done to remove it by an earlier generation, for this noble street was adorned not many years ago by a fine group of trees. Unfortunately a reforming provost arose, who swept them away. Near the cathedral I noticed an inscription which might have called forth Johnson's sarcastic wit had he chanced to see it. It bore the date of 1752, and was in memory of "John Anderson who was Minister of the Gospel of St. Andrews."

While the travellers were strolling about "dinner was mentioned. 'Ay, ay,' said Johnson. 'Amidst all these sorrowful scenes I have no objection to dinner.'" They were to be the guests of the professors, who entertained them at one of the inns.

"An ill natured story was circulated (says Boswell) that, after grace was said in English, Johnson, with the greatest marks of contempt, as if he had held it to be no grace in an university, would not sit down till he had said grace aloud, in Latin. This would have been an insult indeed to the gentlemen who were entertaining us. But the truth was precisely thus. In the course of conversation at dinner, Dr. Johnson, in very good humour, said, 'I should have expected to have heard a Latin grace, among so many learned men: we had always a Latin grace at Oxford I believe I can repeat it."

This grace had been written by the learned Camden for Pembroke College, "to which," to use Johnson's own words, "the zeal or gratitude of those that love it most can wish little better than that it may long proceed as it began."

In the afternoon they went to see the monument to Archbishop Sharpe. His great granddaughter they met at supper. Saint-Fond, confounding him with Cardinal Beaton, says: "Il paraît que les parens du Cardinal Beaton n'ont pas voulu déguiser la paternité du saint archevêque, puisque sa fille est représentée toute en pleurs, les bras tendus vers son père."[1]

The two colleges which formed the University greatly interested Johnson. The natural advantages of St. Andrews for a seat of learning had been pointed out by an earlier traveller, who maintained that it had the best situation he had ever seen for an University, " being out of all common roads, and having fine downs

A DECLINING UNIVERSITY.

or links, as they call them, for exercising the scholars."[1] The golfers who now throng the links and boast that when professors by their learning could not save the ancient city from sinking into decay, they by their idleness have lifted it into prosperity, must have been numerous even in Johnson's time. Of all the old manufactures, that of golf-balls alone was left, and it maintained, or rather helped to destroy, several people. "The trade," says Pennant, "is commonly fatal to the artists, for the balls are made by stuffing a great quantity of feathers into a leathern case, by help of an iron rod with a wooden handle pressed against the breast, which seldom fails to bring on a consumption."[2] To Johnson, though he makes no mention of the Links, "St. Andrews seemed to be a place eminently adapted to study and education." Never-

GOLF AT ST. ANDREWS.

theless, he had to grieve over a declining university. The fault was not, he said, in the professors; the expenses of the students, moreover, were very moderate. For about fifteen pounds, board, lodging, and instruction were provided for the session of seven months for students of the highest class. Those of lower rank were charged less than ten. Percival Stockdale, who was there in 1756, says that "for a good bedroom, coals, and the attendance of a servant, he paid one shilling a week." At this period an Oxford commoner, Johnson says, required a hundred a year and a petty scholarship "to live with great ease."[4] To anyone who could pay for what he bought in ready money, living was made cheaper by the system of giving a discount of a shilling in the pound. A Scotch gentleman who resided much in England finding that this

---

[1] Mackay's *Journey through Scotland*, p. 93.   Stockdale's *Memoirs*, i. 258.
[2] Pennant's *Tour in Scotland*, ii. 197.   [4] Boswell's *Johnson*, vi. xxx.

was not done in that country, "was in the habit when he purchased anything of putting the cash in a piece of paper, on which he wrote what it was to pay. This he kept in his desk twelve months, saying that the English traders are a set of rascals."[1] The poorer Scotch students, however, had to bear great privations. "The miserable holes which some of them inhabit," writes a young English traveller, "their abstemiousness and parsimony, their constant attendance to study, their indefatigable industry, border on romance."[2] At St. Andrews they often were too poor to buy candles, and had to study by fire-light. In spite of the extraordinary cheapness of the life their numbers were dwindling. They did not at this time exceed a hundred, says Johnson. Three years later Wesley was told that there were only about seventy.[3] "To the sight of archi-piscopal ruins," Johnson was reconciled, he said, by the remoteness of the calamity which had befallen them. "Had the University been destroyed two centuries ago we should not have regretted it; but to see it pining in decay and struggling for life fills the mind with mournful images and ineffectual wishes." Some improvement, nevertheless, had of late been made. Defoe, in the year 1727, had described the whole building of St. Salvator's College "as looking into its grave."[4] The account given by Boswell of the fabric is much more cheerful. "The rooms for students," he writes, "seemed very commodious, and Dr. Johnson said the chapel was the neatest place of worship he had seen." Nevertheless, at the beginning of this century some of the lecture-rooms were described as being places "in which a gentleman would be ashamed to lodge his hacks or his terriers."[5] It was fortunate for the reputation of the College that our two travellers had not visited it earlier in the summer, otherwise they would have had to report a disgraceful sight which three years later shocked John Wesley. It was soon after the beginning of the Long Vacation that he was there, before the glaziers had repaired the wreck which marked the end of the yearly course. It was the custom, he was told, for the students to break all the windows before they left. "Where," asks Wesley, indignantly,

---

[1] G. M. Berkeley's *Poems*, p. ccxcvi.
[2] Topham's *Letters from Edinburgh*, p. 218.
[3] G. M. Berkeley's *Poems*, p. ccxlix.
[4] Wesley's *Journal*, iv. 77.
 Tour Through Great Britain. Account of Scotland, iii. 154. Defoe calls it St. Salvador's, and wonders "how it was made to speak Portuguese." Boswell gives it the same name, though he spells it differently—St. Salvador's. By 1807 I find it called in Grierson's *Delineation of St. Andrews*, as it is at present, St. Salvator's.

[5] *Delineation as it was and as it is*, p. 157.

are their blessed Governors in the mean time? Are they all fast asleep?" The young Etonian, Bishop Berkeley's grandson, had the merit of putting an end to this bad practice. On entrance he was required to deposit a crown for window-money; when, model of virtue as he was, he objected that he had never yet broken a window in his life, and was not likely to begin, he was assured that he would before he left St. Andrews. The College porter, who collected "these window-*croons*," told him of a poor student who had shed tears on being called on to pay. His father, a cottar, had sold one of his three cows to find money for his education at the university, and had sent him up with a large tub of oatmeal, a pot of salted butter, and five shillings in his pocket. Sixpence of this money had already been spent, and the rest the porter took.² When the window-breaking time came on, and Berkeley was summoned to take his part in the riot, he refused. As a boy at Eton, he said, though sometimes with more wine in his head than was good for him, he had never performed such a valiant feat, and he was not therefore going to begin as a young man. His comrades yielded to his remonstrances, and the windows were no longer broken.³

At St. Mary's College Johnson was shown the fine library which had been finished within the last few years. Dr. Murison, the Principal, was abundantly vain of it, for he seriously said to him, "You have not such a one in England." Johnson, though he has his laugh at the Doctor for hoping "to irritate or subdue his English vanity," yet admits that if "it was not very spacious, it was elegant and luminous." It is not, of course, to be compared with the largest libraries at Oxford. "If a man has a mind to prance" it is not at St. Andrews, but at Christ Church and All Souls, that he must study.⁴ Nevertheless it confers great dignity on the University, and with its 120,000 volumes there is no English College that it would disgrace. Murison's vanity had therefore some excuse. He was, however, a man "barely sufficient" for the post which he held. Over his slips in Latin the lads sometimes made merry. In the Divinity Hall he one day rebuked a student

---

¹ Wesley's *Journal*, iv. 77.
² Berkeley and his friend, the young Laird of Kinaldrum, raised "a very noble subscription" for the poor lad.
G. M. Berkeley's *Poems*, p. cccxlviii.
³ "On my observing to Dr. Johnson that some of the modern libraries of the university were more commodious and pleasant for study [than the library of Trinity College], as being more spacious and airy, he replied, 'Sir, if a man has a mind to *prance*, he must study at Christ Church and All Souls.'" Boswell's *Johnson*, ii. 67, n. 2.

for delivering a discourse which was too high-flown and poetical. "Lord help him, poor man!" said the indignant youngster, "He knows no better."[1]

On the second day of our travellers' stay "they went," says Boswell, "and saw Colonel Nairne's garden and grotto. Here was a fine old plane tree."[2] Unluckily the Colonel said there was but this and another large tree in the country. This assertion was an

ST. MARY'S COLLEGE LIBRARY.

excellent cue for Dr. Johnson, who laughed enormously, calling to me to hear it." The Colonel's father, Lord Nairne, had been "out in the '45," while the son, who fought in the King's army, had been sent to batter down the old castle of his forefathers. George II. wished to reward his fidelity with the command of a regiment, but

---

[1] *Scotland and Scotchmen in the Eighteenth Century*, 1860, 547. The youngster was Jerome Stone, the author of a poem called *Albin and the Daughter of Mey*, mentioned by Boswell in his *Life of Johnson*, v. 171.

[2] It was probably a sycamore, for, as was pointed out by a writer in the *Gentleman's Magazine* for 1837, p. 343, what the Scotch call sycamores we call planes.

The other tree, according to Sir Walter Scott, was probably the Prior Letham plane, measuring about twenty feet round. It stood in a cold exposed situation apart from every other tree. Croker's *Boswell*, p. 286.

was hindered by the Duke of Cumberland, "who told the King that it was impossible that a man who had suffered so much could ever forget or forgive it."[1] His garden and grotto were at the back of the Chapel. The grotto has disappeared with its "petrified stocks of trees," unless perchance some remains of it are seen in a small building, which looks like a private chapel, and which might have been transformed by that ingenious collector of curiosities, the Colonel. The plane tree survived till about the beginning of the century. An old gentleman still living was told by his grandfather that in the branches a wooden platform had been built, on which tea parties were held.[2] I remember seeing in my boyhood a similar platform in a large willow-tree overhanging Isaac Walton's sedgy Lea. That the good people of St. Andrews have not in their traditions made Johnson drink a dozen or two cups of tea in this airy summer-house is a proof either of their truthfulness or of the sluggishness of their imagination.

Every Scotchman, it was said long ago, thought it his duty once in his life to visit "the city of the scarlet gown" and to see the ruins of the great cathedral.[3] No longer, happily, is the mind of the pilgrim "filled with mournful images and ineffectual wishes;" no longer does he see "a University pining in decay and struggling for life;" no longer does he wander through grass-grown streets, listening to the sound of his own solitary steps. The town is thriving and animated; the University sees the number of its students steadily increasing. It had long been depressed by poverty; but a noble endowment happily has this very year[4] fallen to its lot. If it can never hope to attain to those stately avenues and lawns and gardens and buildings, as beautiful as they are venerable, which are the boast of Oxford, nevertheless in the bracing pureness of its air, in its fine situation on the shores of the northern sea, in its seclusion from that bustle which distracts the student's life, and from that luxury which too often makes poverty, however honest, hang its head, it has advantages which are not enjoyed by any other of our Universities.

---

[1] G. M. Berkeley's *Poems*, p. cxii.
[2] This piece of information I owe to the kindness of Mr. J. Maitland Anderson, the Librarian of the University.
[3] In G. M. Berkeley's *Poems*, p. lvi, a story is told of some people who were at St. Andrews for only one night, and who, rather than miss the ruins, saw them "by the light of an old horn lantern."
[4] Written in 1889.

LEUCHARS AND ARBROTHICK. (AUGUST 20.)

Johnson, closing his description of St. Andrews with his lament over its declining University, goes on to say like a wise man:—

LEUCHARS.

"As we knew sorrow and wishes to be vain, it was now our business to mind our way." Perhaps, as he wrote these words he had in his memory two lines of Matthew Green, though they were originally used of quitting, not what was painful, but what was pleasant

> "Though pleased to see the dolphins play,
> I mind my compass and my way."

He and Boswell started about noon for Montrose on the other side of the Firth of Tay, a distance of a little over forty miles, but with good reason made a halt at Leuchars, on observing the fine old Norman church.¹ They were fortunate enough to see it before it

VIEW ON THE TAY.

was "restored" for nothing ancient remains but the apse and chancel. The new portion in the interior is ugly in the most approved Scottish fashion; in the outside it would be insignificant were it not added as a vast excrescence to the ancient building. It stands on a little hill at the end of the village, with the churchyard round it falling away on the southern side in steep slopes to the road. Hard by are some well-grown trees round the Manse where Boswell waited on the aged minister, a very civil old man, to learn what he could. He was told that the church was supposed to have stood eight hundred years. St. Andrews certainly can show nothing so ancient. The village is built solidly enough of stone,

¹ Boswell *Johnson*, iii. 405.   ² Paterson's *Itinerary*, ii. 307, 581.

but seems careless of pleasing the eye. There are no little gardens before the houses, no roses trained up the walls, scarcely any flowers in the windows. "Take care of the beautiful, the useful will take care of itself," has not been a gospel sounded in Scottish ears.

The road to the Tay, which Boswell enlivened by leading Johnson to discuss the doctrine of transubstantiation, lay through a pleasant undulating country that bears luxuriant crops and at the present time is no longer wanting in trees. Their chaise was taken across the Firth in a ferry-boat at a charge of four shillings. How Johnson, who always delighted in what he called "the accommodations of life," would have exulted in the great bridge which now spans the flood! He would have noticed too with pleasure the long avenue of young trees planted along the bank. Passing through Dundee, "a dirty despicable town" as he describes it, but now the seat of a vast commerce, they came about the close of the day to the ruined abbey of Aberbrothick.[1] The sight of these fragments of "stupendous magnificence" struck Johnson perhaps more than anything which he saw on the whole of his tour. "I should scarcely have regretted my journey," he said, "had it afforded nothing more than the sight of Aberbrothick." John Wesley declared that he "knew nothing like the Abbey in all North Britain. I paced it and found it an hundred yards long. The breadth is proportionable. Part of the west-end which is still standing shows it was full as high as Westminster Abbey."[2] It had been left in much the same state of neglect as the Cathedral of St. Andrews. Boswell, "whose inquisitiveness was seconded by great activity," wanted to climb one of the towers. "He scrambled in at a high window, but found the stairs within broken, and could not reach the top." The entrance to the other tower they could not discern, and as the night was gathering upon them he gave up the attempt. Not clearly remembering Johnson's account, I told the old man who shows the Abbey that I had read in an old book that a hundred years and more ago the staircase was broken down. "Then they *lied*," he answered angrily, indignant for its reputation for antiquity. I learnt from him that an ancient inn, which had been recently pulled down, had been found to have been built of the hewn stones taken from the Abbey. In the ruins no doubt for many a long year the

---

[1] Or *Aberbrothock*, as it is called in Southey's *Ballad of the Inchcape Rock*. The name is now written *Arbroath*, in accordance with the pronunciation.
[2] Wesley's *Journal*, iii. 307.

town had had its quarry. Johnson noticed one room of which he could not conjecture the use, "as its elevation was very disproportionate to its area." I was told that it was the Chapter House, but my informant, a queer little urchin who acted as under-guide, was

ABERBROTHICK.

not trustworthy, for he informed me that the ruins had been caused by a fire in which the Abbey was burnt down a thousand years ago. In this room I found hanging on the wall likenesses of Mary Queen of Scots and of Pope Pius IX. Surely the bitterness of the Reformation has passed away even in Scotland.

The grounds are still used as a graveyard. Here and elsewhere in Scotland I noticed in the inscriptions that the English term *wife* is slowly supplanting the old Scotch term *spouse*. On one side of the great gateway two ugly arches have been lately built as entrances to pompous family burial places. These excrescences should surely be removed and the dead left to their quiet insignificance. On the outside, underneath a lofty wall, a pleasant bowling-green has been laid out for public enjoyment, with flower borders running round. The town was keeping a public holiday the day I was there, and the ground was thronged with players and spectators. I was sorry to see in many places that ivy in the true cockney spirit has been trained up the ruins. Unless the strong sea-breezes, which cut off the tops of the trees as soon as they show their heads too high, come to the rescue, it will in time hide the dark red sandstone beneath a uniform mantle of green. Though the ruins are now cared for, and the ground cleared of the long grass and weeds which hindered Johnson from tracing the foundations, nevertheless the lofty wall close to the main entrance is disgraced by huge advertisements. As the stranger approaches the venerable pile from the High Street he gives one angry thought to the Town Council which leases it to the dealers in sewing machines, in blue, and in Irish whisky for advertising their wares. " Where there is yet shame there may in time be virtue." Would that this protest of mine may rouse a feeling of shame in the unworthy guardians of so glorious a ruin !

MONTROSE, LAURENCEKIRK AND MONBODDO (AUGUST 20-21).

The road along which Johnson and Boswell drove as they journeyed from Dundee through Arbroath to Montrose, is described by Defoe as a " pleasant way through a country fruitful and bespangled, as the sky in a clear night with stars of the biggest magnitude, with gentlemen's houses, thick as they can be supposed to stand with pleasure and conveniency."[1] Our travellers in the latter part of the drive saw nothing of all this, for the sun had set before they left the great Abbey ; it was not till eleven at night that they arrived at Montrose. There they found but a sorry inn, where, writes Boswell, " I myself saw another waiter put a lump of sugar with his fingers into Dr. Johnson's lemonade, for which he called him ' rascal !' It put me in great glee that our

[1] Defoe's *Tour*, p. 179.

landlord was an Englishman. I rallied the Doctor upon this and he grew quiet." The town Johnson praised as "neat"—"neat" last century stood very high among the terms of commendation, though it is now supplanted by "elegant" among Americans, and by "nice" among English people. At the time of the Rebellion

ON THE WAY TO MONTROSE.

of 1745, the townsfolk had been described as "very genteel, but disaffected."[1] To the clerk of the English chapel Johnson gave "a shilling extraordinary, saying, 'He belongs to an honest church.'" He had the great merit also of keeping his church "clean to a degree unknown in any other part of Scotland," so that his shilling was well earned.

[1] James Ray's *History of the Rebellion*, p. 288.

LAURENCEKIRK.

From Montrose the road led through a country rich with an abundant harvest that was almost ripe for the sickle, but bare of everything but crops. Even the hedges, said Johnson, were of stone. Boswell calls this a ludicrous description, but it could have been easily defended as good Scotch, for in the *Scots Magazine* for January of the previous year, we read of "the stone hedges of Scotland."[1] It is strange that Johnson had not noticed these roughly-built walls in Northumberland, for in the northern part of that county, according to Pennant, "hedges were still in their infancy."[2] At Laurencekirk our travellers stopped to dine,

GARDENSTON ARMS.

and "respectfully remembered that great grammarian Ruddiman," who had spent four years there as schoolmaster. More than seventy years before their visit, Dr. Pitcairne, the author of that Latin epitaph on Dundee which Dryden translated, being weather-bound at the village inn, "inquired if there were no persons who could interchange conversation and partake of his dinner." The hostess mentioned Ruddiman. He came, pleased Pitcairne, and was by him brought to Edinburgh. Francis Garden, one of the Scotch judges, under the title of Lord Gardenston, the laird and

[1] *Scots Magazine*, 1772, p. 25.   Pennant's *Tour*, ii. 278.
[2] Chalmers's *Life of Ruddiman*, p. 24.

almost the founder of this thriving village, " had furnished the inn with a collection of books, that travellers might have entertainment for the mind as well as the body. Dr. Johnson praised the design, but wished there had been more books, and those better chosen." The inn still stands with the library adjoining it. Round the room is hanging a series of portraits in French chalk of Gardenston's " feuars," or tenants, who, after the laird, were the chief people of the place when Johnson and Boswell passed through. Many of the books remain on the shelves, though some have been lost through carelessness or the dishonesty of travellers. There are among them a few works of light literature such as Dryden's *Virgil*, and *Gil Blas* in French, but the solid reading which most of them afford makes us think with a feeling of respect that almost amounts to awe, of the learning of the Scotch travellers in those good old days. Tavern chairs were no thrones of human felicity in Laurencekirk if such works as the following were commonly perused by those who chanced to fill them :

Magno's *Observations on Anatomy*, in Latin.
Keill's *Introduction to the Study of Astronomy*.
Aristophanes, with Latin notes.
Boerhaave's *Commentaries on the Aphorisms of Diseases*, naturalized into English.
Tull's *Horse-hoeing Husbandry*.
Watt's *Logic*.
Newton's *Principia*.
Clarke's *Sermons*.
Machiavelli, in Italian.[1]

In Marischal College, Aberdeen, there is a portrait of Lord Gardenston in his judge's robes. He has a somewhat conceited look, such as we might expect in a man who " wrote a pamphlet upon his village, as if he had founded Thebes," and who provided such improving reading for his weary fellow-creatures.

A mile or two off the road from Laurencekirk to Aberdeen lived the famous old Scotch judge, James Burnett, Lord Monboddo. " I knew," wrote Boswell, " that he and Dr. Johnson did not love each other; yet I was unwilling not to visit his Lordship, and was also curious to see them together. I mentioned my doubts to Dr. Johnson, who said he would go two miles out of his way to see

[1] This information I owe to the kindness of my friend Mr. Arthur Galton.

Lord Monboddo." The two men had not much in common except their love of learning, and their precision of speech. Monboddo, according to Foote, was an Elzevir edition of Johnson. In a letter to Mrs. Thrale Johnson thus describes him:

"He has lately written a strange book about the origin of language, in which he traces monkeys up to men, and says that in some countries the human species have tails like other beasts. He inquired for these long-tailed men of Banks, and was not well-pleased that they had not been found in all his peregrinations. He talked nothing of this to me, and I hope we parted friends: for we agreed pretty well, only we disputed in adjusting the claims of merit between a shopkeeper of London and a savage of the American wildernesses. Our opinions were, I think, maintained on both sides without full conviction; Monboddo declared boldly for the savage, and I perhaps for that reason sided with the citizen."

Johnson a few years earlier had contrasted Monboddo with Rousseau, "who talked nonsense so well that he must know he was talking nonsense;" whereas, he added, "chuckling and laughing, 'I am afraid Monboddo does not know that he is talking nonsense.'" He was undoubtedly a man of great learning, but he was almost destitute of the critical faculty. In the six volumes of his *Ancient Metaphysics* we come across such strange passages as the following:

"Not only are there tailed men extant, but men such as the ancients describe satyrs have been found, who had not only tails, but the feet of goats, and horns on their heads. . . . We have the authority of a father of the Church for a greater singularity of the human form, and that is of men without heads but with eyes in their breasts. . . . There is another singularity as great or greater than any I have hitherto mentioned, and that is of men with the heads of dogs."

After stating his readiness to believe that "a tame and gentle animal" once existed, "having the head of a man and the body of a lion," he continues:

"The variety of nature is so great that I am convinced of the truth of what Aristotle says, that everything exists, or did at some time exist, which is possible to exist."

The orang-outang he describes as being "of a character mild and gentle, affectionate, too, and capable of friendship, with the sense also of what is decent and becoming." The ancients, he stoutly maintained, were in every respect better and stronger than their descendants. He shocked Hannah More by telling her that "he loved slavery upon principle." When she asked him "how he could vindicate such an enormity, he owned it was because Plutarch justified it." In one respect he was wise in following

---

[1] *Ancient Metaphysics*, iv. 45.
[2] *Ib.* p. 48.
[3] *Ib.* p. 55.
[4] Hannah More's *Memoirs*, 252.

the example of the ancients. In an age when bathing was very uncommon even among the wealthy, he constantly urged the daily use of the cold bath. He reminded "our fine gentlemen and ladies that the Otaheite man, Omai, who came from a country where the inhabitants bathed twice a day," complained of the offensive smell of all the people of England.[1] It was believed, however, that Monboddo impaired the health of his children by the hardy treatment to which he exposed them. He despised Johnson because "he had compiled a dictionary of a barbarous language, a work which a man of real genius rather than undertake would choose to die of hunger."[2] In the latter part of his life he used every year to pay a visit to London, and he always went on horseback, even after he had passed his eightieth year "A carriage, a vehicle that was not in common use among the ancients, he considered as an engine of effeminacy and sloth. To be dragged at the tail of horses seemed in his eyes to be a ludicrous degradation of the genuine dignity of human nature. In Court he never sat on the Bench with the other judges, but within the Bar, on the seat appropriated for Peers."[3] Yet with all his singularities he was a fine old fellow. There was no kinder landlord in all Scotland. While around him the small farms were disappearing, and farmers and cottagers were making room for sheep, it was his boast that on his estate no change had been made. Neither he nor his father before him had ever turned off a single cottager.

"One of my tenants (he wrote) who pays me no more than £30 of rent has no less than thirteen cottagers living upon his farm. I have on one part of my estate seven tenants, each of whom possesses no more than three acres of arable land, and some moorish land for pasture, and they pay me no more than twelve shillings for each acre, and nothing for the moor. I am persuaded I could more than double the rent of their land by letting it off to one tenant; but I should be sorry to increase my rent by depopulating any part of the country; and I keep these small tenants as a monument of the way in which I believe a great part of the Lowlands was cultivated in ancient times."[4]

He befriended Burns, who repaid his kindness by celebrating his daughter's beauty in his *Address to Edinburgh*, and by the elegy which he wrote on her untimely death. In a note to *Guy Mannering* Sir Walter Scott describes his supper parties, "where there was a circulation of excellent Bordeaux in flasks garlanded with roses, which were also strewed on the table after the manner

---

[1] *Ancient Metaphysics*, vi. 212.
[2] *Origin of Language*, v. 274.
[3] *Scots Magazine*, 1799, pp. 729-731.
[4] *Ancient Metaphysics*, v. 307.

of Horace. The best society, whether in respect of rank or literary distinction, was always to be found in St. John's Street, Canongate. The conversation of the excellent old man; his high gentleman-like, chivalrous spirit; the learning and wit with which he defended his fanciful paradoxes; the kind and liberal spirit of his hospitality, must render these *noctes cœnæque* dear to all who, like the author (though then young), had the honour of sitting at his board."

Boswell's man-servant, who had been sent to ascertain whether Lord Monboddo was at home, awaited the travellers' arrival at the turn in the road, with the news that they were expected to dinner.

"'We drove,' says Boswell, "over a wild moor. It rained, and the scene was somewhat dreary. Dr. Johnson repeated with solemn emphasis Macbeth's speech on meeting the witches. . . . . Monboddo is a wretched place, wild and naked, with a poor old house; though, if I recollect right, there are two turrets, which mark an old baron's residence. Lord Monboddo received us at his gate most courteously, pointed to the Douglas arms upon his house, and told us that his great-grandmother was of that family."

The old arms are still above the door, with the inscription:

"R. I.
E. D.
1635."

"R. I." was Robert Irvine, a colonel in the army of Gustavus Adolphus, the Lion of the North, and possibly the superior officer of Major Dugald Dalgetty. "E. D." was Elizabeth Douglas. Their daughter married one of the Burnetts, of Crathes Castle. There is nothing wretched, wild, or naked about Monboddo in the present day. As I saw it, no thought of a "blasted heath," and of Macbeth's witches could by any freak of the imagination have entered the mind. The land all round has been brought into cultivation, and there is no moor within five miles. The road along which I drove was bordered by a row of beech trees, which might have been planted by Lord Monboddo or his father. The ancient part of the house, which remains much as Boswell saw it, though large additions have been made, so far from striking one as poor and wretched, has a picturesque, old-fashioned look of decent comfort. Close to it stand a holly and a yew, which have seen the lapse of more centuries than one. The lawns are wide and soft, and very pleasant. Hard by a brook prattles along, almost hidden by rhododendrons and firs. The distant view of the Grampians; the pure, bracing air, whether the wind blows it from the sea on the

east or from the mountains on the west; the lawns, the trees, the
old house, picturesque in itself, and interesting in its associations,
render Monboddo a most pleasant abode. In the time of the old
judge it was no doubt bare enough. Where there are now lawns
and flower beds there most likely corn and turnips grew, for he was
almost as fond of farming as he was of the ancients. When he received our travellers, "he was dressed," says Boswell, "in a rustic

MONBODDO.

suit, and wore a little round hat. He told us we now saw him as
Farmer Burnett, and we should have his family dinner—a farmer's
dinner. He produced a very long stalk of corn as a specimen of
his crop, and said, 'You see here the *lætas segetes*.'" An instance of
his "agricultural enthusiasm" used to be recounted by Sir Walter
Scott: "Returning home one night after an absence (I think) on
circuit, he went out with a candle to look at a field of turnips, then
a novelty in Scotland."[1] He had a glimpse, it should seem, of some

Croker's *Boswell*, p. 288.

of the wonders which chemistry was soon to work in agriculture, for being one day at Court, he told George III. that the time would come when a man would be able to carry in his waistcoat pocket manure enough for an acre of land.[1]

The "farmer's dinner" was good enough to satisfy Dr. Johnson, for he made a very hearty meal. Yet with all the pride of a man who has a vigorous appetite, he said, "I have done greater feats with my knife than this." The low, square, panelled room in which they dined is much as they saw it, with its three windows with deep recesses looking on to the lawns and trees. It is a solid, comfortable apartment, which might have recalled to Johnson's memory an Oxford Common-Room, and which harmonized well with the solid talk he had with his host. In it there is a curious clock, so old that it might have told the hours to Colonel Irvine and his wife Elizabeth Douglas, and have attracted Johnson's notice by its antiquity.

ABERDEEN (AUGUST 21-24).

Late in the afternoon our travellers drove on to Aberdeen. "We had tedious driving," writes Boswell, "and were somewhat drowsy." Though they "travelled with the gentle pace of a Scotch driver," nevertheless Johnson, much as he delighted in the rapid motion of the English post-chaise, bore this journey of five-and-twenty miles with greater philosophy than his friend. "We did not," he writes, "affect the impatience we did not feel, but were satisfied with the company of each other—as well riding in the chaise as sitting at an inn." It was not far short of midnight when they arrived at Aberdeen. The "New Inn" at which they stopped was full, they were told. "This was comfortless." Fortunately Boswell's father, when on circuit, always put up there for the five nights during which he was required by law to stay in each assize town.[2] The son was recognized by his likeness to the father, and a room was soon provided. "Mr. Boswell's name," writes Johnson, "overpowered all objection, and we found a very good house, and civil treatment." A few weeks later the old judge went this same

---

[1] This anecdote I had from Lord Monboddo's great grandson, Captain Burnett, of Monboddo House, to whose courtesy I am much indebted.

[2] "In Scotland judges on the circuit are obliged to lay five nights at every town where they open their commission." Howard's *State of Prisons*, ed. 1777, p. 103.

circuit. "Two men being indicted before him at Aberdeen on September 30 for petty thefts, petitioned, and were banished to the plantations for life, their service adjudged for seven years to the transporter."[1] What these poor wretches had "petitioned" was that they might be transported instead of being hanged. The "transporter," who bore the cost of shipping them to America, was rewarded for his outlay by having the use of them as slaves for seven years. At the end of that time they would have their freedom; but if they returned to Scotland, and were seized, in all likelihood they would have been sent to the gallows under their old sentence. It is not at all improbable that these two thieves were in the town prison at the very time of our travellers' visit. If so, they were separated from them merely by a wall or two; for the "New Inn" formed part of the same block of buildings as the common prison. In the central tower the ordinary prisoners were confined, two rooms in the western end being reserved for burgesses, "or any of the better rank who were committed for debt."[2] The judge in all the festivities of his circuit dinner was often close to some poor wretch whom that same day he had sentenced to the gallows, and who was awaiting his dreadful end in the gloom and misery of his dismal cell.

On the other side of the tower, but in the same block, was the Town House, or Town Hall as we should call it in England. When I was in Aberdeen, a man of whom I asked the way to the Town Hall, replied that he did not know where it was; but when I corrected myself, and asked for the Town House, he at once showed it me. Here it was that the freedom of the city was conferred on Johnson.

"At one o'clock (writes Boswell) we waited on the magistrates in the town-hall, as they had invited us in order to present Dr. Johnson with the freedom of the town, which Provost Jopp did with a very good grace. Dr. Johnson was much pleased with this mark of attention, and received it very politely. There was a pretty numerous company assembled. It was striking to hear all of them drinking, 'Dr. Johnson! Dr. Johnson!' in the town-hall of Aberdeen, and then to see him with his burgess-ticket, or diploma, in his hat, which he wore as he walked along the street, according to the usual custom."

The hall in which the ceremony was performed was a room "46 feet long, 29 broad, and 18 high, with five large windows in front, with many elegant sconces double-branched set round it, and three

---

[1] *Scot. Magazine*, Oct. 1773, p. 556.
[2] F. Douglas, *General Description of the East Coast of Scotland*, p. 91.

diamond-cut crystal lustres hanging from the roof."[1] It has been
swept away with the New Inn and the prison, and replaced by the
stately pile which rises on the old site. The Scotch towns last
century seem to have been somewhat lavish in the honours which
they conferred. Pennant was made a freeman of at least three or
four places. Monck Berkeley, the St. Andrew's student, had the
freedom of Aberdeen and some other towns presented to him,
though he was scarcely nineteen when he left Scotland. Like the
dutiful young gentleman that he was, "he constantly presented the
diplomas to his mother requesting her to take great care of them."[2]
George Colman the younger, who, at the age of eighteen was sent
to King's College, says in his *Random Records*;[3] "I had scarcely
been a week in Old Aberdeen, when the Lord Provost of the New
Town invited me to drink wine with him one evening in the Town
Hall; there I found a numerous company assembled. The object
of this meeting was soon declared to me by the Lord Provost, who
drank my health, and presented me with the freedom of the city."
Two of his English fellow-students, of a little older standing, had
received the same honour. A suspicion rises in the mind that it
was sometimes not so much a desire to confer honour as to drink
wine at the public expense which stirred up these town-councillors.
Nevertheless, the testimony of an English gentleman, who a few
years earlier had been made a citizen of Glasgow, goes far towards freeing them from so injurious a supposition. "The magistrates," he wrote, "are all men of so reasonable a size, and so clear
of all marks of gluttony and drunkenness, that I could hardly believe them to be a mayor and aldermen."[4] With the distinction
itself, on whatever account it was given, Johnson was greatly
pleased. "I was presented," he wrote, "with the freedom of the
city, not in a gold box, but in good Latin. Let me pay Scotland
one just praise; there was no officer gaping for a fee; this could
have been said of no city on the English side of the Tweed." In
his own University of Oxford the fee for the honorary degree of
D.C.L. used to be ten guineas. Cox, the Esquire Bedel, records
in his *Recollections of Oxford*, how glum Canning looked when he
was called on to pay it.[5] Wesley, who in the April of the previous
year had been made a freeman of Perth, praised the Latinity in

[1] F. Douglas' *General Description*, &c., p. 89.
[2] G. M. Berkeley's *Poems*, p. cclxxiv.
[3] Vol. ii. p. 99.
[4] *Gentleman's Magazine*, 1766, p. 216.
[5] Cox's *Recollections of Oxford* (ed. 1868), p. 136.

which the honour was conferred on him. "I doubt," he wrote, "whether any diploma from the City of London be more pompous or expressed in better Latin."[1]

The burgess-ticket or parchment on which the freedom was inscribed, after being read aloud in the hall, was made into a roll, and, with the appending seal, was tied on to the new citizen's hat with red riband. "I wore," wrote Johnson, "my patent of freedom *pro more* in my hat from the new town to the old, about a mile." In his narrative he states that it is worn for the whole day. In a town of 16,000 inhabitants—for Aberdeen had no more at that time[2]—it might be supposed that the face of the youngest freeman would thus become known to most of his brother-burgesses. But the population at the present day is seven or eight times as large, and the old custom has died out, perhaps because its use was lost. On those rare occasions when the honour is conferred the diploma is still tied to the hat. The new citizen covers himself for a moment, and then bares his head while he returns thanks. He might, I was told, perhaps wear his ticket for a short distance to his hotel or a club, but certainly not farther. The entry of Johnson's freedom in its good Latin still remains in the City Register. I read it with much interest.

Our travellers, as they passed a Sunday in Aberdeen, went to the English chapel. The word *chapel*, as my friend Dr. Murray has clearly pointed out in his learned Dictionary, which in England was generally used of the places of worship of the Nonconformists, and in Ireland of those of the Roman Catholics, in Scotland was properly and universally applied to the English churches. It is the term used both by Boswell and Johnson. Mrs. Carlyle in one of her early letters describes a certain Haddington Episcopalian as "a man without an arm, who sits in the chapel."[3] "We found," says Boswell, "a respectable congregation and an admirable organ." By *respectable* he meant what would a little later have been described as *genteel*. "The congregation," wrote Johnson, "was numerous and splendid." The volunteer who accompanied the Duke of Cumberland's army in 1747 described the chapel as the finest he had seen in Scotland. "The handsomest young ladies," he adds, "are generally attendants of those meeting-houses (as they call them here), and are generally esteemed as Jacobites by

[1] Wesley's *Journal*, iii. 461. [2] Pennant's *Tour*, i. 121.
[3] *Early Letters of J. W. Carlyle*, p. 45.

the staunch Whigs."[1] Wesley, who had attended the service here a year earlier than Johnson, "could not but admire the exemplary decency of the congregation. This was the more remarkable," he adds, "because so miserable a reader I never heard before. Listening with all attention I understood but one single word, *Balak*, in the First Lesson, and one more, *begat*, was all I could possibly distinguish in the Second."[2] The Aberdeen chapel was no doubt one of those licensed ones "served by clergymen of English or Irish ordination," where alone in Scotland the form of worship of the Church of England could be legally practised. At St. Andrews Boswell recorded that he had seen "in one of its streets a remarkable proof of liberal toleration; a nonjuring clergyman strutting about in his canonicals, with a jolly countenance, and a round belly, like a well-fed monk." By an Act of Parliament passed in 1747, a heavy and cruel blow had been struck at the Scotch nonjurors as a punishment for the support which many of them had given to the young Pretender. Under severe penalties all clergymen were forbidden to officiate who had received their ordination from a nonjuring bishop, even though they took the oaths. They had now to undergo some of the suffering which in their day of triumph they had inflicted on the Covenanters. They in their turn sought the shelter of woods and moors. We read of one of them at Muthill, in Perthshire, "baptising a child under the cover of the trees in one of Lord Rollo's parks to prevent being discovered."[3] Two years later one Mr. John Skinner had been sent to Aberdeen jail for six months for officiating contrary to law. He survived this persecution fifty-five years, and so was contemporary with persons still living.[4] By another act all episcopal clergymen were required, whenever they celebrated worship before five people, to pray for the King and the members of the Royal Family by name, under the penalty of six months' imprisonment for the first offence, and of banishment to America for life for the second. Many under this act were thrown into jail, and so late as 1755 one unhappy man was banished for life.[5] Others complied with the law at the expense of their lungs. An English lady who

[1] *A Journey through Part of England*, &c., p. 134.
[2] Wesley's *Journal*, iii. 461. The lessons were Numbers xxiii. xxiv., and Matthew i. In these chapters *Balak* and *begat* come over and over again.
[3] Chambers's *History of the Rebellion of* 1745 (ed. 1827), ii. 339.
[4] *Scotland and Scotsmen in the Eighteenth Century*, i. 525-8.
[5] Arnot's *History of Edinburgh*, p. 227.

visited Scotland about the year 1778, says: "I have heard a reverend old divine say that he has read the English liturgy so repeatedly over to only four that frequently by evening he has scarce been able to speak to be heard."[1] The persecutions had come to an end by the time of Johnson's visit. The nonjuring ministers were, he says, "by tacit connivance quietly permitted in separate congregations." On the death of the young Pretender on January 31st, 1788, the nonjuring bishops met at Aberdeen and directed that, beginning with Sunday, May 25th, King George should be prayed for by name. His Majesty was graciously pleased to notify his approbation.[2] Even a tutor or "pedagogue" in a gentleman's family was required to take the oaths. This difficulty, however, was easily surmounted. They could be engaged "under the name of factor, or clerk, or comrade," as the Bishop of Moray pointed out in a letter written in 1754.[3]

In Aberdeen there were two Colleges, or rather two Universities, for each had professors of the same parts of learning and each conferred degrees. In 1860 they were incorporated into one body. In old Aberdeen stood King's College. The Chapel and its "Crowned Tower," founded by James IV, who fell at Flodden, has survived time and restorers. They are much as Johnson saw them. Of their architectural beauty and of the ancient richly carved oak screen he makes no mention: "He had not come to Scotland," he said, "to see fine places, of which there were enough in England; but wild objects—peculiar manners; in short, things which he had not seen before." The discipline of the Universities and the method and cost of instruction he examined with attention. In Scotch universities the students generally lived—as they live at present—in lodgings in the town, scarcely under even the pretence of control except in the hours in which they attended lectures. But in King's College a few years earlier the English system had been introduced. Dr. Thomas Reid, the famous Professor of Moral Philosophy, in a letter written in 1755 gives an interesting account of the change which had been made:

"The students have lately been compelled to live within the college. We need but look out at our windows to see when they rise and when they go to bed. They are seen nine or ten times throughout the day statedly by one or other of the masters at public prayers, school hours, meals, and in their rooms, besides occasional visits

---

[1] G. M. Berkeley – *Poems*, p. dxxxviii.   [2] *New Magazine* for 1788, pp. 250, 357.
[3] Dunbar's *Social Life in Former Days*, i. 10.

which we can make with little trouble to ourselves. They are shut up within walls at nine at night. This discipline hath indeed taken some pains and resolution, as well as some expense to establish it. The board at the first table is 50 merks[1] per quarter; at the second, 40 shillings. The rent of a room is from seven to twenty shillings in the session. There is no furniture in their rooms but bedstead, tables, chimney grate and fender—the rest they must buy or hire. They provide fire, and candle, and washing to themselves. The other dues are two guineas to the Master; to the Professors of Greek and Humanity (Latin) for their public teaching, five shillings each. All other perquisites not named, from twelve shillings to seventeen and sixpence."[2]

KING'S COLLEGE, ABERDEEN.

Whether this reformed system lasted in its full extent to the time of Johnson's visit, I do not know; some part of it at all events remained. "In the King's College," he says, "there is kept a public table, but the scholars of the Marischal College are boarded in the town." In Aberdeen, as well as in the other Scotch Universities, students from England were commonly found. Johnson was surprised at finding in King's College a great-grandson of Waller the

---

[1] A Scotch merk was about thirteen pence of English money.
[2] *Dunbar's Social Life in Former Days*, i. 7.

poet. But in the state of degradation into which the English Universities were sunk, what was more natural than that young Englishmen should be sent to places where the Professors still remembered that they had a duty to perform as well as a salary to receive? I have seen in the Royal Society of Edinburgh a manuscript letter written by Dr. Blair from that town to David Hume in 1765, in which he says:—"Our education here is at present in high reputation. The Englishes are crowding down upon us every

MARISCHAL COLLEGE.

season, and I wish may not come to hurt us at last." Excellent though the Aberdeen Professors were as teachers, yet before the great Englishman they seemed afraid to speak. Johnson, writing to Mrs. Thrale, said:—"Boswell was very angry that they would not talk."

In Marischal College scarcely a fragment remains of the old building which our travellers saw, except the stone with the curious inscription:—"Thay haif said; quhat say thay; lat thame say." In the spacious modern library is shown, however, a famous picture which Reynolds was at that time painting. On that very morning when Robertson was showing Johnson Holyrood Palace, Reynolds began the allegorical picture in which he represented Truth and the amiable and harmonious Beattie triumphing together over scepticism and infidelity.[1] It was commonly said that in the group of discomfited figures could be recognized the portraits of Voltaire and Hume. Goldsmith, if we may trust Northcote, reproached Reynolds "for wishing to degrade so high a genius as Voltaire before so mean a writer as Dr. Beattie."[2] If Voltaire's face is to be found in the picture, the likeness is so remote that even he, sensitive though he was, could scarcely have taken offence, while of Hume not even the caricature can be discovered. Feeble though the allegory is, the portrait of Beattie is a very fine piece of workmanship. In Marischal College, by the generosity of his grandnieces it has found its fitting resting-place, for here for many years he was Professor of Moral Philosophy. Here a few years earlier he had been visited by Gray, who, to quote Johnson's words, "found him a poet, a philosopher, and a good man."[3]

SLAINS CASTLE AND THE BULLERS OF BUCHAN.
(AUGUST 24-25.)

At Aberdeen Johnson had found awaiting him a letter from London which must have been six days on the road.[4] He did not receive another till he arrived at Glasgow, nearly ten weeks later. He was now going "to the world's end *extra anni solisque vias*, where the post would be a long time in reaching him," to apply to the Hebrides the words which four years later he used of Brighton. It was only seven and twenty years before he drove out from Aberdeen that the Duke of Cumberland with six battalions of foot and Lord Mark Kerr's dragoons had marched forth along the same road to seek the rebels. With a gentle breeze and a fair wind his transports at the same time moved along shore. Though no

---

[1] Forbes's *Life of Beattie*, p. 160.
[2] Northcote's *Life of Reynolds* (ed. 1819), i. 300.
[3] Johnson's *Works*, viii. 470.
[4] In 1789 the post despatched from Aberdeen on Monday reached London on Saturday. Travellers could reach Edinburgh in a day and a half by the Aberdeen and Edinburgh Fly, which set out from the New Inn at four o'clock in the morning, and arrived at Edinburgh next day to dinner; fare, £2 2s. *Scottish Bibl. and Quern.*, i. 31.

Piozzi Letters, i. 387.
Kay's *History of the Rebellion*, p. 316.

military state waited upon our travellers yet their fame went before them. At Ellon, where they breakfasted, the landlady asked Boswell : " Is not this the great Doctor that is going about through the country ? There's something great in his appearance."   " They say," said the landlord, " that he is the greatest man in England, except Lord Mansfield."   They turned here out of their course to visit Slains Castle, the seat of the Earl of Errol.   The country over which they drove this day was more desolate than any through

ELLON.

which they had as yet passed.   In one place, writes Johnson, " the sand of the shore had been raised by a tempest, and carried to such a distance that an estate was overwhelmed and lost."   Sir Walter Scott, who in the summer of 1814, sailed along the shore in a Lighthouse Yacht, says that northwards of Aberdeen " the coast changes from a bold and rocky to a low and sandy character. Along the Bay of Belhelvie a whole parish was swallowed up by the shifting sands, and is still a desolate waste.   It belonged to the Earls of Errol, and was rented at £500 a year at the time.   When these sands are past the land is all arable. Not a tree to be seen; nor a grazing cow, or sheep, or even a labour-horse at grass, though this be Sunday."[1] The Earl who welcomed Johnson to Slains Castle had done what he could to overcome nature. " He had cultivated his fields so as to bear rich crops of every kind, and he had made an excellent kitchen-garden with a hot-house." His successors have diligently followed in his steps, and taking advantage of a hollow in the ground have even raised an avenue of trees. They can only grow to the height of fifteen or twenty feet, for when the shoots rise high enough to catch the blasts from the North Sea they are cut down the following winter. The situation of the Castle struck Johnson as the noblest he had ever seen.

" From the windows (he said) the eye wanders over the sea that separates Scotland from Norway, and when the winds beat with violence, must enjoy all the terrific grandeur of the tempestuous ocean. I would not for my amusement wish for a storm; but as storms, whether wished or not, will sometimes happen, I may say, without violation of humanity, that I should willingly look out upon them from Slains Castle."

Boswell was also impressed with the position of this old house, set on the very verge of life. "The King of Denmark," he says, "is Lord Errol's nearest neighbour on the north-east." The Castle was built on the edge of the granite cliffs, in one spot not leaving even a foothold for the daring climber. A foolhardy fellow who had tried to get round lost his life in the attempt. I was greatly disappointed at finding that "the excellent old house" which Boswell describes, with its outside galleries on the first and second story, no longer remains. I had looked forward to standing in the very bow-window of the drawing-room fronting the sea where Johnson repeated Horace's Ode, *Jam satis terris*. In the new building, however, the bow-window has not been forgotten, and there I looked out on the wild scene which met his view. I saw "the cut in the rock made by the influx of the sea," into which the rash climber had fallen as he tried to go round the Castle. Below me there were short slopes of grass ending in a precipice. So near was the edge that a child could have tossed a ball over it from the window. Red granite rocks in sharp and precipitous headlands ran out into the sea. A fishing-boat with brown sails was passing close by, while in the distance in a long line lay a fleet of herring-smacks. The sea-birds were hovering about and perching on the

[1] Lockhart's *Life of Scott*, iv. 186.

rocks, mingling their melancholy cries with the dashing of the waves. The dark waters were surging through the narrow chasms formed by rocky islets and the steep sides of the cliffs. For the storm-tost sailor it is a dreadful coast. On a wild night in winter not many years ago one of the maids, as she was letting down the blinds in the drawing-room, heard confused sounds which came, she thought, from the servants' hall beneath. The butler in another part of the house had caught them too. Yet when they reproached their fellow-servants with their noisiness they were told that it was not from them that the sounds had come. They thought no more

SLAINS CASTLE.

about it that night, but next morning when the day broke the masts were seen of a ship-wrecked vessel on the rocks below the Castle. The waves were breaking over it, and not a soul was left alive. Then they understood that it was the despairing cries of the unhappy sailors which had in vain reached their ears. The story, that was told me as I stood looking out on the sea, gave an air of sadness to a room which had already raised sad thoughts in my mind. For on the wall was hanging the portrait of an innocent and pretty boy who, before so many years were to pass over him, on the scaffold on Tower Hill was to pay the penalty of rebellion with his life.

"Pitied by gentle minds Kilmarnock died."

On the table was lying a curious but gloomy collection of the prints of his trial and execution.[1] Boswell's rest was troubled by the thoughts of this unhappy nobleman. He had been kept awake by the blazing of his fire, the roaring of the sea, and the smell of his pillows, which were made of the feathers of some sea-fowl. "I saw in imagination," he writes, "Lord Errol's father, Lord Kilmarnock, who was beheaded on Tower Hill in 1746, and I was somewhat dreary."

In the drawing-room was hanging that fine whole-length picture of Lord Errol, which led Johnson to talk of his friend, the great painter, and "to conclude his panegyric by saying, 'Sir Joshua Reynolds, sir, is the most invulnerable man I know; the man with whom if you should quarrel, you would find the most difficulty how to abuse.'"

In the rebellion of 1745, Lord Errol, following a plan not unknown among the Scotch nobility, had served on the opposite side from his father. At Culloden he had seen him brought in prisoner. "The Earl of Kilmarnock had lost his hat, and his long hair was flying over his face. The son stepped out of the ranks, and taking off his own hat placed it over his father's disordered and wind-beaten locks."[2] The young man in his loyalty to George II., did not follow the example of his forefathers, for he was descended from at least three lines of rebels. "He united in his person the four earldoms of Errol, Kilmarnock, Linlithgow, and Callander." The last two were attainted in 1715, and Kilmarnock in 1746.[3] As we gaze at the haughty-looking man whom Reynolds has so finely painted in the robes of a peer, we call to mind the coronation of George III., where he played his part as High Constable of Scotland—"the noblest figure I ever saw," wrote Horace Walpole.[4] To Johnson he recalled Homer's character of Sarpedon.[5] At the coronation banquet in Westminster Hall, Walpole thought, as well he might, on that "most melancholy scene" which he had witnessed less than fifteen years before in that same hall, when the earl's father, "tall and slender, his behaviour a most just mix-

---

[1] Bound up with them were some interesting and unpublished autograph letters and documents connected with many generations of the earls of Errol. It is greatly to be desired that the present earl, to whose courtesy I am much indebted, would have them edited.

[2] Forbes's *Life of Beattie*, Appendix D.

[3] Chambers's *History of the Rebellion*, ed. 1869, p. 388.

[4] Forbes's *Life of Beattie*, Appendix D. At the time of the rebellion of 1745 the Errol title was held by a woman.

[5] Walpole's *Letters*, iii. 438.

ture between dignity and submission," had in vain pleaded for mercy.[1]

From Slains Castle our travellers drove a short distance along the coast to the famous Bullers of Buchan. "A sight," writes Johnson, "which no man can see with indifference, who has either sense of danger or delight in rarity." Boswell describes the spot as:—

"A circular basin of large extent, surrounded with tremendous rocks. On the quarter next the sea, there is a high arch in the rock, which the force of the tempest has driven out. This place is called Buchan's Buller, or the Buller of Buchan, and the country people call it the Pot. Mr. Boyd said it was so called from the French boudoir. It may be more simply traced from boiler in our own language. We walked round this monstrous cauldron. In some places the rock is very narrow; and on each side there is a sea deep enough for a

THE BULLERS OF BUCHAN.

man-of-war to ride in; so that it is somewhat horrid to move along. However, there is earth and grass upon the rock, and a kind of road marked out by the print of feet: so that one makes it out pretty safely: yet it alarmed me to see Dr. Johnson striding irregularly along."

As the weather was calm they took a boat and rowed through the archway into the cauldron. "It was a place," writes Johnson,

---

[1] Walpole's *Letters*, ii. 38.
[2] *Bouilloire*. According to Dr. Murray the word is connected with " the Swedish *buller*, a noise, roar. But, he adds, "the influence of *boil* is manifest." I remember when I visited the place in my youth I heard it also called Lord Errol's Punch-bowl. The tale was told that a former earl had made a seizure in it of a smuggling ship laden with spirits, and had had the kegs emptied into the water.

"which, though we could not think ourselves in danger, we could scarcely survey without some recoil of mind." He thought that "it might have served as a shelter from storms to the little vessels used by the northern rovers." Sir Walter Scott, however, was told that this was impossible, for "in a high gale the waves rush in with incredible violence. An old fisher said he had seen them flying over the natural wall of the Bullers, which cannot be less than two hundred feet high."[1] In the *Gentleman's Magazine* for 1755 (p. 200), two strange pictures are given of this curious place, which must surely have been drawn in St. John's Gate, Clerkenwell, by an artist who had never seen it.

Not far off is Dun Buy,[2] a lofty island rock placed in an angle of the shore that is formed by no less lofty cliffs. The sea, with its dark waters in endless rise and fall, washes through the narrow channel, its ceaseless murmur answering to the cries of the countless water-fowl who high up on the ledges breed in safety. On one side, where there is a steep, grassy slope, Dun Buy can be scaled. I climbed up it many years ago one hot summer's day, and thought that I had never seen so strange and wild a spot. Johnson had also visited it, but his mind was not affected as was my young imagination, for he said that "upon these rocks there was nothing that could long detain attention."

BANFF AND ELGIN (AUGUST 25-26).

Starting from Slains Castle on the morning of August 25, Boswell and Johnson drove on to Banff, where they spent the night in an indifferent inn. In this little town a dreadful sight had been witnessed when the Duke of Cumberland's army arrived on an early day in April, 1746. The savage way in which the narrative is written, testifies to the ferocity of many of the followers of " the butcher duke."

"At Banff" (writes Ray) "two rebel spies were taken; the one was knotching on a stick the number of our forces, for which he was hanged on a tree in the town; and the other a little out of town, and for want of a tree was hanged on what they call the ridging tree of a house, that projected out from the end, and on his breast

---

[1] Lockhart's *Life of Scott*, iv. 188. it means, it is said, from the colour given to it
[2] Dun Buy means the Yellow Rock. It is so by the dung of the sea birds.

was fixed in writing, *A Rebel Spy*, which, with the addition of *good entertainment*, might have been a very famous sign." [1]

From Banff our travellers drove on to Elgin, passing through Lord Findlater's domain. It is strange that neither of them mentions the passage of the Spey, which ofttimes was a matter of great difficulty and even danger. Wesley describes it as "the most rapid river, next the Rhine, he had ever seen." [2] It was no doubt very low, owing to "that long continuance of dry weather which," as Johnson complained a few days later, "divested the Fall of Foyers of its dignity and terror." At Elgin they dined, and dined badly. "It was," he said, "the first time he had seen a dinner in Scotland that he could not eat." He might have reasonably expected something better, for in the account of Scotch inns given in the *Gentleman's Magazine* for 1771 (p. 544), the Red Lion at Elgin, kept by Leslie, is described as good. It is added that "he is the only landlord in Scotland who wears ruffles." As this was the inn in which the civic feasts were always held, the honour not only of the landlord, but also of the town was wounded by the publication of Johnson's narrative. I am glad to be able to inform the world that a satisfactory explanation has been given, and that Elgin and the Red Lion were not guilty of the inhospitality with which they have so long been reproached, and so unjustly. It seems that for some years before Johnson's visit a commercial traveller, Thomas Paufer by name, used in his rounds to come to this inn.

"He cared little about eating, but liked the more exhilarating system of drinking. His means were limited, and he was in the habit of ordering only a very slender dinner, that he might spend the more in the pleasures of the bottle. This traveller bore a very striking resemblance to Dr. Johnson. When the doctor arrived at the inn, the waiter, by a hasty glance, mistook him for Paufer, and such a dinner was prepared as Paufer was wont to receive. The doctor suffered by the mistake, for he did not ask for that which was to follow. Thus the good name of Elgin suffered, through the mistaking of the person of the ponderous lexicographer. This fact is well known, and is authenticated by some of the oldest and most respectable citizens of the town." [3]

Mr. Paufer's means must have been indeed limited, for unless prices had greatly risen in the previous thirty years, a good dinner and wine could have been provided at a most moderate charge, to

---

[1] James Ray's *History of the Rebellion of 1745*, p. 311.
[2] Wesley's *Journal*, iii. 182.
[3] This account I owe to the kindness of Mr. Lachlan Mackintosh, of Old Lodge, Elgin, who has copied it from a manuscript in his possession which was written at least as early as the year 1837. To him also I am indebted for the sketch of the old piazzas.

judge by the following entries in an Elgin "funeral bill," dated Sept 20, 1742:—

"One dozen strong old claret (bottles being returned) . 14s. 0d.
4 lb. 12 oz. of sugar . . . . 3s. 4d.
five dozen eggs . . . . 5d.
six hens . . . . 2s. 0d."[1]

One pound of sugar, it will be noticed, cost as much as two hens, and a little more than eight dozen eggs. With sugar at such a price it must have given a shock to a careful Scotch housewife to

ELGIN.

see well-sweetened lemonade flung out of the window merely because a waiter had used his dirty fingers to drop in the lumps.

To Johnson Elgin seemed "a place of little trade and thinly inhabited." Yet Defoe, writing only fifty years earlier, had said: "As the country is rich and pleasant, so here are a great many rich inhabitants, and in the town of Elgin in particular, for the gentlemen, as if this was the Edinburgh or the Court for this part of the island, leave their Highland habitations in the winter, and come and live here for the diversion of the place and plenty of provisions."[2]

[1] Dunbar's *Social Life in Former Days*, i. 276.
[2] Defoe's *Tour through Great Britain: Account of Scotland*, iii. 195.

Much of its ancient prosperity has returned to it. If it cannot boast of being a court for the north, it is at all events a pleasant little market-town that shows no sign of decay. The covered ways which in many places ran on each side of the street have disappeared. "Probably," writes Boswell, "it had piazzas all along the town, as I have seen at Bologna. I approved much of such structures in a town, on account of their conveniency in wet weather. Dr. Johnson disapproved of them, 'because,' said he, 'it makes the under story of a house very dark, which greatly overbalances the conveniency, when it is considered how small a part of the year it rains; how few are usually in the street at such times; that many who are might as well be at home; and the little that people suffer, supposing them to be as much wet as they commonly are in walking a street." "They were a grand place for the boys to play at marbles," said an old man to me, who well remembered the past glories of Elgin and the delights of his youth. Even at the time of our travellers' visit, they were frequently broken by houses built in the modern fashion. In many cases they have not been destroyed, but converted into small shops. "There are," writes a local antiquary, "some fine old piazzas in the High Street which have been whitewashed over and hidden." He suggests that some of these might be restored to the light of day.' It would be a worthy deed for the citizens, even in one spot, to bring back the former appearance of their ancient town.

The noble ruins of the great cathedral Johnson examined with a most patient attention, though the rain was falling fast. "They afforded him another proof of the waste of reformation." His indignation was excited even more than by the ruins at St. Andrew's; for "the cathedral was not destroyed by the tumultuous violence of Knox, but suffered to dilapidate by deliberate robbery and frigid indifference." By an order of Council the lead had been stripped off the roof and shipped to be sold in Holland. "I hope," adds Johnson, "every reader will rejoice that this cargo of sacrilege was lost at sea." On this passage Horace Walpole remarks in a letter to Lord Hailes:—" I confess I have not quite so heinous an idea of sacrilege as Dr. Johnson. Of all kinds of robbery that appears to me the lightest species which injures nobody. Dr. Johnson is so pious, that in his journey to your country he flatters himself that all his readers will join him in enjoying the destruction of two Dutch crews, who were swallowed up by the ocean after they had robbed a church. I doubt that uncharitable anathema is more in the spirit of the Old Testament than of the New."[1] While Johnson censured the frigid indifference of the Scotch, he did not forget the ruin that was being slowly worked in England by the avarice and neglect of deans and canons. "Let us not," he wrote, "make

ELGIN CATHEDRAL.

too much haste to despise our neighbours. Our own cathedrals are mouldering by unregarded dilapidation. It seems to be part of the despicable philosophy of the time to despise monuments of sacred magnificence, and we are in danger of doing that deliberately which the Scots did not do but in the unsettled state of an imperfect constitution." He had learnt, there seems good reason to believe, that the chapter of the cathedral of his own town of Lichfield intended to strip the lead off its roof and cover it instead with

[1] Walpole's *Letters*, vii. 484. It was only one ship that was lost, though in it the lead of two cathedrals was conveyed.

slate. As he had first printed his narrative he had much more closely pointed the attack. It had run as follows: "There is now, as I have heard, a body of men not less decent or virtuous than the Scottish council, longing to melt the lead of an English cathedral. What they shall melt, it were just that they should swallow." Before publication he had the leaf cancelled, from the tender recollection that the dean had done him a kindness about forty years before. "He is now very old, and I am not young. Reproach can do him no good, and in myself I know not whether it is zeal or wantonness."[1]

FORRES.

As I turned away from the ruins with my thoughts full of the past—of the ancient glory of the cathedral, of the strange sights which had been seen from its tower when the Young Pretender's Highlanders hurried by, closely followed by the English army, of old Johnson wandering about in the heavy rain—I was suddenly reminded of the vastness of "the abyss of time" by which they are separated from us, by reading in an advertisement placarded on the walls, that for £3 16s. 5d. could be had a ticket from Elgin to Paris and back.

NAIRN AND CAWDOR (AUGUST 27-28).

Leaving Elgin that same afternoon, our travellers drove on to Forres, where they passed the night. Next morning, continuing their journey early, they breakfasted at Nairn. "Though a county town and a royal burgh, it is," writes Boswell, "a miserable place." Johnson also describes it as being "in a state of miserable decay." Nevertheless, "the chief annual magistrate," he says, "is styled Lord Provost." If it sank as a royal burgh, it has raised its head

[1] Boswell-Johnson, vi. xxxiii.

again as a popular bathing place. In this respect it has not its rival, I was told, in the north of Scotland. Here Johnson "fixed the verge of the Highlands; for here he first saw peat fires, and first heard the Erse language."[1] Over the room in the inn where he and Boswell sat "a girl was spinning wool with a great wheel, and singing an Erse song." It was thirty years later that Wordsworth in like manner heard "The Solitary Reaper":

> "Yon solitary Highland lass
> Reaping and singing by herself."

Even so far back as the reign of James VI. both languages were spoken in Nairn. "It was one of that king's witticisms to boast that in Scotland he had a town 'sae lang that the folk at the tae end couldna understand the tongue spoken at the tother.'"[2] Gaelic is no longer heard in its streets. The verge of the Highlands must now be fixed farther to the west. Nine years before Johnson's visit the little town had been stirred up by Wesley. On Monday, June 11, 1762, he recorded in his journal: "While we were dining at Nairn, the innkeeper said, 'Sir, the gentlemen of the town have read the little book you gave me on Saturday, and would be glad if you would please give them a sermon.' Upon my consenting, the bell was immediately rung, and the congregation was quickly in the kirk."[3]

From Nairn our travellers turned a few miles out of their course to visit the Rev. Kenneth Macaulay in his manse at Cawdor. To Johnson he was known by his *History of St. Kilda* —"a very pretty piece of topography" as he called it to the author, "who did not seem much to mind the compliment." To us he is interesting as the great-uncle of Lord Macaulay. "From his conversation," says Boswell, "Dr. Johnson was convinced that he had not written the book which goes under his name. 'There is a combination in it' (he said) 'of which Macaulay is not capable.'" "To those who happen to have read the work," writes Sir George Trevelyan, "Johnson's decision will give a very poor notion of my ancestor's abilities."[4] Let him take comfort. The present minister of Cawdor, to whose civility I am indebted, told

---

[1] The language of the Highlanders is generally called Erse by the English writers of this period; sometimes Irish and Celtic. M'Nicol objected to the term *Erse*. "The Caledonians," he says, "always called their native language Gaelic." *Remarks on Johnson's Journey*, p. 432. Mac-

pherson, in the title-page of *Ossian*, calls it Galic.

[2] Murray's *Handbook for Scotland*, ed. 1867, p. 308.

[3] Wesley's *Journal*, iii. 182.

[4] *Life of Lord Macaulay*, ed. 1877, i. 6.

me that in the Kirk Session Records is a minute by Macaulay "most beautifully expressed." I had hoped to sit in the very parlour where Johnson had reproached him with being "a bigot to laxness," and where he had given his little son a Sallust, promising at the same time to get him a servitorship at Oxford when he was ready for the University. But hopes that are based on the permanence of buildings are often disappointed. Of the old manse nothing remains. The minister, who rejoiced in having a more comfortable home than his predecessors, refused to share in my sentimental regrets. The situation seemed a pleasant one, as I saw it on a fine evening in July, with the sun setting behind the hills on the other side of the Moray Firth. The haymakers were busy at their work close to the house, in a field which is bounded on one side by a deep hollow, with a little brook flowing at the bottom, and in front by a row of old ash trees.

CAWDOR.

In the company of Macaulay Boswell "had dreaded that a whole evening would be heavy. However," he adds, "Mr. Grant, an intelligent and well-bred minister in the neighbourhood, was there, and assisted us by his conversation." His grandson is Colonel Grant, who shares with Captain Speke the glory of having discovered the sources of the Nile. It was indeed an unusual gathering that August evening in the parlour of the quiet manse — Johnson, the first of talkers, Boswell, the first of biographers, the great-uncle of our famous historian, and the grandfather of our famous discoverer. My hopes rose high when I was told that a diary which Mr. Grant kept was still in existence. Of this evening's talk some record surely would have been made. With sorrow I learnt from his grandson that "accounts of expenses, sermons preached, peat-cutting, stipends, washing *twice a year*, births, &c., are the principal things which are mentioned." This washing twice a year must not be taken as a proof that this divine "had no passion for clean linen." A Scotch friend of mine remembers a man who owned three farms in the neighbourhood of Campbeltown. In his house they only washed twice a year, though both he and his three sons who lived with him changed their shirts every second day. A time was chosen when there was a slackness in the ordinary work, and then the female servants were gathered from the three farms for a week's hard washing.

PENANCE-RING, CAWDOR CHURCH.

This same custom exists, I believe, to the present day in Norway. In the churchyard I found Mr. Grant's tombstone. He lived till 1828—fifty five years after he had met Johnson. He used to tell a story about the doctor which happily has been preserved. He had supped with him, as we learn from Boswell, at the inn at Inverness. Johnson, who was in high spirits, gave an account of the kangaroo, which had lately been discovered in New South Wales, "and volunteered an imitation of the animal. The company stared; Mr. Grant said nothing could be more ludicrous than the appearance of a tall, heavy, grave-looking man like Dr. Johnson standing up to mimic the shape and motions of a kangaroo. He stood erect, put out his hands like feelers, and gathering up the tails of his huge brown coat so as to resemble the pouch of the animal, made two or three vigorous bounds across the room."[1]

Near Mr. Grant lies his friend and predecessor Kenneth Macaulay, with an inscription which tells that he was "notus in fratres animi paterni." This *animus paternus* descended in full measure to Lord Macaulay. On the porch of the church is still fastened by an iron chain the old penance-ring which Pennant saw

[1] Boswell's *Journal*, ed. by Carruthers, p. 92.

one hundred and twenty years ago. "Observed," he writes, "on a pillar of the door of Calder church a *joug*, *i.e.*, an iron yoke or ring, fastened to a chain; which was in former times put round the necks of delinquents against the rules of the Church, who were left there exposed to shame during the time of divine service, and was also

DRAWBRIDGE: CAWDOR CASTLE.

used as a punishment for defamation, small thefts, &c., but these penalties are now happily abolished."[1] From such penance as this there was perhaps an escape for those who were well-to-do. From *Hudibras* we learn that the Presbyterian saints could "sentence to stools or poundage of repentance," which passage is explained by the commentator as "doing penance in the Scotch way, upon the stool of repentance, or commuting the penance for a sum of money."[2]

[1] Pennant's *Tour in Scotland*, i. 155.   [2] *Hudibras*, iii. 1, 1477.

CAWDOR CASTLE.

"By the direction of Mr. Macaulay," writes Johnson, "we visited Cawdor Castle, from which Macbeth drew his second title." That they should have needed a direction to visit so beautiful a spot seems strange, for they must have passed close by it on their way to the manse. As I first caught sight of it by the light of a summer evening, I thought that I had rarely seen a fairer spot. This castle hath indeed a pleasant seat, I said. All the barrenness of the eastern coast I had left behind me, and had found in its stead a luxuriance of growth that would have graced the oldest mansion in England. Everything seemed beautiful, and everything harmonious —the ancient castle, with its high-pitched roof and its lofty tower; the swift-flowing river, with its bridge of a single arch; the curve in the road where it crosses it; the avenue of lofty trees, the lawns enclosed by limes, the shrubberies, and the range of mountains in the distance still showing the light of the sun which had set for us.

CAWDOR CASTLE.

The water murmured pleasantly, and a gentle breeze rustled the leaves. I found a little inn close by the park gate, where homely fare and decent lodging are provided. A man of a quiet meditative mind might pass a few days there pleasantly enough if he sought shelter in the woods on the afternoons when the castle is thrown open to visitors. Next morning I watched the school-children, bare-footed, but clean and tidy, carrying on their arms their slates covered with sums in neat figures, trooping merrily by, and winding over the bridge on their way to school. By the kindness of the Earl of Cawdor I was allowed to go over the castle from turret almost to foundation-stone at a time when it was not generally open.

"The old tower," says Boswell, "must be of great antiquity. There is a drawbridge—what has been a moat—and an ancient court. There is a hawthorn-tree, which rises like a wooden pillar through the rooms of the castle; for, by a strange conceit, the walls have been built round it. The thickness of the walls, the small slanting windows, and a great iron door at the entrance on the second story as you ascend the stairs, all indicate the rude times in which this castle was erected. There were here some large venerable trees."

It is surprising that he should have thought that there could ever have been a moat on a rock high above the river. Johnson nevertheless also mentions it. What they mistook for a moat is the

VAULT.

excavation made in quarrying the stone for the castle. In clearing it out some while ago, the workmen came to a place where the masons had left some stones half dressed. Mr. Irving, who visited Cawdor, has had the fine entrance copied, I am told, in his scenery for Macbeth, adding, however, a portcullis, of which no traces remain. I was shown in a kind of vault the trunk of the old hawthorn which Boswell mentions. There is a tradition that "a wise man counselled a certain thane to load an ass with a chest full of gold, and to build his castle with the money at the third hawthorn-tree at which the animal should stop." The ass stopped where Cawdor Castle is built, and the tree was enclosed. The thane's only child, a little girl, was carried off by Campbell of Inverliver, on Loch Awe. In his flight he was overtaken by the Cawdors. Being hard pressed, ' he cried out in Gaelic, 'It is a far cry to Loch Awe, and a distant help to the Campbells,' a saying which

TAPESTRY CHAMBER.

became proverbial in the north to express imminent danger and distant relief."[1] He won the day, however, and the child when she grew up married a son of the Earl of Argyle. From them is descended that "prosperous gentleman," the present Thane or Earl of Cawdor.

I passed through the great iron door which Boswell mentions, and other strong doors too, and climbed up the staircase which is built in the thickness of the wall. I was shown the place in the roof where Lord Lovat, when fleeing from justice early in his bad career, had lain in hiding for some weeks. I saw, moreover, more

[1] Boswell's *Hebrides*, ed. by R. Carruthers, p. 85.

than one chamber hung with old tapestry. In one of them stands the state bed of Sir Hugh Campbell, who in 1672 married Lady Henrietta Stewart. Their initials, with the date, are carved on the outside wall of the court. At one end of the hall runs a gallery which bears the name of the Fiddler's Walk. There the musicians used to play, keeping time with their steps to their tune.

INVERNESS (AUGUST 28-30).

From Cawdor Johnson and Boswell drove to Fort George, "the most regular fortification in the island," according to Johnson; "where," he continues, "they were entertained by Sir Eyre Coote, the Governor, with such elegance of conversation, as left us no attention to the delicacies of his table." Wolfe, who saw it in 1751, when it was partly made, writes : " I believe there is still work for six or seven years to do. When it is finished one may venture to say (without saying much) that it will be the most considerable fortress, and the best situated in Great Britain."[1] In the evening our travellers continued their journey to Inverness a distance of twelve miles. The reviewer of Johnson's narrative in the *Scots Magazine* expresses his wonder that as "he must have passed near the Field of Culloden he studiously avoided to mention that battle."[2] Boswell is equally reticent. The explanation is perhaps merely due to the dusk of evening, in which they passed by the spot. It is not unlikely, on the other hand, that the silence was intentional. Johnson shows a curious reticence in a passage in which he refers to the Rebellion of 1745. In his description of Rasay he writes: " Not many years ago the late laird led out one hundred men upon a military expedition." Had he visited Culloden or described the campaign, his indignation must have flamed forth at the cruelties of the butcher duke. Boswell, Lowlander though he was, said " that they would never be forgotten." With Smollett, in his *Tears of Scotland*, they might well have exclaimed :—

> " Yet when the rage of battle ceased,
> The victor's soul was not appeased :
> The naked and forlorn must feel
> Devouring flames and murd'ring steel."

[1] Wright's *Life of Wolfe*, p. 178. [2] *Scots Magazine*, 1775, p. 26.

THE FIDDLERS' WALK IN THE DRAWING ROOM, CAWDOR CASTLE.

Johnson does indeed speak of "the heavy hand of a vindictive conqueror."[1] It was about this time, or only a little later, that Scott was learning "to detest the name of Cumberland with more than infant hatred."[2] That an Englishman could travel in safety, unarmed and unguarded, through a country which only seven and twenty years before had been so mercilessly treated seems not a little surprising. For the next day or two he was to follow a course where fire and sword had swept along. Wolfe, whose "great name," we boast, was "compatriot with our own," who had so little of the savage spirit of war that he would rather have written Gray's *Elegy* than take Quebec, even he exulted that "as few prisoners were taken of the Highlanders as possible. We had an opportunity of avenging ourselves. The rebels left near 1,500 dead." Yet he did not think that enough had been done. The carnage-pile was not lofty enough. Surveying the battle-field five years later, he writes in a letter to his father, a general in the army, "I find room for a military criticism. You would not have left those ruffians the only possible means of conquest, nor suffered multitudes to go off unhurt with the power to destroy."[3] Ruffians indeed they had shown themselves in their raid into England, but enough surely had been done in the way of slaughter to satisfy the most exacting military critic. How merciless our soldiers had been is proved by the letters that were written from the camp. A despatch sent off from Inverness on April 25, nine days after the battle, says that "the misery and distress of the fugitive rebels was inexpressible, hundreds being found dead of their wounds and through hunger at the distance of twelve, fourteen, and even twenty miles from the field."[4] On June 5 an officer wrote from Fort Augustus: "His Royal Highness has carried fire and sword through their country, and driven off their cattle, which we bring to our camp in great quantities, sometimes 2,000 in a drove. The people are deservedly in a most deplorable way, and must perish either by sword or famine, a just reward for traitors."[5]

On July 26 another officer wrote from the same fort to a friend at Newcastle: "We hang or shoot everyone that is known to conceal the Pretender, burn their houses and take their cattle, of which we have got some 8,000 head within these few days past, so

[1] Johnson's *Works*, ix. 86.
[2] Lockhart's *Life of Scott*, i. 24.
[3] Wright's *Life of Wolfe*, 1864, pp. 84-5, 179.
[4] *Gentleman's Magazine*, 1746, p. 263.
[5] *Ib.*, p. 324.

that if some of your Northumberland graziers were here they might make their fortunes."[1] The author of a *Plain Narrative of the Rebellion*, tells with exultation how "they marched to Loch Yell, the stately seat of old Esquire Cameron," the Lochiel of Campbell's spirited lines. "His fine chairs, tables, and all his cabinet goods were set on fire and burnt with his house. His fine fruit garden, above a mile long, was pulled to pieces and laid waste. A beautiful summer-house that stood in the pleasure garden was also set on fire. From hence the party marched along the sea-coast through Moidart, burning of houses, driving away the cattle, and shooting those vagrants who were found about the mountains. For fifty miles round there was no man or beast to be seen."[2] Andrew Henderson, in his *History of the Rebellion*, after admitting that in the rout several of the wounded were stabbed, and some who were lurking in houses were taken out and shot, urges by way of excuse that "the rebels had enraged the troops; their habit was strange, their language still stranger, and their way of fighting was shocking to the utmost degree."[3] Besides the massacre after the battle and the executions by courts-martial, there were the hangings, drawings and quarterings, and beheadings by judge and jury. Seventy-six had been sent to the scaffold by September, 1747,[4] and above one thousand were transported.[5] Even George II. "said that he believed William had been rough with them."[6] When it was proposed to confer on the duke the freedom of the City of London, an alderman was heard to say that it ought to be the freedom of the Butchers' Company. So late as the summer of 1753 seven rebels were seized in a hut on the side of Loch Hourn, at no great distance from the way along which Johnson was to pass only twenty years later.[7] Nevertheless he everywhere travelled in safety. Among the chieftains, no doubt, "his tenderness for the unfortunate House of Stuart" was known, but to the common people he would only be an Englishman—a man of the race that had slaughtered their fathers and wasted their country. That both he and Boswell were not free from uneasiness they avowed when at Auchnasheal they were surrounded by the wild McCraas. In the memory of men not much past the middle

---

[1] *Gentleman's Magazine*, 1746, p. 420.
[2] Michael Hughes, *Plain Narrative of the Rebellion*, p. 56.
[3] Henderson, *History of the Rebellion*, p. 117.
[4] *Scots Magazine*, 1747, p. 649. According to Smollett the number executed was eighty-one. *History of England*, ed. 1800, iii. 188.
[5] *Gentleman's Magazine*, 1747, p. 246.
[6] *Marchmont Papers*, i. 196.
[7] *Gentleman's Magazine*, 1753, p. 391.

age, tales of the cruel duke used to be told in the winter evenings in the glens of these Western Highlands. They have at last died away, and "infant hatred" is no longer nourished.[1]

Our travellers, whatever may have been their motive, leaving the Field of Culloden unvisited and unnoticed, arrived at Inverness, the capital of the Highlands. They put up at Mackenzie's Inn. Of their accommodation they say nothing; but it can scarcely have been good, if we may trust an English traveller who two years earlier had found, he said, the Horns Inn, kept by Mrs. Mackenzie, dirty and ill-managed.[2] Perhaps they felt as Wolfe did when he was stationed in the town with his regiment. "It would be unmanly," he wrote, "and very unbecoming a soldier to complain of little evils, such as bad food, bad lodging, bad fire. . . . With these reflections I reconcile myself to Inverness, and to other melancholy spots that we are thrown upon." He adds that the post goes but once a week, and that as there are rapid rivers on the road that have neither bridge nor boat, it is often delayed by the floods.[3] Wesley describes Inverness as the largest town he had seen in Scotland after Edinburgh, Glasgow, and Aberdeen. "It stands in a pleasant and fruitful country, and has all things needful for life and godliness. The people in general speak remarkably good English, and are of a friendly, courteous behaviour."[4] Their good English they were said to derive from the garrison which Cromwell had settled among them. It had been noticed by Defoe. "They speak," he said, "perfect English, even much better than in the most southerly provinces of Scotland; nay, some will say that they speak it as well as at London, though I do not grant that neither."[5] Their behaviour had greatly improved in the thirteen years which had elapsed between Wolfe's second and Wesley's first visit, unless the soldier had viewed them with the stern eye of the conqueror, or they had displayed the sullenness of the conquered. "A little while," he wrote, "serves to discover the villainous nature of the inhabitants and brutality of the people in the neighbourhood."[6] Yet the brutality was quite as much on the side of the army, for a year later, five full years after the battle, we find the people still treated with harshness and insolence. The magistrates had invited Lord Bury, the general in

---

[1] My informant is the late Rev. Alexander Matheson, minister of Glenshiel.
[2] *Gentleman's Magazine*, 1771, p. 544.
[3] Wright's *Life of Wolfe*, pp. 182, 195.
[4] Wesley's *Journal*, iv. 181.
[5] Defoe's *Tour*, iii. *Scotland*, p. 197.
[6] Wright's *Life of Wolfe*, p. 177.

command, to an entertainment on the Duke of Cumberland's birthday. "He said he did not doubt but it would be more agreeable to the duke if they postponed it to the day following, the anniversary of Culloden. They stared, said they could not promise on their own authority, but would go and consult their body. They returned, told him it was unprecedented and could not be complied with. Lord Bury replied he was sorry they had not given a negative at once, for he had mentioned it to his soldiers, who would not bear a disappointment, and was afraid it would provoke them to some outrage upon the town. This did; they celebrated Culloden."[1]

The old town had witnessed a strange sight in the first days after the battle. The soldiers had held a fair for the sale of the plunder which they had made. "The traffic on the Rialto Bridge was nothing in comparison to the business done by our military merchants; here being great sortments of all manner of plaids, broad-swords, dirks and pistols, and plaid-waistcoats, officers' laced waistcoats, hats, bonnets, blankets, and oatmeal bags."[2] The severity that was so long exercised by government at length sank into neglect. Only five years before the arrival of our travellers all the prisoners, just before the opening of the Assize, made their escape from the town jail; "so the Lord Pitfour," a writer to the Signet wrote, "will have the trouble only of fugitation and reprimanding the magistrates."[3] How miserable the jail was is shown in a memorial from the Town Council, dated March 17, 1786, stating that "it consists only of two small cells for criminals, and one miserable room for civil debtors. Their situation is truly deplorable, as there are at present and generally about thirty persons confined in these holes, none of which is above thirteen feet square."[4] While the poor prisoners were so cruelly treated, the lawyers had a merry time of it every time that so hospitable a judge as Boswell's father came the circuit:—

"Lord Auchinleck made a most respectable figure at the head of his circuit table. It was his rule to spend every shilling of his allowance for the circuit—a thing less to be expected that in everything else he was supposed to be abundantly economical. He had a plentiful table. He laughed much at the rule laid down by some of his brethren of asking gentlemen but once to dinner. 'It is,' said he, 'treating them like beggars at a burial, who get their alms in rotation.'"

[1] Letters of Horace Walpole, ii. 288.
[2] Ib., p. 89.
[3] M. Hughes's Plain Narrative, p. 51.
[4] Scotland and Scotsmen in the Eighteenth
[5] E. Dunbar's Social Life in Former Days, i. Century, i. 164.
133.

We are not surprised that Boswell found that "everybody at Inverness spoke of Lord Auchinleck with uncommon regard."

The English chapel, which Johnson describes as "meanly built, but with a very decent congregation," was pulled down many years ago. On its site, in the midst of the same old graveyard, another building has been raised in what may be perhaps called the church-warden style. Of Macbeth's castle—"what is called the castle of Macbeth," writes Johnson with his usual caution—nothing remains. If we may trust Boswell, "it perfectly corresponded with Shakespeare's description." It has been replaced by "a modern building of chaste castellated design," to borrow the language of the guide-book. I was told, however, that our travellers had been misinformed, and that "the old original Macbeth's castle" stood on a height a little distance from the town. This "pleasant seat" has been treated, I found, even worse than its rival; for a builder, thinking that the air "might nimbly and sweetly recommend itself" to the public as well as to a king, began the erection of a crescent. Owing to a difficulty about a right of way, the speculation hitherto has not been so successful as might have been feared.

At Inverness the Lowland life came to an end. To the west of that town no road had ever been made till some years after the rising of 1715. All beyond was the work of General Wade and the other military engineers. "Here," writes Johnson, "the appearance of life began to alter. I had seen a few women with plaids at Aberdeen, but at Inverness the Highland manners are common. There is, I think, a kirk in which only the Erse language is used." The plaid, which was not peculiar to the Highlands, had been rapidly going out of fashion. Ramsay of Ochtertyre says that in 1747, when he first knew Edinburgh, nine-tenths of the ladies still wore them. Five years later "one could hardly see a lady in that piece of dress. In the course of seven or eight years the very servant girls were ashamed of being seen in that ugly antiquated garb."[1] The Gaelic language does not seem to have lost much ground in Inverness, for I was told that there are five churches in which it is used every Sunday at one of the services.

[1] Scotland and Scotsmen in the Eighteenth Century, ii. 88.

Inverness to Anoch (August 30-31).

At Inverness Johnson bade farewell to post-chaises, which had brought him in comfort all the way from London. "This day," writes Boswell, "we were to begin our *equitation*, as I said; for I would needs make a word too. We might have taken a chaise to Fort Augustus, but had we not hired horses at Inverness we should not have found them afterwards. We had three horses for Dr.

IN SCAPDIL, A CELEBRATED PASS NEAR FOYERS.

Johnson, myself, and Joseph, and one which carried our portmanteaus, and two Highlanders who walked along with us." They took but little baggage, and soon found the advantage of their moderation "in climbing crags and treading bogs. How often," continues Johnson, "a man that has pleased himself at home with his own resolution, will in the hour of darkness and fatigue be content to leave behind him everything but himself." After leaving the Fort they were "to enter upon a country upon which perhaps no wheel had ever rolled." In the Commercial Map of Scotland, published by J. Knox in 1784, there is not a single road marked in any one of the Hebrides. After long wanderings, and the lapse of almost seven weeks, " Johnson's heart was cheered by the sight of a road marked with cart-wheels as on the mainland, a thing which we had not seen for a long time. It gave us a pleasure similar to that which a traveller feels when, whilst wandering on what he fears is a desert island, he perceives the print of human feet." It was in pleasant weather that they began their ride. "The day though bright was not hot. On the left were high and steep rocks

shaded with birch and covered with fern or heath. On the right
the limpid waters of Loch Ness were beating their bank and waving
their surface by a gentle agitation." In one part of the way, adds
Johnson, " we had trees on both sides for perhaps half a mile. Such
a length of shade, perhaps, Scotland cannot show in any other
place." Boswell, though he thought Fleet Street more delightful
than Tempe, nevertheless felt the cheering powers of this delightful
day. "The scene," he found "as sequestered and agreeably wild

LOCH NESS.

as could be desired." Pennant, who had been there four years
earlier, describes the scenery as "most romantic and beautiful."[1]
Wesley thought the neighbourhood of Inverness one of the
pleasantest countries he had ever seen.[2] In striking contrast with
the enjoyment of these four travellers are the feelings of those who
a few years before had seen the spot when the alarms of war were
still fresh. "On each side of Loch Ness," writes Ray, "is a ridge
of most terrible barren woody mountains. You travel along the
banks through a road made by blowing up monstrous rocks, which

[1] Pennant's *Tour in Scotland*, i. 190.   [2] Wesley's *Journal*, iv. 275.

in many places hang declining over passengers and higher than houses, so that 'tis frightful to pass by them."[1] *A Volunteer* describes the mountains "as high and frightful as the Alps in Spain; so we had nothing pleasant to behold but the sky."[2]

Our travellers halted for dinner at the General's Hut, a small public-house nearly eighteen miles from Inverness.[3] Here, says Johnson, Wade had lodged "while he superintended the works upon the road." I have seen it stated in a guide-book that on its site is built the Foyer's Hotel, but this is a mistake. In the *Map of the King's Roads made by General Wade*, dated 1746, "the General Hutt" (*sic*) is marked just where the road takes a sudden

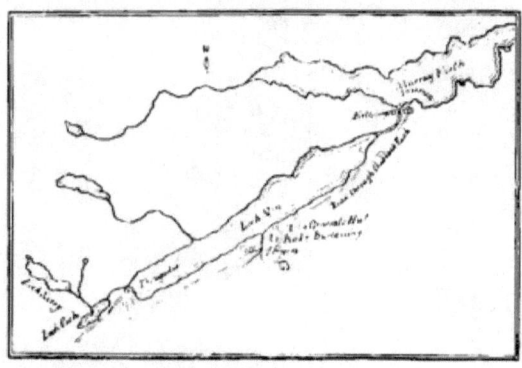

MAP OF FOYERS.

bend to the south, a short distance after which it passes the church of Burlassig. Dr. Garnett, who travelled through the Highlands at the end of the century, says that "the present public-house, which is still called the General's Hut, is very near the place where Wade had a small house, which was afterwards used as an inn. It commands a delightful view up the lake." The change of site must have been made, it would seem, between his visit and Johnson's.

---

[1] Ray's *History of the Rebellion*, p. 362.
[2] M. Hughes's *Plain Narrative*, p. 53. *Alps*, I suppose, he uses as Milton does for lofty mountains in general.
[3] In a *Survey of the Province of Moray*, published at Aberdeen in 1798, on pp. 333-34, the following table is given of the distances along the road which Johnson was following:— "From Inverness to the General's Hut, 17 miles 6 furlongs. From General's Hut to Fort Augustus, 14 miles 2 furlongs. From Fort Augustus to Unach [? Aonach], 9 miles. From Unach to Rattachan, 25 miles 5 furlongs. From Rattachan to Bernera, 9 miles.

The old inn was on the north-east or Inverness side of the church, whereas the Foyers Hotel is a little distance beyond it to the southwest. It is a pity that the ambition of landlords has not allowed the old name to remain. It was the only thing I found wanting in this comfortable hotel. Sir Walter Scott was surprised that "when these roads were made there was no care taken for inns. The King's House and the General's Hut are miserable places," he adds, "but the project and plans were purely military."[1] Johnson, however, was not dissatisfied with his entertainment. "We found," he says, "the house not ill-stocked with provisions. We had eggs and bacon, and mutton, with wine, rum, and whisky. I had water." The little church hard by Boswell describes as "the meanest parish kirk I ever saw. It is a shame it should be on a high road." It might have been pleaded, perhaps, as an alleviation of its disgrace, that the high road had come to it and that it had not come to the high road. His reproach seems to have had some effect, for it has been removed to another place. The ruins, however, still remain. A middle-aged woman who dwells in the neighbourhood told me that "there was an old man living when she first came, who said he did not mind when it was a church, but his father did."

While Boswell mentions the mean kirk, with his indifference to natural objects he passes over in silence the celebrated Falls of Fiers or Foyers. He does not even mention the bridge over the river, or the rocks which on three sides of it rise to a great height. Here Johnson's imagination was deeply impressed, for he describes them as "exhibiting a kind of dreadful magnificence; standing like the barriers of nature placed to keep different orders of being in perpetual separation." Dismounting from their horses, "we clambered," he writes, "over very rugged crags, till we came at last to a place where we could overlook the river, and saw a channel torn, as it seems, through black piles of stone, by which the stream is obstructed and broken, till it comes to a very steep descent, of such dreadful depth, that we were naturally inclined to turn aside our eyes. But we visited the place at an unseasonable time, and found it divested of its dignity and terror. Nature never gives everything at once. A long continuance of dry weather, which made the rest of the way easy and delightful, deprived us of the pleasure expected from the Falls of Fiers." This same month Mason, the poet, was complaining that the cascades at Lodore had

[1] Croker's *Boswell*, 8vo, ed. p. 307

been "reduced by the dry season to a scanty rill, which took away more than half the beauties of the scene."[1]

It was dark when our travellers reached "the wretched inn" at Fort Augustus. Happily it was not in it that they were to lodge, for the governor invited them to sleep in his house. Of the fort, the rebels had made a bonfire on April 15, 1746, the day before Culloden, "to celebrate the Duke of Cumberland's birthday."[2] It had since been rebuilt and greatly strengthened, "being surrounded by two trenches filled with water, and having draw-bridges, strong

INVERMORISTON.

walls, and bastions."[3] Nothing is left of it. Where rough soldiers once carried things with a high hand, now smooth priests rule. On the site of the old fortifications which bore the second name of the butcher duke has been raised a college and monastery dedicated to St. Benedict. Johnson long remembered the rest which he enjoyed in the governor's hospitable home. Nearly four years later he recorded in his diary: "I passed the night in such sweet uninterrupted sleep as I have not known since I slept at Fort Augustus." The following year, writing to Boswell, he said, "The best night that I have had these twenty years was at Fort Augustus." From

[1] Walpole's *Letters*, v. 501. [2] Ray's *History of the Rebellion*, p. 325. [3] *Ib.*, p. 362.

this spot to the sea-shore opposite Skye they had about forty-four miles of highland paths to traverse. This part of their journey they were forced to divide very unequally, as Anoch, the only place where they could find entertainment, was scarcely a third of the way. Crossing the mountains by a road which had been made "with labour that might have broken the perseverance of a Roman legion," early in the afternoon they came "through a wild country" to Glenmorison.[1] They did not, as the guide-book says, follow the course of the river Moriston from Invermoriston, but joined it some miles higher up, above the fine scenery and the wild tumble of water which are shown in the accompanying sketch. This fact I did not discover till too late. Anoch Johnson describes as "stand-

THE RUINS OF THE HOUSE AT ANOCH.

ing in a glen or valley pleasantly watered by a winding river. It consists of three huts, one of which is distinguished by a chimney." It was in the house thus distinguished that they lodged. When I visited this spot last summer, we halted at a farmhouse hard by to rest our horses and take some lunch. We sat on the bank of a dried-up brook, beneath a row of witch-elms. A cuckoo was flying about, resting now and then on the garden wall. "Its two-fold shout" it scarcely uttered, thinking, perhaps, that as it was the month of June, it would be "heard, not regarded." The wind rustled in the leaves, the river, blue beneath a blue sky, ran swiftly by, now under a shady bank, and now round a stony foreland, till it lost itself at last from our sight behind a bend. To the west rose lofty mountains; on the other side of the valley were sloping hills. We lunched on frothing milk, oat-cakes, scones, and butter; the sheep dogs playing around us, and with wistful gaze asking for their share of the feast. We lay on the ground and looked across the little ravine at an old hut that was "distinguished by a chimney." This

---

[1] Judge Boswell's spelling. Johnson calls it Glenmollison. It is now generally written Glenmoriston.

we all voted, and very likely with truth on our side, was the very place where our travellers had lodged. Talking of "far-off things," of Johnson and the copy of Cocker's Arithmetic which he gave to his landlord's "gentle and pleasing daughter," of her father's library of odd volumes, and of the old hut and the old life, an hour slipped quickly and pleasantly by.

As our travellers "passed on through the dreariness of solitude" on their way hither, they had come upon a party of soldiers working on the road, to whom they gave a couple of shillings to spend in drink. "With the true military impatience of coin in their pockets," these men had followed them to the inn, "having marched at least six miles to find the first place where liquor could be bought." There they made merry in the barn. "We went and paid them a visit," writes Boswell; "Dr. Johnson saying, 'Come,

THATCHED HOUSE.

let's go and give 'em another shilling a-piece.' We did so, and he was saluted 'MY LORD' by all of them." Johnson avows that one cause of his generosity was regard to his and Boswell's safety. "Having never been before in a place so wild and unfrequented, I was glad of their arrival, because I knew that we had made them friends; and to gain still more of their good-will, we went to them when they were carousing in the barn, and added something to our former gift." The money was ill-bestowed. "The poor soldiers got too much liquor. Some of them fought and left blood upon the spot, and cursed whisky next morning." Perhaps Johnson had them in his mind when, a few years later, he said, "Why, sir, a common soldier is usually a very gross man." To the degradation of one of the English regiments which had been stationed in the Highlands, testimony is borne by Wolfe, who on his return from Scotland in 1753, wrote: "If I stay much longer with the regiment I shall be perfectly corrupt; the officers are loose and profligate, and the soldiers are very devils."[1] Johnson soon found that he had no need of a guard. His host had indeed fought in the Highland army at Culloden, but he was a quiet honest fellow. The account which he gave of the campaign moved Boswell to tears. If he

[1] Wright's *Life of Wolfe*, p. 279.

told them the following story which I have found in Henderson's *History of the Rebellion*, he would have moved also Johnson to anger. A party of the Grants of Glenmorison had joined the Pretender's army at Edinburgh. The laird, who had remained loyal, came, after the battle of Culloden, "with about five hundred of his vassals to Inverness, whence they were sent into the country of the Macintoshes. Hereupon the Grants in the rebellion begged his intercession. He repaired to the Duke of Cumberland, and said, 'Here are a number of men come in with their arms, who would have submitted to none in Britain but to me.' 'No!' answered the duke; 'I'll let them know that they are my father's subjects, and must likewise submit to me.' So he gave orders to embark them with the other prisoners, and they were shipped off to Tilbury Fort."[1] Smollett tells how great numbers of the miserable captives who were sent to London by sea, being crowded in the holds of the vessels, "perished in the most deplorable manner for want of necessaries, air, and exercise."[2] If the Grants escaped this fate, very likely they were transported to America.

Anoch to Glenelg (September 1).

It was a long and heavy journey that this day lay before our travellers, so that they rose in good time and started about eight o'clock. Boswell, who had awakened very early, had been a little scared by the thought that "their landlord, being about to emigrate, might murder them to get their money, and lay it upon the soldiers in the barn." "When I got up," he adds, "I found Dr. Johnson asleep in his miserable stye, as I may call it, with a coloured handkerchief round his head. With difficulty could I awaken him." So miserable had their beds looked that "we had some difficulty," writes Johnson, "in persuading ourselves to lie down in them. At last we ventured, and I slept very soundly in the vale of Glenmorison amidst the rocks and mountains." The road which they were to follow is but little traversed at the present day, for tourists either keep to the south by the Caledonian Canal, or to the north by the railway to Strome Ferry. They thereby miss, to use Boswell's words, "a scene of as wild nature as one

[1] Henderson's *History of the Rebellion*, p. 122.   [2] Smollett's *History of England*, iii. 185.

could see." To this part of my tour I had long looked forward. It is many a year since I first formed the wish to visit that "narrow valley not very flowery, but sufficiently verdant," where Johnson planned the history of his tour.

"I sat down on a bank (he says) such as a writer of romance might have delighted to feign. I had indeed no trees to whisper over my head, but a clear rivulet streamed at my feet. The day was calm, the air was soft, and all was rudeness, silence, and solitude. Before me and on either side were high hills, which by hindering the eye from ranging, forced the mind to find entertainment for itself. Whether I spent the hour well I know not, for here I first conceived the thought of this narration."

In a letter to Mrs. Thrale he describes the same scene, but makes no mention of the book which he had in mind.

"I sat down to take notes on a green bank, with a small stream running at my feet, in the midst of savage solitude, with mountains before me, and on either hand covered with heath. I looked around me, and wondered that I was not more affected, but the mind is not at all times equally ready to be put in motion. If my mistress and master, and Queeney[1] had been there, we should have produced some reflections among us either poetical or philosophical, for though solitude be the nurse of woe,[2] conversation is often the parent of remarks and discoveries."

My hopes of finding this classical rivulet were great. A kind correspondent, the Rev. Alexander Matheson, minister of Glen Shiel, had been told by some old people of the neighbourhood that they knew by tradition the exact spot. Though he had nearly twenty miles to come, he undertook to show me it. I arrived at the little inn at Clunie earlier than he had expected, and there meeting him found to my disappointment that I had passed the spot some six or seven miles. Both horses and travellers were too weary to retrace their steps. The tradition of the old people had on further investigation proved to be worthless. Like myself he had been at first misled by Boswell's narrative, which places this happy valley at the western end of Glen Shiel. But on looking at Johnson's account, aided too by his own knowledge of the locality, he had detected the error. The rivulet by which they had made their noonday halt must have been in Glen Clunie, near the eastern end of the loch, for Johnson describes how after their rest "they continued their journey along the side of a loch which at last ended in a river broad and shallow. Beyond it is a valley called Glen Shiel." For my disappointment there was some con-

---

[1] He means Mr. and Mrs. Thrale and their eldest daughter.

[2] Johnson is quoting Parnell — *Hymn to Con-*

tentment. Pope, in *Donne's Satire Versified* (iv. 185), calls "solitude the nurse of sense."

solation to be found. The long drought of nearly two months which had preceded my tour had dried up those rivulets which Johnson crossed, running, as he describes them, "with a clear, shallow stream over a hard, pebbly bottom." The main river had still water in it; but we saw few indeed of "the streams rushing down the steep" which fed it. In that part of the narrow valley where he reposed we should have had only a choice of dried-up watercourses, had we tried to select the

bank on which he sat. For me Yarrow still remains unvisited. I have still to see

"Its silvery current flow
With uncontrolled meanderings."

Passing through Glen Clunie, which now boasts of a little inn where the traveller can find clean, if homely lodgings, they reached Glen Shiel. It is worth notice that though the word *Glen* is in Johnson's Dictionary, so unfamiliar was it at this time to English ears, that using it in the letter in which he describes this day's journey, he adds, "so they call a valley." In Glen Shiel, writes Boswell, they saw "where the battle was fought in 1719." It was in the second and last of the Spanish invasions of our island that this fight took place. An armament of ten ships of war and transports, having on board 6,000 regular troops with arms for 12,000 men, had sailed from Cadiz under the command of the Duke of Ormond, in the hope of restoring the Stuarts to that throne which they had forfeited by their tyranny and their folly. The winds and waves fought for us, as they had fought long before in the time of the Great Armada. Two ships only succeeded in reaching the coast of Scotland. They landed their troops near Eilan Donan Castle on Loch Duich, the seat of the chief of the Mackenzies. Four years earlier the fighting men of

EILAN DONAN.

this clan had gone off to join the forces of the Earl of Mar, and had taken part in the battle of Sheriffmuir. The grandfather of the present minister of the parish in which Eilan Donan stands, had known an aged parishioner, who had seen the clansmen dance on the leads of the castle the evening before they started on their expedition. There were among them four chieftans, each bearing the name of John, and known as "the four Johns of Scotland." They all danced at Eilan Donan, and all fell at Sheriffmuir. I was told also of a tradition which still exists among the people, that at Glen Shiel the clansmen had sent their women and children to wave flags on the hills as if they were a fresh body of men. Deceived by this appearance, the regular troops had at first retreated. The battle with the Spaniards was fought at a spot where on both sides the mountains draw close, and the valley

narrows to a ravine through which the river when swollen by the
rains rushes foaming along in fine cascades. Along the right bank
the rocks were so steep that till the present road was cut no passage was possible; on the left bank there was a narrow opening
beneath a precipitous crag. A little above the uppermost of the
waterfalls the country folks still point out "the black colonel's
grave"—some swarthy Spaniard, perhaps, who fell that day far
from the cork-groves of Southern Spain. They tell too how the
Spanish soldiers who surrendered themselves as prisoners of war

GLEN SHIEL BATTLE-FIELD.

first cast their arms into the deep pool below. A dreadful story
has been recorded by an Englishman who lived for many years at
Inverness. "He had been assured," he writes, "by several
officers who were in the battle, that some of the English soldiers
who were dangerously wounded were left behind for three or
four hours. When parties were sent to them with hurdles made
to serve as litters, they were all found stabbed with dirks in twenty
places."[1] The story may not be true. If it is, the clansmen were
as savage after Glen Shiel, as were the regular troops twenty-seven
years later after Culloden.

[1] *Letters from a Gentleman in the North of Scotland*, ii. 179.

In the warm sunshine of a day in June we sat on a bank above the dark pool beneath whose eddying waters some of the arms perhaps still lie. There was a gentle breeze, the larks were singing over our heads, the water was sparkling and splashing, the sides of the torrent were overhung with the mountain ash and were green with ferns, but below us and in front lay a scene of wild desolation. Far off to the west was the mountain which Boswell had pointed out to Johnson as being like a cone. "No, Sir," said Johnson,

FAOCHAG.

"It would be called so in a book, and when a man comes to look at it, he sees it is not so. It is indeed pointed at the top; but one side of it is larger than the other." Its Gaelic name, *Faochag*, which signifies *whelk*, shows that though Johnson's objection may have been a proof of his "perceptive quickness," yet Boswell's description was quite accurate enough for two men out on a tour. We tried in vain to distinguish which among the mountains was "the considerable protuberance." Perhaps the Johnson Club may not disdain to appoint a committee who shall be instructed to bid farewell for a time to the delights of Fleet Street and visit Glen Shiel, with full powers to come to a final decision in this important matter.

A long drive down the steep pass brought us to the place which Boswell said was "a rich green valley, comparatively speaking." A little way beyond it lay the twenty huts which formed the village of Auchnasheal. "One of them," says Johnson, "was built of loose stones, piled up with great thickness into a strong, though not solid wall. From this house we obtained some great pails of milk, and having brought bread with us were very liberally regaled." The curious scene which they witnessed here is thus described by Boswell:—

"We sat down on a green turf-seat at the end of a house; they brought us out two wooden dishes of milk,[1] which we tasted. One of them was frothed like a syllabub. I saw a woman preparing it with such a stick as is used for chocolate, and in the same manner. We had a considerable circle about us, men, women, and children, all M'Craas, Lord Seaforth's people. Not one of them could speak English. I observed to Dr Johnson, it was much the same as being with a tribe of Indians. Johnson: 'Yes, sir, but not so terrifying.' I gave all who chose it snuff and tobacco. Governor Trapaud had made us buy a quantity at Fort Augustus, and put them up in small parcels. I also gave each person a piece of wheat bread, which they had never tasted before. I then gave a penny apiece to each child. I told Dr. Johnson of this; upon which he called to Joseph and our guides, for change for a shilling, and declared that he would distribute among the children. Upon this being announced in Erse, there was a great stir: not only did some children come running down from neighbouring huts, but I observed one black-haired man, who had been with us all along, had gone off and returned, bringing a very young child. My fellow-traveller then ordered the children to be drawn up in a row, and he dealt about his copper, and made them and their parents all happy."

"It was the best day the McCraas declared they had seen since the time of the old laird of Macleod." He, no doubt, had made a halt in their valley on his way to or from Skye. The snuff and tobacco must have won their hearts more even than the money. "Nothing," Johnson was told, "gratified the Highlanders so much." Knox recorded a few years later that "any stranger who cannot take a pinch of snuff or give one is looked upon with an evil eye."[2] So uncommon was wheaten bread even a quarter of a century later, that Dr. Garnett, after leaving Inverary, tasted none till he reached Inverness.[3] At present it can be had in most places, being brought by the steamers in large boxes from Glasgow, and transported inland in the country carts. The way in which the villagers had gathered round the travellers had startled even

[1] Johnson calls them *potts*. In his time pails were only made of wood, if we construct his definition of the word in his Dictionary.

[2] J. Knox's *Tour through the Highlands in* 1786, p. 255.

[3] T. Garnett's *Observations*, etc., ii. 12.

Johnson, stout-hearted though he was. "I believe," he says, "they were without any evil intention, but they had a very savage wildness of aspect and manner." My friend, the minister of Glen Shiel, pointed out to me that it was no doubt mere curiosity which brought them round him. Johnson was as strange a sight to them as they were to Johnson. An earlier traveller in the Hebrides has expressed this very well. "Every man and thing I met with," he writes, "seemed a novelty. I thought myself entering upon a new scene of nature, but nature rough and unpolished. Men, manners, habits, buildings, everything different from our own; and if we thought them rude and barbarous, no doubt the people had the same opinion of what belonged to us, and the wonder was mutual."[1]

Auchnasheal has been swept away; nothing of it is left but a few banks of earth and the foundations of the one stone house. The same fate has befallen it which befell that other village near Fort Augustus where Coleridge heard a Highland widow mourn over the desolation of the land:

"'Within this space,' she said, 'how short a time back! — there lived a hundred and seventy-three persons, and now there is only a shepherd and an underling or two. Yes, Sir! One hundred and seventy-three Christian souls, man, woman, boy, girl, and babe, and in almost every home an old man by the fire-side, who would tell you of the troubles before our roads were made; and many a brave youth among them who loved the birthplace of his forefathers, yet would swing about his broad-sword, and want but a word to march off to the battles over sea: aye, Sir, and many a good lass who had a respect for herself. Well, but they are gone, and with them the bristled bear [barley] and the pink haver [oats], and the potato plot that looked as gay as any flower-garden with its blossoms! I sometimes fancy that the very birds are gone — all but the crows and the gleads [kites]. Well, and what then? Instead of us all, there is one shepherd man, and it may be a pair of small lads — and a many, many sheep! And do you think, Sir, that God allows of such proceedings?'"[2]

The desolation had already begun even at the time of our travellers' visit. Their host of the evening before was following seventy of the dalesmen to America, whither they had been driven by a rack-renting landlord. "I asked him," writes Johnson, "whether they would stay at home if they were well-treated. He answered with indignation, that no man willingly left his native country."

Taking leave of these inoffensive, if wild-looking people, our travellers rode on, much refreshed by their repast. They had, as Johnson complained, "very little entertainment, as they travelled

---

[1] W. Sacheverell's *Account of the Isle of Man*, ex., p. 128. [2] *Lay Sermon*, ed. 1839, p. 427.

either for the eye or ear. There are, I fancy," he adds, "no singing birds in the Highlands." It is odd that he should have looked for singing birds on the 1st of September. Had it been earlier in the summer he would have found melody enough. Nowhere have I heard the thrushes sing more sweetly than at Glenelg. Wesley, visiting Inverness on an early day of May, "heard abundance of birds welcoming the return of spring."¹ If so late in the summer there was no music for the ear, the eye surely should have been something more than entertained, when in the evening light the first sight was caught of Loch Duich and the waters of the Atlantic, and the barrier of mountains which so nobly encloses them. Yet they are passed over in silence by both our travellers. So fine is the scenery here that I longed to make a stay in the comfortable inn at Shiel, near the head of the loch. But we were forced to press on, having first witnessed, however, sheep-shearing on a large scale on a farm close by. In front of a storing-house for wool fifteen men were seated all hard at work with their shears, their dogs lying at their feet. They wore coloured jerseys in which the shades of blue and green were all the pleasanter to the eye because they were somewhat faded. Young lads were bringing up the sheep from the fold. The forelegs of each animal were tied, it was then lifted on to a narrow bank of turf which had been raised in front of each shepherd, thrown on its back, and in a moment the busy shears were at work. In the long summer day a quick hand could finish eighty, we were told. As soon as the fleece fell loose, an old woman came forward, folded it up tight, and carried it into the store-house; while a boy, dipping the branding-iron into boiling pitch, scored the side of each sheep with a deep black mark. From time to time the farmer went round with a bottle and a small glass, and gave each man a dram of pure whisky. Not far from here on the banks of the loch was an old house where it was said that Johnson made a halt. It is so pleasant a place, with its grove of trees and its garden of roses, and so kindly was I welcomed, that I would willingly believe the tradition. I could wish, however, that he and Boswell had not treated it with the same neglect as they did the view. Had their reception been as kind as mine they would certainly have expressed their gratitude. It was here that I was told of the address which he made to the mountain at the foot of which the house stands, and up which he was now to climb, "Good-bye, Mam Rattakin, I hope never to see your face again."[1] They did not reach it till late in the afternoon. Both Johnson and the horses were weary, and they had "a terrible steep to climb." Going down was almost worse than going up, for his horse now and then stumbled beneath his great weight. On the edge of one of the precipices he was, he thought, in real danger. He grew fretful with fatigue, and was not comforted by the absurd attempt made by his guide to amuse him.

"Having heard him, in the forenoon, express a pastoral pleasure on seeing the goats browsing, just when the doctor was uttering his displeasure, the fellow cried, with a very Highland accent, 'See, such pretty goats!' Then he whistled *whu!* and made them jump. Little did he conceive what Dr. Johnson was. Here now was a common ignorant Highland clown imagining that he could divert, as one does a child, *Dr. Samuel Johnson!* The ludicrousness, absurdity, and extraordinary contrast between what the fellow fancied, and the reality, was truly comic."

At the bottom of the mountain a dreary ride of six or seven long miles through a flat and uninteresting country still awaited them. They were too tired even for talk. Boswell urged on his horse so that some preparation might be made for the great man at the inn at Glenelg.

"He called me back," he writes, "with a tremendous shout, and was really in a passion with me for leaving him. I told him my intentions, but he was not satisfied, and said, 'Do you know, I should as soon have thought of picking a pocket, as doing so.' BOSWELL. 'I am diverted with you, Sir.' JOHNSON. 'Sir, I could never be diverted with incivility. Doing such a thing makes one lose confidence in him who has done it, as one cannot tell what he may do next.'"

Even after he had reached the inn his violence continued. "Sir," he said, "had you gone on, I was thinking that I should have returned with you to Edinburgh, and then have parted from you, and never spoken to you more." The next morning "he owned that he had spoken in passion ; that he would not have done what he threatened ; and that if he had, he should have been ten times worse than I ; and he added, 'Let's think no more on't.'" As we drove down the mountain on a summer afternoon the peacefulness of the pastoral scene, the sheep dotted about quietly nibbling the grass, with their lambs by their side, the hazy air on the hills, all seemed to contrast strangely with the violence of his passion. To an old man, however, tired with a long day's ride over rough ways, and in want of his dinner, something must be forgiven. He is not

---

[1] See *ante*, p. 2. Boswell calls the mountain *Rattakin*, Johnson *Rattiken*. Its name I was told is properly written *Rattagan*.

the only tourist who, in his need of rest and food, has relieved his feelings by quarrelling with his companion.

When they were not far from the end of their ride they passed the barracks at Bernera. "I looked at them wistfully," writes Boswell; "as soldiers have always everything in the best order; but there was only a sergeant and a few men there." Pennant, who had visited them a year earlier, describes them as "handsome and capacious, designed to hold two hundred men; at present occupied only by a corporal and six soldiers. The country lament this neglect. They are now quite sensible of the good effects of the military, by introducing peace and security; they fear lest the evil days should return, and the ancient thefts be renewed as soon as the banditti find this protection of the people removed."[1] The banditti were the Highlanders of this district in general. Less than thirty years earlier "the whole country between Loch Ness and the sea to the west had been," he says, "a den of thieves. The constant petition at grace of the old Highland chieftains was delivered with great fervour in these terms: 'Lord, turn the world upside down, that Christians may make bread out of it.'"[2]

The country had to lament a loss of trade as well as of security. The cottagers who had been drawn together to supply the wants of the soldiers are described by Knox, a few years later, as being in the utmost poverty. The barracks had fallen into so ruinous a state, that it justified the report that the building of them had been "a notorious job." Even the sergeant and his six soldiers had been removed. "I was entertained," says Knox, "by the commanding officer and his whole garrison. The former was an old corporal, and the latter was the corporal's wife: the entertainment snuff and whisky."[3]

When at length our travellers, "weary and disgusted," reached Glenelg, "our humour," writes Johnson, "was not much mended by our inn, which, though it was built of lime and slate the Highlander's description of a house which he thinks magnificent, had neither wine, bread, eggs, nor anything that we could eat or drink. When we were taken upstairs a dirty fellow bounced out of the bed where one of us was to lie. Boswell blustered, but nothing could be got. At last a gentleman in the neighbourhood, who heard of

---

[1] *Voyage to the Hebrides*, ed. 1774, p. 336.
[2] *Ib.*, p. 345.
[3] *Tour through the Highlands in* 1786, pp. cxx, 103. I do not know whether an earlier instance can be found of the expression "notorious job" than the above.

our arrival, sent us rum and white sugar. Boswell was now provided for in part, and the landlord prepared some mutton chops which we could not eat, and killed two hens, of which Boswell made his servant broil a limb, with what effect I know not. We had a lemon and a piece of bread, which supplied me with my supper." Boswell's account of the place is no less dismal. "There was no provender for our horses; so they were sent to grass with a man to watch them. A maid showed us upstairs into a room damp and dirty, with bare walls, a variety of bad smells, a coarse black greasy fir table, and forms of the same kind; and out of a

SKYE, FROM GLENELG.

wretched bed started a fellow from his sleep, like Edgar in *King Lear*, 'Poor Tom's a-cold.'" Johnson slept in his clothes and great coat, on a bed of hay; "Boswell laid sheets upon his bed which he had brought from home, and reposed in linen like a gentleman."

Here, again, was I struck by the contrast between the past and the present. Of the old inn, with all its magnificence of lime and slate, not even the site is known. In its place stands a roomy and comfortable hotel. It was on the 21st of June when we visited

BERVEY'S BARRACKS, GIENJIG.

it, and we found it half asleep and almost empty, for the season had not yet begun. At the most delightful time of the year, when the days were at their longest and no candles were burnt, there was scarcely a single stranger to enjoy the quiet and the beauty. There were woods and flowering shrubs, rhododendrons and the Portugal laurel, and close to the water's edge the laburnum in full bloom. There were all the sights of peaceful country life—the cocks crowing, the sheep answering with their bleats their bleating lambs, the cows with their calves in the noonday heat seeking the shade of the tall and wide-spreading trees. The waves lapped gently on the shore, and in the distance, below the rocky coast of Skye, the waters were whitened by the countless sea-birds. We drove up a beautiful valley to the Pictish forts, and saw an eagle hovering high above us.

CORRICHATACHIN (SEPTEMBER 6-8; 25-28.)

On the morning of Thursday, September 2, our travellers took boat at Glenelg, "and launched into one of the straits of the Atlantic Ocean." Rowing along the Sound of Slate towards the south-west, they reached the shore of Armidale in Skye early in the afternoon. They had intended to visit in his castle the owner of half the island,

THE SOUND OF SLATE.

Sir Alexander Macdonald. But, wrote Johnson, "he had come from his seat in the middle of the island to a small house on the shore, as we believe, that he might with less reproach entertain us meanly." Boswell was so much disgusted with this chieftain's parsimony, that he "meditated an escape from his house the very next day; but Dr. Johnson resolved that we should weather it out till Monday." When the day of escape at length came, they started on horseback in a north-westerly direction for Corrichatachin, a farm-house near Broadford,[1] belonging to Sir A. Macdonald, but tenanted by a Mackinnon, a clan to which all this district had formerly belonged. "Here they were entertained better than at the landlord's;" here "they enjoyed the comfort of a

[1] Boswell calls the place Broadfoot.

table plentifully furnished, and here for the first time they had a specimen of the joyous social manners of the inhabitants of the Highlands." Books, too, were not wanting, both Latin and English; among them was a copy of the abridgment of Johnson's Dictionary. He might have said here, as four years later with some eagerness he said at Lord Scarsdale's, when he discovered the same book in his lordship's dressing-room, "Quæ regio in terris nostri non plena laboris?" Here, too, he wrote that Latin Ode to Mrs. Thrale, which so caught Sir Walter Scott's imagination, that when he first set foot on Skye, it was the thing which first came into his thoughts. And here on their return after a lapse of nearly three weeks, Boswell got so tipsy and so piously penitent next day. He had not gone to bed till nearly five o'clock on a Sunday morning, by which time four bowls of punch had been finished.

"I awaked at noon," he records, "with a severe headache. I was much vexed that I should have been guilty of such a riot, and afraid of a reproof from Dr. Johnson. I thought it very inconsistent with that conduct which I ought to maintain, while the companion of the *Rambler*. About one he came into my room, and accosted me, 'What, drunk yet?' His tone of voice was not that of severe upbraiding; so I was relieved a little. 'Sir,' said I, 'they kept me up.' He answered, 'No, you kept them up, you drunken dog.' This he said with good-humoured English pleasantry. Soon afterwards, Corrichatachin, Col, and other friends, assembled round my bed. Corri had a brandy-bottle and glass with him, and insisted I should take a dram. 'Ay,' said Dr. Johnson, 'fill him drunk again. Do it in the morning, that we may laugh at him all day. It is a poor thing for a fellow to get drunk at night, and sculk to bed, and let his friends have no sport.' Finding him thus jocular, I became quite easy; and when I offered to get up, he very good-naturedly said, 'You need be in no such hurry now.' I took my host's advice, and drank some brandy, which I found an effectual cure for my headache. When I rose, I went into Dr. Johnson's room, and taking up Mrs. M'Kinnon's Prayer-book, I opened it at the Twentieth Sunday after Trinity, in the epistle for which I read, 'And be not drunk with wine, wherein there is excess.' Some would have taken this as a divine interposition."

Before the afternoon was over, by the help of good cheer and good society, he felt himself comfortable enough, and his piety was drowned in philosophy.

"I then thought," he says, "that my last night's riot was no more than such a social excess as may happen without much moral blame; and recollected that some physicians maintained, that a fever produced by it was, upon the whole, good for health."

The Highlanders were more seasoned drinkers than he was, for the following night they had another drinking-bout.

"They kept a smart lad lying on a table in the corner of the room, ready to spring up and bring the kettle whenever it was wanted. They continued drinking,

and singing Erse songs, till near five in the morning, when they all came into my room, where some of them had beds. Unluckily for me, they found a bottle of punch in a corner, which they drank; and Corrichatachin went for another, which they also drank. They made many apologies for disturbing me. I told them, that, having been kept awake by their mirth, I had once thoughts of getting up and joining them again. Honest Corrichatachin said, 'To have had you done so, I would have given a cow.'

Johnson was better lodged than Boswell, for he had a room to himself at night, though in the day it was the place where the servants took their meals. Yet he was pleased with the kindness shown him, and discovered no deficiencies. "Our entertainment," he wrote, "was not only hospitable but elegant." The company he describes as being "more numerous and elegant than it could have been supposed easy to collect." He gave as much pleasure as he received, and when he left, "the Scottish phrase of *honest man*, which is an expression of kindness and regard, was again and again applied to him."

The house he describes as "very pleasantly situated between two brooks, with one of the highest hills of the island behind it." Boswell with good reason remarks on the entire absence of a garden. "Corrichatachin," he writes, "has not even a turnip, a carrot, or a cabbage." Where these were wanting, there would be no roses clustering on the porch, no flower-beds before the door. This scene of hospitality and jovial riot is now a ruin. We walked to it from Broadford across a moorland, the curlews flying round us with their melancholy cry. The two brooks were shrunk with the long drought, and flowed in very quiet streams. Yet one of them, I was told, in a time of flood once broke into Mackinnon's house. We crossed it on a bridge formed of two trees, with a long piece of iron wire for a railing. There we rested awhile, now looking down at the sunlight dancing in the shallows, and now gazing at the ruined farm and the mountain rising behind in steep crags of barren rock. Far up the valley to the west a flock of sheep was coming white from the shearing, bleating as they spread out along the hill-side. Another flock the dogs were gathering into what had been the yard of the old house. It had been solidly built, two stories high, about thirty-six feet long by fifteen broad in the inside measurements. On the outside, over the door, was carved:—

L. M. K.   J. M. K.
1747.

Johnson's host was Lachlan Mackinnon, and the initials are, I suppose, his and his wife's. It was but a small place to hold the large and festive company that was gathered at the time of our traveller's visit; but, as Boswell says, "it was partly done by separating man and wife, and putting a number of men in one room and of women in another." As I looked up at the windows which still remain, though the floors have fallen in, I wondered which was the room which was Johnson's chamber at night, and the ladies' parlour by day, where Boswell sat among them writing his journal.

At the Hotel at Broadford, I was struck by the change that has come about since Johnson's time "in this verge of European life," to use the term which he applied to Skye. Corrichatachin remains almost as he saw it. A house had fallen in ruins and had been replaced by another, and a small grove of trees had been planted. A garden had been made, and patches of ground which once were pasture had been ploughed up. But the broad face of nature is unchanged. This "region of obscurity," is, however, obscure no longer. Where he was nearly ten weeks without receiving letters, now even the poor, far from their homes, by means of the telegraphic wire can, as it were, "live along the line." A maid-servant who goes to distant services, on her arrival, by means of a telegram, at once frees her mother from her "heart-struck anxious care." The owner of the hotel, from whom I learnt this fact, said that "Rowland Hill had done more for the poor man than all the ministers since, and that many of the Highlanders in gratitude had called their sons after him."

CORRICHATACHIN.

RAASAY (SEPTEMBER 8-12).

From Corrichatachin our travellers rode down to the sea-side at Broadford, two miles off, where they took boat for the island of Raasay. The Macgillichallum, or laird of Raasay, John Macleod, had politely sent his coach and six, as he called his six-oared boat, to fetch them over. Though it was " thus dignified with a pompous name," writes Johnson, " there was no seat, but an occasional bundle of straw. I never," he adds, " saw in the Hebrides a boat furnished with benches." In it had come the learned Donald M'Queen, a minister, and old Malcolm Macleod, who had been out in the '45, and had aided the Young Pretender in his escape. I had at one time thought that it was to him that Johnson alludes when he speaks of having met one man, and one only, who defied the law against wearing the Highland dress. " By him," he adds, " it was worn only occasionally and wantonly."[1] I now believe, however, that it was Macdonald of Kingsburgh who was meant. Ever since the last rebellion the national garb had been suppressed. It had been enacted that "no person whatsoever should wear or put on those parts of the Highland clothes, garb, or habiliments which are called the plaid, philibeg,[2] or little kilt, or any of them." Any offender " not being a landed man, or the son of a landed man " shall be tried before a justice of the peace " in a summary way, and shall be delivered over to serve as as a soldier."[3] Even the loyal Highlanders in the Duke of Cumberland's army had been compelled in part to adopt the southern garb. " Near Linlithgow," writes Henderson, " the whole army passed in review before their illustrious General. When the Highlanders passed he seemed much delighted with their appearance, saying, 'They look very well; have breeches, and are the better for that."[4] Some years later when Pitt " called for soldiers from the mountains of the North," "to allure them into the army it was thought proper to indulge them in the continuance of their national dress."[5] Numerous were the devices to evade the law, and great must have been the perplexities of the magistrates. One of Wolfe's officers wrote in 1752,

[1] Johnson's Works, ix. 47.
[2] The philibeg, or filibeg, is defined as " the dress or petticoat reaching nearly to the knees."
[3] An Act to Amend the Diswarm, etc. 19 G. II., made in the 21 Geo. II. Edinburgh, 1748. p. 15.
[4] Henderson's History of the Rebellion, p. 99.
[5] Johnson's Works, ix. 94.

that "one of his serjeants had taken a fellow wearing a blanket in form of a philibeg. He carried him to Perth, but the Sheriff-substitute did not commit him, because the blanket was not a tartan. On his return he met another of the same kind; so, as he found it needless to carry him before a magistrate, he took the blanket-philibeg and cut it to pieces." Another officer wrote two months later: "One of my men brought me a man to all appearance in a philibeg; but on close examination I found it to be a woman's petticoat, which answers every end of that part of the Highland dress. I sent him to the Sheriff-substitute, who dismissed him."[1]

Smollett, in his *Humphry Clinker*, pleads the cause of the dejected Highlanders, who had not only been deprived of their ancient garb, but, "what is a greater hardship still, are compelled to wear breeches, a restraint which they cannot bear with any degree of patience; indeed the majority wear them, not in the proper place, but on poles or long staves over their shoulders."[2] In 1782 the Marquis of Graham brought in a bill to repeal this prohibitory Act. One of the English members asked that if it became law, the dress should still be prohibited in England. When six Highland soldiers had been quartered at a house in Hampshire, "the singularity of their dress," he said, "so much attracted the eyes of the wife and daughters of the man of the house that he found it expedient to take a lodging for them at another place."[3] A Lowland friend tells me that one day at church her grandfather turned two Highland officers out of his pew, as he thought their dress improper where there were ladies. This she learnt from her aunt who had been present. Old Malcolm Macleod, if he did not return altogether to the ancient dress, nevertheless broke the law. "He wore a pair of brogues; tartan hose which came up only near to his knees, and left them bare; a purple camblet kilt; a black waistcoat; a short green cloth coat bound with gold cord; a yellowish bushy wig; a large blue bonnet with a gold thread button." Sir Walter Scott tells us that "to evade the law against the tartan dress, the Highlanders used to dye their variegated plaids and kilts into blue, green, or any single colour."[4] Malcolm had done this with his kilt, but in his hose he asserted his independence. Yet so early as the beginning of last century, according to Martin, the Highland dress was fast dying out in Skye. "They

---

[1] Wright's *Life of Wolfe*, pp. 216-18.   *Gentleman's Magazine*, 1782, p. 307.
[2] *Humphry Clinker*, iii. 20.   Croker's *Boswell*, p. 316.

now," he writes, "generally use coat, waistcoat, and breeches, as elsewhere. Persons of distinction wear the garb in fashion in the south of Scotland."[1]

While Johnson in the voyage to Raasay "sat high on the stern of the boat like a magnificent Triton," old Malcolm, no less magnificent through his attire, took his turn at tugging the oar, "singing an Erse song, the chorus of which was *Hatyin foam foem eri*, with words of his own." The original was written in praise of Allan of Muidart, a chief of the Clanranald family. The following is a translation of the complete chorus:

> "Along, along, then haste along,
> For here no more I'll stay;
> I'll braid and bind my tresses long,
> And o'er the hills away."

In the sound between Scalpa and Raasay, "the wind," writes Boswell, "made the sea very rough. I did not like it. 'This now,' said Johnson, 'is the Atlantic. If I should tell, at a tea-table in London, that I have crossed the Atlantic in an open boat, how they'd shudder, and what a fool they'd think me to expose myself to such danger.'" In his letter to Mrs. Thrale he makes light of the roughness of the waves. "The wind blew enough to give the boat a kind of dancing agitation." For a moment or two his temper was ruffled, for by the carelessness of their man-servant his spurs were carried overboard. "There was something wild," he said, "in letting a pair of spurs be carried into the sea out of a boat." What a fine opening we have here for the enthusiasm of the Johnson Club! An expedition properly equipped should be sent to dredge in this sound for the spurs, with directions to proceed afterwards to the Isle of Mull, and make search for that famous piece of timber, his walking-stick, which was lost there.

As the boat drew near the land the singing of the reapers on shore was mingled with the song of the rowers. It was frequently noticed by travellers how the Highlanders loved to keep time with their songs to whatever they were doing. Gray heard the masons singing in Erse all day long as they were building the park wall at Glamis Castle.[2] An earlier writer tells how "the women in harvest work keep time by several barbarous tones of the voice; and stoop and rise together as regularly as a rank of soldiers when they

---

[1] Martin's *Description of the W. Ern Islands*, pp. 206-7.
[2] Croker's *Boswell*, p. 364.   Gray's *Works*, iv. 55.

ground their arms. They proceed with great alacrity, it being disgraceful for anyone to be out of time with the sickle."[1] According to Pennant, "in the songs of the rowers the notes are commonly long, the airs solemn and slow, rarely cheerful, it being impossible for the oars to keep a quick time: the words generally have a religious turn, consonant to that of the people."[2] Ramsay of Ochtertyre says that "the women's songs are in general very short and plaintive. In travelling through the remote Highlands in harvest, the sound of these little bands on every side has a most pleasing effect on the mind of a stranger." The custom, we learn from him, was rapidly dying out at the end of last century.[3] I did not myself hear any of this singing in my wanderings; but a Scotch friend tells me that more than forty years ago she remembers seeing a field in which thirty Highland reapers were at work in couples, a man and a woman together, all singing their Gaelic songs.

Three or four hours' stout rowing brought the boat to the shore below the Laird of Raasay's house. "The approach to it," says Boswell, "was very pleasing. We saw before us a beautiful bay, well defended by a rocky coast; a good family mansion; a fine verdure about it, with a considerable number of trees; and beyond it hills and mountains in gradation of wildness." At the entrance to the bay is a rocky islet, where we landed, when we visited Raasay on the afternoon of a bright June day. As it was unoccupied, we took formal possession, with a better claim than the European nations have to the well-peopled islands of the Southern Seas. Its name, we learnt from our boatman, was Goat Island, and just as Johnson was addressed as Island Isa, so we were willing to derive our title from our new acquisition. We passed a full half an hour in our domain with great satisfaction. Who, we asked, "would change the rocks of Scotland for the Strand?" The waves beat on our coast, breaking in white crests far away in the open sound. We looked across the little bay on the sunny shore of our nearest neighbour, the Laird of Raasay, and did not envy him the pleasant grassy slope, almost ready for the scythe, which stretched from his mansion to the edge of the sea, or the fine woods which covered the hills at the back of his house. We thought how much the scene is changed since our travellers saw it. Then there was no landing-place;

---

[1] *Letters from a Gentleman in the North of Scotland,* ii. 142.
[2] *Voyage to the Hebrides,* ed. 1774, p. 291.
[3] *Scotland and Scotsmen in the Eighteenth Century,* ii. 410, 415.

steps had not been even cut in the natural rock. "The crags," Johnson complained, "were irregularly broken, and a false step would have been very mischievous." Yet "a few men with pick-axes might have cut an ascent of stairs out of any part of the rock in a week's time." There is now a small stone pier. The hayfield, in the memory of people still living, was all heathland down to the water's edge, with a rough cart-track running across it. Trees have been everywhere planted, and the hill-sides are beautifully wooded. Even before Johnson's time something had been done in the way

RAASAY.

of improvement. Martin, in his *Description of the Western Isles*,[1] mentions "an orchard with several sorts of berries, pot-herbs, &c." In the copy of Martin's work in the Bodleian Library, Toland has entered in the margin: "Wonderful in Scotland anywhere." Boswell mentions "a good garden, plentifully stocked with vegetables, and strawberries, raspberries, currants, &c." The house—that "neat modern fabric," which Johnson praises as "the seat of plenty, civility, and cheerfulness"—still remains, but it is almost hidden beneath the great additions which have in later years been made. In a letter to Mrs. Thrale, he says: "It is not large, though we

[1] Page 164.

were told in our passage that it had eleven fine rooms, nor magnificently furnished, but our utensils[1] were most commonly silver. We went up into a dining room about as large as your blue room, where we had something given us to eat, and tea and coffee." The blue room, less fortunate than its rival at Raasay, has been swept away, with all the beauty and the associations of Streatham Park. I was shown his chamber, with his portrait hanging on the wall. A walking stick which he had used is treasured up. From his windows he looked down into the garden. However productive it may have been, it was not, I fear, so gay with flowers as it was when I saw it, or so rich in shrubs. I walked between fuchsia hedges that were much higher than my head. One fuchsia bush, or rather tree, which stood apart, covered with its branches a round of sixty feet. Its trunk was as thick as a man's thigh. The Western Islands are kept free from severe frosts by the waters of the Gulf Stream, so that in the spots which face the southern suns, and are sheltered from the north and east, there is a growth which rivals, and perhaps outdoes, that of Devonshire and Cornwall.

Not far from the house is the ruined chapel which provoked Johnson's sarcasm. "It has been," he writes, "for many years popular to talk of the lazy devotion of the Romish clergy; over the sleepy laziness of men that erected churches we may indulge our superiority with a new triumph, by comparing it with the fervid activity of those who suffer them to fall." Boswell took a more cheerful view. "There was something comfortable," he wrote, "in the thought of being so near a piece of consecrated ground." Here they looked upon the tombs of the Macleods of Raasay, that ancient family which boasted that "during four hundred years they had not gained or lost a single acre;" which was worthily represented in their host; which lasted for two generations longer, and then sank in ruins amidst the wild follies of a single laird. Whilst rack-renting landlords were driving their people across the wide Atlantic, Macleod of Raasay could boast " that his island had not yet been forsaken by a single inhabitant." Pleased with all he saw, "Johnson was in fine spirits. 'This,' he said, 'is truly the patriarchal life; this is what we came to find.'" He was delighted with the free and friendly life, the feasting and the dancing, and all

---

[1] Johnson seems to use this word in much the same sense as Caliban does when he speaks of Prospero's "brave utensils" (*The Tempest*, act iii. sc. 2). In his *Journey*, he says that in the Hebrides "they use silver on all occasions where it is common in England, nor did I ever find a spoon of horn but in one house."

"the pleasures of this little Court." The evening of their arrival, as soon as dinner was finished, "the carpet was taken up, the fiddler of the family came, and a very vigorous and general dance was begun." According to Boswell, "Johnson was so delighted with this scene, that he said, 'I know not how we shall get away.' It entertained me to observe him sitting by, while we danced, sometimes in deep meditation, sometimes smiling complacently, sometimes looking upon Hooke's *Roman History*, and sometimes talking a little, amidst the noise of the ball, to Mr. Donald M'Queen, who anxiously gathered knowledge from him." The same accommodating hospitality was shown here as at Corrichatachin in finding sleeping room for the large party that was assembled. "I had a chamber to myself," writes Johnson, "which in eleven rooms to forty people was more than my share. How the company and the family were distributed is not easy to tell. Macleod, the chieftain of Dunvegan, and Boswell and I had all single chambers on the first floor. There remained eight rooms only for at least seven-and-thirty lodgers. I suppose they put up temporary beds in the dining-room, where they stowed all the young ladies. There was a room above stairs with six beds, in which they put ten men." The patriarchal life was so complete that in this island, with a population estimated at nine hundred,[1] there was neither justice of the peace nor constable. Even in Skye there was but one magistrate, and, so late as forty years ago, but one policeman. Raasay is still without a justice. The people, I was told, settle all their disputes among themselves, and keep clear of crime. Much of the land is still held on the old tribal system. "I have ascertained," writes Sir Henry Maine, "that the families which formed the village communities only just extinct in the Western Highlands had the lands of the village re-distributed among them by lot at fixed intervals of time."[2] In Raasay there are little plots of land which every year are still distributed by lot. So small are they, and so close together that it often happens that five or six families are all at the same time getting in their harvest on a strip not much larger than a couple of lawn tennis grounds.

Boswell with three Highland gentlemen spent one day in exploring the island, and in climbing to the top of Dun Can, or

---

[1] This was Johnson's estimate, based on the number of men who took part in the Rebellion of 1745. The population in 1881 was 750.

Raasay's Cap, as sailors called the mountain, to whom far away at sea it was a conspicuous landmark. On the top they danced a Highland reel. If we may trust the statement of a young English tourist, the dance was just as enjoyable, though there were no ladies for partners. "The Scotch," he writes, "admire the reel for its own merit alone. A Scotchman comes into an assembly room as he would into a field of exercise, dances till he is literally tired, possibly without ever looking at his partner. In most countries the men have a partiality for dancing with a woman: but here I have frequently seen four gentlemen perform one of these reels seemingly

DUN CAN.

with the same pleasure as if they had had the most sprightly girl for a partner. They give you the idea that they could with equal glee cast off round a joint-stool or set to a corner cupboard."[1] Beyond Dun Can to the north-west the travellers visited the ruins of the old castle, once the residence of the lairds of Raasay. On their return from their walk of four-and-twenty miles over very rugged ground, "we piqued ourselves," Boswell writes, "at not being outdone at the nightly ball by our less active friends, who had remained at home."

Of the ancient crosses which he mentions I fear but one is

[1] E. Topham's *Letter from Edinburgh*, p. 264.

remaining. Martin, who looked upon them as pyramids to the deceased ladies of the family, found eight. Malcolm Macleod thought that they were "false sentinels—a common deception to make invaders imagine an island better guarded." The learned M'Queen maintained that they "marked the boundaries of the sacred territory within which an asylum was to be had." In this opinion Boswell concurred.

Delightful as the mansion at Raasay seemed to the travellers, with "the rough ocean and the rocky land, the beating billows and the howling storm without, while within was plenty and elegance, beauty and gaiety the song and the dance," yet it had seen another sight only seven-and-twenty years earlier. In the island the Young Pretender "in his distress was hidden for two nights, and the king's troops burnt the whole country, and killed some of the cattle. You may guess," continues Johnson, "at the opinions that prevail in this country; they are, however, content with fighting for their king; they do not drink for him. We had no foolish healths." Pleased as our travellers were with their four days' residence here, in the midst of storms and rain, how much would their pleasure have been increased could they have seen it as I saw it in the bright summer weather! No one who visited it then would have said with Johnson that "it has little that can detain a traveller, except the laird and his family." It has almost everything that Nature can give in the delightfulness of scenery and situation.¹ Like Boswell, as I gazed upon it, I might "for a moment have doubted whether unhappiness had any place in Raasay;" but, like him, I might "soon have had the delusion dispelled," by recalling Johnson's lines :—

"Yet hope not life from grief or danger free,
Nor think the doom of man reversed for thee.

PORTREE AND KINGSBURGH (SEPTEMBER 12-13).

Much as Johnson had delighted in the patriarchal life at Raasay, yet after four days' stay he became impatient to move. "There was," writes Boswell, "so numerous a company, mostly young people, there was such a flow of familiar talk, so much noise,

¹ I am much indebted to Mr. A. L. Stewart, of Raasay, for his kindness in showing me what-ever there was to see, and for a present of the photograph of the old castle.

and so much singing and dancing, that little opportunity was left for his energetic conversation. He seemed sensible of this; for when I told him how happy they were at having him there, he said, 'Yet we have not been able to entertain them much.'" The weather, which had been very wet and stormy, cleared up on the morning of September 12. "Though it was Sunday," says Johnson, "we thought it proper to snatch the opportunity of a calm day." A row of some five or six miles brought them to Portree in Skye, a harbour whose name commemorated the visit of King James V. The busy little town on the top of the cliff, with its

PORTREE HARBOUR.

Court House, hotels, banks, and shops, which has grown up at the end of the land-locked harbour, did not then exist. Sir James Macdonald, "the Marcellus of Scotland," as Boswell called him, had intended to build a village there, but by his untimely death the design had come to nothing. There seems to have been little more than the public-house at which the travellers dined. "It was," Johnson believed, "the only one of the island." He forgot, however, as Boswell pointed out to him when he read his narrative, another at Sconser, and a third at Dunvegan. "These," Boswell adds, "are the only inns properly so called. There are many huts where whisky is sold."[1] On the evening which I spent at Portree,

[1] Croker's *B. & J.* p. 826.

a company of Highland volunteers were going through their yearly inspection, in tartan plaids and kilts, with the bagpipes playing as only bagpipes can. Had it been as it was in the days of their forefathers, when twelve Highlanders and a bagpipe made a rebellion, there was ample provision made here for at least five or six. Each volunteer, in addition to his guilt as a rebel, both for the arms which he carried, and the garb which he wore, would have been liable to be sent off by summary process to serve as a common soldier. But happily we live in loyal days, and under milder laws.

KINGSBURGH.

These bold citizen-soldiers ran but one risk, which no doubt was averted by a good-natured and sympathetic magistracy. To a fine of five shillings for being drunk and disorderly some of them certainly became exposed as the evening wore away. Let us hope that their excess was little more than an excess of loyalty, in drinking the health of a Hanoverian queen.

At Portree our travellers took horse for Kingsburgh, a farmhouse on Loch Snizort, whither they went, though a little off their road, in order to see Flora Macdonald. She had married a gentleman of the same clan, and so had not changed her name. "Here," writes Johnson, "I had the honour of saluting the far-famed Miss

Flora Macdonald, who conducted the Prince, dressed as her maid, through the English forces, from the island of Lewis; and when she came to Skye, dined with the English officers, and left her maid below. She must then have been a very young lady—she is now not old—of a pleasing person and elegant behaviour. She told me that she thought herself honoured by my visit; and I am sure that whatever regard she bestowed on me was liberally repaid." Boswell describes her as "a little woman of a genteel appearance, and uncommonly mild and well-bred. To see Dr. Samuel Johnson, the great champion of the English Tories, salute Miss Flora Macdonald in the Isle of Skye was a striking sight." By *salute* I have little doubt that both Boswell and Johnson meant *kiss*. Johnson in his *Dictionary* gives it as the third meaning of the word, though he cites no authority for the usage. "The Scotch," wrote Topham in 1774, "have still the custom of salutation on introduction to strangers. It very seldom happens that the salute is a voluntary one, and it frequently is the cause of disgust and embarrassment to the fair sex."[1] By the uncouth appearance of the man who thus saluted her, Flora Macdonald might with good reason have been astonished, for "the news had reached her that Mr. Boswell was coming to Skye, and one Mr. Johnson, a young English buck, with him." Her husband, "a large stately man, with a steady, sensible countenance," who was going to try his fortune in America, was perhaps for that reason the more careless of obeying the laws of the country he was leaving. This evening he wore the Highland costume. "He had his tartan plaid thrown about him, a large blue bonnet with a knot of black riband like a cockade, a brown short coat of a kind of duffil, a tartan waistcoat with gold buttons and gold button-holes, a bluish philibeg, and tartan hose." The bed-curtains of the room in which our travellers slept were also of tartan. Johnson's bed had whatever fame could attach to it through its having been occupied for one night "by the grandson of the unfortunate King James the Second," to borrow Boswell's description of him. The grandson, before many years passed over his head, proved not unworthy of the grandfather—equally mean and equally selfish. 'The happy failure of the rebels hindered him from displaying his vices, with a kingdom for his stage. His worthlessness, which though it might have been suspected from his stock, could not have been known in his youth,

[1] *Letters from Edinburgh*, pp. 34, 35.

takes away nothing, however, from the just fame of Flora Macdonald, "whose name will be mentioned in history, and, if courage and fidelity be virtues, mentioned with honour." Johnson, after recounting how "the sheets which the Prince used were never put to any meaner offices, but were wrapped up by the Lady of the house, and at last, according to her desire, were laid round her in her grave," ends the passage with much satisfaction, by observing: "These are not Whigs." Upon the table in the room he left a piece of paper "on which he had written with his pencil these words: *Quantum cedat virtutibus aurum*."[1] He was thinking, no doubt, of the reward of £30,000 set upon Charles Edward's head, and of the fidelity of the poor Highlanders who one and all refused to betray him. To more than fifty people he was forced in his wanderings to trust his life, many of them "in the lowest paths of fortune," and not one of them proved faithless. It was well for him that he had not had to trust to fifty hangers on of a Court.

The old house in which he had taken shelter for one night, and where Boswell and Johnson were so hospitably received, where they heard from their hostess the strange story of her adventures this interesting old house no longer exists. Some of the trees which surround the modern residence must be old enough to have seen not only our two travellers, but also the fugitive Prince. As we looked upon it from the opposite shore of the narrow loch it seemed a pleasant spot, nearly facing the west, sheltered from the east by hills, and embosomed in trees, with meadows in front sloping down to the sea. In the rear rose barren dreary hills, but all their lower slopes were green with grass and with the young crops of oats. Far down the loch the green slopes ended in a steep rocky coast. In the distance the mountains of Lewis fringed the northern sky. The steep headland on which we sat was beautiful with grasses and flowers and ferns and heather. Of wild flowers we gathered no less than thirty-six varieties on this one small spot. We found even a lingering primrose, though June was rapidly drawing to its close. How different were our thoughts as we watched this peaceful scene from those which, one hundred and forty-three years earlier, had troubled the watchers as the young Wanderer slept! As the morning wore on, and he did not awake, one of them, in her alarm lest the soldiers should surprise him, roused her father, who was also in hiding, and begged that "they

[1] "With virtue weighed what worthless trash is gold."

should not remain here too long. He said, 'Let the poor man repose himself after his fatigues! and as for me, I care not, though they take off this old grey head ten or eleven years sooner than I should die in the course of nature.' He then wrapped himself in the bed clothes, and again fell fast asleep." That same afternoon the two fugitives set off for Portree, where the Prince took boat for Raasay.

DUNVEGAN CASTLE (SEPTEMBER 13-21).

Had our travellers ridden the whole distance from Kingsburgh to Dunvegan they would have travelled a weary way in rounding

THE FERRY TO KINGSBURGH.

Lochs Snizort and Grishinish. But they sent their horses by land to a point on the other shore of the further loch, and crossed over themselves in Macdonald of Kingsburgh's boat. "When," said Johnson, "we take into computation what we have saved and what we have gained by this agreeable sail, it is a great deal." They had still some miles of dreary riding through the most melancholy of moorlands. There were no roads or even paths. "A guide," writes Boswell, "explored the way, much in the same manner as, I suppose, is pursued in the wilds of America, by observing certain marks known only to the inhabitants." In some places the ground

was so boggy that it would not bear the weight of horse and rider, and they were forced to dismount and walk. It was late in the afternoon when they reached Dunvegan Castle "that hospitable home where Johnson "tasted lotus, and was in danger," as he said, "of forgetting that he was ever to depart." This ancient seat of the Macleods was less beautiful, but far more interesting as he saw it than it is at the present day. The barrenness of nature has been covered with a luxuriant growth, and the land all around "which presented nothing but wild, moorish, hilly, and craggy appearances," is now finely wooded. But while the setting is so greatly improved, the ancient building which is enshrined has suffered beneath the hand of a restorer. It is true that some great improvements have been made. The wing which had so long been left unfinished, through a superstitious fear that the owner would not long outlive the completion—"this skeleton of a castle," as Johnson describes it—has been completed. A fine approach has been formed from the side of the land. But in the alterations which were made about fifty years ago an architect was employed who must surely have acquired his mischievous art in erecting sham fortresses on the banks of the Clyde for the wealthy traders of Glasgow. It is greatly to be wished that a judicious earthquake would bring to the ground his pepper-box turrets. Nevertheless, in spite of all that he has done—and he did his worst,—it still remains a noble pile, nobly placed. It is built on the rocky shore of a small bay, and well sheltered from the violence of the waves by an island which lies across the mouth, and by headlands on both sides. Through narrow inlets are seen the open waters of Loch Follart, and beyond them the everlasting hills. We saw it on a fine summer evening, when the long seaweeds were swaying in the gentle heaving of the tiny waves. Outside the bay two yachts were furling their sails, for the morrow was the day of rest. The sea-birds were hovering and screaming all around. A great heron was standing on a rock, with his white breast reflected in the water. A little to the north a long mast was lying on the beach, washed up from a wreck which, black with seaweed, is discovered at low tide. The old castle, the finely wooded hills, the rocks covered with fern and heath, the clear reflections in the sea of the mountains across the loch, the island, the inlets, the white sails of the yachts, the tranquil beauty of the summer evening—all moved us deeply. One thing only was wanting. The delightful weather which the country had so long enjoyed had silenced "Rorie More's Nurse." There was not water enough in it to have caught that good knight's ear; still less to have lulled him to sleep. Johnson had seen it "in full perfection." It was "a noble cascade," he said. But he paid dearly for the fineness of the sight; for during the whole of his stay the weather was dreary, with high winds and violent rain. "We filled up the time as we could," he writes; "sometimes by talk, sometimes by reading. I have never wanted books in the Isle of

RORIE MORE'S NURSE.

Skye." So comfortably was he situated that he could hardly be persuaded to move on. "Here we settled," he writes, "and did not spoil the present hour with thoughts of departure." When on Saturday Boswell proposed that they should leave on the following Monday, when their week would be completed, he replied: "No, Sir, I will not go before Wednesday. I will have some more of this good."

He was fortunate in his hosts. The Laird, a young man of nineteen, quickly won his friendship. He had been the pupil at University College, Oxford, of George Strahan, who had been known to Johnson from his childhood. Boswell describes Macleod as "a most promising youth, who with a noble spirit struggles with difficulties, and endeavours to preserve his people. He has been left with an incumbrance of forty thousand pounds debt, and annuities to the amount of thirteen hundred pounds a year. Dr. Johnson said, 'If he gets the better of all this, he'll be a hero; and I hope he will. I have not met with a young man who had more desire to learn, or who has learnt more. I have seen nobody that I wish more to do a kindness to than Macleod." According to Knox, who was an impartial witness, he was an excellent landlord. Distressed though he was by this heavy burthen of debt, "he raised no rents, turned out no tenants, used no man with severity, and in all respects, and under the most pressing exigences, maintained the character of a liberal and humane friend of mankind."[1] He formed at one time the design of writing his own Life. Unhappily he left but a fragment. His father had died early, so that on the death of his grandfather, the year before Johnson's visit, he had succeeded to the property—the estates in Skye, the nine inhabited isles and the islands uninhabited almost beyond number. "He did not know to within twenty square miles the extent of his territories in Skye." But vast as these domains were, the revenue which they produced was but small. One estate of eighty thousand acres was only rented at six hundred pounds a year.

"His grandfather," he writes, "had entered upon his inheritance in the most prosperous condition; but the course of his life was expensive, his temper convivial and hospitable, and he continued to impair his fortune till his death. He was the first of our family who was led to leave the patriarchal government of the clan, and to mix in the pursuits and ambition of the world. He had always been a most beneficent chieftain, but in the beginning of 1772, his necessities having lately induced him to raise his rents, he became much alarmed by the new spirit which had reached his clan. Aged and infirm he was unable to apply the remedy in person; he devolved the task on me, and gave me for an assistant our nearest male relation, Colonel Macleod, of Talisker. The estate was loaded with debt, encumbered with a numerous issue from himself and my father, and charged with some jointures. His tenants had lost in that severe winter above a third of their cattle. My friend and I were empowered to grant such deductions in the rents as might seem reasonable; but we found it terrible to decide between the justice to creditors, the necessities of an ancient family, and the distresses of an impoverished tenantry. I called

---

[1] Knox's *Tour through the Highlands*, p. 142. "In the year seventy-one they had a severe season remembered by the name of the Black Spring, from which the island has not yet recovered. The snow lay long upon the ground, a calamity hardly known before.' Johnson's *Works*, ix. 74.

the people together; I laid before them the situation of our family; I acknowledged the hardships under which they laboured; I reminded them of the manner in which their ancestors had lived with mine; I combated their passion for America; I promised to live among them. I desired every district to point out some of their most respected men to settle with me every claim, and I promised to do everything for their relief which in reason I could. Our labour was not in vain. We gave considerable abatements in the rents; few emigrated; and the clan conceived the most lively attachment to me, which they most effectually manifested.

'I remained at home till the end of 1774, but I consider this as the most gloomy period of my life. Educated in a liberal manner, bred with ambition, fond of society, I found myself in confinement in a remote corner of the world; without any hope of extinguishing the debts of my family, or of ever emerging from poverty and obscurity. I had also the torment of seeing my mother and sisters immured with me.

"In 1774 [1773] Dr. Samuel Johnson, with his companion, Mr. Boswell, visited our dreary regions; it was my good fortune to be enabled to practise the virtue of hospitality on this occasion. The learned traveller spent a fortnight at Dunvegan; and indeed amply repaid our cares to please him by the most instructive and entertaining conversation. I procured for him the company of the most learned clergymen and sagacious inhabitants of the islands."¹

Macleod's high praise of Johnson is in curious contradiction to Sir Walter Scott's account, that " when winter-bound at Dunvegan, Johnson's temper became most execrable, and beyond all endurance save that of his guide (Boswell)." ² Mr. Croker, on receiving this account from Sir Walter, applied to the Laird's son and successor, " who assured him emphatically they were all *delighted* with him." ³ Nevertheless, as I have already stated,⁴ the young ladies of the family do not seem to have shared in this delight. The true Johnsonian must look upon them as " a set of wretched un-idea'd girls," and so forgive their want of taste.

Macleod, two or three years after our traveller's visit, raised a company of his own Highlanders, and entered the army. In the war against our colonists in America he and his wife, who had accompanied him, were taken prisoners. In their captivity they made the acquaintance and won the friendship of George Washington. Let us hope that the heart of the founder of the great American Commonwealth was softened towards the author of *Taxation no Tyranny* by the anecdotes which he heard of him from his warm friend, the young Scottish chief. On his return home he raised the second battalion of the forty-second Highlanders, and served with distinction in India as their colonel. Zoffany painted him in his soldier's dress, surrounded with elephants,

¹ Croker's *Boswell*, ed. 1835, iv. 322-9. ² Croker's *Boswell*, p. 334.
³ Croker Correspondence, ii. 33. ⁴ *Ante*, p. 3.

camels, and Hindoos, with Highland scenery in the background. Just before he started for the East he dined at the house of one of his *tacksmen*, or chief tenants, "who said that all the dishes should be the produce of Macleod's estate and the shores thereof. Amongst a profusion of other dishes there were thirteen different kinds of fish."[1] He died in 1802 at the early age of forty-six.

Fortunate as Johnson was in having this amiable and high-spirited youth for his host, scarcely less fortunate was he in his hostess, the Laird's mother, Lady Macleod. The title which she bore was one of courtesy. Up to this time the wives of Highland lairds, and also of Scotch judges, seem commonly to have been addressed as *Lady*. Johnson's hostess at Lochbuie, the wife of the laird, is called Lady Lochbuie by Boswell. The change to the modern usage had, however, begun; for Ramsay of Ochtertyre, speaking of the year 1769, says that, "Somebody asked Lord Auchinleck before his second marriage if the lady was to be called Mrs. Boswell, according to the modern fashion."[2] Johnson was not wholly a stranger to his hostess. "I had once," he writes, "attracted her notice in London." She was able to render his stay pleasant, for from her long residence in England, "she knew all the arts of southern elegance, and all the modes of English economy." In his talk she took great delight, though when one day she heard him maintain "that no man was naturally good more than a wolf, and no woman either," she said in a low voice, "This is worse than Swift.'" Knox, who visited Dunvegan in 1786 records the following anecdote:—

"Lady Macleod, who had repeatedly helped Dr. Johnson to sixteen dishes or upwards of tea, asked him if a small basin would not save him trouble, and be more agreeable. 'I wonder, Madam,' answered he roughly, 'why all the ladies ask me such impertinent questions. It is to save yourselves trouble, Madam, and not me.' The lady was silent and went on with her task."

It is not likely that Knox had the story at first hand, for when he visited Dunvegan, the Castle was occupied by a Major Alexander Macleod, who had married a daughter of Flora Macdonald. It is probable, therefore, that Lady Macleod was not living there at the time. The number of cups of tea may have grown as the story passed from one to another. We shall find in the next chapter that at Ulinish Johnson was reported to have

---

[1] Knox's *Tour*, p. 152.   [2] *Scotland and Scotsmen of the Eighteenth Century*, i. 173. Knox's *Tour*, p. 143.

exceeded even this feat in tea drinking. Lady Eldon used to
relate that one evening at Oxford she had helped him to fifteen.
Cumberland, who was not famed for accuracy, did not go beyond
a dozen as the number supplied to the great man by Mrs. Cumberland. Short even of this Johnson might very well "have turned
his cup," as he had done at Aberbrothick, and muttered, "*claudite
jam rivos, pueri.*"

Lady Macleod was discontented with the barrenness of Dunvegan, and longed to move the seat of the family to a spot about
five miles off, "where she could make gardens and other ornaments. She insisted that the rock was very inconvenient; that
there was no place near it where a good garden could be made;
that it must always be a rude place; that it was a *Herculean*
labour to make a dinner here." "I was vexed," writes Boswell,
"to find the alloy of modern refinement in a lady who had so much
old family spirit. 'I have all the comforts and conveniences of life
upon it. I said, 'but never leave Rorie More's cascade.' 'It is
very well for you,' she replied, 'who have a fine place, and everything easy, to talk thus, and think of chaining honest folks to a
rock. You would not live upon it yourself.' 'Yes, Madam,' said
I, 'I would live upon it, were I Laird of Macleod, and should be
unhappy if I were not upon it.' JOHNSON (with a strong voice and
most determined manner). 'Madam, rather than quit the old rock,
Boswell would live in the pit; he would make his bed in the
dungeon.' The lady was puzzled a little. She still returned to
her pretty farm—rich ground—fine garden. 'Madam,' said Dr.
Johnson, 'were they in Asia, I would not leave the rock.'"

Her visitors were in the right. The scene was too noble a
one to be lightly deserted. There was no need to go five miles
for trees and gardens. The reproaches which Johnson cast on the
Scotch for their carelessness in adorning their homes did not here
fall on deaf ears. His host and his host's son planted largely, and
the fruit of his advice and of their judicious labours is seen in the
beautiful woods and shrubberies which surround the Castle.
Rorie More's Cascade is almost hidden by trees. A Dutch garden
has been formed, where, under the shelter of the thick beech hedge
which encloses it, the roses bloom. Close to the ruins of an ancient
chapel, with glimpses through the trees of the waters of the Loch,
a conservatory has been built. Had Johnson seen the beautiful and
rare flowers which grow in it, he would surely never have main-

tained that "a green-house is a childish thing." What a change has come since the day when he wrote that "the country about Dunvegan is rough and barren. There are no trees except in the orchard, which is a low sheltered spot, surrounded with a wall." The rough old fellow passed over the land with his strong common sense and his vigorous reproofs, and the rudeness of nature has been tamed, and its barrenness changed into luxuriance. He deserved better of mankind even than he "who made two ears of corn, or two blades of grass, to grow upon a spot of ground where only one grew before;"[1] for he made trees and flowers to grow where before there had been none. He did that which a king of Scotland had tried to do and failed. James the Fifth's command that round every house plantations should be made had resulted, I was told, in the few trees which Johnson saw. But where the king's could be almost counted on the fingers of the two hands, Johnson's cover whole hill-sides. I was informed by Miss Macleod, of Macleod, for whose kindness I am most grateful, that she had no doubt that it was his reproaches which stirred up her grandfather to plant so widely. How luxuriantly nature can deck the ground when she is aided by art, was seen in the strange variety of flowers which we noticed in the grounds. Two seasons seemed to be mingled into one, for we found at the same time wild roses, the hawthorn, blue bells, cuckoo flowers, heather, lupins, laburnums, and rhododendrons.

In ancient days the only access to the castle, says Sir Walter Scott, was "from the sea by a subterranean staircase, partly arched, partly cut in the rock, which winding up through the cliff opened into the court."[2] These steps Johnson oddly describes as "a pair of stairs," just as if they were in an Oxford college or the Temple. When the tide was up access was cut off, so that a visitor who had arrived by land must at the very end of his journey have taken boat in order to gain the entrance. A little above the lower gate, on the side of the passage, there was an old well, with uncovered mouth. At the christening of the present laird, one of the guests who had drunk too freely, going down the steps to his boat, fell in and was drowned. The well was at once enclosed, and has never been used since. Even in Johnson's time its water, though not brackish in spite of its being so near to the sea, was not much used. The stream which formed Rorie More's Cascade was thought to

[1] Swift: *Voyage to Brobdingnag*, chap. vii.   [2] Croker: *Boswell*, p. 342.

afford a purer supply. It was not by this staircase that our travellers entered the castle, but by a long flight of steps which the last laird had made on the side of the land. They were not guarded by hand-rails. Many years ago a milkmaid coming up them with her pails on a stormy day, was carried over by a high wind, and much hurt. They have given place to the present approach by a carriage-road carried over the chasm which cut off the castle from the neighbouring land.

On the walls of the " stately dining-room " where our travellers were first received, I saw hanging some fine portraits by Raeburn, their host and his wife and their eldest son, a lad with a sweet honest face, who was lost with his ship, the Royal Charlotte, in the Bay of Naples. Near them hang " the wicked laird " and his two wives. There is a tradition that his first wife had fled from him on account of his cruelty, but had been enticed back by a friendly letter. When her husband had caught her, he starved her to death in the dungeon. It was no doubt the sight of these pictures which one day at table led the company to talk of portraits; when Johnson maintained that "their chief excellence is being like. One would like," he added, " to see how Rorie More looked. Truth, Sir, is of the greatest value in these things."

In the same room stands a handsome old sideboard, bearing the date of 1603. Though it goes back to the year of the union of the two Crowns, yet of all the festive gatherings which it has witnessed, perhaps there is none that was more striking than that evening when the Highland gentlemen listened to Johnson's "full strain of eloquence. We were," writes Boswell, " a jovial company at supper. The laird, surrounded by so many of his clan, was to me a pleasing sight. They listened with wonder and pleasure while Dr. Johnson harangued." It was very likely in this same room that Sir Walter Scott breakfasted that August morning forty-one years later, " when he woke under the castle of Dunvegan. I had," he writes, " sent a card to the laird of Macleod, who came off before we were dressed, and carried us to his castle to breakfast."[1]

DRAWING-ROOM, DUNVEGAN CASTLE.

The noble drawing-room, with the deep recesses for the windows in walls nine feet thick, is not the one described by Boswell. The drawing-room which he saw " had formerly been," he says, " the bed-chamber of Sir Roderick Macleod, and he chose it because behind it there was a cascade, the sound of which disposed him to sleep." At the time of Sir Walter Scott's visit it had again become a bed-room, for here he slept on a stormy night. He had accepted, he says, " the courteous offer of the haunted apartment," and this

[1] Lockhart, v. 2, p. 192.

was the room which was given him. "An autumnal blast, sometimes clear, sometimes driving mist before it, swept along the troubled billows of the lake, which it occasionally concealed and by fits disclosed. The waves rushed in wild disorder on the shore, and covered with foam the steep pile of rocks, which rising from the sea in forms something resembling the human figure have obtained the name of Macleod's Maidens. The voice of an angry

PORTRAIT OF SARAH, LADY MACLEOD, BY RAEBURN.

cascade, termed the nurse of Rorie More, was heard from time to time mingling its notes with those of wind and wave. Such was the haunted room at Dunvegan; and as such it well deserved a less sleepy inhabitant."[1] This account Sir Walter wrote many years later from memory. The rocks which he saw were not Macleod's Maidens; from them he was separated by nearly ten miles of mountains and lochs.

In the present drawing-room a small portrait of Johnson, as-

[1] Lockhart's Scott, iv. 305.

cribed to Reynolds, but, as I was told, by Zoffany, hangs in a place
of honour. Here, too, is kept his letter of thanks to Macleod,
endorsed "Dr. Johnston's." He wrote it "on the margin of the
sea, waiting for a boat and a wind. Boswell," he continues "grows
impatient; but the kind treatment which I find wherever I go
makes me leave with some heaviness of heart an island which I am
not very likely to see again." Among other treasures in the same
room is Rorie More's horn, "a large cow's horn, with the mouth of
it ornamented with silver curiously carved. It holds rather more
than a bottle and a half. Every laird of Macleod, it is said, must,
as a proof of his manhood, drink it off full of claret without laying
it down." It is curious that Boswell makes no mention of the

ancient cup described by Scott in a note to the second canto of
The Lord of the Isles, or of the fairy flag. "Here," writes Pennant, "is preserved the *Braolanch shi*, or fairy-flag of the family,
bestowed on it by the queen of the fairies. She blessed it with
powers of the first importance, which were to be exerted on only
three occasions; on the last, after the end was obtained, an invisible
being is to carry off standard and standard-bearer, never more to be
seen. The flag has been produced thrice. The first time in an
engagement against the Clan-Ronald, to whose sight the Macleods
were multiplied ten-fold; the second preserved the heir, being
then produced to save the longings of the lady; and the third
time to save my own; but it was so tattered, that Titania
did not seem to think it worth sending for. This was a super-

stition derived from the Norwegian ancestry of the house."[1] Sir Walter describes it as "a pennon of silk, with something like round red rowan-berries wrought upon it."[2] In the gallery I saw Rorie More's claymore, "of a prodigious size," as Boswell called it. He wrote this some years before he heard from old Mr Edwards that Johnson, when an undergraduate of Oxford, "would not let them say prodigious at college, for even then he was deli-

ARMOUR.

cate in language." If it is not prodigious, nevertheless it is a real *claymore* or *great sword*, for that is what the Gaelic word means. Unfortunately the point is broken off. The sight of it did not console me for my disappointment at finding that Rorie More's bed is no longer in existence, with the inscription above it, " Sir Roderick M'Leod of Dunvegan, Knight. God send good rest." I would rather have seen it than a dozen swords, whether great or small.

Johnson slept in the Fairy Bedroom in the Fairy Tower. The legend runs that this part of the castle was built 450 years ago by

[1] Pennant's *Voyage to the Hebrides*, 1774, p. 295.   Lockhart's *Life of Scott*, iv. 304.

that very uncommon being, a fairy grandmother. Godmothers among the fairies have often been heard of, but grandmothers, we believe, never before or since. Had Puck peeped in and seen Johnson wearing his wig turned inside out and the wrong end in front as a substitute for a night-cap,[1] he might well have exclaimed that his mistress kept a monster, not only rear but in "her close and consecrated bower." From this room a winding stone staircase led up to the battlements, but without mounting so high Johnson commanded a fine view. From his window he could see, far

MACLEOD'S TABLES.

away across the lochs, Macleod's Tables, two lofty hills with round flat tops, which on all sides form a striking landmark. Much nearer was the Gallows Hill, where in the bad old times many a poor wretch, dragged from his dark and dismal dungeon, caught his last sight of loch and mountain and heath, doomed to death by the laird. Only thirty-three years before our travellers' visit a man was hanged there by the grandfather of their host. He was a Macdonald who had murdered his father, and escaped into Macleod's country. But the old tribal feuds were long since over, and

[1] See *ante*, p. 3.

he found no safety there. At Macdonald's request he was at once seized and hanged.[1]

The dungeons and the pit are not described by either Boswell or Johnson, though the sight of them, we would willingly believe, must have roused their indignation. In these old castles there are few things more shocking than the close neighbourhood of festivity and misery. It shows a callousness to human suffering which almost passes belief. If a prisoner is in a remote part of a great castle, the imagination then must come into play to bring his sufferings before the mind; but when he is close at hand, when his sorrowful sighing is only kept by the thickness of a single wall from mingling with the prattle of children and the merriment of feasters, then the heart must be hard indeed which is not touched. At Dunvegan a door to the left opened into a pleasant sitting-room, and to the right into the chief dungeon. In it there was no window, not even one of those narrow slits by which a few rays can struggle in. But there was something worse even than the dungeon. In the floor there was an opening by which the unhappy prisoner could be lowered into a deep pit. Here he would dwell in ever-during dark, never cheered by the hurried glimpse of daylight such as broke the long night in the prison above whenever the jailer paid his visit. The door of the other dungeon—for there was yet another—is in the wall of a bedroom, which is furnished in so old a style that it is likely enough that the curious bed and hangings were gazed at by many a prisoner as he was hurried by.

As we wandered through these old rooms and staircases and passages, we were told of a poor woman from St. Kilda, who like ourselves was shown over the castle. As she went on she became so bewildered by the number of the rooms, that she begged to be allowed to keep fast hold of the hand of the person who was conducting her, for fear she might get lost and never find her way out. The story called to my mind a man from the same remote island mentioned by Martin. He was taken to Glasgow, and though in those days it was but a small town, nevertheless he was so much scared that in like manner he clung to his guide's hand as long as he was in the streets.[2] The poor woman must have breathed more freely when she at length reached the court-yard and looked out over the familiar sea. The platform, then, no doubt was rough

[1] See *p. ?* in the chapter on Lochbuie for an account of the hereditary jurisdictions.
[2] Martin's *Western Island.*, p. 297.

with stone, but now it is soft with green turf. I looked there for the false stone cannons which Boswell mentions, but I learnt that they had been moved to the top of one of the towers. In their place are some of iron, venerable by their antiquity, but unfit for service. Against one of the low walls which enclose this pleasant court leans a piece of old sculpture, the effigy probably of some lady of the family.

Three or four miles down the loch, and out of sight of the castle, lies the little island of Isa or Issay, "which Macleod said he would give to Dr. Johnson, on condition of his residing on it three months in the year; nay, one month. Dr. Johnson was highly amused with the fancy. He talked a great deal of this island; how he would build a house there—how he would fortify it—how he would have cannon—how he would plant—how he would sally out, and *take* the Isle of Muck; and then he laughed with uncommon glee, and could hardly leave off. Macleod encouraged the fancy of Dr. Johnson's becoming owner of an island; told him that it was the practice in that country to name every man by his lands, and begged leave to drink to him in that mode, '*Island Isa,* your health.' Ulinish, Talisker, M'Queen, and I all joined in our different manners, while Dr. Johnson bowed to each with much good humour." To Mrs. Thrale he wrote: " Macleod has offered me an island; if it were not too far off I should hardly refuse it; my island would be pleasanter than Brighthelmstone if you and my master could come to it; but I cannot think it pleasant to live quite alone.

ELLEVE.

'Obliitusque meorum, obliviscendus et illis.'[1]

Much as he wished to visit it, he was hindered even from seeing it

---

[1] "Your friends forgetting, by your friends forgot."
Francis's *Horace, Epistles,* i. xi. 9.

by the stormy weather. We were more fortunate, for though we
did not land yet we saw it from the high ground on the opposite
shore. The greater part of the way to this spot a rough road has
been made along which we drove, passing a great heronry. It
was curious to watch the huge nests and the great birds in the
trees. For nearly three miles of country they were the chief
inhabitants. Island Isa would certainly have lived in great
solitude, for after we had passed the gamekeeper's cottage close to
the castle, we saw no signs of habitation except the herons' nests,
till we reached a farm house nearly three miles off. Here the road
ended. In the little garden stood some large laburnum trees, all
drooping with their golden flowers. Our way led across a wide

HERONRY.

heath to a fine breezy
headland. Below us
another stretch of
heath-land sloped
down to the shore of
the loch. On the
other side of a narrow
channel lay Isa, with
fine rocky cliffs to the
west and the north,
but lying open to the
south-east. It was
Midsummer Day.
The sea was calm, a
blue haze softened the outline of the neighbouring hills, but let the
mountains in the farther Hebrides be but faintly seen. The little
isle lay before us with no signs on it of human habitation. Buchanan
describes it as "fertilis frugum,"[1] and Martin says that it was
"fruitful in corn;"[2] but it must be many a year since the plough
turned up its soil. It is a land of pastures. In the hot, drowsy
air there was nothing but the song of the lark and the bleating
of the lambs "to break the silence of the seas." Far below us
a shepherd with his two dogs was gathering a small flock of sheep.
They, and the larks, and the sea-birds were the only things that
seemed alive. We had reached, as it were, the antipodes of "that
full tide of human existence" in which Johnson delighted. For
not a single day would he have endured the lonely dignity of

[1] Buchanani *Opera Omnia*, ed. 1725, i. 40.   [2] Martin's *Western Islands*, p. 170.

ISLAND ISA, OFFERED TO DR. JOHNSON BY THE LAIRD OF M'LEOD.

such a domain. The road to the headland had not been quite free from danger, for on our return we found coiled up asleep on the path half hidden in the heather an adder. It was killed by a blow of a stick which I had brought with me from Corsica.

On the Sunday, which we spent at Dunvegan, we chanced to see a sight interesting in itself, but doubly so to anyone who came from the South. The Free Kirk congregations of three parishes met in a field to take the Sacrament. It was one of the three great

SACRAMENT SUNDAY.

religious gatherings of the year, and the people flocked in from all the country side. Many came by water from far-off glens that sloped down to the sea. From the windows of our inn we watched the heavy boats fully laden coming round a distant point, and rowing slowly up to a ledge of rocks just below us. In one we counted twenty-one people. Women as well as men tugged at the oars, and when the boat was run aground helped to drag it up the beach. When this was done, they all set about completing their toilettes. The beach served them for their tiring-house, though it was a good deal more open to view than a hawthorn brake. In one of the boats we had noticed a man distinguished from all the rest by a tall black hat, *pictate gravem ac meritis*. To him had been entrusted the clean white collars and neckties of the rowers. Many of the men knelt down while their wives fastened them on for them and smoothed their hair. One man even went so far as to put on his shirt in public. The women too, who were almost all in black, had their dresses to arrange, for in the boats they had kept their skirts tucked up. Some of the girls even had to get their bustles adjusted. Carlyle or his wife once made merry over their maid-of-all-work at Chelsea, who with two or three kitchen-dusters made the best substitute she could for that monstrous and most "considerable protuberance." What would he have said had he seen the lasses in Skye thus making themselves as ridiculous as even the finest lady in town?

When at length every one was ready, the whole party moved slowly along the road towards the church. Others came driving up in light and heavy carts, while across the moors we could see single wayfarers, or more often three or four together, coming in by different paths. There was greeting of old friends and shaking of hands. The church stood on the road-side, a plain building with the manse close by. In it was gathered that part of the congregation which spoke English. On the other side of the road the ground fell away to a little brook which had eaten its way through the dark-coloured peat, and here made a sudden bend. On the other side of the water, within the bend, there was a grassy slope ending in a low ridge, and dotted with little hillocks. Here the people sat down on the ground, facing an erection which looked like a large sentry-box. It was occupied by the minister, who addressed the people in Gaelic, speaking in a kind of musical recitative which carried the voice far, and must have made every syllable distinct. It often had a very pleading and plaintive sound. Below him stood two long rows of tables, and a cross table, all covered with white cloths. On the other side of the stream by the roadside twenty carts or more were standing, while the horses were quietly grazing on the moor tethered each to an iron peg. One horse nibbled through the cord, and came up to the outskirts of the meeting, but a lad left his seat and caught it. In the background the dreary moorland sloped upwards, blackened here and there with heaps of peat drying in the sun and wind. I thought how in the old days watchers would have been posted on the most distant ridges to give warning of the approach of the persecutors. How many people were gathered together I do not know—certainly many hundreds, perhaps a thousand. All were decently, though some poorly dressed. Almost all had good warm clothing, with strong boots and shoes, none of them in holes. Very many of the women had tartan shawls, and one or two boys wore the kilt. One man I saw with tartan stockings, but the dress of all the rest differed in no respect from that worn in England. In costumes an act of uniformity seems to have been passed not only for the British Isles, but also for Western Europe in general.

A CROFTER'S HUT IN SKYE.

Travelling is losing part of its interest by the great sameness in clothing everywhere met with. There will soon, I fear, be no country left which can boast of a national dress. Though the meeting was out of doors, yet all were decent and sober in their behaviour. There was no talking or giggling, no fringe of rude lads and silly girls. Where the little moorland path ended that led from the church a table was set, on which stood a large metal basin to receive the offerings. Every one seemed to put in something, even the poorest, but in the great pile of pence and halfpence I saw but one piece of silver. When the service in the church was over, the minister and people joined those on the moor, for it was there that the Sacrament was taken by both congregation, together. The service began between eleven and twelve o'clock. Soon after four we saw the people come trooping down to the shore. The boats were launched, sails were set, and with a gentle breeze they were slowly carried down the loch and round the headland out of our sight.

ULINISH AND TALISKER (SEPTEMBER 21-25).

On the morning of Tuesday, September 21, our travellers took advantage of a break in the stormy weather to continue their journey to Ulinish, a farm-house on Loch Bracadale, occupied by

TALISKER HEAD AND ORONSAY.

"a plain honest gentleman," the Sheriff-substitute of the island. Here they passed the night, and here, if we may trust report, Johnson's powers as a drinker of tea were exerted to their utmost pitch. "Mrs. Macleod of Ulinish," writes Knox, "has not forgotten the quantity of tea which she filled out to Dr. Johnson, amounting to twenty-two dishes."[1] Surely for this outrageous statement some of those excuses are needed "by which," according to Boswell, "the exaggeration of Highland narratives is palliated." From an old tower near the house a fine view was had of the Cuillin, or Cuchullin Hills, "a prodigious range of mountains, capped with rocky pinnacles in a strange variety of shapes," which with good reason reminded Boswell of the mountains he had seen near Corte in Corsica.

[1] Knox's *Tour*, p. 139.

On the afternoon of the following day "an interval of calm sunshine," writes Johnson, "courted us out to see a cave on the shore famous for its echo. When we went into the boat one of our companions was asked in Erse by the boatmen who they were that came with him. He gave us characters, I suppose, to our advantage, and was asked in the spirit of the Highlands whether I could recite a long series of ancestors. The boatmen said, as I perceived afterwards, that they heard the cry of an English ghost. This, Boswell says, disturbed him. We came to the cave, and clambering up the rocks came to an arch open at one end, one hundred and eighty feet long, thirty broad in the broadest part, and about thirty feet high. There was no echo; such is the fidelity of reports; but I saw what I had never seen before, mussels and whelks in their natural state. There was another arch in the rock open at both ends." This cave was not on the shore of Skye, as Johnson's account seems to imply, but in the little island of Wia. From Boswell we learn that it was to an island they were taken. We were fortunate enough on our visit to this wild part of the coast to have as our guide one of Macleod's gamekeepers. " A man," to borrow from Johnson the praise which he bestowed on one of his guides, ' of great liveliness and activity, civil and ready-handed."[1] We had passed the night in the lonely little inn at Struan on the shore of an arm of Loch Bracadale, where we had found decent, if homely, lodging. In a fisherman's boat we rowed down the loch, sometimes in mid-channel and sometimes skirting the cliffs, which rose like a wall of rock to a great height above us. We passed little islets, and the mouths of caverns which filled with clouds of spray as the long rolling waves swept in from the Atlantic. On the ledges of the rocks, hovering over our heads, swimming and diving in the sea, were cormorants, puffins, oyster catchers, gulls, curlews and guillemots. We had none of us looked upon a wilder scene. When we reached our island we were pleased to find that the narrow beach at which we were to land was guarded by a huge headland from the swell of the sea. Whether we visited the cave which our travellers saw I do not feel at all sure, for it does not correspond with their description. My friend, the gamekeeper, was sure that it was the place, and I was willing to advance my faith more than half-way to meet his assertion We scrambled up

[1] For his services and for many other acts of kindness, I am indebted to the Rev. Roderick Macleod of Macleod.

the steep beach, and then over rocks covered with grass and ferns, between the sides of a narrow gorge. At the top a still steeper path led downwards to a cave, at the bottom of which we could see a glimmer of light. Scrambling upwards again, we reached a place where we could hear the sea murmuring on the other side. We afterwards climbed to the top of the cliff and sat down on the ground which formed the roof of the cavern. It was covered with heather and ferns, and patches of short grass; a pleasant breeze was blowing, the sea birds were uttering their cries, far beneath us we could hear the beating of the surge. Across the Loch on both sides, the dark cliffs rose to a great height, and in the background stood the mountains of Skye and of the mainland. Had the air been very clear, we might have seen on the north-west the wooded hills of Dunvegan.

Two or three days later, when I was giving two Highlanders an account of this cavern, one of them asked with a humorous smile: "Did they not tell you it was Prince Charlie's Cave? He must, I am thinking, have been sleeping everywhere." His companion laughed and said: "They have lately made a new one near an hotel which they have opened at ———." The innkeepers should surely show a little originality. Why should they not advertise Dr. Johnson's Cave, and show the tea-pot out of which he drank his two-and-twenty cups of tea when he picnicked there? They would do well also to discover the great cave in Skye which Martin tells of. "It is supposed," he writes, "to exceed a mile in length. The natives told me that a piper who was over-curious went in with a design to find out the length of it, and after he entered began to play on his pipe, but never returned to give an account of his progress."[1]

From Ulinish our travellers sailed up Loch Bracadale on their way to Talisker. "We had," says Boswell, "good weather and a fine sail. The shore was varied with hills, and rocks, and cornfields, and bushes, which are here dignified with the name of natural *wood*." They landed at Ferneley, a farm-house about three miles from Talisker, whither they made their way over the hills, Johnson on horseback, the rest on foot. The weather, no doubt, had been too uncertain for them to venture into the open sea round the great headland at the entrance of the loch. Skirting the stern and rock-bound coast, a few miles' sail would have brought

[1] M. Martin's *Western Island*, p. 150.

them to Talisker Bay, within sight of Colonel Macleod's house. Yet, had the wind risen, or had there been a swell from the Atlantic, they would have been forced to keep out to sea. Boswell describes "the prodigious force and noise with which the billows break on the shore." "It is," says Johnson, "a coast where no vessel lands but when it is driven by a tempest on the rocks." Only two nights before his arrival two boats had been wrecked there in a storm. "The crews crept to Talisker almost lifeless with wet, cold, fatigue, and terror." What could not be safely done

LANDING PLACE.

near the end of September, might, we thought, be hazarded in June. As the day was fine and we had a good sea-boat, an old fisherman to manage it, our trusty gamekeeper to help in rowing, and an accomplished yachtsman in our artist, we boldly sailed forth into the Atlantic. We passed in sight of Macleod's Maidens, beneath rocks such as Mr. Brett and Mr. Graham delight to paint. In one spot we were shown where, a few years before, a huge mass had come tumbling down. At the entrance to the Bay we passed through a narrow channel in the rocks with the waves foaming on each side. Even our stout-hearted gamekeeper for a moment looked uneasy, but with a few strong strokes of the oars the worst was past, and we were out of the broken waters, and in full sight of the little bay with its beach of great black stones, its rugged and steep headlands, and its needle rocks, with one of the sunniest of valleys for its background. Johnson thought it "the place, beyond all he had seen, from which the gay and the jovial seem utterly excluded; and where the hermit might grow old in meditation without possibility

VIEWS AT TALISKER.

of disturbance or interruption." To us on that fine June day, with the haze lying on the hills, it was as if

"We came unto a land
In which it seemed always afternoon."

One sight, to which I had long looked forward, I missed. It was no longer "a land of streams." There was no spot where

"The slender stream
Along the cliff to fall and pause and fall did seem."

Boswell had counted "fifteen different waterfalls near the house in the space of about a quarter of a mile." "They succeeded one another so fast," said Johnson, "that as one ceased to be heard another began." This one thing was wanting on that beautiful afternoon which we spent in this delightful spot. The voice of the cascades was still. There were no waterfalls streaming down the lofty hills. One indeed we found by following the course of a river up a fine glen, but owing to the long drought its roar had sunk into a murmur.

Johnson's host, Colonel Macleod, was the good kinsman who had befriended the young Laird in the troubles which he encountered on his succession to the property.

"He had," writes Boswell, "been bred to physic, had a tincture of scholarship in his conversation, which pleased Dr. Johnson, and he had some very good books; and being a colonel in the Dutch service, he and his lady, in consequence of having lived abroad, had introduced the ease and politeness of the continent into this rude region."

Pennant, writing in the year 1774, thus describes these Scotch regiments in the Dutch service:

"They were formed out of some independent companies sent over either in the reign of Elizabeth or James VI. At present the common men are but nominally national, for since the scarcity of men occasioned by the late war, Holland is no longer permitted to draw her recruits out of North Britain. But the officers are all Scotch, who are obliged to take oaths to our government, and to qualify in presence of our ambassador at the Hague."[1]

In the war which broke out between England and Holland in 1781, this curious system, which had survived the great naval battles between the two countries in the seventeenth century, at last came to an end. In the *Gentlemen's Magazine* for December, 1782, we read, that on the first of that month :

"The Scotch Brigade in the Dutch service renounced their allegiance to their lawful Sovereign, and took a new oath of fidelity to their High Mightinesses. They are for the future to wear the Dutch uniform, and not to carry the arms of the enemy any longer in their colours, nor to beat their march. They are to receive the word of command in Dutch, and their officers are to wear orange-coloured sashes, and the same sort of spontoons as the officers of other Dutch regiments."

Colonel Macleod, if he was still living, lost, of course, his command. At the time of our travellers' visit he was on leave of absence, which had been extended for some years, says Johnson, "in this time of universal peace." The knowledge which he had gained in Holland he turned to good account in Skye. He both drained the land which lay at the foot of the mountains round Talisker, and made a good garden. "He had been," says Knox, "an observer of Dutch improvements. He carried off in proper channels the waters of two rivers which often deluged the bottom. He divided the whole valley by deep and sometimes wide ditches into a number of square fields and meadows. He now enjoys the

[1] Pennant's *Voyage to the Hebrides*, ed. 1774, p. 289.   *Gentleman's Magazine*, 1782, p. 595.

fruits of his ingenuity in the quantity of grain and hay raised thereon." He had made it "the seat of plenty, hospitality, and good nature."[1] To few places in our islands could Dutch art have been transplanted where it would find nature more kindly. Johnson noticed the prosperous growth of the trees, which, though they were not many years old, were already very high and thick. Could he have seen them at the present day he would have owned that even in the garden of an Oxford College there are few finer. The soil is so good, we were told, "that things have only to be planted and they grow." So sheltered from all the cold winds is the position, and so great is the warmth diffused by the beneficent Gulf Stream, that the whole year round flowers live out of doors which anywhere but on the southern coasts of Devonshire and Cornwall would be killed by the frosts. The garden is delightfully old-fashioned, entirely free from the dismal formality of ribbon-borders. Fruit trees, flowers, shrubs, and vegetables mingle together. It lies open to the south-west, being enclosed on the other sides with groves of trees. A lawn shaded by a noble sycamore stretches up to the house. Boswell would have been pleased to find that smooth turf now covers the court which in his time was "most injudiciously paved with round blueish-grey pebbles, upon which you walked as if upon cannon-balls driven into the ground." The house "in its snug corner" has been greatly enlarged, but the old building still remains. Unfortunately no tradition has been preserved of the room occupied by Johnson. Much as he admired this sequestered spot—"a place where the imagination is more amused cannot easily be found," he said—nevertheless it was here that he quoted to Boswell the lines of the song:

"Every island is a prison
Strongly guarded by the sea;
Kings and princes, for that reason,
Prisoners are as well as we."

If Talisker is a prison, it is a goodly one. There are few places which linger more pleasantly in my memory. To the beauty of the scenery and the delightfulness of the weather was added the hospitality which we received from our kind hostess, Mrs. Cameron. Time, alas, failed us to climb "the very high rocky hill" at the back of the house, whence Boswell had "a view of Barra, the Long

[1] Knox's *Tour*, p. 140.

Island, Bernera, the Loch of Dunvegan, part of Rum, part of Raasay, and a vast deal of the Isle of Skye." According to Pennant, who had made the ascent the year before:

"It has in front a fine series of genuine basaltic columns, resembling the Giant's Causeway. The ruins of the columns at the base made a grand appearance; they were the ruins of the creation. This is the most northern basalt I am acquainted with; the last of four, all running from south to north—the Giant's Causeway, Staffa, the rock Humbla, and Briis-mhawl. The depth of ocean in all probability conceals the lost links of this chain."

This mountain, which he calls Briis-mhawl, in Boswell's narrative appears as Prieshwell.

At Talisker Johnson made the acquaintance of young Macleane of Col, that amiable man whose death by drowning the following year he so much lamented. Under his guidance, taking leave of their kind hosts, they rode across the island to Sconser, on the coast opposite to Raasay. Of this part of their journey they tell us next to nothing, though they passed through the wildest scenery. For the first two or three miles their path wound up a valley that is not unworthy of the most delightful parts of Cumberland. It is altogether free from the utter desolation which casts a gloom over so much of Skye. The sloping sides of the hills are covered with short grass and fragrant herbs. All about in summer time are dotted the sheep and lambs, answering each other with their bleats. When we travelled along this way we passed a band of five-and-twenty shearers who had been hard at work for many days. The farm of Talisker keeps a winter stock of between five and six thousand Cheviot sheep, and the clipping takes a long time. Dropping into the valley on the other side of the hills the road leads beyond the head of Loch Harport across the island to Sligachan, where amidst gloomy waste now stands a comfortable hotel. In the little garden which surrounds it is the only trace of cultivation to be anywhere seen. It would have seemed impossible to add anything to the dreariness of the scenery; nevertheless something has been added by the long line of gaunt telegraph posts which stretches across the moor. Perhaps at this spot stood the little hut where our travellers made a short halt, as they watched an old woman grinding at the *quern*. With one hand she rapidly turned round the uppermost of two mill-stones, while with the other she poured in the corn through a hole pierced through it. A ride of a few more miles brought the party, through the gloom of evening, to Sconser, where they dined at the little inn.

CORRICHATACHIN TO TOBERMORIE (SEPTEMBER 25—OCTOBER 16).

At Sconser our travellers took boat for Strolimus, on their way to the friendly farmhouse at Corrichatachin, where they had been

ON THE ROAD TO SCONSER.

so hospitably received nearly three weeks earlier. Their horses they sent round a point of land to meet them further down the coast.

"It was seven o'clock," writes Boswell, "when we got into our boat. We had many showers, and it soon grew pretty dark. Dr. Johnson sat silent and patient. Once he said, as he looked on the black coast of Skye—black, as being composed of rocks seen in the dusk—'This is very solemn.' Our boatmen were rude singers, and seemed so like wild Indians, that a very little imagination was necessary to give one an impression of being upon an American river. We landed at Strolimus, from whence we got a guide to walk before us, for two miles, to Corrichatachin. Not being able to procure a horse for our baggage, I took one portmanteau before me, and Joseph another. We had but a single star to light us on our way. It was about eleven when we arrived. We were most hospitably received by the master and mistress, who were just going to bed, but, with unaffected ready kindness, made a good fire, and at twelve o'clock at night had supper on the table.

Here, as I have already described, they rested that twentieth Sunday after Trinity, when Boswell, recovering from his drinking bout, "by divine interposition, as some would have taken it," opened his Prayer Book at the Apostles' injunction against drunkenness contained in the Epistle for that day. Here, too, the Highlanders, drinking their toasts over the punch, won by Johnson's easy and social manners, "vied with each other in crying out, with a strong Celtic pronunciation, 'Toctor Shonson, Toctor Shonson, your health!'" The weather was so stormy that it was not till the afternoon of Tuesday, September 28, that they were able to

SAILING PAST THE ISLE OF RUM.

continue their journey. That night they arrived at Ostig, on the north-western side of the promontory of Slate, and found a hospitable reception at the Manse. Here, too, they were kept prisoners by wind and rain. "I am," writes Johnson, "still confined in Skye. We were unskilful travellers, and imagined that the sea was an open road which we could pass at pleasure; but we have now learned with some pain that we may still wait for a long time the caprices of the equinoctial winds, and sit reading or writing, as I now do, while the tempest is rolling the sea or roaring in the mountains." Nevertheless, so good was the entertainment which they received that, as Boswell tells us, "the hours slipped along imperceptibly." They had books, and company, and conversation. In strange contrast to the wildness of the scenery and the roughness of the weather was their talk one day about Shenstone and his Love Pastorals. It was surely not among the stormy Hebrides that the poet of the Leasowes, whose "ambition was rural elegance," would have expected to be quoted. Yet here it was, in the midst of beating winds and dashing showers, with the storm-tossed sea in view of the windows, that Boswell repeated the pretty stanza:

> "She gazed as I slowly withdrew:
> My path I could hardly discern:
> So sweetly she bade me adieu,
> I thought that she bade me return."

On Friday, October 1, they took advantage of a break in the weather to move on to Armidale, about a mile from the Sound of Slate, where they waited for a favourable wind to carry them to Iona. It came, or rather seemed to come, on the following Sunday.

ARDNAMURCHAN POINT.

"While we were chatting," writes Boswell, "in the indolent style of men who were to stay here all this day at least, we were suddenly roused at being told that the wind was fair, that a little fleet of herring-busses was passing by for Mull, and that Mr. Simpson's vessel was about to sail. Hugh M'Donald, the skipper, came to us, and was impatient that we should get ready, which we soon did. Dr. Johnson, with composure and solemnity, repeated the observation of Epictetus, that 'as man has the voyage of death before him, whatever may be his employment, he should be ready at the master's call; and an old man should never be far from the shore, lest he should not be able to get himself ready.'"

For some hours they sailed along with a favourable breeze, catching sight of the Isle of Rum as they rounded the point; but when they had got in full view of Ardnamurchan, the wind changed. They tried tacking, but a storm broke upon them, night came on, and they were forced to run through the darkness for Col. Boswell's account of this dangerous voyage is too long to quote, and too good

to abridge. In this dreary spot they were weather-bound for more
than a week. "There is," writes Johnson, "literally no tree upon the
island; part of it is a sandy waste, over which it would be really
dangerous to travel in dry weather, and with a high wind." The
sight of these hills of sand struck him greatly. "I heard him,"
writes Boswell, "after we were in the house, repeating to himself,
as he walked about the room,

"And smothered in the dusty whirlwind dies."

Over this low-lying island the Atlantic blasts swept in all their

fury. On Sunday October 10, Boswell recorded:—"There was this
day the most terrible storm of wind and rain that I ever remember.
It made such an awful impression on us all, as to produce, for some
time, a kind of dismal quietness in the house."

The rough weather spread far. In London, as the old weather
tables tell us, it was "a stormy day with heavy rains and with little
intermission night and day."[1] On the previous Friday Horace
Walpole had come home in a tempest from Bushey Park. "I

[1] *Gentleman's Magazine*, 1774, p. 394.

hope," he wrote. "Jupiter Pluvius has not been so constant at Ampthill. I think he ought to be engraved at the top of every map of England."[1] Happily in the young Laird of Col our travellers had the kindest of hosts. His house "new-built and neat" still stands; Grissipol, which they visited, is in ruins. It was not till the morning of Thursday, the 14th, that they were able to set sail. With a fair breeze they were soon carried over to Tobermory, or Mary's Well, a beautiful bay in the Isle of Mull.

"There are (writes Boswell) sometimes sixty or seventy sail here: to-day there were twelve or fourteen vessels. To see such a fleet was the next thing to seeing a town. The vessels were from different places; Clyde, Campbeltown, Newcastle, &c. One was returning to Lancaster from Hamburgh. After having been shut up so long in Col, the sight of such an assemblage of moving habitations, containing such a variety of people engaged in different pursuits, gave me much gaiety of spirit.

COL: THE LAIRD'S HOUSE.

When we had landed, Dr. Johnson said, 'Boswell is now all alive. He is like Antæus; he gets new vigour whenever he touches the ground.'"

No such fleet is, I imagine, ever to be seen there at the present day, for one steamer does the work of many small vessels. The beauty of this little haven has been long celebrated. Sacheverell, who visited it two hundred years ago, thus describes it :—

"To the landward it is surrounded with high mountains covered with woods, pleasantly intermixed with rocks, and three or four cascades of water, which throw themselves from the top of the mountain with a pleasure that is astonishing, all which together make one of the oddest and most charming prospects I ever saw. Italy itself, with all the assistance of art, can hardly afford anything more beautiful and diverting."[2]

He had been sent there to fish for sunken treasure. Martin,

[1] Walpole's *Letters*, v. 512.
[2] W. Sacheverell's *Account of the Isle of Man*, ed. 1702, p. 126.

whose *Description of the Western Isles* was published the year after Sacheverell's book, gives the following account of this expedition:—

"One of the ships of the Spanish Armada, called the Florida, perished in this Bay, having been blown up by one Smollet, of Dumbarton, in the year 1588. There was a great sum of gold and money on board, which disposed the Earl of Argyle and some Englishmen to attempt the recovery of it. Some pieces of gold and money and a golden chain was taken out of her. I have seen some fine brass cannon, some pieces of eight, teeth, beads and pins that had been taken out of that ship. Several of the inhabitants of Mull told me that they had conversed with their relations that were living at the harbour when the ship was blown up."

"One Smollet" was an ancestor of the great novelist, who in his *Humphry Clinker* artfully brings old Matthew Bramble to Tobermory so that he may celebrate the great deed of his forefather. According to his account "the divers found the hull of the vessel still entire, but so covered with sand that they could not make their way between decks."[2] Mr. Froude mentions the loss of this great Spanish galleon, but

COLVAY.

did not know the name of the harbour.[3] Sir Walter Scott, who visited Tobermory a century and a quarter after Sacheverell, said that, "the richness of the round steep green knolls, clothed with copse and glancing with cascades, and a pleasant peep at a small fresh-water loch embosomed among them—the view of the bay surrounded and guarded by the island of Colvay—the gliding of two or three vessels in the more distant sound—and the row of the gigantic Ardnamurchan mountains closing the scene to the north, almost justify his eulogium who in 1688 declared the Bay of Tobermory might equal any prospect in Italy."[4] With one thing Sacheverell was not content, and that was the weather. "With the dog-days," he says, "the autumnal rains began, and for six weeks we had scarce a good day. The whole frame of nature seemed inhospitable, bleak, stormy, rainy, windy."

---

[1] Martin's *Western Islands*, p. 254.
[2] *Humphry Clinker*, iii. 57.
[3] *History of England*, ed. 1870, xii. 441.
[4] Lockhart's *Life of Scott*, iv. 138.

There was a tolerable inn, where "a dish of tea and some good bread and butter" restored Johnson's good humour, which had been somewhat ruffled by the miserable accommodation which he had had on shipboard. They did not pass the night here, but became the guests of a Dr. Macleane who lived close by. "Col," wrote Johnson, "made every Macleane open his house where we came, and supply us with horses when we departed." Here they were once more kept prisoners by the weather. Not only was there wind and rain, but the rivers, they were told, were impassable. They had books and good talk. In the daughter of the house Johnson at last found "an interpreter of Erse poetry." At Dunvegan he complained that "he could never get the meaning of a song explained to him." Miss Macleane had been bred in the Lowlands, and had gained Gaelic by study. She therefore understood the exact nature of his inquiries.

"She is," he said, "the most accomplished lady that I have found in the Highlands. She knows French, music, and drawing, sews neatly, makes shell-work, and can milk cows: in short, she can do every thing. She talks sensibly, and is the first person whom I have found, that can translate Erse poetry literally."

Ulva's Isle (October 16-17).

On Saturday, October 16, the weather changed for the better, owing to a new moon, as Boswell thought. A long day's journey lay before them, for they hoped to reach Inchkenneth, a little island which lies at the mouth of Loch Na Keal, close to the western coast of Mull. Here they were to be the guest of Sir Allan Macleane.

"We set out," writes Boswell, "mounted on little Mull horses. Dr. Johnson was not in very good humour. He said, it was a dreary country, much worse than Skye. I differed from him. 'O, Sir,' said he, 'a most dolorous country!' We had a very hard journey. I had no bridle for my sheltie, but only a halter; and Joseph rode without a saddle. At one place, a loch having swelled over the road, we were obliged to plunge through pretty deep water. Dr. Johnson observed, how helpless a man would be, were he travelling here alone, and should meet with any accident; and said, 'he longed to get to a *country of saddles and bridles*.'"

When he called the country "most dolorous" he had no doubt in mind the lines which describe the march of "the adventurous bands" in *Paradise Lost*:

"Through many a dark and dreary vale
They passed and many a region dolorous."

Writing to Mrs. Thrale he speaks of this day's journey "as difficult and tedious over rocks naked and valleys untracked through a country of barrenness and solitude. We came almost in the dark to the sea side, weary and dejected, having met with nothing but water falling from the mountains that could raise any image of delight." Sacheverell had found the same ride no less gloomy.

"We proceeded on our journey (he writes) over a country broken, rocky, boggy, barren, and almost wholly unarable. Wet and weary at last we came to a Change-

LOCH NA KEAL.

House (so they call a house of entertainment); if a place that had neither bed, victuals, or drink may be allowed that name. Our servants cut us green fern, wet as it was, for bedding. We set forward early next morning. If I thought the first day's journey hard and unequal, this was much worse; high and craggy mountains, horrid rocks and dreadful precipices; Pelion upon Ossa are trifling and little if compared to them."[1]

Our travellers made their way so slowly over this rough country

---

[1] Account of the Isle of Man, p. 130.

that though they started at eleven, they did not reach the coast till seven at night. Yet they had been told that the distance was but eight miles. To add to the gloom, it was here that Johnson discovered that he had lost that famous piece of timber, his huge oak-stick. Seeing how late it was, Col, who throughout had been their guide, "determined that they should pass the night at Macquarrie's, in the Island of Ulva, which lies between Mull and Inchkenneth." The ferry-boat unfortunately was on the other side of the narrow channel. The wind was so high that their shouts could not be heard, and the darkness was too great for their signals to be seen. They might have been forced to spend the night on the shore had there not chanced to be lying in the little Sound of Ulva a ship from Londonderry. In its long-boat they were ferried over. In this same Sound less than a year later, on the night of September 25, 1774, poor Col lost his life. "His boat," says Sir Walter Scott, "was swamped by the intoxication of the sailors, who had partaken too largely of Macquarrie's wonted hospitality." Here, perhaps, the Macleanes will some day set up a memorial to the unhappy youth. "Col does every thing for us," said Johnson: "We will erect a statue to Col. He is a noble animal. He is as complete an islander as the mind can figure. He is a farmer, a sailor, a hunter, a fisher; he will run you down a dog; if any man has a tail, it is Col. He is hospitable; and he has an intrepidity of talk whether he understands the subject or not." His untimely end was regretted by those who only knew "this amiable man" by the reports of our two travellers. "At the death of Col," said Boswell, "my wife wept much."[1] "There is great lamentation here," wrote Johnson from Lichfield, "for the death of Col. Lucy is of opinion that he was wonderfully handsome." Though they were in the land of second-sight there was no shadow thrown by coming events on the very liberal entertainment provided by their host. Nevertheless the Chief of Ulva's Isle had a sea of troubles of his own to oppose. He was almost overwhelmed with the stormy waters, not of Loch Gyle, but of debt. "His ancestors," wrote Johnson to Mrs. Thrale, "had reigned in Ulva beyond memory, but he has reduced himself by his negligence and folly to the necessity of selling this venerable patrimony." His house was a strange mixture of luxury and squalor. The room in which Johnson slept was unboarded, and through a broken

[1] Croker's *Boswell*, p. 826.

window the rain had driven in and turned the floor to mud. He thus describes his night's lodging : "The house and the furniture are not always nicely suited. We were driven once, by missing a passage, to the hut of a gentleman where, after a very liberal supper, when I was conducted to my chamber, I found an elegant bed of Indian cotton, spread with fine sheets. The accommodation was flattering ; I undressed myself, and felt my feet in the mire. The bed stood upon the bare earth which a long course of rain had softened to a puddle."

INCHKENNETH, MACKINNON'S CAVE, AND IONA (OCTOBER 17-20).

Our travellers having stayed but one night at Ulva, on the morning of Sunday, October 17, took boat and rowed to Inchkenneth, "an island about a mile long, and perhaps half a mile broad, remarkable for pleasantness and fertility. It is verdant and grassy, and fit both for pasture and tillage ; but it has no trees." The only inhabitants were " the chief of the ancient and numerous clan of Macleane, his daughter and their servants." In a letter to Mrs. Thrale Johnson says : " Sir Allan, a chieftain, a baronet, and a soldier, inhabits in this insulated desert a thatched hut with no chambers. He received us with the soldier's frankness and the gentleman's elegance, and introduced us to his daughters, two young ladies who have not wanted education suitable to their birth, and who in their cottage neither forgot their dignity nor affected to remember it. His affairs are in disorder by the fault of his ancestors, and while he forms some scheme for retrieving them, he has retreated hither." By *chambers*, Johnson seems to mean rooms on an upper floor. Boswell describes the habitation as commodious, "though it consisted but of a few small buildings only one story high." In two of these huts were the servants' rooms and the kitchen. " The dinner was plentiful and delicate. Neither the comforts nor the elegancies of life were wanting. There were several dishes and variety of liquors." Sir Walter Scott many years later visited the island in company with a Gloucestershire baronet, Sir George Onesiphorus Paul :

" He seemed to me,' writes Sir Walter, "to suspect many of the Highland tales which he heard, but he showed most incredulity on the subject of Johnson's having been entertained in the wretched huts of which we saw the ruins. He took me aside, and conjured me to tell him the truth of the matter. 'This Sir Allan,' said he, 'was he a *regular baronet*, or was his title such a traditional one as you find in Ireland? I assured my excellent acquaintance that, 'for my own part, I would have paid more respect to a knight of Kerry, or knight of Glynn: yet Sir Allan Macleane was a *regular baronet* by patent;' and, having given him this information, I took the liberty of asking him, in return, whether he would not in conscience prefer the worst cell in the jail at Gloucester (which he had been very active in overlooking while the building was going on) to those exposed hovels where Johnson had been entertained by rank and beauty. He looked round the little islet, and allowed Sir Allan had some advantage in exercising ground; but in other respects he thought the compulsory tenants of Gloucester had greatly the advantage. Such was his opinion of a place, concerning which Johnson has recorded that 'it wanted little which palaces could afford.'"

Johnson, by the way, did not write "*it* wanted," but "*we* wanted little that palaces afford." We have from Sir Walter also an amusing story which shows how the chief of the Macleanes in the embarrassment of his affairs had learnt to hate the sight of an attorney—*writers*, as they are called in Scotland:

"Upon one occasion he made a visit to a friend residing at Carron lodge, on the banks of the Carron, where the banks of that river are studded with pretty villas: Sir Allan, admiring the landscape, asked his friend whom that handsome seat belonged to. 'M——, the writer to the signet,' was the reply. 'Umph!' said Sir Allan, but not with an accent of assent, 'I mean that other house.' 'Oh! that belongs to a very honest fellow, Jamie ——, also a writer to the signet.' 'Umph!' said the Highland chief of Macleane, with more emphasis than before, 'And yon smaller house?' 'That belongs to a Stirling man; I forget his name, but I am sure he is a writer too; for ——.' Sir Allan, who had recoiled a quarter of a circle backward at every response, now wheeled the circle entire, and turned his back on the landscape, saying, 'My good friend, I must own you have a pretty situation here; but d——n your neighbourhood.'"[1]

In his dislike of lawyers he would have found a common feeling in Johnson, who one day, "when inquiry was made concerning a person who had quitted a company where he was, observed that he did not care to speak ill of any man behind his back, but he believed the gentleman was an attorney." Happily there was nothing to disturb the tranquillity of the scene during the visit of our travellers. The Sunday which Johnson spent on Inchkenneth was, as he told Boswell, "the most agreeable he had ever passed." He thus describes it to Mrs. Thrale: "Towards evening Sir Allan told us that Sunday never passed over him like another day. One of the ladies read, and read very well, the evening service, 'and Paradise was opened in the wild.'"[2] Such was the impression produced on him that he commemorated the day in some pretty Latin lines

[1] Croker's *Boswell*, p. 384.   [2] Pope, *Eloisa to Abelard*, l. 135.

entitled, *Insula Sancti Kennethi*. Though he would not attend a Scotch church and hear Robertson preach, yet a woman's reading the English service did not shock him.

> "Quid quod sacrifici versavit femina libros?
> Legitimas faciunt pectora pura preces."

> "A woman's hand, 'tis true, turned o'er the sacred leaves,
> But prayer from hearts so pure God's sanction sure receives."

He thus prettily ends his verses:

> "Quo vagor ulterius? quod ubique requiritur hic est;
> Hic secura quies, hic et honestus amor."

> "Why should we further roam? here what all seek we gain,
> Both peace without a care, and love without a stain."

INCHKENNETH CHAPEL.

Sir Allan had chosen well his hermitage. The landing-place is on the south-eastern side of the island, in a little bay with a sandy beach, sheltered by a low point from the storms coming from the north-west, while the cold blasts from the north and the north-east are kept off by a low hill. The ground slopes up from the shore in pleasant meadow land. At the bottom of the slope, a little above the beach, Sir Allan, I conjecture, had his habitation. Here are the ruins of a farmhouse which was burnt down a few years ago. It is very likely that it occupied the same site as his cottages.

The road marked with cart-wheels, as on the main land, at the sight of which Dr. Johnson's heart was cheered, I failed to discover. We wandered up the little path to where on the rising ground the ruined chapel stands within the hearing of the wave.

> "We walked uncovered into the chapel," writes Johnson, "and saw in the reverend ruin the effects of precipitate reformation. The floor is covered with ancient gravestones, of which the inscriptions are not now legible. The altar is not yet quite demolished; beside it, on the right side, is a *bas relief* of the Virgin with her child, and an angel hovering over her. On the other side still stands a hand-bell, which, though it has no clapper, neither Presbyterian bigotry nor barbarian wantonness has yet taken away. The chapel is thirty-eight feet long and eighteen broad. Boswell, who is very pious, went into it at night to perform his devotions, but came back in haste for fear of spectres. Near the chapel is a fountain, to which the water, remarkably pure, is conveyed from a distant hill through pipes laid by the Romish clergy, which still perform the office of conveyance though they have never been repaired since Popery was suppressed."

Our boatman, whom I had in vain questioned about Johnson's host, led me up to the tomb of an old knight, clothed in armour, with a dog lying at his feet, and said, "That is Sir Allan." The little fountain, in spite of the lapse of years and the long drought, still ran with a stream of pure water. Besides the chapel, there had once been on the island a seminary of priests. "Sir Allan," writes Johnson, "had a mind to trace the foundations of a college, but neither I nor Mr. Boswell, who bends a keener eye on vacancy, were able to perceive them." Where they failed we could not hope to succeed. We next explored, as they had done, a neighbouring islet.

"Even Inchkenneth," says Johnson, "has a subordinate island, named Sandiland, I suppose in contempt, where we landed, and found a rock, with a surface of perhaps four acres, of which one is naked stone, another spread with sand and shells, some of which I picked up for their glossy beauty, and two covered with a little earth and grass, on which Sir Allan has a few sheep. I doubt not but when there was a college at Inchkenneth, there was a hermitage upon Sandiland."

The shells, perhaps, he kept to add to the collection of Mrs. Thrale's eldest daughter. "I have been able," he wrote later on, "to collect very little for Queeney's cabinet." The name which our boatman gave to the island was, so far as I could catch it, not Sandiland, but Sameilan. At the time of our visit it had for inhabitants four sheep, and flocks of sea-birds who made it their breeding ground. They flew circling and screaming over our heads, while a mother bird led off a late brood of little ones into the sea. Before each of the burrows in which they made their nests was a litter of tiny

SANDBANG.

shells thrown up like sand before a rabbit warren. The sun shone
brightly, the little waves beat on the shore, while all around us
there were mountains, islands, and lochs. As I picked up a few
shells, I thought that on this lonely rock, perhaps, none had been
gathered since the day when they caught Johnson's eye by

MACKINNON'S CAVE.

their glossy beauty. In sailing back to the mainland of Mull
we saw four seals popping up their heads in the water near the
shore.

So pleasant did Johnson find the life in Inchkenneth that he
remained a day longer than he had intended. "We could have
been easily persuaded," he writes, "to a longer stay, but life will
not be all passed in delight. The session at Edinburgh was

approaching from which Mr. Boswell could not be absent." On the morning of Tuesday, October 19, they started for Iona in a good strong boat, with four stout rowers under the guidance of the chief of the Macleanes. On the shore they took their last farewell of poor Col, "who," wrote Johnson, "had treated us with so much kindness, and concluded his favours by consigning us to Sir Allan." On the way they visited Mackinnon's Cave, on the opposite coast of Mull, the greatest natural curiosity," said Johnson, "he had ever seen." He thus describes it in a letter to Mrs. Thrale.

"We had some difficulty to make our way over the vast masses of broken rocks that lie before the entrance, and at the mouth were embarrassed with stones, which the sea had accumulated as at Brighthelmstone; but as we advanced we reached a floor of soft sand, and as we left the light behind us walked along a very spacious cavity vaulted overhead with an arch almost regular, by which a mountain was sustained, at least, a very lofty rock. From this magnificent cavern went a narrow passage to the right hand, which we entered with a candle, and though it was obstructed with great stones, clambered over them to a second expansion of the cave, in which there lies a great square stone, which might serve as a table. The cave goes onward to an unknown extent, but we were now one hundred and sixty yards under ground; we had but one candle, and had never heard of any that went further and came back: we therefore thought it prudent to return."

"Tradition," according to Boswell, "says that a piper and twelve men once advanced into this cave, nobody can tell how far; and never returned." It is indeed a wonderful place. As we sat on the rocks near the entrance, with the huge cliffs rising sheer above us, and the waves breaking at our feet, we could see in the distance Iona, with its beach of white sand, Staffa with its lofty masses of dark rock, Little Colonsay with the waves dashing in foam upon it, and on the horizon a coast which we took to be the island of Col. Vast masses of rock lay along the beach in huge and wild disorder. Beyond the cavern they came to an end; for there the cliff rose from the sea steep as the wall of a house. The cascade near the cave, which Boswell mentions, was falling in a very slender stream. Hard by a huge crag was covered almost to the top by the fresh young leaves of a great ivy-tree. It called up to my memory the ivy-mantled ruins of Kenilworth Castle.

Our travellers, taking boat again, continued their voyage along the shore of Mull. "The island of Staffa," writes Boswell, "we saw at no very great distance, but could not land upon it, the surge was so high on its rocky coast." It is strange that Sir James Mackintosh, with this passage before him, should have accused

Johnson of having visited Iona, "without looking at Statfa, which lay in sight, with that indifference to natural objects, either of taste or scientific curiosity, which characterised him."[1] As they sailed along, "Sir Allan, anxious for the honour of Mull, was still talking of its *woods*, and pointing them out to Dr. Johnson, as appearing at a distance on the skirts of that island. 'Sir,' he answered, 'I saw at Tobermory what they called a wood, which I unluckily took for *heath*. If you show me what I shall take for *furze*, it will be something.'"

They dined at "a cluster of rocks, black and horrid,' near to which was a public-house where they had hoped to procure some rum or brandy for the boatmen; "but unfortunately a funeral a few days before had exhausted all their store." Smollett in his *Humphry Clinker*, tells how a Highland gentleman, at his grandmother's funeral, "seemed to think it a disparagement to his family that not above a hundred gallons of whisky had been drunk upon such a solemn occasion."[2]

MULL.

The rest of this day's voyage Johnson thus finely described in one of his letters: "We then entered the boat again; the night came upon us; the wind rose; the sea swelled. We passed by several little islands in the silent solemnity of faint moonshine, seeing little, and hearing only the wind and the water. At last we reached the island; the venerable seat of ancient sanctity, where secret piety reposed, and where fallen greatness was reposited." Boswell adds that as they "sailed along by moonlight in a sea somewhat rough, and often between black and gloomy rocks, Dr. Johnson said, 'If this be not roving among the Hebrides nothing is.'"

Iona, which of old belonged to the Macleanes, in their recent embarassments had been sold to the Duke of Argyle. Though

[1] *Life of Sir Jas. Mackintosh,* i. 257.   [2] *Humphry Clinker*, iii. 27.

the tie of property was broken yet the feeling of clanship remained entire. "Whatever was in the island," writes Johnson, "Sir Allan could demand, for the inhabitants were Macleanes; but having little they could not give us much." A curious scene described by Boswell bears witness to the strength of the devotion of these poor people.

"Sir Allan had been told that a man had refused to send him some rum, at which the knight was in great indignation. 'You rascal!' (said he,) don't you know that I can hang you, if I please?' Not adverting to the Chieftain's power over his clan, I imagined that Sir Allan had known of some capital crime that the fellow had committed, which he could discover, and so get him condemned; and said, 'How so?' 'Why, (said Sir Allan,) are they not all my people?' Sensible of my inadvertency, and most willing to contribute what I could towards the continuation of feudal authority, 'Very true,' said I. Sir Allan went on : 'Refuse to send rum to me, you rascal! Don't you know that, if I order you to go and cut a man's throat, you are to do it?' 'Yes, an't please your honour! and my own too, and hang myself too.' The poor fellow denied that he had refused to send the rum. His making these professions was not merely a pretence in presence of his Chief; for after he and I were out of Sir Allan's hearing, he told me, 'Had he sent his dog for the rum, I would have given it: I would cut my bones for him.' It was very remarkable to find such an attachment to a Chief, though he had then no connection with the island, and had not been there for fourteen years. Sir Allan, by way of upbraiding the fellow, said, 'I believe you are a *Campbell*.'"

The memory of the power so lately exercised throughout the Highlands by the chiefs was not soon forgotten. It was noticed so late as 1793, that in Scotland *master* was still, for the most part, the term used for *landlord*. As an instance of this it was mentioned that in a sermon preached in the High Church of Edinburgh in 1788, the minister thus described the late Earl of Kinnoul in relation to his tenants.[1] Even after the abolition of the jurisdictions of the chiefs the powers left in the hands of the justices were very great. "An inferior judge in Scotland," wrote the historian of Edinburgh in the year 1779, "makes nothing of sentencing a man to whipping, pillory, banishment from the limits of his jurisdiction, and such other trifling punishments, without the idle formality of a jury."[2]

In Iona, however, there was no need of threats. The poor people were devoted to their former chief. "He went," says Johnson, "to the headman of the island whom fame, but fame delights in amplifying, represents as worth no less than fifty pounds. He was, perhaps, proud enough of his guests, but ill prepared for

[1] J. L. Buchanan, *Travels in the Western Highlands from 1782 to 1790*, p. 5.
[2] *History of Edinburgh*, p. 445.

our entertainment; however, he soon produced more provision than men not luxurious required." There was not a single house in which, with any comfort, they could have been lodged. Pennant, who had been there a year earlier, "had pitched a rude tent formed of oars and sails." There was but one house which had a chimney. "Nevertheless, even in this," says Johnson, "the fire was made on the floor in the middle of the room, and notwithstanding the dignity of their mansion the inmates rejoiced like their neighbours in the comforts of smoke." Though the soil was naturally fruitful, yet the poverty of the people was great. "They are," he adds, "remarkably gross and remarkably neglected; I know not if they are visited by any minister. The island, which was once the metropolis of learning and piety, has now no school for education nor temple for worship, only two inhabitants that can speak English, and not one that can write or read." The population was probably not less than four hundred souls.[1] Sacheverell, who was there in 1688, mentions a class of "hereditary servants. They are," he adds, "miserably poor. They seem an innocent, simple people, ignorant and devout; and though they have no minister, they constantly assemble in the great church on Sundays, where they spend most part of the day in private devotions."[2] According to Pennant they were "the most stupid and the most lazy of all the islanders." "They used," he says, "the Chapel of the Nunnery as a cow-shed; the floor was covered some feet thick with dung, for they were too lazy to remove this fine manure, the collection of a century, to enrich their grounds."[3] Boswell, however, gives a much better report. "They are industrious," he says, "and make their own woollen and linen cloth; and they brew a good deal of beer, which we did not find in any of the other islands." In July, 1798, Dr. Garnett and his companion, Mr. Watts, the painter, passed a night in the public house. The floor of their chamber was liquid mud; the rain fell on their beds. For fellow-lodgers they had several chickens, a tame lamb, a dog, some cats, and two or three pigs. Next morning they invited the schoolmaster to breakfast, and found that the inn could boast of only two tea-cups and one spoon, and that of wood.[4] Sir Walter Scott, who visited Iona in 1810 mentions "the squalid and dejected poverty of the

---

[1] See Johnson's *Works*, ix. 149. Pennant, however, gives the number of inhabitants as only one hundred and fifty. Pennant's *Tour*, ed. 1774, p. 243.

[2] *An Account of the Isle of Mon,* p. 136.

[3] Pennant's *Tour*, ed. 1774, pp. 243, 246.

[4] Dr. Garnett's *Observation*, vol. i. 244, 245.

inhabitants the most wretched people he had anywhere seen."[1] With such houses and such people Sir Allan Macleane certainly did wisely in choosing a barn for the lodgings of himself and his two friends. "Some good hay," writes Boswell, " was strewed at one end of it, to form a bed for us, upon which we lay with our clothes on; and we were furnished with blankets from the village. Each of us had a portmanteau for a pillow. When I awaked in the morning, and looked round me, I could not help smiling at the idea of the chief of the Macleanes, the great English Moralist, and myself, lying thus extended in such a situation."

The smile might have passed into a sigh, had Boswell contrasted the splendours of Iona's past with the meanness of her present lot. They had come to

"Where, beneath the showery west,
The mighty kings of three fair realms are laid."

Like the pilgrim

"From the Blue Mountains, or Ontario's Lake,"

amidst the ruins of fallen greatness and fallen learning they had sought

"Some peasant's homely shed,
Who toils unconscious of the mighty dead."

Whether with Johnson among "those illustrious ruins," we look upon Iona as the instructress of the west, or with Gibbon as the island whence was "diffused over the northern regions a doubtful ray of science and superstition," in either case it is surely a spot where we are forced to pause, and with pensive mind "revolve the sad vicissitude of things." I must not, however, be unjust to Boswell. It was his enthusiasm which had led them hither. It was he who had longed to survey Iona. "I," said Johnson, "though less eager did not oppose him." To him then we owe that splendid passage in which the great Englishman celebrates the power exerted over the mind by the sight of places where noble deeds were done, and noble lives were lived.

"We were now treading that illustrious Island, which was once the luminary of the Caledonian regions, whence savage clans and roving barbarians derived the benefits of knowledge, and the blessings of religion. To abstract the mind from all local emotion would be impossible, if it were endeavoured, and would be foolish if it were possible. Whatever withdraws us from the power of our senses, whatever makes the past, the distant, or the future, predominate over the present, advances us in the dignity of thinking beings. Far from me, and from my friends, be such frigid

[1] Lockhart's *Life of Scott*, iii. 285; iv. 324.

philosophy as may conduct us indifferent and unmoved over any ground which has been dignified by wisdom, bravery, or virtue. That man is little to be envied, whose patriotism would not gain force upon the plain of Marathon, or whose piety would not grow warmer among the ruins of Iona."

Boswell surely not without good reason maintains that "had their tour produced nothing else but this sublime passage the world must have acknowledged that it was not made in vain."

RUINS IN IONA.

THE SOUTHERN COAST OF MULL AND LOCHBUY
(OCTOBER 20-22).

Sailing from Iona about midday on Wednesday, October 20, our travellers landed in the evening on the southern coast of Mull, near the house of the Rev. Neal Macleod, who gave them lodgings for the night. Johnson oddly described him as "the cleanest-headed man that he had met with in the Western Islands." The talk ran on English statesmen. Here it was that Johnson called Mr. Pitt a meteor, and Sir Robert Walpole a fixed star, and main-

tained that Pulteney was as paltry a fellow as could be. Continuing
their journey on the morrow, they dined at the house of a physician,
"who was so much struck with the uncommon conversation of
Johnson, that he observed to Boswell, 'This man is just a hogshead of sense.'" This doctor's practice could scarcely have been
very lucrative, for there came a time when he had no successor.
Garnett writing of Mull at the end of the century, says, "There is
at present no medical man in the island; the nearest surgeon of
eminence is at Inverary."[1] The distance from that town to the

MACADAM'S ARCH ; MULL.

farthest points in Mull, as the crow flies, is not less than sixty miles,
but by the route taken would be perhaps one hundred. In the
afternoon our travellers rode, writes Boswell, "through what
appeared to me the most gloomy and desolate country I had ever
beheld." "It was," said Johnson, "a country of such gloomy
desolation that Mr. Boswell thought no part of the Highlands
equally terrific." Faujas Saint-Fond, a few years later, describes
Mull as a country "without a single road, without a single tree,
where the mountains have heather for their only covering."[2]
Amidst the beautiful plantations and the fine trees with which this

[1] Dr. T. Garnett's Observation, vol. ii. 148. [2] Faujas de St. Fond, vol. ii. 86.

island is now in so many parts adorned, the modern tourist fails to recognize the truthfulness of these gloomy descriptions. Our travellers were to spend the night at Moy, the seat of the Laird of Lochbuy,[1] at the head of the fine loch from which he takes his title. I approached it from the north-eastern side of the island, having driven over from Craignure, a little port in the Sound of Mull. Perhaps the country through which I passed was naturally finer than that which they had traversed in coming from the south-west. Perhaps, on the other hand, the difference was chiefly due to the trees and to better weather. Certainly the long drive, though in places dreary, was for a great part of the road on a bright, windy summer day, one of remarkable beauty. I passed lochs of the sea with the waves tossing, the sea-fowl hovering and settling and screaming, great herons standing on the shore, and the sea-trout leaping in the waters. But far more beautiful was Loch Uisk, an inland lake embosomed among the mountains, its steep shores covered with trees. The strong wind was driving the scud like dust over the face of its dark waters. As I drew near Lochbuy, I caught sight of the ivy-mantled tower across a meadow, where the mowers were cutting the grass, and the hay-makers were tossing it out to the sun and wind. Beyond the castle there was a broad stretch of white sand; a small vessel lay at anchor, ready at the next tide to run ashore and discharge the hamlet's winter stock of coal. Tall trunks of fir-trees were lying near the water's edge ready for shipping. At the head of the loch are two beautiful bays, each with its pastures and tilled lands, its low-wooded heights and its lofty circling mountains, each facing the south-west and sheltered from the cold winds. Between these two bays rise fine crags, hidden in places beneath hazels and ivy. For most of the year it is a land streaming with waterfalls. In beautiful ravines, half hidden by the trees, wild cascades rush down, swollen by the storms that have burst on the mountains; but at the time of my visit their voice was hushed by the long drought. So dry had the springs become in some places, that I was told at Lochbuy that to one of the neighbouring islands water had to be carried in boats.

Close to the ruined Castle stood "the mansion, not very spacious or splendid," where Macleane of Lochbuy, "a true Highland laird, rough and haughty, and tenacious of his dignity," entertained our travellers.

[1] The name is now commonly written Lochbuie.

"We had heard much,' writes Boswell, "of Lochbuy's being a great roaring braggadocio, a kind of Sir John Falstaff, both in size and manners; but we found that they had swelled him up to a fictitious size, and clothed him with imaginary qualities. Col's idea of him was equally extravagant, though very different: he told us he was quite a Don Quixote; and said, he would give a great deal to see him and Dr. Johnson together. The truth is, that Lochbuy proved to be only a bluff, comely, noisy, old gentleman, proud of his hereditary consequence, and a very hearty and hospitable landlord. Lady Lochbuy was sister to Sir Allan Maclean, but much older. He said to me, 'They are quite *Antediluvians*.' Being told that Dr. Johnson did not hear well, Lochbuy bawled out to him, 'Are you of the Johnstons of Glencro, or of Ardnamurchan?' Dr. Johnson gave him a significant look, but made no answer; and I told Lochbuy that he was not John*ston*, but John*son*, and that he was an Englishman." [1]

According to Sir Walter Scott, Boswell misapprehended Lochbuy's meaning.

"There are,' he says, "two septs of the powerful clan of M'Donald, who are called Mac Ian, that is *John's-son*; and as Highlanders often translate their names when they go to the Lowlands, as Gregor-son for Mac-Gregor, Farquhar-son for Mac-Farquhar, Lochbuy supposed that Dr. Johnson might be one of the Mac-Ians of Ardnamurchan, or of Glencro. Boswell's explanation was nothing to the purpose. The *Johnstons* are a clan distinguished in Scottish border history, and as brave as any Highland clan that ever wore brogues; but they lay entirely out of Lochbuy's knowledge—nor was he thinking of them."

I have little doubt, however, that whatever Lochbuy was thinking of he pronounced the name *Johnston*. In this both Boswell and Johnson agree. This too was the name which I commonly found given to the great man in the Highlands and Lowlands alike.

"The following day (writes Boswell) we surveyed the old castle, in the pit or dungeon of which Lochbuy had some years before taken upon him to imprison several persons; and though he had been fined in a considerable sum by the Court of Justiciary, he was so little affected by it, that while we were examining the dungeon, he said to me, with a smile, 'Your father knows something of this;' (alluding to my father's having sat as one of the judges on his trial). Sir Allan whispered me, that the laird could not be persuaded that he had lost his heritable jurisdiction."

Up to the year 1747 "in the Highlands," to quote Johnson's words, "some great lords had an hereditary jurisdiction over counties, and some chieftains over their own lands." This subjection of the people to their chiefs was rightly regarded as one of the main sources of the rebellions of 1715 and 1745. He who by law was privileged to keep a pit, a dungeon, and a gallows, was not likely to meet with much resistance when he summoned his people to follow him to the field. Advantage was therefore taken of the

[1] See *ante*, p. 5.

defeat of the clansmen at Culloden, "to crush all the Local Courts and to extend the general benefits of equal law to the low and the high, in the deepest recesses and obscurest corners." The heritable jurisdiction had been divided into regalities, ordinary baronies, and baronies which had the right of pit and gallows.

> "The lowest criminal jurisdiction," says a Scotch legal author, "is what we call for Battery and Bloodwits, viz., Offences whereby a party is beaten, or blood drawn of him, but no greater harm done; and this is implied in all Baronies. But if the erection of the Barony contain a power of Pit and Gallows, it imports a jurisdiction in ordinary capital cases, but not in the excepted crimes, which go under the name of the *Four Pleas of the Crown*, viz., Murder, Robbery, Rape, and wilful Fireraising. It is so called from the manner of execution of criminals, viz., by hanging the men upon the Gallows or Gibbet, and drowning the women, sentenced in a capital crime, in a pit, it not being thought decent of old to hang them."[1]

In old law Latin this right was known under the name of *furca et fossa*.[2] A person invested with the jurisdiction of a regality had power also in the Four Pleas of the Crown. "The sentences in civil cases are subject to the review of the Lords of Session, and in criminal to the Court of Justiciary. In criminal trials thirty days were allowed before execution of the sentence on this [the southern] side of the Forth, and forty on the other." From this appeal there was one regality which was exempt. The jurisdiction of the Duke of Argyle was absolute even in cases of life and death. From his sentences there was no appeal.[3] Each barony had its Gallows Hill, and its dempster or hangman.[4] Pennant, in 1772, saw "on a little flat hill near the village of Kilarow in Islay the remains of the gallows."[5] At Dunvegan men had been hanged on the sentence of the laird, so late as 1740. No doubt this power was sometimes most oppressively exercised. A chief who lived near Inverness was charged with having rid himself at a profit of men on his estate who had given him trouble. He charged them with theft, threatened them with the gallows, and so brought them "to sign a contract for their banishment." They were then put on board a ship bound to the West Indies, "the master paying so much a head for them."[6] In other words,

---

[1] *An Essay upon Feudal Holdings, Superiorities, and Hereditary Jurisdiction in Scotland.* London, 1747, p. 16.

[2] "Baro dicitur qui gladii potestatem habet, id est imperium merum; apud nos furcæ et fossæ nomine significamus."—Craig, *De Feudis*, i. 12, 16, quoted in Arnot's *History of Edinburgh*, p. 224.

[3] *An Essay upon Feudal Holdings*, &c., pp. 18, 28.

[4] Dunbar's *Social Life*, &c., ii. 141.

[5] Pennant's *Voyage to the Hebrides*, ed. 1774, p. 221.

[6] *Letter from a Gentleman in the North of Scotland*, i. 54.

they were sold for slaves, if not for life, at all events for a certain number of years.

No change had been made by the Act of Union of 1706, for it was expressly provided in it that all these heritable jurisdictions "should be reserved to the owners as rights and property."[1] When in 1747 these powers had been swept away, two unhappy classes of men were excepted from the full benefit of the Act. The workers in any kind of mine or in salt-works were to remain as they had hitherto been—serfs for life. These men were found only in the Lowlands, chiefly in the neighbourhood of Edinburgh. Nevertheless, even they were not left altogether without relief. "All jurisdiction in any case inferring the loss of life or demembration, was abrogated."[2] A collier or a salter therefore could no longer be hanged or drowned, or even mangled by his master. It was not till the last year of the century that they were finally and fully freed. One of these emancipated serfs lived till the year 1844.[3]

The Act of 1747 not only abolished jurisdictions, but also alleviated the prisoner's lot. Till it was passed, "all over Scotland pits were accounted legal prisons for thieves and other meaner criminals."[4] Lady Margaret Bellenden in *Old Mortality* praises her pit. "It is not more than two stories beneath ground," she says, "so it cannot be unwholesome, especially as I rather believe there is somewhere an opening to the outer air."[5] But henceforth—so the Act ran—"the prison shall have such windows or grates, as that it may be practicable for any friend of the prisoner to visit, see, and converse with him when he shall be so minded."[6] In out of the way places, where there were no justices within reach, the laird, no doubt, to some extent, continued to exercise his old powers. Thus in Col, more than sixteen years after the Act was passed, the laird put a woman into "the family prison" for theft.[7] There have been men who regarded, or affected to regard with indignation the abolition of these injurious hereditary powers. "By the nation at large," writes Dr. Robert Chambers, "the measure was contemplated as a last stab to the independence of Scotland, previously almost destroyed by the Union."[8] There is

---

[1] Smollett's *History of England*, ii. 79.
[2] An Act for Abolishing the Heritable Jurisdiction, 1747, p. 19.
[3] Boswell's *Johnson*, iii. 207, n. 1.
[4] *Scotland and Scotsmen*, &c., ii. 94.
[5] *Old Mortality*, ed. 1860, ii. 14.
[6] An Act for Abolishing, &c., p. 17.
[7] Boswell's *Johnson*, v. 292.
[8] *History of the Rebellion in Scotland*, ed. 1827, ii. 295.

happily no reason to believe that the nation at large was at any period of its history a set of sentimental fools.

To most of the chiefs this loss of their ancient jurisdictions must have come as a terrible shock. Lochbuy, as has been seen, had refused to believe it, and so had got into trouble with the Court of Justiciary. After some search I was fortunate enough to discover a report of his case. He had, as I was informed by his descendant, the present laird, with the help of his piper let down a man into the pit. But here, for once, tradition has not been guilty of amplification. Aided by his servant, his piper and son, the innkeeper in Moy, and two other tenants, he had seized two men of the name of Maclean, and had imprisoned them two days "in an old ruinous castle." Two of the accused did not appear to the indictment, "they were therefore fugitated (outlawed) and their moveables escheated to the king for their contempt." The trial took place on August 15, 1759. It lasted twelve hours. "The jury (of which a majority was landed gentlemen) returned their verdict unanimously, finding the pannels (prisoners at the bar) guilty; but verbally recommending the four servants and tenants to the mercy of the court, it appearing that what they did was by order of Lochbuy, their master. The lords pronounced sentence, decerning Lochbuy in £180 sterling of expenses and damages to the private prosecutors, and 500 marks Scots (about £27) of fine; and condemning the whole pannels to seventeen days' imprisonment."[1]

Lochbuy had no doubt been the more unwilling to believe in the abolition of his jurisdiction as he had, it should seem, no share in that "valuable consideration in money which was granted to every nobleman and petty baron who was thus deprived of one part of his inheritance."[2] On what principle of justice this compensation was given is not clear, unless we agree with Johnson in his assertion that "those who have long enjoyed dignity and power ought not to lose it without some equivalent."[3] Professor Thorold Rogers informs me that we have here, he believes, the first instance in our history where compensation is paid by the country at large for the vested interests of a class. The claims which were made were excessive, partly no doubt in the hope that when much was demanded at all events something would be given, but partly,

[1] *Scots Magazine*, 1759, p. 441. [2] Smollett's *History of England*, iii. 206.
[3] Johnson's *Works*, ix. 91.

it was said, with the intention of "obstructing the Act, and raising discontents in the country."¹ The total sum asked for was £587,000, but only £152,000 was granted. Among the claimants I found "Maclean of Lochbuie, Bailie of the Bailiery of Morovis and Mulerois, £500." His name does not appear among the list of those whose claims were allowed.²

Though in 1759 the castle was described as ruinous, nevertheless it had been inhabited by the laird a few years earlier. Over the entrance of the house in which he received Johnson is inscribed: "Ha c domus [a word effaced] erat per Johannem M'Laine De Lochbuy Anno Dom. 1752." It has, in its turn, given way to a more modern mansion, and has been converted into stables, coach-houses, and hay-lofts. The castle was built on the edge of the sea, "four-square to all the winds that blew." The walls, nine or ten feet thick, "are probably as old as the fourteenth century, but the upper part seems to have been modified in the seventeenth."³ The ivy has climbed up to the top, nevertheless much of the stonework is still seen. It would be a pity if it were suffered to cover the walls on all sides. Hard by a little stream shaded with trees makes its way into the loch. To the north-west rises the steep hill of Dun Buy. "*Buy* in Erse," says Boswell, "signifies yellow. The hill being of a yellowish hue, has the epithet of *buy*." This hue I altogether failed to discover; perhaps it is only seen in the autumn. On the bright summer's day in which I saw the castle, it seemed to be almost unsurpassed in the pleasantness of its seat. Tall trees grew near it, their leaves rustling in the wind, and the lights and shadows dancing on the ground as the branches swayed to and fro, while in front lay the loch with its foaming waves. The old ruin looked as if it had been set there to add to the beauty of the scene, not for a place where lairds and their pipers should let down luckless folk into dismal pits. In the inside there was gloom enough. A few well-worn stone steps lead up to the entrance. The strong old door studded with iron nails which had withstood the storms of many a long year, has at length yielded to time, and been replaced. Behind it is an iron grate secured by bolts and by an oaken bar that is drawn forth from a hole in the wall. Passing on I went into a gloomy vault known as the store-room Not a

---

[1] *Marchmont Papers*, i. 234, 248.
[2] *Scots Magazine*, 1747, p. 587, and 1748, p. 136.
[3] Macgibbon and Ross's *Architecture of Scotland*, iii. 127.

ray of light entered save by the open door. In the rocky floor there is a shallow well, which in the driest seasons is always full of water. The arched roof is built of huge boulders gathered from the beach, the spaces between being filled up with thin layers of stone after the fashion of Roman masonry. A dark staircase in the thickness of the wall leads up through another strong door to a second vaulted chamber, dimly lighted by narrow slits at the end of two slanting recesses, on each side of which are stone benches. This I was told was the court-room or judgment-hall. Opening out of it on one side is a very small chamber, in which was a kind of cupboard, a hiding-place perhaps for title-deeds and plate, for it could be so closed with stones as to look like solid wall. On the other side is the door to the dungeon, dismal enough, but not so dismal as the pit below, with its well in which women could be put to death with decency. On either side of the mouth of the well is a narrow ledge some eighteen inches wide, but not long enough to allow the prisoner to stretch himself at full length. On the floor above the court-room was the kitchen, with walls more than seven feet thick. It occupied the whole of the story. On the freestone joints of the great hearth can be seen the deep marks made by sharpening knives. Above the kitchen was the family sitting-room, which was entered from a gallery running all round it outside, and built in the overhanging part of the tower. Here at length I arrived at what may be called the front door. There was some attempt at ornament in the carving on the stones at the top and each side of the doorway. There was, moreover, light enough to see it clearly, for the gallery can boast of fair-sized windows. From one of them the laird could look out on the Hangman's Hill, about a third of a mile off, now covered with fir-trees, but then bare. Some stones remain, in which the gallows were set up. The view from the castle, except when a hanging was going on, must on a fine day have been always beautiful, even when the country was bare of trees. To the north and east they looked over fields, once yellow every autumn with grain, but now pleasant meadow-land, shut in with hills and mountains down whose sides in rainy weather rivers stream and cascades leap. From one corner of the gallery a turret projects with two narrow windows, where the watchman could see anyone approaching from the side of the land. Not far from it was "the whispering hole," where, by removing a stone which exactly fits into an opening, a suspicious laird could overhear the talk in the kitchen beneath. Above the sitting-room was another story divided into small rooms, the bed-chamber of the family. So solidly had the roof been built, that unrepaired it withstood all the blasts of heaven, till that terrible storm burst upon it and brought it down, which swept away the Tay Bridge.

In these two upper stories there were, no doubt, cheerful rooms, but they were reached through gloomy doors and iron grates, up dark staircases, with rough sides and well-worn steps, past the gloomy dungeon. Everything shows signs of danger and alarm. " It was sufficient for a Laird of the Hebrides," as Johnson says, " if he had a strong house in which he could hide his wife and children from the next clan." At the present day, as I was told by my guide, no one thinks of locking his door at night-time. My bag and great-coat and travelling rug were left in perfect safety for a couple of hours by the road-side while I wandered about. Of the modern mansion Johnson would never have said what he said of the second house, that " it was built with little regard to convenience, and with none to elegance or pleasure." He would have been delighted not only with it, but with its large garden full of flowers and vegetables and fruits that testify to the mildness of the climate. The peaches ripen on the walls, though they do not attain to a large size. The hot-houses were full of choice plants, and clustering grapes. One bunch, I was told, had weighed nearly five pounds. But there are far greater changes than those worked by builders and gardeners. Here, where the rough old Laird in his out-of-the-way corner of the world used to rule his people with the help of gallows, pit and dungeon, I found a money-order office, a savings bank, a telegraph office, and a daily post. There is a good school, governed by a School Board, and a large reading room where the dulness of the long winter nights is relieved by various kinds of entertainments. There is besides an infirmary under the management of a qualified nurse, the daughter of a medical man, who has learnt her art by some years' study in a hospital. She is provided with a chest of surgical instruments and a large stock of drugs. On her little pony she sometimes has to attend sick people at a distance of eight miles. Forty-three cases of measles had lately been under her care and none of them ended fatally. There is a salmon-hatching house, and a museum both of antiquities and natural curiosities. In it I saw a thumbscrew, with an iron ring at one end through which a thong could be passed. Used in this way it would have served much the same purpose as hand-cuffs. I looked with interest on an old Highland spinning-wheel, the gift of my intelligent and friendly guide, Mr. Angus Black. It had belonged to his grandmother. He had given it, he said, "to be kept there as a present for ages and generations to come." When a little before I drank water from "the well by the river side," such was the name of the spring in Gaelic, he told me that it was the spring "whence the Lairds had drunk for ages and generations past." One thing I in vain looked for in the Museum. Boswell had been told much of a war-saddle, on which Lochbuy, "that reputed Don Quixote, used to be mounted; but we did not see it," he adds, "for the young Laird had applied it to a less noble purpose, having taken it to Falkirk Fair *with a drove of black cattle*." He took it much farther—to America, whither he went with his regiment. There he lost his life in a duel, and it was lost too. Perhaps it is preserved as a curiosity in some collection on the other side of the Atlantic.

I was shown also at a short distance eastwards from the Castle, at the bottom of a crag by the roadside, a place known as the Cheese Cave. Here at every funeral the refreshments used to be placed for the mourners, who had often come twenty miles across the hills. In former days, when there were more men and fewer sheep some hundreds would assemble. "Two old respectable friends were left behind to take care of the food and drink. When the people came back from the grave-yard they refreshed themselves. I have seen them," continued my guide, "sitting on these rocks by the cave having their luncheon." Ramsay of Ochtertyre tells how "the women of each valley through which the funeral passed joined in the procession, but they attended but part of the way and then returned. The whole company seemed to be running; and wherever they rested small cairns or heaps of stones were raised to commemorate the corpse having halted on that spot."[1] These heaps were pointed out to us on the side of Rattachan as we drove down to Glenelg. The silence of the Scotch funeral shocked Wesley, who recorded on May 20, 1774: "When I see in Scotland a coffin put into the earth and covered up without a word spoken, it reminds me of what was spoken concerning Jehoiakin, 'He shall be buried with the burial of an ass.'"[2]

[1] *Scotland and Scotsmen*, &c., ii. 489. [2] Wesley's *Journal*, iv. 14.

It is not with accounts of funerals that I must take my leave of a place where I spent so pleasant a day, and had so hospitable a reception. Here I saw not only the dead past but a vigorous and hopeful present. Even the old Laird, we are told, "was a very hearty and hospitable landlord," though with his belief in his rights of *furca et fossa* he certainly was an ante-diluvian. His descendant does not yield to him in heartiness and hospitality, but has other ways of guiding his people than gallows, pit and dungeon. By his schools, his reading-room, his infirmary and his schemes for developing the fisheries he has won their affections. An old lady who had been allowed to visit the Castle, meeting him by chance as she came out, full of anger at what she had seen, exclaimed : "You ought, Sir, to be ashamed of your ancestors." "No," he replied, "I am not ashamed of them. They led their lives, and I lead mine." They were at all events as good as the men of their time, perhaps better. Old Lochbuy does not seem to have been a bad fellow, though he was slow in learning that he had lost his right to imprison his tenants. "May not a man do what he likes with his own ?" we can fancy him asking in the words used more than seventy years later by an English duke. Much as his descendant has done, there is one thing more which I would ask him to do. He dreads, no doubt, the throng of noisy tourists, but he might surely build a modest inn where the pensive wanderer could find lodging, and enjoy the scenery of Lochbuy.

"The guiltless eye
Commits no wrong, nor wastes what it enjoys."

OBAN AND INVERARY (OCTOBER 22-26).

On the morning of Friday, October 22, our travellers set out for the ferry by which they were to cross to Oban—a distance of about twelve miles. According to Dr. Garnett, travellers were conveyed first to Kerrera, an island lying off the mainland. Crossing this on foot or horseback they found awaiting them another boat to take them to Oban. At Auchnacraig in Mull there was an inn about half a mile from the ferry. Here he and his companion could procure, he says, neither oats for their horses nor straw for their litter. They wanted to give them a mess of oatmeal and water, but the woman, who acted as hostler, at first refused, "asking whether

THE FERRY FROM MULL TO OBAN.

it was proper to give the food of Christians to horses." After a long dispute she yielded. "In these islands," he adds, "horses seldom taste oats."[1] "The bottom of the ferry-boat," says Boswell, "was strewed with branches of trees or bushes upon which we sat. We had a good day and a fine passage, and in the evening landed at Oban, where we found a tolerable inn." This place, which I have seen recommended to cockney tourists in huge advertisements as The Charing Cross of the North, was then a little hamlet. In 1786 Knox found "about twenty families collected together with a view to the fisheries."[2] It boasted of a custom-house and a

KERRERA ISLAND.

post-office. In the islands no customs were paid, for there was no officer to demand them. Faujas Saint-Fond gives a curious account of his stay in the inn, a few years after Johnson's visit. He would have got on very well, for the food though simple was good, and his bed though hard was clean, had it not been for a performer on the bag-pipes—" un maudit joueur de cornemuse " who played "une musique d'un genre nouveau, mais bien terrible pour mon oreille." The day of their arrival this man had strutted up and down before the inn with haughty and warlike looks, and had stunned them with his airs. "Nous crûmes d'abord que ce personnage était une espèce d'insensé qui gagnait sa vie à ce métier." They were informed that he was an accomplished musician, "de l'école

---

[1] T. Garnett *Observations*, &c., i. 145.   Knox's *Tour*, p. 44.
Johnson's *Works*, ix. 52.

highlanders," and that in this display of his talents he was shewing the joy which he felt on seeing strangers in a place where they came so rarely. Touched by his friendly sentiments Saint-Fond had not only applauded him, but had even pressed on him "quelques shelings," which he accepted, it almost seemed, merely out of complaisance. Taking pity on the stranger's solitude he came and played under his bed room window in the silence of the night. It was all in vain that Saint-Fond rose, went out of doors, took him by the hand and led him away. "Il revint au même moment, me donnant à entendre qu'il n'était point fatigué, et qu'il jouerait toute la nuit pour me plaire, et il tint parole."[1]

The bagpiper was surely the direct ancestor of those bands of musicians who at Oban distress the peaceful tourist. But there are things worse even than musicians. How melancholy is the change which has come over the whole scene in the last quarter of a century! A beautiful bay ruined by man! That it should become thronged was inevitable; it need not have been made vulgar. It was on no scene of overgrown hotels that Johnson looked, as, with the tear starting in his eye, he repeated those fine lines in which Goldsmith describes the character of the British nation:

DUNOLLY CASTLE, OBAN.

> "Stern o'er each bosom reason holds her state,
> With daring aims irregularly great,
> Pride in their port, defiance in their eye,
> I see the lords of humankind pass by,
> Intent on high designs, a thoughtful band,
> By forms unfashion'd, fresh from Nature's hand;
> Fierce in their native hardiness of soul,
> True to imagin'd right, above control,
> While e'en the peasant boasts these rights to scan,
> And learns to venerate himself as man."

The *Traveller* had formed the subject of their talk at breakfast, and it was while Boswell helped Johnson on with his great-coat that

[1] *Voy. en Angleterre*, &c., i. 360-373.

he recited these lines. They had a long ride before them through heavy rain to Inverary. Loch Awe they crossed by the ferry at Portsonachan—"a pretty wide lake," as Boswell describes it, not knowing its name. Towards evening they came to a good road made by the soldiers, the first which they had seen since they left Fort Augustus more than seven weeks before. Unwearied by his long journey, Johnson that same night wrote a letter to Mrs. Thrale in which he thus describes both what he saw and what he felt.

"About ten miles of this day's journey were uncommonly amusing. We travelled with very little light in a storm of wind and rain; we passed about fifty-five streams that crossed our way, and fell into a river that, for a very great part of our road foamed and roared beside us. All the rougher powers of nature, except thunder, were in motion, but there was no danger. I should have been sorry to have missed any of the inconveniences, to have had more light or less rain, for their co-operation crowded the scene and filled the mind."

When an old man describes such a journey as "uncommonly amusing" it is clear that he uses the term in a sense which it does not bear at present. In his *Dictionary* he defines *amuse*, "to entertain with tranquillity; to fill with thoughts that engage the mind without distracting it." The thoughts which this stormy evening in late autumn engaged his mind amidst the wilds of Argyleshire he put forth in a fine passage when, in the quietness of his study, he came to write the account of his journey.

"The night came on while we had yet a great part of the way to go, though not so dark but that we could discern the cataracts which poured down the hills on one side, and fell into one general channel, that ran with great violence on the other. The wind was loud, the rain was heavy, and the whistling of the blast, the fall of the shower, the rush of the cataracts, and the roar of the torrent, made a nobler chorus of the rough musick of nature than it had ever been my chance to hear before.

The man who wrote this noble passage had not surely that insensibility to nature which is so often laid to his charge. He was sixty-four years old; mounted on a pony scarcely strong enough to bear his weight, he had had a long and hard day's ride through wind and rain; he had dined in his wet clothes in a hut warmed by a smoky turf fire, and yet at the end of the day he could say with the enthusiasm of a young poet that neither darkness nor storm would he willingly have had lessened. He was supported, no doubt, in his recollections by the comforts of the inn at Inverary which was, he said, "not only commodious, but magnificent." Perhaps he was inspired also by the gill of whisky which he called for—"the first fermented liquor," says Boswell, "that he tasted during his travels." He forgets, however, the brandy which he was prevailed on to drink at Dunvegan when he was suffering from cold. "Come, (said Johnson) let me know what it is that makes a Scotchman happy." He thought it preferable to any English malt brandy. "What was the process," he writes, "I had no opportunity of enquiring, nor do I wish to improve the art of making poison pleasant." To the excellence of the inn at Inverary, Pennant also bears testimony. Far otherwise does Burns speak of it, in his in-

INVERARY CASTLE.

dignation at the incivility of the landlord, whose whole attention was occupied by the visitors of the Duke of Argyle.

"Whoe'er he be that sojourns here,
 I pity much his case,
Unless he comes to wait upon
 The Lord their God his Grace.

"There's naething here but Highland pride,
 And Highland scab and hunger;
If Providence has sent me here,
 'Twas surely in an anger."

At Inverary our travellers rested from Saturday evening till Tuesday morning. This pleasant little town had a very different look from that which it now bears. "This place," wrote Pennant, "will in time be very magnificent; but at present the space between the front of the castle and the water is disgraced with the old town,

SUNDAY ON LOCH FYNE.

composed of the most wretched hovels that can be imagined."[1] These have long been cleared away, so that there is now an unbroken view over a finely wooded lawn of the loch and the hills beyond. It was in the beginning of September, 1769, that he visited the place. "Every evening," he says, "some hundreds of boats cover the surface of Loch Fyne. On the week-days the cheerful noise of the bag-pipe and dance echoes from on board; on the Sabbath each boat approaches the land, and psalmody and devotion divide the day." Our travellers were perhaps too late in the year to witness this curious scene; at all events they make no mention of it. Had they heard the psalm-singing on the Sunday they would not have left it unnoticed. The forenoon of that day they "passed calmly and placidly." Of all the Sundays which I passed in Scotland, nowhere did I find such an unbroken stillness as here. It was far quieter than the towns, for the people were as still as mice, and it was quieter than the country, for there was an absence of country noises. We were alone in our hotel.

ELIZABETH GUNNING.

It was the last day of June, but there were scarcely any other strangers in the place to enjoy the beautiful scenery and the long summer days.

Boswell hesitated, or affected to hesitate, about calling on the Duke of Argyle. "I had reason to think," he writes, "that the duchess disliked me on account of my zeal in the Douglas cause; but the duke had always been pleased to treat me with great civility." The duchess was that famous beauty, Elizabeth Gunning,

[1] *Tour in Scotland*, ed. 1774, i. 218.

THE DUKE AND DUCHESS OF ARGYLE.

the wife of two dukes and the mother of four. Her sister had married the Earl of Coventry. "The two beautiful sisters," says Horace Walpole, "were going on the stage, when they are at once exalted almost as high as they could be, were countessed and double-duchessed."[1] The duchess, by her first husband, the Duke of Hamilton, was the mother of the unsuccessful competitor for the Douglas estates, and was therefore "prejudiced against Boswell,

JOHNSON BOCE.

who had shown all the bustling importance of his character in the Douglas cause."[2] Johnson, on hearing the state of the case, "was clear that Boswell ought to pay his respects at the castle. I mentioned," continues Boswell, "that I was afraid my company might be disagreeable to the duchess. He treated the objection with a manly disdain, '*That*, Sir, he must settle with his wife.' He insisted that I should not go to the castle this day before dinner, as it

would look like seeking an invitation. 'But,' said I, 'if the duke invites us to dine with him to-morrow, shall we accept?' 'Yes, Sir,' I think he said, 'to be sure.' But he added, 'He won't ask us.'" By the duke, who was sitting over his wine, Boswell was most politely received; but when he was taken into the drawing-room and introduced, neither the duchess nor the ladies with her took the least notice of him. The following day he and Johnson were shown through the castle. "It is a stately place," said Johnson.

[1] Walpole *Letters*, v. 358. [2] Boswell's *Johnson*, v. 353, n. 1.

"What I admire here is the total defiance of expense." In a low one-horse chair our two travellers were driven through "the duke's spacious park and rising forests." "I had," writes Boswell, "a particular pride in showing Dr. Johnson a great number of fine old trees, to compensate for the nakedness which had made such an impression on him on the eastern coast of Scotland." Pennant noticed pines nine feet, and beeches from nine to twelve feet in girth, planted, it was said, by the Earl of Argyle who was beheaded in 1685. They have grown to a noble size, and in one part form a long avenue, which would grace that English county which takes its name from its beech woods. Even in the Black Forest I do not

THE AVENUE OF BEECHES.

know that I have seen larger pines. The planting still goes on. A fine young Spanish chestnut boasts in the inscription which it bears that in the year 1858 it was planted by Lord Tennyson. "Would," I exclaimed as I read the words, "that twin chestnuts of stately growth in like manner commemorated the visit of Johnson and Boswell." But Johnson's trees are scattered broadcast over Scotland. *Si monumentum quæris, circumspice.*

The fine collection of arms of which he took much notice still adorns the hall. Of the pictures no mention is made by either of the travellers, though in more than one they might have recognized the work of their friend Sir Joshua. Here is his full-length portrait of the beautiful duchess, "about whom the world had gone mad" one and twenty years before. When she was presented at

K K

Court, "the crowd was so great," writes Horace Walpole, "that even the noble mob in the drawing-room clambered upon chairs and tables to look at her." As she passed down to Scotland, "seven hundred people," it was reported, "sat up all night in and about an inn in Yorkshire to see her get into her post-chaise next morning."[1] Here, too, is a small but lovely picture of her sister, the Countess of Coventry. On her going down to her husband's

THE HALL, INVERARY CASTLE.

country seat near Worcester, "a shoemaker in that town got two guineas and a half by showing a shoe that he was making for her at a penny a-piece."[2] In striking contrast with the two sisters are many of the portraits which hang on the walls. It is a strange company which is brought together: Mary, Queen of Scots, and her half-sister, a Countess of Argyle; Oliver Cromwell; the Marquis of Argyle, and just below him Charles II., who sent him to the scaffold; the earl, his son, who was beheaded by James II.; and

---

[1] Horace Walpole, *Letters*, ii. 281, 285.   [2] *Ib.* p. 295.

John, the great duke, who broke the neck of the rebellion in 1715, and rendered desperate the cause of James II.'s son.

The room in which our travellers dined is much in the state in which they saw it; the walls panelled with the same festoons, and the chairs adorned with the same gilding and the same tapestry. But it is turned to other uses. No "splendid dinner" is served up in it such as Johnson enjoyed and praised; no "luxuries" such as

THE OLD DINING ROOM.

he defended. No Lady Betty Hamilton can quietly take her chair after dinner, and lean upon the back of it, as she listens eagerly to the great talker, who is unaware that she is just behind him. No Boswell can with a steady countenance have the satisfaction for once to look a duchess in the face, as with a respectful air he drinks to her good health. The tables are covered with books and magazines, and pamphlets, and correspondence. It is the duke's business-room where he sees his chamberlain,[1] and where his librarian

---

[1] "I went to renew my lease, but my Lord's *Chamberloun* was not at home. Steward. The

receives and sorts the new publications which are ever coming in, before he transfers them to the shelves of the library.

The noble drawing-room remains unchanged—the gilded ceiling, the old French tapestry covering the walls, the gilt tapestry chairs, the oaken floor, up and down which the duke and Boswell walked conversing, while her grace made Dr. Johnson come and sit by her. All is the same, except that time has dealt kindly by the tapestry and the gilding, and refined them in their fading.

Faujas Saint Fond, who spent three days in the castle a few years later, is full of praise of everything which he saw. The duke and his family, he says, spoke French with a purity not unworthy

TAPESTRY BEDROOM.

of the highest society in Paris. The cookery, with the exception of a few dishes, was French, and was excellent. There was an abundance of hot-house fruits. There were silver forks instead of "ces petits tridens d'acier bien aigus, en forme de dard, fixés sur un manche, dont on se sert ordinairement en Angleterre, même dans les maisons où l'on donne de fort bons diners."[1] Still more did he rejoice at seeing napkins on the table, a rare sight in England. The hours of meals were, breakfast at ten o'clock, dinner at half-past four, and supper at ten. At dinner, after the ladies had withdrawn, "la cérémonie des toasts" lasted at least three-quarters of an hour.[2]

At Inverary Johnson met not only the descendants of a long line

---

person who receives the rents and revenues of some corporations is still called chamberlain; as the chamberlain of London." Beattie's Scot tournes, p. 24.

[1] Voyage en Angleterre, &c., i. 290.

[2] He gives the following curious account of an accommodation which we should scarcely have expected to find in the dining-room of In-

verary: "Si pendant les libations, le champagne mousseux fait ressentir son influence apéritive, le cas est prévu, et sans quitter la compagnie, on trouve dans de jolies encoignures placées dans les angles de la salle, tout ce qui est nécessaire pour satisfaire à ce petit besoin." Voyage en Angleterre, &c., i. 234.

of famous statesmen, but also the ancestor of a great historian. Lord Macaulay's grandfather was at this time Minister of Inverary. He passed the evening with our travellers at their inn after they had returned from dining at the Castle, and got somewhat roughly handled in talk.

> "When Dr. Johnson spoke of people whose principles were good, but whose practice was faulty, Mr. Macaulay said, he had no notion of people being in earnest in their good professions, whose practice was not suitable to them. The doctor grew warm, and said, 'Sir, are you so grossly ignorant of human nature, as not to know that a man may be very sincere in good principles, without having good practice?'"

On this Sir George Trevelyan remarks in his life of his uncle: "When we think what well-known ground this was to Lord Macaulay it is impossible to suppress a wish that the great talker had been at hand to avenge his grandfather and grand-uncle."[1] "A hundred to one on Sam Johnson," say we. It is a pity that it was not at the Manse that they spent that Sunday evening; for there the little child who was one day to make the name of Zachary Macaulay famous as the liberator of the slaves would have gazed with eager open eyes on the great Englishman, who had startled the grave men at Oxford by giving as his toast: "Here's to the next insurrection of the negroes in the West-Indies."

GLENCROE, LOCH LOMOND, AND GLASGOW (OCTOBER 26-30).

The Duke of Argyle, who had heard Dr. Johnson complain that the shelties were too small for his weight, "was obliging enough to mount him on a stately steed from his Grace's stable." Joseph (Boswell's servant), said:—"He now looks like a bishop." Leaving Inverary on the morning of Tuesday, October 26, they rode round the head of Loch Fyne through Glencroe to Tarbet on Loch Lomond. Boswell, who was becoming somewhat indolent in keeping his journal, passes over this part of their tour in silence. Saint-Fond speaks of the Glen as "ce triste passage." Pennant describes it as "the seat of melancholy," and Johnson as "a black and dreary region. At the top of the hill," he adds, "is a seat with this inscription, 'Rest and be thankful.' Stones were placed to mark the distances, which the inhabitants have taken away, resolved,

[1] *Life of Lord Macaulay*, ed. 1877, i. 7.

they said, to have no new miles." The road was that at which Wolfe's men had been working twenty years earlier.

"He that has gained at length the wished for height," still finds

"REST AND BE THANKFUL."

as Wordsworth many years later found "this brief, this simple wayside call," *Rest and be Thankful;* but there is no longer a seat where his weary limbs may repose. Perhaps some day it will be restored with the old inscription and the following addition:—"James Wolfe, 1753. Samuel Johnson, 1773. William Wordsworth, 1831." It is on a mile-stone, or on what looks like a mile-stone, that the inscription is now read. Beneath is carved.

> MILITARY ROAD REPD.
> BY 93D REGT. 1768.
> TRANSFERRED TO
> COMMRS FOR H. R. & B.[1]
> IN THE YEAR 1814.

One of the earlier tablets, which were believed to have been put up by Wolfe's men, was pulled down many years ago by a farmer at Ardvoirlich, and transformed into a hearth stone.[2] Glencoe is but little changed since Johnson looked upon it. It is still lonely and grand. The tourist's carriage breaks the quiet from time to time, but it soon sinks back into "sublimity, silence and solitude." When we passed through it there was no succession of cataracts and no roaring torrent such as Johnson described. The long drought had made a silence in the hills. We met only one tourist—a lad on his bicycle who had escaped that morning from the smoke of Glasgow, and full of eagerness and life, was pressing on to the inn where his long ride of fifty miles would find its pleasant termination in dinner and a bed. I called to mind how seven and thirty years before when I was just such another youngster, as I was crossing the top of the Glen, I had seen in the distance

---

[1] Commissioners for Highland Roads and Bridges. [2] Wright's *Life of General Wolfe*, p. 269.

something white fluttering in the wind. It was a big Highlander returning, as he told us, from Glasgow. Overcome by the heat of the day, and incommoded by a garment to which he was not much accustomed, he had taken off his trousers and was carrying them on his shoulders. It was his shirt that had caught my eye.

At Tarbet our travellers dined at the little inn on the bank of Loch Lomond. Here, a few years later, Saint-Fond and his party

MILESTONES ON THE TARBET ROAD.

arrived very late on a rainy night in September. They were on their way from Glasgow to Inverary, and had meant to rest at Luss. Unfortunately for them it was the the time of the autumn circuit. The inn looked like a fisherman's hut. The landlady coming out made them a sign that they must not utter a sound. They were thrust into a stable, where she said:—"Le lord juge me fait l'honorable faveur dans sa tournée de loger chez moi; il est là; chacun doit respecter ce qu'il fait, il dort." She added that she could take in neither them nor their horses. They remonstrated,

"Point de bruit, ne troublez pas le sommeil du juge, respect à la loi ; soyez heureux et partez." They had no help for it, but drove on with their weary horses through the night and the heavy rain to Tarbet, where they arrived between three and four next morning. There they found all the beds occupied by jurymen, who were on their way to Inverary. The landlady did what she could to make them comfortable, and gave them some good tea in a set of China cups which had been given her by the Duchess of Argyle.[1]

At Stuckgown, close to Tarbet, Lord Jeffrey for many years passed a few weeks of every summer, in a quietness and solitude which have for ever fled the place. Writing from Tarbeton August 5, 1818, he says: "Here we are in a little inn on the banks of Loch

ROSSDHU.

Lomond, in the midst of the mists of the mountains, the lakes, heaths, rocks, and cascades which have been my passion since I was a boy, and to which, like a boy, I have run away the instant I could get my hands clear of law, and review, and Edinburgh. They have no post-horses in the Highlands, and we sent away those that brought us here, with orders to come back for us to morrow, and so we are left without a servant, entirely at the mercy of the natives." He goes on to mention a steam-boat "which circumnavigates the whole lake every day in about ten hours. It was certainly very strange and striking to hear and see it hissing and roaring past the headlands of our little bay, foaming and spouting like an angry whale ; but on the whole it rather vulgarises the scene too much, and I am glad that it is found not to answer, and

[1] *Voyage en Angleterre*, etc. i. 268.

is to be dropped next year."[1] At Tarbet the tourist who is oppressed with the size of the hotel and the army of waiters, and who sees the pier as I saw it crowned with an automatic sweet-meat machine, may well wish that the steam-boat had never been found to answer. The scene is hopelessly vulgarised. It is fast sinking into the paradise of cockneys. I asked for that variety of bread which I remember to have seen served up there thirty-seven years ago. I was scornfully told that in those days the Scotch had not known how to bake, but that now they could make a large loaf as well as anyone. At Inverary I had in vain asked for oat-cakes at my hotel. If Johnson were to make his journey in these present times, and were confined to the big tourists' hotels, he would certainly no longer say that an epicure, wherever he had supped, would wish to breakfast in Scotland.

From Tarbet he rode along the shores of Loch Lomond to Rosedew,[2] the house of Sir James Colquhoun. "It was a place," says the historian of Dumbartonshire, "rich in historic associations, but about 1770 it was super-seded by a new mansion, to which large additions have since been made."[3] Here Boswell passed in review Johnson's courteous behaviour at Inverary, and said, "You were quite a fine gentleman when with the duchess.' He answered in good humour, 'Sir, I look upon myself as a very polite man.'" Next morning "we took," writes Johnson, "a boat to row upon the lake. It has about thirty islands, of which twenty belong to Sir James. Young Colquhoun[4] went into the boat with us, but a little agitation of the water frighted him to shore. We passed up and down and landed upon one small island,[5] on which are the ruins of a castle; and upon another much larger, which serves Sir James for a park, and is remarkable for a large wood of yew trees." Just one hundred years later, on December 18, 1873, that very fate befel one of his descendants which the young Colquhoun dreaded

INCH GALBRAITH.

---

[1] Cockburn's *Life of Jeffrey*, ed. 1852, ii. 180.
[2] Rosedhu.
[3] J. Irving' *Book of Dumbarton his.*, ii. 242. See ib. p. 257, where it is stated that it was in 1774 (the year after Johnson's visit), that "a re-moval was made from the old castle to the centre portion."
[4] Johnson spells the name as it was pronounced Cohoon.
[5] Inch Galbraith.

for himself. In the darkness of a winter's evening his boat was upset as he was coming home from the Yew Island, and he was drowned with three of his gamekeepers and a boy. It was never known how the accident happened, for no one escaped; but the boat was heavily laden with the dead bodies of some stags, which they had shot in the island, and the unhappy men were weighed down with their accoutrements and the ammunition which they carried. The yew trees were planted, it was said, on the advice of King Robert Bruce, in order to furnish the Lennox men with

YEW TREE ISLAND.

trusty bows.[1] The old castle, "on which the osprey built her annual nest," is so much buried in ivy that it is not easily distinguished from the surrounding woods. We hired a boat at Luss and in our turn roved upon the lake. We landed on one of the islands and lunched on the top of a rock by the ruins of a second castle. Loch Lomond, studded with islands, lay like a mirror beneath us, with the huge Ben Lomond for a noble background. From time to time a boat broke the smoothness of the water, and the cry of a gull, or the bark of a far-away dog, the stillness of the air. We spoke of the heat and bustle of the world, but imagination almost refused to picture them in so peaceful a spot. Our boat-

[1] Irving's *Book of Dumbartonshire*, i. 347.

man was a man of a strong mind, which had not been suffered to lie barren. He bore his part well in a talk on books. I had chanced to mention the serfs who worked in the coal mines and salt pans in Scotland; he at once struck into the conversation. "Sir Walter Scott," he said, "makes one of his characters say, 'he would not take him back like a collier on a salter.' This made me look the matter up for I did not understand what he meant." He praised the old Scotch common schools. "We Scotchmen," he proudly said, "have had education for three hundred years. A Scotch working-man would starve to death to give his son a good education." The present race of schoolmasters who are "paid by results," he contrasted unfavourably with those whom he had known in his boyhood. "The old Dominies would willingly teach all that they knew, and grudged no time to a boy who was eager for knowledge; but now they are like other people, and when they have done their day's work they will do no more." In the village club to which he belonged, they had in the last two or three winters engaged for a few weeks a young Glasgow student to teach them elocution, "for how could they enjoy Shakespeare if they did not know how to read him properly?" He praised the Colquhouns. "They would never send any of their tenants to prison for poaching. They might fine them, but the money they would give away in charity." He spoke of the old clan feeling, and of the protection given by the laird. His grandfather, who was a farmer, a Macpherson by name, had married a Macqueen.[1] On a rapid fall in the price of Highland cattle he fell into money difficulties, and was harshly threatened with a forced sale by one of his creditors. The Laird of the Macqueens said significantly to this man: "You may do whatever you like against Macpherson, but remember that his wife is a Macqueen." The hint was enough, and the proceedings were at once dropped. Our boatman had read Johnson's *Journey to the Western Islands*, but said that Scotchmen feel too sore about him to like reading him. I opened the book, for I had it with me, and read the concluding words in which he says: "Novelty and ignorance must always be reciprocal, and I cannot but be conscious that my thoughts on national manners are the thoughts of one who has seen but little." My boatman was much struck with his modesty, and seemed to think that he had formed too severe a judgment.

[1] I have intentionally altered the names.

Boswell was not so careful in recording Johnson's talk on the Lake as I was with our boatman's. "I recollect," he writes, "none of his conversation, except that, when talking of dress, he said, 'Sir, were I to have any thing fine, it should be very fine. Were I to wear a ring, it should not be a bauble, but a stone of great value. Were I to wear a laced or embroidered waistcoat, it should be very rich. I had once a very rich laced waistcoat, which I wore the first night of my tragedy.'" Johnson, nearly five and twenty years before, sat in one of the side-boxes of Drury Lane Theatre, in a scarlet waistcoat, with rich gold lace, and a gold-

CAMERON.

laced hat, listening to the catcalls whistling before the curtain rose; how little could he have thought that one day he would boast of his costume as he was roving in a boat upon Loch Lomond!

In the evening they drove to Cameron, the seat of Commissary Smollett. It was the first drive which they had taken since at Inverness they began their *equitation* full two months earlier. "Our satisfaction," says Boswell, "of [*sic*] finding ourselves again in a comfortable carriage was very great. We had a pleasing conviction of the commodiousness of civilisation, and heartily laughed at the ravings of those absurd visionaries who have attempted to persuade us of the superior advantages of a *state of nature*." With these visionaries Boswell himself sometimes sided. The people of

Otaheite especially had won his admiration. "No, Sir;" said Johnson to him on one such occasion: "You are not to talk such paradox; let me have no more on't. It cannot entertain, far less can it instruct." "Don't cant in defence of savages," he said, on another occasion. At Cameron they had none of this fanciful talk. Their host "was a man of considerable learning, with abundance of animal spirits; so that he was a very good companion for Dr. Johnson, who said, 'We have had more solid talk here than at any place where we have been.'" He was a relation of the great novelist, and one of the four judges of the Commissary Court in Edinburgh. It was the sole court in Scotland which took cognisance of actions about marriage, and the Supreme Court in all questions of probate. "It sat," says the lively Topham, "in a little room of about ten feet square; from the darkness and dirtiness of it you would rather imagine that those who were brought into it were confined there." The judges were paid rather by perquisites than by salaries. In each cause they fixed the amount which the litigants should pay them for the sentence which they pronounced.[1]

SMOLLETT'S PILLAR.

Smollett, in his *Humphry Clinker*, brings Matthew Bramble and his nephew to Cameron, who describe it as "a very neat country house, but so embosomed in an oak wood that we did not see it till we were within fifty yards of the door." "If I was disposed to be critical," Mr. Bramble continues, "I should say it is too near the Lake, which approaches on one side to within six or seven yards of the window."[2] The Commissary had erected a pillar by the side of the high road to Glasgow, "to the memory of his ingenious kinsman," who two years earlier had died in Italy, "Eheu! quam procul a patria!" The Latin inscription for this monument was shown to Johnson, and revised by him "with an ardent and liberal earnestness." The copy with the corrections

---

[1] Topham's *Letters from Edinburgh*, p. 296, and Arnot's *History of Edinburgh*, p. 401.
[2] *Humphry Clinker*, iii. 17, 19.

in his handwriting is preserved among the family papers at Cameron.[1]

On Thursday, October 28, a postchaise which Boswell had ordered from Glasgow, "came for us," he says, "and we drove on in high spirits." On their way they stopped at Dunbarton, then "a small but good old town, consisting principally of one large street in the form of a crescent;"[2] but now a smoky seat of the iron ship-building industry. The steep rock on which the Castle stands Johnson "ascended with alacrity." At Glasgow they stayed at the "Saracen's Head," "the paragon of inns in the eyes of the Scotch," says a writer in the *Gentleman's Magazine*, "but most wretchedly

DUNBARTON.

managed."[3] Our two travellers seem to have been contented. Johnson, no doubt, was kept in the best of humours by the sight of a great many letters from England, after the long interval of sixty-eight days during which not a line had reached him. "He enjoyed in imagination the comforts which we could now command, and seemed to be in high glee. I remember, he put a leg up on each side of the grate, and said, with a mock solemnity, by way of soliloquy, but loud enough for me to hear it: 'Here am I, an ENGLISH man, sitting by a *coal* fire.'" Of fires made by peat, that "sullen fuel," he had had enough in the last two months. All along the sea-board coal was made artificially dear by the folly of

[1] Irving's *Book of Dumbartonshire*, ii. 200. [2] Pennant's *Tour in Scotland*, ed. 1774, i. 228.
[3] *Gentleman's Magazine*, 1771, p. 545.

Parliament. A duty of five shillings and fourpence per chaldron, says Knox, was levied on coal at ports; none on inland coal. It had to be landed at a port where there is a custom-house, and might then be re-shipped for some other place in the neighbourhood.[1] Custom-houses were few and far between, so that in many cases, if coal was used at all, it would have had to be twice landed and twice shipped. On this mischievous regulation Adam Smith remarks: "Where coals are naturally cheap they are consumed duty free; where they are naturally dear, they are loaded with a heavy duty."[2]

The "Saracen's Head" with its coal fire has disappeared. My boatman had heard the old people talk of it. In this inn the following morning Dr. Reid, the philosopher, and two of the other professors of the University breakfasted with Johnson. He met some of them also at dinner, tea, and supper. "I was not much pleased with any of them," he wrote to Mrs. Thrale. Boswell unfortunately was again lazy with his journal, and kept no record of the talk. Writing long afterwards, he says: "The general impression upon my memory is, that we had not much conversation at Glasgow, where the professors, like their brethren at Aberdeen, did not venture to expose themselves much to the battery of cannon which they knew might play upon them." Reid's silence was perhaps merely due to that reserve which he generally shewed among strangers.[3] Had fate been kinder, the great Clow might have been still among them, who twenty-two years before had been preferred both to Hume and Burke as Adam Smith's successor in the Chair of Logic.[4] The story of the Billingsgate altercation between Smith and Johnson, recorded by Sir Walter Scott, is wholly untrue. Smith was not at this time in Glasgow. It is, no doubt, one of those tales about Johnson in which Scotch invention was humorously displayed. It was, perhaps, meant as a reply to the question which one day, in London, he put to Adam Smith, who was boasting of Glasgow, "Pray, sir, have you ever seen Brentford?" Boswell says: "I put him in mind of it to-day while he expressed his admiration of the elegant buildings, and whispered him, 'Don't you feel some remorse?'" Smith's pride in the city where he had spent more than three years as a student, and twelve as a professor, was assuredly well-founded. Johnson calls it

[1] Knox's *Tour*, pp. cli-iii.
[2] *Wealth of Nations*, ed. 1811, iii. 335.
[3] Tytler's *Life of Lord Kames*, ii. 230.
[4] Burton's *Life of Hume*, i. 351.

"opulent and handsome," and Boswell "beautiful." Nearly two centuries earlier Camden had said that "for pleasant situation, apple-trees, and other like fruit trees, it is much commended."[1] Defoe describes it as "indeed a very fine city; the four principal streets are the fairest for breadth, and the finest built that I have ever seen in one city together. It is the cleanest, and beautifullest, and best built city in Britain, London excepted."[2] Another traveller of about the same date says that "it is the beautifullest little city he had seen in Britain. It stands deliciously on the banks of the River Clyde."[3] In June, 1757, John Wesley went up to the top of the cathedral steeple. "It gave us a fine prospect," he writes, "both of the city and the adjacent country. A more fruitful and better cultivated plain is scarce to be seen in England."[4] Smollett swells the general chorus of praise: "Glasgow is the pride of Scotland. It is one of the prettiest towns in Europe."[5] Pennant, who visited it the year before Johnson, calls it "the best built of any second-rate city I ever saw. The view from the Cross has an air of vast magnificence."[6]

At the Rebellion of 1745 the citizens had shown the greatest loyalty. They raised and supported at their own expense two battalions of six hundred men each, who joined the duke's army. Their town was occupied by the Pretender's forces, who for ten days lived there at free quarters. They had had to pay, moreover, two heavy fines, amounting to more than nine thousand pounds, imposed on them for their fidelity to the Hanoverian Family. In 1749, in answer to their petition for relief, they received a grant from Parliament of ten thousand pounds.[7] On April 24 of that same year a stage-coach began to run between Glasgow and Edinburgh, starting from Edinburgh every Monday and Thursday, and from Glasgow every Tuesday and Friday. "Every person pays nine shillings fare, and is allowed a stone weight of luggage"[8] By the year 1783 far greater facilities were afforded. In John Tait's *Directory for Glasgow* of that year (p. 77) it is announced that "three machines set out from each town every day at eight morning. They stop on the road and change horses. Tickets, 10s. 6d.

---

[1] Camden's *Description of Scotland*, 2nd ed. p. 81.
[2] Defoe's *Tour through Great Britain: Scotland*, p. 83.
[3] J. Macky's *Journey through Scotland*, ed. 1723, p. 295.
[4] Wesley's *Journal*, ii. 410.
[5] *Humphry Clinker*, iii. 14, 33.
[6] *Voyage to the Hebrides*, ed. 1774, p. 127
[7] *Scots Magazine*, 1749, p. 202.
[8] *Scots Magazine*, 1749, p. 253.

each." There was another daily "machine" belonging to a different set of proprietors, besides one which ran only three times a week, and charged but 8s. 6d. "The Carlisle Diligence," it is announced, "sets out every lawful day."

As we gaze on the filthy river which runs by the large city, on the dense cloud of smoke which hangs over it, on the grimy streets which have swallowed up the country far and wide, while we exult in the display of man's ingenuity and strength, and in the commerce by which the good things of earth are so swiftly and cheaply interchanged, we may mourn over the beautiful little town among the apple-trees which stood so deliciously on the banks of the fair and pure stream that ran to seawards beneath the arches of the old stone bridge. How far removed from us are those days when Glasgow was pillaged by the wild rabble of Highlanders! Yet I have an uncle[1] still living who remembers his grandfather and his grandfather's brother, one of whom had climbed up a tree to see the other march with a body of Worcestershire volunteers against the Young Pretender.

Johnson, after seeing the sights of the city, visited the college. "It has not had," he writes, "a sufficient share of the increasing magnificence of the place." From the account which Dr. Alexander Carlyle gives of the citizens, as he had known them about thirty years earlier, they were not likely to trouble themselves much about the glory of their University. With a few exceptions they were "shopkeepers and mechanics, or successful pedlars, who occupied large warerooms full of manufactures of all sorts to furnish a cargo to Virginia. In those accomplishments and that taste that belong to people of opulence, much more to persons of education, they were far behind the citizens of Edinburgh." There was not a teacher of French or of music in the whole town. Nevertheless, in the University itself he found "learning an object of more importance, and the habit of application much more general" than in the rival institution in the capital.[2] Wesley compared the two squares which formed the college with the small quadrangles of Lincoln College, Oxford, of which he was a Fellow, and did not think them larger, or at all handsomer. He was surprised at the dress of the students. "They wear scarlet gowns, reaching only to their knees. Most I saw were very dirty, some very ragged,

---

[1] Mr. Frederic Hill, late Assistant-Secretary to the Post Office. [2] Dr. A. Carlyle's *Autobiography*, pp. 71, 74.

and all of very coarse cloth." [1] How much more surprised would he have been at the far shorter gowns now worn by the commoners in his own university, showing, as they do, a raggedness which is not the effect of age and wear, but of intentional mutilation! There is an affectation of antiquity quite as much in a freshman's gown, as in the pedigree of some upstart who boasts that he is sprung from the Plantagenets. The college numbered at this time about four hundred students, most of whom lived in lodgings, but some boarded with the professors. [2]

The principal was Dr. Leechman, whose sermon on prayer had once raised a storm "among the high-flying clergy." [3]

"In his house Dr. Johnson had the satisfaction of being told that his name had been gratefully celebrated in one of the parochial congregations in the Highlands, as the person to whose influence it was chiefly owing that the New Testament was allowed to be translated into the Erse language. It seems some political members of the Society in Scotland for propagating Christian Knowledge had opposed this pious undertaking, as tending to preserve the distinction between the Highlanders and Lowlanders."

Johnson, in a letter full of generous indignation, had maintained that "he that voluntarily continues ignorance, is guilty of all the crimes which ignorance produces," and had compared these political Christians to the planters of America, "a race of mortals whom, I suppose, no other man wishes to resemble." [4] Though he was no doubt struck by Leechman's appearance, "which was that of an ascetic, reduced by fasting and prayer," yet in his talk he could have had no pleasure. "He was not able to carry on common conversation, and when he spoke at all, it was a short lecture." The young students who were invited to his house, longed to be summoned from the library to tea in the drawing-room, where his wife "maintained a continued conversation on plays, novels, poetry, and the fashions." [5]

DUNDONALD CASTLE, AUCHANS (OCTOBER 30—NOVEMBER 2).

On Saturday, October 30, our travellers set out on their way to Boswell's home at Auchinleck, in Ayrshire. Part of the way must

[1] Wesley's *Journal*, ii. 286.
[2] Pennant's *Voyage to the Hebrides*, ed. 1774, p. 136.
[3] Dr. A. Carlyle's *Autobiography*, p. 69, and Johnson's *Boswell*, v. 68.
[4] Boswell's *Johnson*, ii. 27.
[5] Dr. A. Carlyle's *Autobiography*, pp. 68, 83.

have been over a wild country, for a few years earlier, in his "Instructions" for his friend Temple on his tour to Auchinleck, he writes: "Set out [from Glasgow] for Kingswell, to which you have a good road; arrived there, get a guide to put you through the muir to Loudoun."[1] He and Johnson did not go the whole distance in one day, though they had but thirty-four miles to travel. They broke their journey at the house of Mr. Campbell, of Treesbank, who had married Mrs. Boswell's sister. Here they rested till Tuesday. At a few miles distance Robert Burns, a lad of thirteen, "a dexterous ploughman for his age," was spending his boyhood "in unceasing moil" and hardship, not having as yet "committed the sin of rhyme." Boswell, I believe, much as he admired Allan Ramsay's poem in the Scottish dialect, *The Gentle*

DUNDONALD CASTLE.

Shepherd, never makes mention of Burns, and Burns only once mentions him. In the *Author's Earnest Cry and Prayer*, written before the year 1786, he says:

> "Alas! I'm but a nameless wight,
> Trode i' the mire an' out o' sight!
> But could I like Montgomeries fight,
>   Or gab[2] like Boswell,
> There's some sark-necks[3] I wad draw tight,
>   An' tie some hose well."

Dundonald Castle, in which Robert II. lived and died, our travellers visited on Monday morning. "It has long been unroofed," writes Boswell, "and though of considerable size we could not by any power of imagination, figure it as having been a suitable habitation for majesty. Dr. Johnson, to irritate my *old Scottish* enthusiasm,

---

[1] Boswell's *Letters to Temple*, p. 98.   [2] To prate.   [3] Shirt-collars.

was very jocular on the homely accommodation of "King *Bob*," and roared and laughed till the ruins echoed."

The castle belongs to two periods. The original keep was eighty-one feet long, forty broad, and seventy high. It was afterwards lengthened at the southern end by seventeen feet. "The great hall has been a very noble apartment."[1] Boswell justly praises the view. "It stands," he says, "on a beautiful rising ground, which is seen at a great distance on several quarters, and from whence there is an extensive prospect of the rich district of Cuninghame, the western sea, the isle of Arran, and a part of the northern coast of Ireland." Camden quaintly says that "the name *Cunninghame*, if one interpret it, is as much as the *King's Habitation*, by which a man may guess how commodious and pleasant it is."[2] As I sat on the Castle hill, and looked over the fine country to the north-west, I could have wished that the tall chimneys of Irvine, pouring forth clouds of smoke, had been out of sight. In the plain, at the distance of about a mile, a thin line of steam showed where a heavy train was creeping along the railway. Just beneath us the low spire of the church rose among the trees, while in the gardens of the cottages that clustered around it there was an abundance of fruit trees and of vegetables which would have delighted Johnson's heart, such as "King Bob" never saw or even dreamt of. Beyond the village were undulating fields of well-cultivated land. To the west, almost within bow-shot, stands a steep rocky hill—a counterpart of that on which the castle is placed—all covered with wood. High over the old ruins the swifts were flying and screaming. The sole tenants of the great hall were some black cattle whom my entrance disturbed. Where kings once kept their court, and frowned and were flattered,

"There but houseless cattle go
To shield them from the storm."

High up on the wall of the keep there are two stone shields, on which still can be traced the royal and the Stewart arms. Little did they who carved them think that the day was to come when they would have sunk into the ornaments of a cow-house.

From Dundonald our travellers rode on a short distance to Auchans, the house of the Dowager Countess of Eglintoune. Johnson, in a letter to Mrs. Thrale, describes her as "a lady who

[1] Macgibbon and Ross's *Castellated and Domestic Architecture of Scotland*, i. 167, 171.
[2] *Description of Scotland*, 2nd ed. p. 68.

for many years gave the laws of elegance to Scotland. She is in full vigour of mind, and not much impaired in form. She is only eighty-three. She was remarking that her marriage was in the year eight; and I told her my birth was in nine. 'Then,' says she, 'I am just old enough to be your mother, and I will take you for my son.' She called Boswell the boy. 'Yes, Madam,' said I, 'we will send him to school.' 'He is already,' said she, 'in a good

OLD AUCHANS.

school;' and expressed her hope of his improvement. At last night came, and I was sorry to leave her." "She had been," writes Boswell, "the admiration of the gay circles of life, and the patroness of poets." To her Allan Ramsay had dedicated his *Gentle Shepherd*, and Hamilton of Bangour had addressed verses. With his reception Johnson was delighted, so congenial were their principles in church and state. "In her bed-rooms," says Dr. Robert Chambers, "was hung a portrait of her sovereign *de jure*, the ill-starred Charles Edward, so situated as to be the first object which met her sight on awaking in the morning."[1] She who

[1] R. Chambers' *Traditions of Edinburgh*, ed. 1869, p. 217.

had patronised poets and worshipped princes in her last years amused herself by taming rats. "She had a panel in the oak wainscot of her dining-room, which she tapped upon and opened at meal-times, when ten or twelve jolly rats came tripping forth and joined her at table." She died in 1780, at the age of ninety-one.[1]

Auchans—Old Auchans as it is now called—since the countess's death has been chiefly inhabited by caretakers. It was built in 1644, at a time when in the houses of the great comfort was more studied than means of defence. Nevertheless "we find some shot-holes near the entrance doorway."[2] It is finely placed among the trees, with views of Dundonald Castle on one side and of the sea in the distance on the other. The interior has been greatly altered

OLD AUCHANS.

by the division of rooms and blocking up of windows and passages. We were only shown a small part of it, and looked with sadness on the broken ceiling in what by tradition is known as the dining-room. It is a pity that so interesting and so fine a building should have suffered under the neglect of a whole century. It is so strongly built that it looks as if it could, at no excessive expense, be once more made habitable. Johnson had not been easily persuaded to visit it, but "he was so much pleased with his entertainment, that he owned," says Boswell, "that I had done well to force him out." No less pleased was the old countess, "who, when they were going away, embraced him, saying, 'My dear son, farewell.'" Neither of this visit nor of one which he had paid two days earlier to the Earl of Loudoun, who "jumped for joy" at the thought of seeing him, does he make any mention in his book. He was the last man to indulge "in that vain ostentatious importance," which he censured in many people, "of quoting the authority of dukes and lords." He merely says that, "on our way from Glasgow to Auchinleck we found several

---

[1] R. Chambers's *Traditions of Edinburgh*, ed. 1869, p. 217.

[2] Macgibbon and Ross's *Castellated Architecture of Scotland*, ii. 174.

places remarkable enough in themselves, but already described by those who viewed them at more leisure, or with much more skill."

AUCHINLECK (NOVEMBER 2-8).

On Tuesday, November 2, our travellers having ordered a chaise from Kilmarnock drove to Auchinleck, where they arrived in time for dinner. "We purpose," wrote Johnson that same evening, "to stay here some days, more or fewer, as we are used." He said "we" advisedly, for he knew that not only between Lord Auchinleck and himself there was little in common, but that also between the father and son there was no freedom of intercourse. "My father," Boswell once complained, "cannot bear that his son should talk with him as a man."[1] How uncomfortable was his position at home is shown by a letter which he wrote to his friend the Rev. Mr. Temple in September, 1775:

"I came to Auchinleck on Monday last, and I have patiently lived at it till Saturday evening.... It is hardly credible how difficult it is for a man of my sensibility to support existence in the family where I now am. My father, whom I really both respect and affectionate (if that is a word, for it is a different feeling from that which is expressed by *love*, which I can say of you from my soul), is so different from me. We *divaricate* so much, as Dr. Johnson said, that I am often hurt when, I dare say, he means no harm; and he has a method of treating me which makes me feel myself like a *timid boy*, which to *Boswell* (comprehending all that my character does in my own imagination and in that of a wonderful number of mankind) is intolerable. His wife too, whom in my conscience I cannot condemn for any capital bad quality, is so narrow-minded, and, I don't know how, so set upon keeping him under her own management, and so suspicious and so sourishly tempered that it requires the utmost exertion of practical philosophy to keep myself quiet. I however have done so all this week to admiration: nay, I have appeared good humoured; but it has cost me drinking a considerable quantity of strong beer to dull my faculties."[2]

It can scarcely be doubted that he is describing the position which he himself held at home, in an essay which he published in the *London Magazine* in 1781 (p. 253):

"I knew a father who was a violent Whig, and used to attack his son for being a Tory, upbraiding him with being deficient in 'noble sentiments of liberty,' while at the same time he made this son live under his roof in such bondage, that he was not only afraid to stir from home without leave, like a child, but durst scarcely open

[1] *Letters of Boswell to Temple*, p. 255.   [2] *Ib.*, p. 215.

his mouth in his father's presence. This was sad living. Yet I would rather see such an excess of awe than a degree of familiarity between father and son by which all reverence is destroyed."

Lord Auchinleck had taken unto himself a second wife on the very day of his son's marriage. She was, in all likelihood, in the house at the time of Johnson's visit, but neither by him nor Boswell is she once mentioned. She remained, no doubt, silent and insignificant. With their reception they must have been satisfied on the whole, as they prolonged their stay till the sixth day, in spite of the famous altercation which Boswell's piety forbade him to record at any length. That only one such scene should have occurred speaks well for the self-control both of host and guest. To Boswell Johnson had quickly become attached. "Give me your hand," he said to him in the first weeks of their acquaintance, "I have taken a liking to you." A month or so later he added, "There are few people to whom I take so much as to you." But Lord Auchinleck, though he might have respected he never could have liked. No men were more unlike in everything but personal appearance, than Boswell and his father. The old man had none of that "facility of manners," of which, according to Adam Smith, the son "was happily possessed."[1] Whence he got it we are nowhere told—perhaps from his mother. It certainly was not from his paternal grandfather, the old advocate, "who was a slow, dull man of unwearied perseverance and unmeasurable length in his speeches. It was alleged he never understood a cause till he had lost it thrice."[2] There were those who attributed Boswell's eccentricities to his great grandmother, Veronica, Countess of Kincardine, a Dutch lady of the noble house of Sommelsdyck. "For this marriage," writes Ramsay of Ochtertyre, "their posterity paid dear, for most of them had peculiarities which they had better have wanted." He adds that "Boswell's behaviour on the occasion of the riots in Edinburgh about the Douglas cause, savoured so much of insanity, that it was generally imputed to his Dutch blood."[3] Why madness was supposed to come from Holland I do not know. Sir William Temple, writing of that country, says: "In general all appetites and passions seem to run lower and cooler here than in other countries where I have conversed. Their tempers are not airy enough for joy or any unusual strains of

[1] *Correspondence of Boswell and Erskine*, ed. 1879, p. 26.
[2] *Scotland and Scotsmen of the Eighteenth Century*, i. 161.
[3] *Scotland and Scotsmen of the Eighteenth Century*, i. 161, 173.

pleasant humour, nor warm enough for love. This is talked of sometimes among the younger men, but as a thing they have heard of rather than felt; and as a discourse that becomes them rather than affects them."[1] All this was the very reverse of Boswell's eager and wild youth, though perhaps not unlike the character of his father and grandfather. There was one thing in common between Johnson and the old judge, both were sound scholars. At Auchinleck there was a library "which," says Boswell, "in curious editions of the Greek and Roman classics is, I suppose, not excelled by any private collection in Great Britain."

[1] Temple's *Works*, ed. 1757, i. 160.

AUCHINLECK.

Here Johnson found an edition of Anacreon which he had long sought in vain. "They had therefore much matter for conversation without touching on the fatal topics of difference." In all questions of Church and State they were wide as the poles asunder. In the perfect confidence which each man had in his own judgment there was nothing to choose between them.

"My father," writes Boswell, "was as sanguine a Whig and Presbyterian as Dr. Johnson was a Tory and Church-of-England man; and as he had not much leisure to be informed of Dr. Johnson's great merits by reading his works, he had a partial and unfavourable notion of him, founded on his supposed political tenets; which were so discordant to his own, that instead of speaking of him with that respect to which he was entitled, he used to call him '*a Jacobite fellow*.' Knowing all this, I should not have ventured to bring them together, had not my father, out of kindness to me, desired me to invite Dr. Johnson to his house. I was very anxious that all should be well; and begged of my friend to avoid three topics, as to which they differed very widely, Whiggism, Presbyterianism, and Sir John Pringle. He said courteously, 'I shall certainly not talk on subjects which I am told are disagreeable to a gentleman under whose roof I am; especially, I shall not do so to *your father*.'"

Yet with all Lord Auchinleck's gravity and contempt of his son's flightiness, he had known what it was not only to be young, but to be foolish. Like so many of the young Scotchmen of old, he had been sent to Holland to study civil law. Thence he had made his way to Paris, where he had played the fop. Years afterwards one of the companions of his youth, meeting his son at Lord Kames's table, "told him that he had seen his father strutting abroad in red-heeled shoes and red stockings. The lad was so much diverted with it that he could hardly sit on his chair for laughing."[1] His appointment as judge he owed to that most corrupt of Whig ministers, the Duke of Newcastle,[2] and he was as Whiggish as his patron. King William III., "one of the most worthless scoundrels that ever existed," according to Johnson, was to him the greatest hero in modern times. Presbyterianism he loved all the more because it was a cheap religion, and narrowed the power of the clergy. He laid it down as a rule that a poor clergy was ever a pure clergy. He added that in former times they had timber communion cups and silver ministers, but now we were getting silver cups and timber ministers.[3] According to Sir Walter Scott he carried "his Whiggery and Presbyte-

---

[1] *Scotland and Scotsmen*, i. 161. The Earl of Chesterfield, writing to his son in the year 1751, says: "I do not indeed wear feathers and *red heels*, which would ill suit my age; but I take care to have my clothes well made." *Letters to his Son*, ed. 1774, iii. 227.

[2] *Historical Manuscripts Commission*, 1874, p. 531.

[3] *Scotland and Scotsmen, &c.*, i. 170; ii. 556.

rianism to such a height, that once, when a countryman came in to state some justice business, and being required to make his oath, declined to do so before his lordship, because he was not a *covenanted* magistrate.—' Is that a' your objection, mon?' said the judge: 'come your ways in here, and we'll baith of us tak the solemn league and covenant together.' The oath was accordingly agreed and sworn to by both, and I dare say it was the last time it ever received such homage."[1] He would have nothing to do with clearing his tongue of Scotticisms, or with smoothing and rounding his periods on the model of the English classical authors. "His Scotch was broad and vulgar."[2] In one thing at all events he was sure of receiving Johnson's warm approval. He was a great planter of trees. "It was," he said, "his favourite recreation. In his vacations he used to prune with his own hands the trees which he himself had planted. Beginning at five in the morning, he wrought with his knife every spare hour. Of Auchinleck he was passionately fond."[3] He was not the man to prefer Fleet Street to the beauties of Nature. "I perceive some dawnings of taste for the country," wrote his son on one of his visits to his old home. "I will force a taste for rural beauties."[4] He never succeeded in the attempt, and though he often boasted of "waking among the rocks and woods of his ancestors," it was from a distance that he most admired them.

Rarely were two men more unlike. The old man had in excess that foresight which in Boswell was so largely wanting. He had built himself a new house, which Johnson describes as "very magnificent and very convenient;" but he had proceeded "so slowly and prudently that he hardly felt the expense."[5] Across the front of it he put the inscription—

"Quod petis hic est,
Est Ulubris, animus si te non deficit aequus."

"It is," writes Boswell, "characteristic of the founder; but the *animus aequus* is, alas! not inheritable, nor the subject of devise. He always talked to me as if it were in a man's own power to attain it; but Dr. Johnson told me that he owned to him, when they were alone, his persuasion that it was in a great measure constitutional, or the effect of causes which do not depend on ourselves, and that Horace boasts too much when he says, *aequum mi animum ipse parabo*.

---

[1] Boswell's *Johnson*, v. 382, n. 2.
[2] *Scotland and Scotsmen*, &c., ii. 513.
[3] *Ib.* i. 166.
[4] *Letters of Boswell to Temple*, pp. 216, 219. *Scotland and Scotsmen*, &c. i. 166.
[5] "The peace you seek is here — where is it not? If your own mind be equal to the lot." — CROKER.

He had, too, that sobriety of character in which his son was so conspicuously wanting. "His age, his office, and his character, had given him an acknowledged claim to great attention in whatever company he was, and he could ill brook any diminution of it." He was by no means deficient in humour, and in this respect father and son were alike. "He had a great many good stories, which he told uncommonly well, and he was remarkable for 'humour, *incolumi gravitate*,' as Lord Monboddo used to characterize it."

The contrast between his dignity and gravity, and Boswell's bustling and most comical liveliness, must have been as amusing as it was striking. His ignorance of his son's genius, and the contempt for him which he did not conceal, heightened the picture. Johnson's presence would have greatly added to the interest of the scene, for Boswell must have constantly wavered between his admiration of his idol and his awe of his father. A few years later Miss Burney met Boswell at Streatham, and thus describes him, no doubt with a good deal of exaggeration:

"He spoke the Scotch accent strongly. He had an odd mock solemnity of manner, that he had acquired imperceptibly from constantly thinking of and imitating Dr. Johnson. There was something slouching in his gait and dress, that wore an air, ridiculously enough, of purporting to personify the same model. His clothes were always too large for him; his hair or wig was constantly in a state of negligence; and he never for a moment sat still or upright upon a chair. When he met with Dr. Johnson he commonly forbore even answering anything that was said, or attending to anything that went forward, lest he should miss the smallest sound from that voice to which he paid such exclusive homage. His eyes goggled with eagerness; he leant his ear almost on the shoulder of the Doctor; and his mouth dropt open to catch every syllable that might be uttered. The Doctor generally treated him as a schoolboy, whom without the smallest ceremony he pardoned or rebuked alternately."[1]

It is probable that this description is heightened by Miss Burney's wounded vanity. Boswell had not read her *Evelina*, and when he was reproached by Johnson with being a Brangton—one of the characters in the novel—he did not know what was meant. She was as careful in recording the conversation that was about herself as Boswell was in recording Johnson's. Her great hero was herself. The voices to which she paid her homage were those in which she was praised and flattered.

In another place she describes "the singularity of his comic-serious face and manner."[2] He himself has more than once drawn

[1] *Memoirs of Dr. Burney*, ii. 191-4.   [2] Madame d'Arblay's *Diary*, ed. 1843, v. 166

his own character. He was, he flattered himself, a citizen of the world; one who in his travels never felt himself from home. In that impudent *Correspondence* which he and his friend Andrew Erskine published when they were still almost lads, he thus describes himself:

"The author of the *Ode to Tragedy* is a most excellent man: he is of an ancient family in the west of Scotland, upon which he values himself not a little. At his nativity there appeared omens of his future greatness. His parts are bright; and his education has been good. He has travelled in post-chaises miles without number. He is fond of seeing much of the world. He eats of every good dish, especially apple-pie. He drinks old hock. He has a very fine temper. He is somewhat of an humorist, and a little tinctured with pride. He has a good manly countenance, and he owns himself to be amorous. He has infinite vivacity, yet is observed at times to have a melancholy cast. He is rather fat than lean, rather short than tall, rather young than old. His shoes are neatly made, and he never wears spectacles."[1]

We have a later description of him again by his own hand, as he was at the time of his tour with Johnson.

"Think, then (he says), of a gentleman of ancient blood, the pride of which was his predominant passion. He was then in his thirty-third year, and had been about four years happily married. His inclination was to be a soldier; but his father, a respectable judge, had pressed him into the profession of the law. He had travelled a good deal, and seen many varieties of human life. He had thought more than anybody supposed, and had a pretty good stock of general learning and knowledge. He had all Dr. Johnson's principles, with some degree of relaxation. He had rather too little, than too much prudence; and, his imagination being lively, he often said things of which the effect was very different from the intention. He resembled sometimes

'The best good man, with the worst natur'd muse.'"

Johnson celebrated his good humour and perpetual cheerfulness, his acuteness, his gaiety of conversation, and civility of manners. "He was," he said, "the best travelling companion in the world." According to Burke, "his good nature was so natural to him that he had no merit in possessing it. A man might as well assume to himself merit in possessing an excellent constitution." Reynolds loved him so well that "he left him £200 in his will, to be expended, if he thought proper, in the purchase of a picture at the sale of his paintings, to be kept for his sake."[2] In a memoir of him in the *Scots Magazine* he is described as "a most pleasant companion, affectionate and friendly; but, particularly in his latter days, he betrayed a vanity which seemed to predominate." Tytler

---

[1] Boswell's *Correspondence with Erskine*, ed. 1879, p. 36.

[2] Boswell's *Johnson*, i. 11; iii. 362; v. 52. *Scots Magazine*, 1797, p. 292.

praises "his sprightly fancy and whimsical eccentricity," which "agreeably tempered the graver conversation" of Adam Smith or Hugh Blair at the small and select parties given by Lord Kames.[1]

He was welcome everywhere but at his own father's house. Neither was he the better thought of by the old man on account of the great Englishman whom he brought with him. Everything however went off smoothly for a day or two, but the host and his guest at length came in collision over Lord Auchinleck's collection of medals. The scene is thus described by Boswell, who witnessed it:

"Oliver Cromwell's coin unfortunately introduced Charles the First and Toryism. They became exceedingly warm and violent, and I was very much distressed by being present at such an altercation between two men, both of whom I reverenced; yet I durst not interfere. It would certainly be very unbecoming in me to exhibit my honoured father and my respected friend, as intellectual gladiators, for the entertainment of the public; and, therefore, I suppress what would, I dare say, make an interesting scene in this dramatic sketch—this account of the transit of Johnson over the Caledonian Hemisphere."

Ramsay of Ochtertyre says, that the year after this famous altercation, Lord Auchinleck "told him with warmth that the great Dr. Johnson, of whom he had heard wonders, was just a dominie, and the worst-bred dominie he had ever seen."[2] The account which Sir Walter Scott gives is very dramatic, though no doubt somewhat embellished.

"Old Lord Auchinleck (he writes) was an able lawyer, a good scholar, after the manner of Scotland, and highly valued his own advantages as a man of good estate and ancient family; and, moreover, he was a strict Presbyterian and Whig of the old Scottish cast. This did not prevent his being a terribly proud aristocrat; and great was the contempt he entertained and expressed for his son James, for the nature of his friendships and the character of the personages of whom he was *engoué* one after another. 'There's nae hope for Jamie, mon,' he said to a friend. 'Jamie is gaen clean gyte.' What do you think, mon? He's done wi' Paoli –he's off wi' the land-louping' scoundrel of a Corsican; and whose tail do you think he has pinned himself to now, mon?' Here the old judge summoned up a sneer of most sovereign contempt. 'A *dominie*, mon—an auld dominie: he keeped a schule, and ca'd it an acaadamy."

The full force of Lord Auchinleck's contempt is only seen when we understand the position of a *dominie*. The character of a schoolmaster, generally, according to Johnson, was less honour-

---

[1] Tytler's *Life of Lord Kames*, ii. 228.
[2] *Scotland and Scotsmen*, i. 176.
[3] Croy.

Loup is a cognate word with *leap*, and signifies to run. A *landlouper* is a runagate; one constantly shifting from one place to another.

able in Scotland than in England.[1] But the dominie, or tutor in a family, was still less esteemed. "He was raised," writes Sir Walter Scott, "from a humble class to a society where, whatever his personal attainments might be, he found himself placed at a humiliating distance from anything like a footing of equality. His remuneration was scanty in the extreme, and consisting (as if to fill up the measure of his dependence) not entirely of a fixed salary, but partly of the precarious prospect of future preferment in the Church. The Scotch *dominie* was assuredly one of the most pitiable of human beings."[2] It is a curious and perhaps a somewhat suspicious fact, that a very few years before Sir Walter supplied Mr. Croker with this amusing story about the old judge, he had put on record in the pages of the *Quarterly Review* the following anecdote: "When the old Scots judge Lord Auchinleck first heard of Johnson's coming to visit him at his rural *castellum*, he held up his hands in astonishment, and cried out, 'Our Jeemy's clean aff the hooks now! would ony body believe it? he's bringing down a *dominie* wi' him—an auld dominie.'"[3] This looks like a different version of the same story. Moreover, Boswell tells us that his father had desired him to invite him to his house. When Johnson called his school at Lichfield an academy, he does not seem to have used the term pretentiously, for in his *Dictionary* he defines the word under one of its meanings as "a place of education in contradistinction to the universities or public schools." It does not seem likely, moreover, that Lord Auchinleck had any feeling of contempt for Pascal Paoli, a man of good family, who for years had headed a rebellion against the tyranny first of Genoa and afterwards of France. He had visited Auchinleck two years before Johnson, and had been well received. Boswell, writing to Garrick on September 18, 1771, said: "I have just been enjoying the very great happiness of a visit from my illustrious friend, Pascal Paoli. He was two nights at Auchinleck, and you may figure the joy of my worthy father and me at seeing the Corsican hero in our romantic groves. Count Burgynski, the Polish ambassador, accompanied him."[4] Poland's days of sending ambassadors had nearly drawn to an end, for the first partition of the country was made in the following year. It was a strange chance which brought the last Corsican patriot and the last Polish ambas-

---

[1] Johnson's *Works*, ix. 158.   [3] *Ib.*
[2] *Quarterly Review*, No. 71, p. 225.   [4] *Garrick Correspondence*, i. 436.

sador to this Ayrshire mansion. One thing only was wanting. Would that Burns that day had played truant and had wandered up "Lugar's winding stream" as far as Auchinleck! It would, indeed, have formed an interesting group—the stiff old Scotch judge and his famous son, the great Corsican patriot and the Pole, with the peasant lad gazing at them with his eyes full of beauty and wonder. Paoli's name is well nigh forgotten now, but he and his Corsicans deeply stirred the hearts of our forefathers. Boswell, by a private subscription in Scotland, had sent out to him in one week £700 worth of ordnance—"a tolerable train of artillery."[1] His account of his tour in that island had been widely read. Even his father "was rather fond of it. 'James,' he said, 'had taken a *tout* on a new horn.'"[2] Whether Lord Auchinleck abused Paoli "as a land-louping scoundrel of a Corsican," or admired him as he admired other great patriots, the rest of Sir Walter Scott's account of the great altercation may be true enough:

"The controversy between Tory and Covenanter raged with great fury, and ended in Johnson's pressing upon the old judge the question, what good Cromwell, of whom he had said something derogatory, had ever done to his country; when, after being much tortured, Lord Auchinleck at last spoke out, 'God, Doctor! he gart kings ken that they had a *lith* in their neck.' he taught kings they had a *joint* in their necks."

This story did not, I believe, appear in print till the year 1831, when it was given as a note by Scott in Mr. Croker's edition of *Boswell*. Fifty years earlier it had been told in somewhat different words of Quin the player, who had said that "on a thirtieth of January every king in Europe would rise with a crick in his neck." Davies, who records the anecdote, says that it had been attributed to Voltaire, but unjustly. It is possible, and even not unlikely, that we have but a Scotch version of an English saying. Cromwell himself, in his letter to the governor of Edinburgh Castle, had shown that he too saw this consequence of his great deed. "The civil authority," he writes, "turned out a Tyrant in a way which the Christians in aftertimes will mention with honour, and all Tyrants in the world look at with fear."[4]

In one happy though impudent retort, Lord Auchinleck was very successful.

"Dr. Johnson challenged him (writes Boswell) to point out any theological

---

[1] *Letters of Boswell to Temple*, p. 156.   [3] *Davies' Life of Garrick*, ii. 115.
[2] *Scotland and Scotsmen*, &c., i. 172. *Tout* is the blast of a horn.   [4] *Cromwell's Letters and Speeches*, ed. 1857, ii. 209.

works of merit written by Presbyterian ministers in Scotland. My father, whose studies did not lie much in that way, owned to me afterwards, that he was somewhat at a loss how to answer, but that luckily he recollected having read in catalogues the title of *Durham on the Galatians*; upon which he boldly said, 'Pray, Sir, have you read Mr. Durham's excellent commentary on the Galatians?' 'No, Sir,' said Dr. Johnson. By this lucky thought my father kept him at bay, and for some time enjoyed his triumph; but his antagonist soon made a retort, which I forbear to mention."

In the long list of Durham's theological works in the British Museum catalogue I find no mention of this book on the Galatians. The old judge, it is clear, had not forgotten in the years which he had sat on the bench the arts of the advocate. In Rowlandson's Caricatures there is a humorous picture of *The Contest at Auchinleck*. Johnson is drawn felling his opponent with a huge liturgy, having made him drop two books equally big, entitled *Calvin* and *Whiggism*. On the floor are lying the medals over which the dispute had begun, while Boswell is at the door in an attitude of despair, with his *Journal* falling from his hands.

One figure was wanting to make the picture complete. Of the three topics on which Johnson had been warned not to touch only two had been introduced. "In the course of their altercation," writes Boswell, "Whiggism and Presbyterianism, Toryism and Episcopacy, were terribly buffeted. My worthy hereditary friend, Sir John Pringle, never having been mentioned, happily escaped without a bruise." We could have wished that he had been mentioned, for though we know of the dislike which existed between the two men, yet as he has never "hitched" in one of Johnson's strong sayings, he has scarcely attained that fame which he deserved.

Towards Lord Auchinleck Johnson bore no resentment. With him the heat of altercation soon passed away, but not the memory of the hospitality which he had received in his house. In not a single word spoken or written has he attacked him. On the contrary, in his *Journey to the Western Islands*, he only mentions him to praise him. When, six years later, he published the first four volumes of his *Lives of the Poets*, he wrote to Boswell: "Write me word to whom I shall send sets of *Lives*; would it please Lord Auchinleck?" A few months after this he wrote to him: "Let me know what reception you have from your father, and the state of his health. Please him as much as you can, and add no pain to his last years." The old lord was not so placable. He had that "want of tenderness which," said Johnson, "is want of parts." This part of his character is seen in the following anecdote recorded of him by his son:

> "I mentioned to Johnson a respectable person of a very strong mind, who had little of that tenderness which is common to human nature; as an instance of which, when I suggested to him that he should invite his son, who had been settled ten years in foreign parts, to come home and pay him a visit, his answer was, 'No, no, let him mind his business.' JOHNSON. 'I do not agree with him, Sir, in this. Getting money is not all a man's business: to cultivate kindness is a valuable part of the business of life.'"

He had what Boswell calls "the dignified courtesy of an old Baron," and when Johnson left "was very civil to him, and politely attended him to his post-chaise." But he was not in the least soothed by the compliments which he paid him in his book. Boswell had hoped that he might be moved. Writing to Johnson just after it had been published, he said: "You have done Auchinleck much honour, and have, I hope, overcome my father, who has never forgiven your warmth for monarchy and episcopacy. I am anxious to see how your pages will operate upon him."[1] His anxious wish was grievously disappointed. A few months later he wrote to his friend Temple: "My father is most unhappily dissatisfied with me. . . . He harps on my going over Scotland with a brute (think how shockingly erroneous!) and wandering (or some such phrase) to London. How hard it is that I am totally excluded from parental comfort! I have a mind to go to Auchinleck next autumn, and try what living in a mixed stupidity of attention to common objects and restraint from expressing any of my own feelings can do with him."[2] When his father and Johnson were both dead he indulged in the pious hope that "as they were both worthy Christian men, they had met in happiness. But I must observe," he adds, "in justice to my friend's political principles and my own, that they have met in a place where there is no room for *Whiggism.*" Johnson, it is true, "always said the first Whig was the Devil," but on the other hand, some Presbyterian who drew up an epitaph on Lochiel, declared in it that he "is now a Whig in heaven."[3]

That pride in his ancient blood, which Boswell boasted was his predominant passion, was very strong in the old lord. In the son, if it really existed in any strength, it was happily overpowered by

---

[1] Croker's *Boswell*, 8vo. ed. p. 826. [2] *Letters of Boswell to Temple*, p. 207.
[3] *Quarterly Review*, No. 71, p. 209.

a host of other and better feelings. He had travelled widely, he had seen a great variety of men, some of them among the most famous of their age, and had learnt to value genius without troubling himself about its pedigree. His successors at Auchinleck had something of the narrowness of the old judge. "His eldest son, Sir Alexander Boswell," wrote Sir Walter Scott, "was a proud man, and like his grandfather, thought that his father lowered himself by his deferential suit and service to Johnson. I have observed he disliked any allusion to the book or to Johnson himself, and I have heard that Johnson's fine picture by Sir Joshua was sent upstairs out of the sitting apartments."[1] He was not too proud a man to write a poem on the anniversary of the Accession of George IV., and what is George IV. now? It was not from any dulness of mind that he did not value his father's book. "He had," says Lockhart, "all *Bozzy's* cleverness, good-humour, and joviality, without one touch of his meaner qualities, wrote some popular songs, which he sang capitally, and was moreover a thorough bibliomaniac."[2] It was due to him and a friend, that the Burns monument at Ayr was erected. They summoned a public meeting, but no one attended except themselves. Little daunted they appointed a chairman, proposed resolutions, carried them unanimously, passed a vote of thanks, and issued subscription lists. More than £2,000 was subscribed, and the monument was opened by Sir Alexander shortly before his death. That he was not wanting in tenderness of heart is shown by some of his poems. How pretty is the following verse in an address by an aged father to his children:—

> "The auld will speak, the young maun hear,
>   Be cantie, but be gude and leal;
> Your ain ills aye hae heart to bear,
>   Anither's aye hae heart to feel.
>
> So, ere I sat, I'll see ye shine;
>   I'll see ye triumph ere I fa';
> My parting breath shall boast you mine—
>   Good night, and joy be wi' ye a'."[3]

Lockhart goes, however, too far when he exalts him in comparison with his father. Boswell, I feel sure, would never have been guilty of the act which involved his son in the unhappy duel in which he lost his life. In two scurrilous newspapers he had

---

[1] Croker's *Correspondence*, ii. 32.
[2] Lockhart's *Life of Scott*, v. 336.
[3] C. Rogers's *Modern Scottish Minstrel*, 1870, p. 158.

secretly defamed his kinsman, Mr. James Stuart, of Dunearn, "with whom he had long been on good terms." Though the articles were written in a disguised hand, the authorship was detected. He received a challenge from the injured man, and at the first shot fell mortally wounded. He dined with Scott a day or two before the duel, and "though Charles Matthews (the famous comedian) was present, poor Sir Alexander Boswell's songs, jokes, and anecdotes exhibited no symptom of eclipse."[1]

His only son, Sir James Boswell, the last male descendant of the author of the immortal *Life*, shared his father's illiberal feelings about Johnson. Miss Macleod of Macleod told me that when she was on a visit at Auchinleck, he said to her one day that he did not know how he should name one of his race-horses. She suggested Boswell's Johnsoniana, which made him very angry. He was, I learnt, a man of great natural ability, who, had he chosen, might have become distinguished. His feeling of soreness against his grandfather was partly due to another cause than dislike of hero-worship. Boswell, in an access of that particular kind of folly which he called "feudal enthusiasm," had entailed his estates on the heirs male of his father to the exclusion of his own nearer female descendants. Sir James, who had no sons, saw that Auchinleck on his death would pass away from his daughters to his cousin, Thomas Alexander Boswell, Lord Auchinleck's grandson by his second son David. He managed to get the settlement upset on the plea that in the deed the first five letters of the word *irredeemably* were written upon an erasure.[2] It is not impossible that the lawyer who drew it up, not liking the provision, intentionally contrived this loop-hole.

Among Boswell's male descendants, his second son James was, so far as I know, the only one who was not ashamed of the *Life of Johnson*. He supplied notes to the later editions. His father, writing of him when he was eleven years old, says : " My second son is an extraordinary boy ; he is much of his father (vanity of vanities)."[3] Croker describes him as " very convivial, and in other respects like his father—though altogether on a smaller scale."[4] According to Lockhart, he was "a man of considerable learning and admirable social qualities. To him Sir Walter Scott

---

[1] Lord Cockburn's *Memorials*, pp. 380, 392, and Lockhart's *Scott*, vii. 33.
[2] Rogers' *Boswelliana*, p. 195, and *Notes and Queries*, 3rd Series, vii. 197.
[3] *Letters of Boswell to Temple*, p. 315.   [4] Croker's *Boswell*, p. 620.

was warmly attached. He died suddenly in the prime of life, about a fortnight before his brother."[1]

When Boswell, at the age of twenty-seven, published his *Account of Corsica*, he boasted in his preface that "he cherished the hope of being remembered after death, which has been a great object to the noblest minds in all ages." When he saw his *Life of Johnson* reach its second edition, he said with a frankness which is almost touching, "I confess that I am so formed by nature and by habit, that to restrain the effusion of delight on having obtained such fame, to me would be truly painful. Why then should I suppress it? Why 'out of the abundance of the heart' should I not speak?" He goes on to mention the spontaneous praise which he has received from eminent persons, "much of which," he adds, "I have under their hands to be reposited in my archives at Auchinleck." How little did he foresee that his executors, with a brutish ignorance worthy of perpetual execration, would destroy his manuscripts! If Oliver Goldsmith had had children and grandchildren, they too, when they read of his envy and his vanity, when they were told that "in conversation he was an empty, noisy, blundering rattle,"[2] might have blushed to own that they were sprung from the author of *The Deserted Village* and *The Vicar of Wakefield*.

It is a melancholy thing that Boswell's descendants should have seen their famous ancestor's faults so clearly as to have been unable to enjoy that pride which was so justly their due, in being sprung from a man of such real, if curious genius. Was it nothing to have written the best biography which the world has ever seen? Nothing to have increased more than any writer of his generation "the public stock of harmless pleasure?" Nothing to have "exhibited" with the greatest skill "a view of literature and literary men in Great Britain for near half a century?" Nothing to have been the delight of men of the greatest and most varied genius? Nothing to be read wherever the English tongue is spoken, and, as seems likely, as long as the English tongue shall last? *Sume superbiam quaesitam meritis*, "Assume the honours justly thine," we would say to each one of his race.

How widely Boswell's influence is felt is shown in a story which was told me by Sir Charles Sikes, the benevolent inventor

---

[1] Lockhart's *Life of Scott*, vii. 35.
[2] Macaulay's *Miscellaneous Writings*, ed. 1871, p. 369.

of the Post Office Savings Banks, and no mean Johnsonian. One
day he had gone under an archway in Fleet Street to shun a
shower, as Burke might have gone.¹ Being "knowing and con-
versible," he fell into talk with a sergeant of police who was also
taking shelter, and whose tongue showed that he was an Irishman.
He came, he said, from the west of Ireland. When he was a boy
the parish priest had lent him a copy of the *Life of Johnson*. He
had read it again and again, till at last the wish grew so strong
upon him to see with his own eyes the scenes which in the pages
of the book were so familiar to him, that he came to London, not
knowing what employment he should find, but bent on seeing
Fleet Street. What pilgrimages have not men made from the
other side of the Atlantic to the same spots! With their Boswell
in their hands they have wandered by Charing Cross, "with its
full tide of human existence;" up the Strand, "through the greatest
series of shops in the world;" under Temple Bar, where Johnson's
and Goldsmith's names did *not* mingle with those of the Scotch
rebels²; along Fleet Street, with "its very animated appearance,"
to the courts and lanes and taverns where the spirits of the men
who gathered round the great Lexicographer seem still to linger.
The Boswells are proud of their descent from a man who fell at
Flodden Field. There are thousands and ten thousands of Scotchmen who got knocked on their heads in border forays, but only one
who wrote the *Life of Johnson*. "The chief glory of every people
arises from its authors," and among Scotch authors Sir Walter
Scott alone equals Boswell in the extent of his popularity. The
genius of Burns lies hidden from most Englishmen in the dialect
in which his finest poetry is written. Never did one man of letters
do another a more shameful wrong than when Macaulay laboured
at the ridiculous paradox that the first of biographers was "a man
of the meanest and feeblest intellect." He was thirty years old
when he wrote this. Yet, to borrow Johnson's words, it was such
stuff as a young man talks when he first begins to think himself a
clever fellow, and he ought to have been whipped for it. The

---

¹ Johnson imagines Burke falling into chance conversations on two occasions; once on shun-
ning a shower under a shed, and another time on stepping aside to take shelter from a drove of
men.—*Life of Johnson*, iv. 275; v. 34.

² "JOHNSON. I remember once being with Goldsmith in Westminster Abbey. While we
surveyed the Poets' Corner I said to him,

'Forsitan et nostrum nomen miscebitur istis.'

When we got to Temple Bar he stopped me, pointed to the heads upon it, and slily whispered
me,

'Forsitan et nostrum nomen miscebitur istis.'"

Ib. ii. 238.

worst of it is that Macaulay, like Rousseau, talked his nonsense so well that it still passes for gospel with all those who have advanced as far as reading, but have not as yet attained to thinking. We may feel thankful that he did not with his overpowering common sense go on to overwhelm the memory of Goldsmith.

In the price set on autographs we have a means of measuring in some fashion the estimation in which men are held by posterity. The standard is but a rough one, however, for it is affected by the number of their writings which chance to have been preserved: judging by it, Boswell's rank is very high. There were, probably, few men whose career he more envied than that of Lord Bute's "errand-goer," Alexander Wedderburne, who rose to be Lord Loughborough, Earl of Rosslyn and Lord High Chancellor of England. Yet a letter of his I have recently seen offered for sale at ten shillings and sixpence, while Boswell's was marked nine guineas. While I exult at seeing that one author equals eighteen Lord Chancellors, I sometimes sigh over the high prices which have hitherto kept me from obtaining a specimen of the handwriting of a man at whose works I have so long laboured.

It is to be hoped that the day will at length come when those in whose veins Boswell's blood still flows will take that just and reasonable view of their famous forefather which will lead them, from time to time, to throw open "the rocks and woods," and even "the stately house" of Auchinleck to strangers from afar. It was he who "Johnsonised the land," and they therefore should have some indulgence for the enthusiasm which he created. "The sullen dignity of the castle with which Johnson was delighted" they should not keep altogether to themselves. Another famous man had beheld those ruins also. "Since Paoli stood upon our old castle," wrote Boswell to a friend, "it has an additional dignity." Who would not like to stand upon it also, and to see the Lugar running beneath, "bordered by high rocks shaded with wood?" Into this beautiful stream falls "a pleasing brook," to use Johnson's odd description of a rivulet which has cut a deep passage through the sandstone. "It runs," he adds, "by a red rock, out of which has been hewn a very agreeable and commodious summer-house." I have been told that the meeting of the waters is a scene of striking beauty. Then there are "the venerable old trees under the shade of which," writes Boswell, "my ancestors had walked," and the groves where, as he told Johnson, it was his intention to erect a monument to his "reverend friend." "Sir," he answered, little flattered by the prospect of "a lapidary inscription," "I hope to see your grand children." Who would not gladly stroll along Lord Auchinleck's *via sacra*, "that road which he made to the church, for above three miles, on his own estate, through a range of well-inclosed farms, with a row of trees on each side of it?" The avenue is composed mainly of oaks and beeches, planted alternately; but the finest of the trees were brought down a few years ago in a great storm which swept over the country. Only one or two small farms remain, but there are the ruins of another. From the road a most pleasant view is seen, grassy slopes running down to the Lugar, with hedge-rows and trees growing in them after the English fashion. Across the river the ground rises rapidly in tilled fields and meadows and groves to a high range of hills. To the south-west lies the village of Ochiltree, whence Scott perhaps derived old Edie's name in the *Antiquary*.

The manse still stands where Johnson dined with the Rev. John Dun, who had been Boswell's *dominie*, and had been rewarded for his services by the presentation to the living of Auchinleck. He rashly attacked before his guest the Church of England, and "talked of fat bishops and drowsy deans. Dr. Johnson was so highly offended, that he said to him, 'Sir, you know no more of our church than a Hottentot.'" Dun must have complained to Boswell of being thus publicly likened to the proverbial Hottentot, for in the second edition of the *Tour to the Hebrides* his name is suppressed. The manse has been enlarged since those days, and surrounded with a delightful garden which might excite the envy, if not of a drowsy dean, at all events of a south country vicar. In the venerable minister, Dr. James Chrystal, who has lived there for more than fifty years, Johnson would have found a man "whom, if he should have quarrelled with him, he would have found the most difficulty how to abuse."

The parish church where Johnson refused to attend Boswell and his father at public worship has been rebuilt. In the churchyard stands a fine old beech which might have been called venerable even a hundred years ago. There, too, is the vault of the Boswells with their coat-of-arms engraved on it, and their motto, *Vraye Foy*. In a niche cut in the solid rock lies Boswell's body. He died in London, at his house in Great Portland Street, but in accordance with the direction in his will he was buried "in the family burial-place in the church of Auchinleck." Though the vault is now at a little distance from the church, yet in the old building, which did not occupy precisely the same site, it was under a room at the back of the Boswells' pew. On a wall in the churchyard I noticed a curiously-carved stone with the following inscription:

<pre>
              M
         G.   W.
            1621
           M. G.
     HUNC TUMULUM CONIUNX
     POSUIT DILECTA MARITO.
     QUEMQUE VIRO POSUIT
     DESTINAT HORA SIBI.
     ─────
     THIS STONE WAS ERECTED
             1621
       IN MEMORY OF THE
     REVD. GEORGE WALKER
     WHO WAS PASTOR OF THIS PARISH.
     REPAIRED BY OLD MORTALITY
            IN HIS DAY
     AND RENEWED AND PLACED HERE IN
             1855.
</pre>

"Auchinleck," said the landlady of my inn, "is the very heart of the Covenanters' district." Hard by, at Airdsmoss, the founder of the Cameronians, with seven or eight of his followers, was slain in July, 1681. In the churchyard lies buried a man of a very different type of character—William Murdoch, the inventor of gas. Two of Boswell's tenants were James and William Murdoch. They and their forefathers had possessed their farms for many generations.[1] Perhaps not only the *Life of Boswell*, but illumination by gas takes its rise from Auchinleck.

The village consists mainly of one long street of solidly-built stone houses; the older ones thatched and often white-washed, the modern ones slated. At the back are good gardens well stocked with fruit trees. Bare feet are far more common here than in the Highlands or Hebrides. All the children, with scarcely an exception, and many of the women, go bare-footed. As I passed down the street a "roup," or sale by auction, was going on before the house of a deceased "baker, violin-maker, clock-mender, blood-letter, dentist, geologist, and collector of coins." The auctioneer, standing on the doorstep of this departed worthy, who at one and

[1] See Boswell's will in Rogers's *Bo*s*wellia*n*a*, p. 185.

the same time had played many parts, dispersed his motley goods to the four quarters of heaven. The best of his violins, for he had had some of considerable value, had been sent for sale to Glasgow. I stayed in the Railway Hotel, a curious old house, which boasted of two sitting-rooms and one bed-room. It was clean and comfortable, and in my courteous landlady I found a woman of sense and education. She quoted *Sartor Resartus*, and spoke with anger of Mr. Froude's *Life of Carlyle*. In Scotland the traveller finds book learning far more generally diffused than in England.

In Boswell's time Auchinleck, he tells us, was pronounced Affléck. His grand-daughter, who died in 1836, informed Mr. Croker that in her time it had come to be pronounced as it is written. I learnt however from Dr. Chrystal that "the name Affléck is still quite common as applied to the parish, and even Auchinleck House is as often called Place Affléck as otherwise." A lad whom I questioned on the subject told me that the old people call it Affléck but the young Auchinleck. The old pronunciation will no doubt soon disappear.

Boswell had been a kind landlord. Johnson, in the early days of their acquaintance, "had recommended to him a liberal kindness to his tenantry, as people over whom the proprietor was placed by Providence." The advice was congenial to his natural disposition. In his will, which he made ten years before his death, he says : " As there are upon the estate of Auchinleck several tenants whose families have possessed their farms for many generations, I do by these presents grant leases for nineteen years and their respective lives to" —here follow the names of eight tenants. He continues :
" And I do beseech all the succeeding heirs of entail to be kind to the tenants, and not to turn out old possessors to get a little more rent." We may venture to express a hope that his descendants, if they have slighted him as an author, have always honoured and followed him as a landlord.

HAMILTON, EDINBURGH, NEW HAILES, BALLENCRIEFF, AND CRANSTON, NOVEMBER 8—22.

Leaving Auchinleck on the morning of November 8, our travellers arrived that night at Hamilton on the road to Edinburgh. They had crossed Drumclog Moor, the scene of the skirmish nearly one hundred years earlier where Claverhouse was beaten by the Covenanters. Scott in *Old Mortality* has told how in the fight John Balfour of Burley struck down Sergeant Bothwell. Fifty years or so after our travellers crossed the Moor, Thomas Carlyle and Edward Irving passed over it on foot. "It was here," says Carlyle, "as the sun was sinking, Irving drew from me by degrees, in the softest manner, the confession that I did not think as he of

NEW HAILES.

the Christian religion, and that it was vain for me to expect I ever could or should."[1] Boswell's record of this day's journey is of the briefest. "We came at night to a good inn at Hamilton. I recollect no more." A writer in the *Gentleman's Magazine* gives us a humorous description of the innkeeper. "Hamilton Arms, kept by Burns, tolerable. The landlord from pure insipidity will laugh at you if you come in wet through; yet he can tell a good deal about the Duke's family."[2] Smollett gives the little town the highest praise in his vocabulary, by calling it "one of the neatest he had seen in any country." Whatever nature could do, the force of art could no farther go last century than make a place neat. Boswell, before they left next morning, in vain tried to move

[1] Carlyle's *Reminiscences*, ed. 1881, i. 178. [2] *Gentleman's Magazine*, 1771, p. 545.
[3] *Humphry Clinker*, ii. 85.

Johnson to visit the Palace of Hamilton, as the Duke's castle is called. "He had not come to Scotland to see fine places of which there were enough in England." He would do nothing more than view the outside. That same night "they arrived at Edinburgh after an absence of eighty-three days. For five weeks together of the tempestuous season," adds Boswell, "there had been no account received of us." Yet, as the crow flies, they had never at their farthest been two hundred miles away. How vast is the change since those days! I received the other day at my house in Oxford, a letter which had been posted in Bombay just fifteen days before. Johnson would have hurried on to London had he followed his own wishes. "I long to come under your care," he wrote to Mrs. Thrale a day or two after his arrival in Edinburgh, "but for some days cannot decently get away." He had his morning levees to hold, and his dinner and supper parties to attend. "'Sir,' he said one evening, 'we have been harassed by invitations.' I acquiesced. 'Ay, sir,' he replied, 'but how much worse would it have been if we had been neglected!'" There was one man who did not harass him. Boswell nowhere mentions that he visited Lord Auchinleck at his house in Parliament Close.

He paid a visit to New Hailes, four miles east of Edinburgh, the seat of Sir David Dalrymple, better known by the title of Lord Hailes, which he bore as one of the judges of Scotland. "Here," says Boswell, "we passed a most agreeable day, but," he adds, "again I must lament that I was so indolent as to let almost all that passed evaporate into oblivion." Johnson had first heard of his host ten years earlier. One evening, when he and Boswell were supping in a private room at the Turk's Head Coffee-house in the Strand, "he drank a bumper to Sir David Dalrymple as 'a man of worth, a scholar, and a wit. I have,' said he, 'never heard of him, except from you; but let him know my opinion of him; for, as he does not show himself much in the world, he should have the praise of the few who hear of him.'" They did not meet till Johnson came to Edinburgh, but then they at once took to each other. "I love him better than any man whom I know so little," wrote Johnson eighteen months later. His love was no doubt increased by the decision which his friend gave a few years later in that famous case in which it was decided, by a majority of the judges, that a slave who had been brought from Jamaica to

Scotland became thereby free. "Dear Lord Hailes was on the side of liberty," Johnson wrote to Boswell.[1] He would have loved him still more for the tenderness of heart which, unlike so many of his brethren, he showed on the Bench. "When called to pass sentence of death he addressed the unfortunate convicts in a pathetic, dignified strain of piety and commiseration that made a deep impression on the audience."[2] Many of the old judges, as is shown by the stories recorded of them, were in criminal trials little better than ruffians in ermine. If "robes and furred gowns hide all," in many a case they had far more cruelty to cover than the unfortunate prisoner had been guilty of who was sent to the gallows. Lord Hailes, with all his kindness, was by no means faultless as a judge. He too often allowed his pedantry to override his good sense. This failing in his friend, Boswell took off in his comic poem *The Court of Session Garland*:

> "'This cause,' cries Hailes, 'to judge I can't pretend,
> For *justice*, I perceive, wants an *e* at the end.'"

According to Dr. Robert Chambers "a story was told of his once making a serious objection to a law-paper, and in consequence to the whole suit, on account of the word *justice* being thus spelt."[3] Lord Braxfield, one of the ruffian judges, but a man of strong mind, "hearing him praised as a good judge, said, in his vulgar way, 'Him! he knows nothing but the nooks of a cause.' He was not without his crotchets. One day when he sat as President, he reprimanded a lawyer very sharply for making a ludicrous application of some text in the Gospels or Epistles. 'Sir,' said he, 'you may take liberties with the Old Testament, but I will not suffer you to meddle with the New.'"[4]

As an historian he had considerable merits. Johnson revised the proof-sheets of his *Annals of Scotland*, and found them "a new mode of history in our language." "They are very exact," he added, "but they contain mere dry particulars. They are to be considered as a Dictionary. You know such things are there, and may be looked at when you please."[4] Gibbon praised him as "a diligent collector, and an accurate critic;" but he complained that when he came to criticise "the two invidious chapters" in the *Decline and Fall*, "he scrutinized each separate passage with the

---

[1] Boswell's *Johnson*, iii. 212, 216.
[2] *Scotland and Scotsmen, &c.*, i. 398.
[3] *Traditions of Edinburgh*, ed. 1825, ii. 161.
[4] *Scotland and Scotsmen, &c.*, i. 397, 407. Boswell's *Johnson*, ii. 383, iii. 404.

dry minuteness of a special pleader; and as he was always solicitous to make, he may have succeeded sometimes in finding a flaw."[1] Hume spoke of him with contempt. "He is a godly man; feareth the Lord and escheweth evil, and works out his salvation with fear and trembling. None of the books he publishes are of his writing; they are all historical manuscripts, of little or no consequence."[2] "Nothing delighted him more," writes Ramsay of Ochtertyre, "than to demolish some historical fabric which length of time had rendered venerable. I lent an old lady the first volume of his *Annals*. She was so ill pleased with the rejection of some popular stories of Wallace, that she said she would drive the powder out of his lordship's wig if she were by him."[3] With all his critical power he was a believer in Ossian. Burke, who once met him at dinner, "found him a clever man, and generally knowing."[4]

He had been educated at Eton, and there one day had noticed a little black-looking boy, who had come up "*to show for college, i.e.*, to stand for a scholarship on the foundation."

"After being examined he was found entitled to be placed high in the fourth form, if he could make a copy of Latin verses in a given time. As he knew nothing of the matter, his friend bade him throw the theme assigned him over the window in a quill, and he would convey him the verses ere they were wanted. He told the door keeper to carry a pen-case to the lad under examination, who exhibited the theme, and was elected. For some months Dalrymple lent him his aid in versifying. Dr. Hallam, now Dean of Bristol and Canon of Westminster, confessed many years after, with tears in his eyes, that next to the providence of God he owed all that he had to the philanthropy of Sir David Dalrymple.'

If, as seems likely, the examination was competitive, the boy who did not get the scholarship might not have taken altogether the same view of the matter as the pious and tearful dean. Dr. Hallam was the father of the historian, and the grandfather of Arthur Hallam. Had it not been for Lord Hailes's good-natured roguery the *In Memoriam* might never have been written.

New Hailes, as Johnson's host told Ramsay of Ochtertyre, "had been first made by Mr. Smith, a Popish architect employed in fitting up King James's chapel at the Abbey. He planted the oldest trees. It was acquired by Lord Hailes's grandfather, the Lord Advocate, who gave it its present name."[7] We may wonder

---

[1] Gibbon's *Miscellaneous Works*, ed. 1814, i. 232.
[2] Hume's *Letters to Strahan*, p. 74.
[3] *Scotland and Scotsmen*, &c., i. 402.
[4] Burke's *Correspondence*, iii. 301.
[5] A Scotticism for *out of the window*. See *ante*, p. 46.
Scotland and Scotsmen, &c., i. 394.
Scotland and Scotsmen, &c., i. 411.

where poor Mr. Smith sought shelter that day when the news reached Edinburgh that James II. had fled from London. He may well have been in danger, for "the rabble," writes Burnet, "broke into the church of Holyrood House, which had been adorned at a great charge to be a royal chapel, defaced it quite, and seized on some that were thought great delinquents."[1] When Lord Hailes came into the property, "his first care was to fit up the library—a

LIBRARY, NEW HAILES.

magnificent room. The furnishing of it with an ample store of books was the great object of his ambition."[2] The library is now the drawing-room—the most noble and learned drawing-room that I have ever seen, for the great and well-filled book-shelves still go round it from the floor almost to the lofty ceiling. If it was in this room that Johnson was received, no doubt he behaved as he did that April day, a year or two later, when he drove down to

---

[1] Burnet's *History of his own Time*, ed. 1818, ii. 443. [2] *Scotland and Scotsmen, &c.*, i. 409.

dine with Mr. Cambridge at Twickenham. "No sooner," says Boswell, "had we made our bow to Mr. Cambridge in his library than Johnson ran eagerly to one side of the room, intent on poring over the backs of the books." Perhaps he turned to Lord Hailes, as he turned to Dr. Burney, on seeing his library, and said, " You are an honest man to have formed so great an accumulation of knowledge."[1]

The house, like so many in Scotland, is built more after the continental than the English fashion. In the front is a square courtyard, on a level with which are the offices. The hall is reached by a flight of stone steps. As I came up to it a peacock was perched on the top. Above the door is inscribed the motto, *Laude manentem*. Johnson's bedroom was at one end of the house, on the same floor as the hall; but as the ground is higher on this side, it was on a level with the flower-garden, which was just beneath the windows. He had also a dressing-room, whence I looked out on pleasant hayfields, where the haymakers were hard at work. All about the house are fine trees, many of them planted, no doubt, by the old Popish architect; while on one side there is a lofty grove of beeches with a column in the middle, inscribed—

>   " Joanni Comiti de Stair
>   De Patria et Principe optime merito
>   Viventi positum
>   MDCCXLVI."

The Earl of Stair was a Dalrymple. At the Jacobite rebellion in 1745 he had been appointed Field-Marshal and Commander-in-Chief of the Forces in South Britain.[2] Horace Walpole did not think highly of his services at this time for, after describing in the November of that year how "the Prince of Wales, the night of his son's christening, had the citadel of Carlisle in sugar at supper, and the company besieged it with sugar-plums," he continues, " One thing was very proper; old Marshal Stair was there, who is grown child enough to be fit to war only with such artillery."[3] We can picture to ourselves Johnson walking up and down under the beech trees, reading the inscription, and telling how kindly he had been welcomed a few days earlier by the earl's sister, the Countess of Loudoun, an old lady, "who in her ninety fifth year had all her faculties entire. This," adds Boswell, "was a very cheering

---

[1] Boswell's *Johnson*, ii. 364.   [2] Smollett's *History of England*, iii. 169.
[3] Walpole's *Letters*, i. 407.

sight to Dr. Johnson, who had an extraordinary desire for long life."

With such a pleasant spot as this to live at, it is not surprising that Lord Hailes for many years would not take a house in Edinburgh, but resided constantly at New Hailes summer and winter "driving in every morning in session time before breakfast, and returning before dinner." Dr. Alexander Carlyle, who was no bad judge of conviviality, said, "that nowhere did he get more good wine or more good *cracks* than from Lord Hailes."[1] Besides his learning and his hospitality he had, like so many of Johnson's Scotch friends, deserved the praise of being a good landlord. He did not raise his rents.[2] On his death his will could not be found. He had no sons, and the heir-male was about to take possession of his estates to the exclusion of his daughter, Miss Hailes. She had made her preparations for leaving her old home, and had sent some of her servants to lock up his town house in New Street. As one of them was closing the shutters of a window the will dropped out upon the floor from behind a panel. It was found to secure her in the possession of the estates. She enjoyed them for upwards of forty years.[3]

Johnson paid a visit also to Patrick, Lord Elibank, and stayed two nights "at his seat in the country." I at first thought that this was Darnhall, near Peebles, and accordingly visited that most delightful spot. But I have little doubt that it was at Ballencrieff, in the neighbourhood of Haddington, where he stayed.[4] Smollett, when he takes Matthew Bramble through this part of the country, makes him say : "I intended to pay my respects to Lord Elibank, whom I had the honour to know at London many years ago. He lives in this part of Lothian, but was gone to the North on a visit. I have long revered him for his humanity and universal intelligence, over and above the entertainment arising from the originality of his character."[5] He was a Jacobite, and a member of that famous Cocoa Tree Club, which, according to Boswell, "was sacred of old to loyalty." The loyalty, by the way, was rather towards the third James than the second George. Horace Walpole tells how, after

---

[1] *Scotland and Scotsmen*, &c., i. 407
[2] *Ib.*, p. 411.
[3] Chambers's *Traditions of Edinburgh*, ed. 1869, p. 145.
[4] Darnhall is at present Lord Elibank's seat; but in Paterson's *British Itinerary* (ed. 1800, i. 227; ii. 557) it is described as the seat of the Hon. George Murray, while Ballencrieff is mentioned as Lord Elibank's. Murray is the family name of the Elibanks.
[5] *Humphry Clinker*, ii. 219.

Culloden, "the Duke of Cumberland gave Brigadier Mordaunt the Pretender's coach, on condition he rode up to London in it. 'That I will, Sir,' said he, 'and drive till it stops of its own accord at the Cocoa Tree.'"[1] Lord Elibank had been deeper in the cause than was known at the time. According to Sir Walter Scott, the Stuart Papers show that "he carried on a correspondence with the Chevalier after 1745, which was not suspected by his most intimate friends."[2] He probably was made to pay dearly for his attachment to the exiled family. Lord Cromartie, one of the rebel lords, "had been," says Walpole, "receiver of the rents of the king's second son in Scotland, which it was understood he should not account for, and by that means had six hundred pounds a year from the Government. Lord Elibank, a very prating, impertinent Jacobite, was bound for him in nine thousand pounds, for which the duke is determined to sue him."[3] If the money was exacted, the loss must have been severely felt, for Elibank was somewhat parsimonious. "When he heard of John Home's pension, he said, 'It is a very laudable grant, and I rejoice at it; but it is no more in the power of the king to make John Home rich than to make me poor.'"[4] Perhaps when he said this he was thinking how the king had done his best to impoverish him by exacting "the penalty and forfeit of his bond," and had failed.

One day he and Dr. Robertson called on Johnson at Boswell's house, and the talk turned on the Rebellion. Lord Elibank, addressing the historian, said : "Mr. Robertson, the first thing that gave me a high opinion of you was your saying in the Select Society, while parties ran high, soon after the year 1745, that you did not think worse of a man's moral character for his having been in rebellion. This was venturing to utter a liberal sentiment, while both sides had a detestation of each other." Such a sentiment must have been particularly comforting to a man who perhaps was still plotting treason. The Select Society had been founded in 1754 by Allan Ramsay the painter, aided by Robertson, Hume, and Adam Smith. "It rubbed off all corners by collision," says Dr. Carlyle, "and made the *literati* of Edinburgh less captious and pedantic than they were elsewhere."[5] If collision always rubbed off corners, there was enough between Elibank and Hume to have

---

[1] Walpole's *Letters*, ii. 32.
[2] *Quarterly Review*, No. 71, p. 191.
[3] Walpole's *Letters*, ii. 40.
[4] Home's *Work*, i. 54.
[5] Dr. A. Carlyle's *Autobiography*, p. 298, and D. Stewart's *Lfp. of Robertson*, ed. 1802, p. 5.

produced the greatest smoothness and even polish. The historian, in the fifth volume of his *History of England*, speaks of him as "a person that has writ an *Enquiry historical and critical into the evidence against Mary Queen of Scots*." He goes on to accuse him with having "almost directly called him a liar," and charges him in his turn with being guilty of "scandalous artifices." He concludes with that well-known passage, in which he maintains that "there are indeed three events in our history which may be regarded as touchstones of party-men. An English Whig, who asserts the reality of the Popish Plot, an Irish Catholic, who denies the massacre in 1641, and a Scotch Jacobite, who maintains the innocence of Queen Mary, must be considered as men beyond the reach of argument or reason, and must be left to their prejudices."[1] In a letter to Robertson, written some years earlier than this note, Hume says : " I desire my compliments to Lord Elibank. I hope his lordship has forgot his vow of answering us, and of washing Queen Mary white. I am afraid that is impossible ; but his lordship is very well qualified to gild her."[2] Hume, with all his good nature, was not a little touchy, and perhaps took offence where no offence was meant. Lord Elibank had been "the early patron of Robertson and Home, the tragick poet, who when they were ministers of country parishes, lived near his seat. He told me," continues Boswell, "'I saw these lads had talents, and they were much with me.' I hope they will pay a grateful tribute to his memory." According to Dr. Carlyle, they found a far better way of showing their gratitude, for "they cured him of his contempt for the Presbyterian clergy, made him change or soften down many of his original opinions, and prepared him for becoming a most agreeable member of the Literary Society of Edinburgh, among whom he lived during the remainder of his life, admiring and admired."[3] Besides his *Enquiry*, he published several other "small pieces of distinguished merit," according to Boswell. National Debts and the Currency were among the subjects of which he treated.[4] Dr. Carlyle describes him as "rather a humourist than a man of humour; one who defended paradoxes and uncommon opinions with a copiousness and ingenuity that was surprising." This part of his character would have endeared him to Johnson, who liked a tavern because, as he said, "wine there prompts me

---

[1] *History of England*, ed. 1773, v. 504.
[2] Robertson's *Works*, ed. 1802, i. 46.
[3] Dr. A. Carlyle's *Autobiography*, p. 267.
[4] Horace Walpole's *Letters*, ix. 103.

to free conversation, and an interchange of discourse with those whom I most love; I dogmatise and am contradicted, and in this conflict of opinions and sentiments I find delight."[1] Though Johnson was fond of his society, and once said "that he was never in his company without learning something," yet speaking of him on another occasion he said, "Sir, there is nothing conclusive in his talk." Lord Elibank's admiration of Johnson was very high. Yet he need not have gone so far as to flatter him at the expense of his own country. Having missed seeing him on his first visit to Edinburgh, he wrote to Boswell: "I could not persuade myself there was anything in Scotland worthy to have a summer of Samuel Johnson bestowed on it; but since he has done us that compliment, for heaven's sake inform me of your motions. I will attend them most religiously, and though I should regret to let Mr. Johnson go a mile out of his way on my account, old as I am, I shall be glad to go five hundred miles to enjoy a day of his company." Johnson, in his plain truthfulness, on the very day on which Lord Elibank wrote this extravagant letter, said that "he would go two miles out of his way to see Lord Monboddo." As five hundred was to two, so perhaps was Johnson's accuracy of talk to Lord Elibank's. To the mean way in which his lordship spoke of Scotland, as if it were beneath the great Englishman's notice, I much prefer the spirit of his countryman, who, according to Boswell, "would say of Dr. Johnson, 'Damned rascal! to talk as he does of the Scotch!'" However, he had none of that smallness of mind common enough among the high-born, which would not let him enjoy Johnson's strong talk. He was "one of the great who sought his society. He well observed that if a great man procured an interview with him, and did not wish to see him more, it showed a mere idle curiosity, and a wretched want of relish for extraordinary powers of mind." Such an idle curiosity and such a wretched want of relish were shown by George III.

The old house at Ballencrieff, in which Johnson "passed two nights and dined thrice," as Boswell accurately records, is now a melancholy ruin. It was burnt down about twenty years ago. For many years previously, deserted by its owners, it had been left in the care of a woman who lived in an outbuilding, which in the old days had formed the kitchen. It was here, I believe, that

---

[1] When I had the honour of meeting Mr. Gladstone in his visit to Oxford early this year, he quoted this passage in his strong deep voice, and praised it highly.

were prepared those "performances of a nobleman's French cook which so much displeased Johnson, that he exclaimed with vehemence, 'I'd throw such a rascal into the river.'"[1] Though the flames no longer roared up the chimney as they had done for many a long year, still a fire was kept up and soot accumulated. One day the old woman tried to get rid of it by setting it alight, a primitive mode of chimney-sweeping not uncommon in that part of the country. A spark, it is conjectured, was carried into the main building through a broken pane, and falling on some straw brought in by the birds who nested there, set an upper room on fire. The summer had been unusually dry. The flames spread rapidly from one end of the house to the other; so fierce was the blaze that a large beech-tree which stood at some little distance was burnt also. Part of the house is evidently of considerable antiquity, being very solidly built, with vaulted chambers and walls many feet in thickness. In the year 1625, as I judge from an inscription on the wall, great additions were made. It is pleasantly placed, with meadow-land on three sides, and at a little distance from a fine range of hills, which boasts of a Roman camp and of a lofty column to one of Wellington's generals.

BALLENCRIEFF.

So strangely do the ages mingle here. From the upper windows on a clear day a delightful view most have been enjoyed of the Forth, with the little island of Inch Keith and the hills of Fife beyond. Near the house there is a row of yew-trees which could not have looked young in Johnson's time, and holly hedges leading up to it, between which, perhaps, he walked, for they too look old. The land is in the occupation of a market-gardener, who cultivates it with a success which would have won his praise, and made him allow that something beside the sloe is brought to perfection in Scotland. The whole district abounds in fruitful gardens and orchards, and fine plantations of trees. As I looked at the luxuriance of growth, and meditated on the change that had been wrought in a century and a quarter, I thought that to Johnson, who had shown the nakedness of the land, a grateful and penitent people, who had profited by his exhorta-

[1] At Ballencrieff there is no river, but perhaps Johnson was thinking of the Firth of Forth.

tions, should raise a memorial as the god of gardens. According to a tradition which has come down to our time, a group of ash-trees was planted by Lord Elibank on his suggestion.[1] Planting had begun earlier than he thought. "It may be doubted," he said, "whether before the Union any man between Edinburgh and England had ever set a tree." The market-gardener told me that he had counted one hundred and ninety rings on some tall trees near the house, which had been cut down fourteen years before. This would show that they were planted not only before the Union, but also before the Revolution, for though a ring marks the growth of a year, yet in an old tree many of the rings cannot be distinguished.

As I wandered about the ruins, and listened to the jackdaws chattering overhead "with nothing conclusive in their talk," how much I regretted that Boswell's indolence had kept him from recording the conversation which passed here in those three November days between the old Jacobite lord and his famous guest.

Johnson's tour was rapidly drawing to a close. Brundusium is at hand.

"Brundusium longæ finis chartæque viæque."[2]

He wrote from Edinburgh to Mrs. Thrale on Thursday, November 18: "I long to be at home, and have taken a place in the coach for Monday; I hope, therefore, to be in London on Friday, the 26th, in the evening. Please to let Mrs. Williams know." On Saturday he accepted the invitation of Sir John Dalrymple, a cousin of Lord Hailes, and author of *Memoirs of Great Britain and Ireland*, to visit him at his house at Cranston, twelve miles from Edinburgh on the middle road to Newcastle. There he was to be taken up by the London coach. Three years earlier Boswell had described Dalrymple as "a very knowing, lively companion;"[3] but his feelings towards him were changed. He had not worshipped the image which he had set up. Nevertheless, "he was ambitious," Boswell writes, "of having such a guest; but as I was well assured, that at this very time he had joined with some of his prejudiced countrymen in railing at Dr. Johnson, and had said, he

---

[1] This interesting tradition comes to me from my friend General Cadell, C.B., of Cockenzie House, to whom I am indebted for the accompanying sketch of the trees.

[2] "From thence our travels to Brundusium bend,
Where our long journey and my paper end."
FRANCIS'S *Horace*, i. Sat. v. 103.

[3] *Letters of Boswell to Temple*, p. 168.

wondered how any gentleman of Scotland could keep company with him, I thought he did not deserve the honour; yet, as it might be a convenience to Dr. Johnson, I contrived that he should accept the invitation, and engaged to conduct him." The convenience consisted in the fact that, as his house was on the London road, Johnson would not have to rise so early by two hours to catch the coach. Dalrymple had lately made a good deal of stir both in the world of literature and politics by the publication of his *Memoirs*. From these it had been learnt for the first time that Algernon Sidney had been a pensioner of the King of France. Horace Walpole had been roused to anger by the exposure of a man whose memory he revered. " Need I tell you," he wrote to Mason, "that Sir John Dalrymple, the accuser of bribery, was turned out of his place of Solicitor of the Customs for taking bribes from brewers?"[1] Hume was astonished at "the rage against him, on account of the most commendable action in his life," but he despised "his ranting, bouncing style."[2] Johnson had an equal contempt for it, calling it "his foppery." Boswell records in the spring of the year:

> "I mentioned Sir John Dalrymple's *Memoirs of Great Britain and Ireland*, and his discoveries to the prejudice of Lord Russell and Algernon Sidney. JOHNSON. 'Why, Sir, every body who had just notions of government thought them rascals before. It is well that all mankind now see them to be rascals. . . . This Dalrymple seems to be an honest fellow; for he tells equally what makes against both sides. But nothing can be poorer than his mode of writing, it is the mere bouncing of a schoolboy: Great He! but greater She! and such stuff.'"

In describing the last scene between Lord and Lady Russell he had said, "they parted for ever—he great in this last act of his life, but she greater."[3]

His portrait, which I saw in the Loan Exhibition of the Scottish National Portrait Gallery, shows a cold conceited face. Dr. Carlyle gives an unpleasing account of him. After recounting how at a dinner he had once had "to divide a haunch of venison among fifteen without getting any portion of fat for himself," he continues, "But what signifies that, when you have an opportunity of obliging your friends? as Sir J. Dalrymple said to me one day when we had a haunch at the Poker, flattering me for a good piece, for he was a gourmand."[4] How must the indignation of this flattering

---

[1] Walpole's *Letters*, v. 441.   [2] Boswell's *Johnson*, ii. 210.
[3] *Letters of Hume to Strahan*, pp. 174, 265.   [4] Dr. A. Carlyle's *Autobiography*, p. 437.

glutton have been excited at the careless and even rude treatment which he received from our travellers, who had engaged to dine with him on the day they left Edinburgh! They were very late in starting, for Johnson in his good-nature had let himself be detained "by young Mr. Tytler who came to show some essays which he had written." They did not leave till one o'clock, and then Boswell insisted on their going to see Rosslyn Castle and the Chapel. They dined and drank tea at the inn. As if this were not enough, and as if no baronet were waiting dinner, they next went to Hawthornden, and "had *Rare Ben* in mind" who one hundred and forty-three years earlier had there visited the poet Drummond. "It was very late," writes Boswell, "before we reached the seat of Sir John Dalrymple, who, certainly with some reason, was not in very good humour. Our conversation was not brilliant. We supped, and went to bed in ancient rooms, which would have better suited the climate of Italy in summer, than that of Scotland in the month of November." Dalrymple was alive when this account was published. Not finding their quarters to their mind they went on next evening two miles further to the inn at Blackshiels. Pennant, who had passed a night there in September of the previous year, describes "the country as good, full of corn, and decked with numbers of small woods. The inn is good."[1] Just one year and two days before our travellers arrived there, on November 19, 1772, one Mr. John Scott of Newcastle had married, in this same village and most probably in the inn, pretty Miss Elizabeth Surtees. She had escaped by a ladder from her father's house and had run with him across the Border. He was twenty-one and she eighteen. "Jack Scott," said a friend on hearing of it, "has run off with Bessy Surtees, and the poor lad is undone." In the end he became Lord Chancellor and Earl of Eldon. The certificate of marriage shows that the ceremony was performed in the presence of James and Thomas Fairbairn. From a paper in the *Gentleman's Magazine* I know that Fairbairn was the innkeeper's name.

On the morning of Monday, November 22, the coach took up Johnson and off he drove homewards. On the following Saturday he wrote to Boswell from London:—"I came home last night, without any incommodity, danger, or weariness, and am ready to begin a new journey. I shall go to Oxford on Monday." There

---

[1] *Tour in Scotland*, ed. 1776, ii. 259. 260.
[2] Twiss's *Life of Lord Eldon*, ed. 1846, i. 57, and the *Gentleman's Magazine*, 1771, p. 543.

he met Mr. John Scott and his young bride, and perhaps compared notes about Blackshiels and the Newcastle road.[1] To his friend, Dr. Taylor, he wrote that "he had traversed the east coast of Scotland from south to north, from Edinburgh to Inverness, and

HAWTHORNDEN.

the west-coast from north to south, from the Highlands to Glasgow."[2]

"The time he spent in his Tour, was," he often said, "the

[1] Boswell's *Johnson*, ii. 268.
[2] The original letter of which a facsimile is given is in my possession. See Appendix B.

K K

pleasantest part of his life." I too have rarely spent my time more pleasantly than when I was following his traces both in that beautiful country through which he wandered, and in those old books in which still live the people, the manners, and the Scotland which he saw.

APPENDIX A.

(Pages 18 and 117.)

Dr. Johnson's Burgess Ticket of Aberdeen.

BERDONIÆ vigesimo tertio Die mensis Augusti 1773 pnt [in præsentia] magistratuum. Quo Die vir generosus ac Doctrina Clarus Samuel Johnson LL.D. receptus et admissus fuit in municipes et fratres Guildæ præfati Burgi de Aberdeen in devotissimi affectus et amoris ac eximiæ observantiæ tesseram quibus dicti magistratus illum amplecturitur."

APPENDIX B.

(Page 305.)

Dr. Johnson's Letter to Dr. Taylor.

"Dear Sir,

"WHEN I was at Edinburgh I had a letter from you, telling me that in answer to some enquiry you were informed that I was in the Sky. I was then I suppose in the western islands of Scotland; I set out on the northern expedition August 6, and came back to Fleet-street, November 26. I have seen a new region.

"I have been upon seven of the islands, and probably should have visited many more, had we not begun our journey so late in the year, that the stormy weather came upon us, and the storms have I believe for about five months hardly any intermission.

"Your Letter told me that you were better. When you write do not forget to confirm that account. I had very little ill health while I was on the journey, and bore rain and wind tolerably well. I had a cold and deafness only for a few days, and those days I passed at a good house. I have traversed the east coast of Scotland from south to north from Edinburgh to Inverness, and the west coast from north to south, from the Highlands to Glasgow, and am come back as I went.

"Sir,
"Your affectionate humble servant,
"SAM. JOHNSON.

"*Jan. 15, 1774.*

"To the Reverend Dr. Taylor,
 "in Ashbourn,
  "Derbyshire."

Dear Sir

When I was at Edinburgh I had a letter from [Mr Jessop?] telling me that in answer to some enquiry you were informed that I was in the Sky. I was then I suppose in the western Islands of Scotland. I set out on the northern expedition August 6. and came back to Fleet-Street, November 26. I have seen a new region.

I have been upon seven of the Islands, and probably should have visited many more, had we not begun our journey so late in the year, that the stormy weather came upon us, and the storms have I believe for about five months hardly any intermission.

Your father told me that you were better. When you write do not forget to confirm that account.

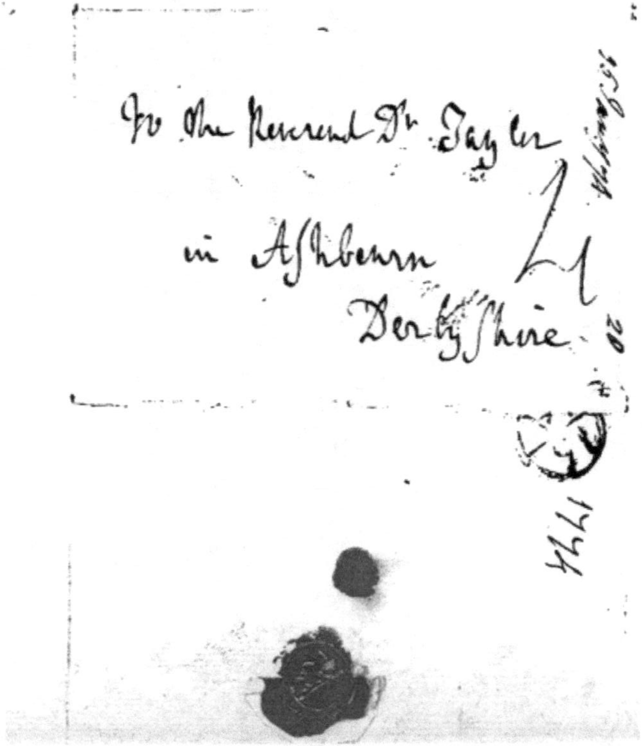

25 Jany 74 20   1774

To the Reverend Mr Taylor
  in Ashburn
    Derbyshire

INDEX.

ABERBROTHICK, 94, 105-7, 190.
Aberdeen, 115-123; freedom of the city, 18, 116; population, 118; King's College, 120; Marischal College, 120, 121; professors, 122.
Academy, 279.
Adams, Rev. Dr. William, 66.
Addison, Joseph, 5, 62.
Airdsmoss, 289.
Allan of Muidart, 173.
Amuse, 245.
Anderson, Rev. John, 97.
Anoch, 153.
Arbroath. *See* ABERBROTHICK.
Arbuthnot, Dr., 89.
Ardnamurchan, 5, 214.
Ardvoirlich, 254.
Argyle, Archibald, second Earl of, 141.
Argyle, Archibald, ninth Earl of, 217, 249.
Argyle, Archibald, Marquis of, 250.
Argyle, Elizabeth Gunning, Duchess of, 247, 249-252, 256.
Argyle, Jane, Countess of, 250.
Argyle, John, second Duke of, 251.
Argyle, John, fifth Duke of, 227, 246-253.
Armidale, 23, 167, 214.
Auchans, 268.
Auchinleck, Lord, 18, 56, 62, 74, 79, 80, 115, 146, 189, 234, 271-286, 292.
Auchinleck, 271-290; house, 273-5; old castle, 287; *via sacra*, manse, church, 288; village, 289; pronounced Affleck, 290.

Auchnacraig, 242.
Auchnasheal, 144, 161.
Authors, 60-3, 66.

Bagpipes, 243.
Ballencrieff, 297.
Balliol College, 84.
Banff, 129.
Banks, Sir Joseph, 24.
Bare feet, 289.
Baronial turrets, 113.
Bathing, 112.
Bayle, Peter, 19.
Beaton, Cardinal, 94, 97.
Beattie, Rev. Dr. James, 13, 14, 28, 62, 123.
Beauclerk, Topham, 66.
Bedford, Duke of, 29.
Beggars, 43.
Bellhaven, Lord, 39, 79.
Bentham, Jeremiah, 71.
Berkeley, Bishop, 92.
Berkeley, G. M., 92, 100, 117.
Bernera, 165.
Black, Adam, 77.
Black, Mr. Angus, 241.
Black Spring of 1771, 187.
Blacklock, Dr. Thomas, 75.
Blackshields, 304.
Blair, Rev. Dr. Hugh, 10, 14, 63, 65, 74, 81, 122, 278.
Boats, 171.
Boswell, Alexander (the author's father). *See* LORD AUCHINLECK.
Boswell, Sir Alexander (the author's eldest son), 283.

Boswell, David (the author's brother), 282, 284.
Boswell, James (author of *The Life of Johnson*), activity, 105, 178; ancestry, 272; autograph, 287; *Court of Session Garland*, 293; descendants, 283-7; described by Miss Burney, 276; and by himself, 277; drunk, 4, 168, 213; facility of manners, 272; family pride, 282; fear of ghosts, 205; feudal enthusiasm, 284; funeral, 288; good landlord, 290; indifference to scenery, 86, 275; interested in the Douglas cause, 56, 247, 272; *Life of Johnson*, 285-6; love of London, 149; manuscripts, 285; mentioned by Burns, 267; no memorial of him, 77; praises savage life, 261; pronunciation, 63; *Tour to Corsica*, 280, 285; will, 284, 290.
Boswell, James (the author's grandfather), 272.
Boswell, James (the author's second son), 284.
Boswell, Sir James (the author's grandson), 284.
Boswell, Thomas Alexander, 284.
Boswell, Veronica (the author's eldest daughter), 75.
Boswell, Mrs. (Lord Auchinleck's second wife), 271.
Boswell, Mrs. (the author's wife), 55, 75, 220, 267.
Boswell family, 286.
Bothwell, Earl of, 69.
Boyd, Hon. Charles, 128.
Boyd, James, 69.
Braxfield, Lord, 293.
Breadalbane, Lord, 34.
Breakfasts, 20.
Brentford, 263.
Brett, John, R.A., 207.
Brighton, 123, 199.
Broadford, 3, 167, 169-171.
Bruar Water, 24, 33.
Bruce, King Robert, 258.
Buccleugh, fifth Duke of, 77.
Buchanan, George, 37, 91, 200.
Bullers of Buchan, 128.
Burgynski, Count, 279.
Burke, Edmund, 66, 76, 263, 277, 286, 294.

Burlassig, 150.
Burnet, Bishop, 295.
Burney, Dr., 296.
Burney, Miss, 276.
Burns, Robert, *Bruar Water*, 24, 33; Ayrshire scenery, 31; Scotch militia, 64; Holyrood House, 85; Miss Burnet, 112; Inverary, 246; *Earnest Cry and Prayer*, 267; "Lugar's winding stream," 280; monument, 283; his genius hidden by his dialect, 286.
Bury, Lord, 145.
Bute, Earl of, 37.
Byron, Lord, 25.

Cadell, General, C.B., 302, *n.* 1.
Cambridge, R. O., 296.
Camden, William, 27, 97, 264, 268.
Cameron, 260.
Cameron of Lochiel, 144, 282.
Cameron, Mrs., of Talisker, 210.
Cameronians, 289.
Campbell, Rev. Dr. Archibald, 90, *n.* 2.
Campbell, Sir Hugh, 142.
Campbell, Dr. John, 14.
Campbell of Inverliver, 141.
Campbell of Treeshank, 267.
Campbell, ——, 4, *n.* 2.
Candles, 4.
Canning, George, 117.
Carlisle, fifth Earl of, 26.
Carberry Hill, 69.
Carlyle, Rev. Dr. Alexander, 43, 65, 69, 265, 297-9, 303.
Carlyle, Jane Welsh, 96, 118.
Carlyle, Thomas, 39, 52, 68, 79, 86, 88, 89, 202, 291.
Caroline, Queen, 48.
Cathedrals, 133.
Caves, 205-6, 226.
Cawdor, 135-142.
Cawdor, Earl of, 141.
Chamberlain, 251.
Chambers, Sir Robert, 68.
Chambers, Dr. Robert, 97, 236, 269, 293.
Chambers, William, 77.
Change-house, 219.
Chapels, 118.
Charles I., 278, 280.

INDEX.

Charles II., 250.
Charles Edward, Prince, the Young Pretender, 53, 64, 119-20, 129, 182-84, 206, 269.
Charlotte, Queen, 77.
Chatham, Earl of, 64, 171, 231.
Chesterfield, Earl of, 15, n. 3, 274, n. 1.
Chrystal, Rev. Dr. James, 288, 290.
Churches, 43, 81, 108, 176.
Civility, 19.
Clan feeling, 259.
Clarke, Rev. Dr. Samuel, 19
Climate, 20, 30.
Clow, Professor, 263.
Coaches, 264.
Coal, 262.
Cockburn, Lord, 58, 59, 80, 81.
Cockburn, Sheriff, 56.
Cocker's Arithmetic, 154.
Cocoa Tree Club, 297.
Col, Isle of, 24, 214-6, 236.
Col, Macleane of. *See* MACLEANE.
Coleridge, S. T., 162.
Colliers, 69, 236, 259.
Colman, George, 117.
Colquhoun, Sir James, 257.
Colvay, 217.
Commissary Court, 261.
Coote, Sir Eyre, 142.
Copyright, 61.
Corrichatachin, 4, 21, 167-70, 212.
Corsica, 201, 204, 280.
Court of Session, 78.
Court of Session Garland, 293.
Covenanted magistrates, 275.
Coventry, Countess of, 248, 250.
Cox, G. V., 117.
Craig, James, 57.
Craigie, Lord President, 58
Craignure, 4, 233.
Cranston, 302.
Cromartie, Earl of, 298.
Cromwell, Oliver, 35, 68, 145, 250, 278.
Crosbie, Andrew, 64.
Cuchullin Hills, 204.
Culloden, 60, 127, 142, 146, 152, 155, 298.
Cumberland, Richard, 190.
Cumberland, William, Duke of, 27, 102, 118, 123, 129, 142-6, 152, 155, 171, 298.

Cunninghame, 268.
Cupar, 88.

Dalrymple, Sir David. *See* LORD HAILES
Dalrymple, Sir John, 63, 302-4.
Dancing, 178.
Darnhall, 297.
Davies, Thomas, 280.
Defoe, Daniel, 34, 36, 51, 99, 107, 131, 135, 264.
Dempster, 235.
Dempster, George, 8.
Dinner hour, 65.
Discounts, 98.
Doge of Genoa, 23.
Dominies, 278.
Douglas, Duchess of, 63.
Douglas, Elizabeth, 113.
Douglas Cause, 56, 247, 272.
Drinking, 91.
Drumclog Moor, 290.
Drummond of Hawthornden, 304.
Drummond, George, of Blair, 35, 44 n. 3.
Drummore, Lord, 58.
Dryden, John, 109.
Dun, Rev. John, 288.
Dun Buy, 129, 238.
Dun Can, 2, 177.
Dunbar, 68.
Dunbarton, 262.
Dundas, Henry. *See* VISCOUNT MELVILLE.
Dundee, 12, 105.
Dundee, Marquis of, 109.
Dundonald Castle, 267, 270.
Dungeons and pits, 198, 234-9.
Dunolly Castle, 244.
Dunvegan, 1-3, 19, 184-204, 235.
Durham, 87.
Durham on the Galatians, 281.
Dutch Scotch Regiments, 209.

Edinburgh, Advocates' Library, 80; Bridge, 58; Cadies, 54; Castle, 85; Chessel's Buildings, 72; College Wynd, 82; Cowgate, 82; Cross, 53, 81; English residents, 37; Grass Market, 53; Guard House, 78; hackney coaches, 65; High Street, 51-4; Holyrood House, 77, 85, 295; hotbed of genius, 9; houses, 45;

312   INDEX.

inns and taverns, 45, 49-51; 69-72;
James's Court, 57, 67, 72-7; Laigh
Parliament House, 80; Luckenbooths,
52, 78; Mound, 58; New Town, 57,
59; Parliament-House, 78; Pleasance,
50; poor, 42; Post-House Stairs,
82; printing-houses, 61; robberies,
54; Royal Infirmary, 84; scavengers,
46; "Scotch scene," 60; Sedans, 65;
Select Society, 48, 298; St. David's
Street, 57; St. Giles, 81; St. John's
Street, 113; Stage-coaches, 60, 123 n.
4, 264; Sunday, 53; suppers, 65;
Tolbooth, 53, 78; University, 58, 83;
Weigh House, 78; White Horse Inn,
68-72; workhouse, 43, 85.
Edwards, Oliver, 196.
Eglinton, Earl of, 35.
Eglington, Dowager Countess of, 268-70.
Eilan Donan Castle, 158.
Eldon, Earl of, 304.
Eldon, Countess of, 190, 304.
Elgin, 36, 130-4.
Elibank, Patrick, Lord, 42, 65, 74, 75,
85, 297-302.
Ellon, 124.
Emigration, 162, 176.
Epictetus, 214.
Errol, Earl of, 49, 124-27.
Erse, 135, 147, 218, 266.
Erskine, Hon. Andrew, 277.
Erskine, Hon. Henry, 78.
Erskine, John, 55 n. 1.
Eton, 294.
Executions, 53.

Fairbairn, James, 304.
Faorhag, 160.
Farming, 32, 34.
Farms, small, 112.
Fergusson, Dr. Adam, 9, 63, 65.
Ferneley, 206.
Fielding, Sir John, 54.
Findlater, Lord, 130.
Firth of Tay, 104.
Fleet Street, 275, 286.
Foote, Samuel, 111.
Forbes, Sir William, 76.
Fore-stairs, 92.

Fores, 134.
Forrest, Henry, 93.
Fort Augustus, 143, 148, 152, 162.
Fort George, 142.
Foster-children, 4.
Foyers, 130, 150-51.
Franklin, Benjamin, 74, 77.
Frederick, Prince of Wales, 296.
Freedom of towns, 117.
Froude, Mr. J. A., 217, 290.
Funeral bill, 131.
Funerals, 227, 241.
Furca et fossa, 235.

Gaelic. *See* Erse.
Garden, Francis (Lord Gardenstone), 109.
Gardens, 32, 35, 42, 105, 169, 175-76,
  190, 210, 240, 301.
Gardenstone Arms, 109.
Garnett, Dr. T., 150, 161, 229, 232, 242.
Garrick, David, 76.
Geddes, Jenny, 81.
General's Hut, 150.
George I., 69.
George II., 48, 101, 127, 144.
George III., 115, 120, 127, 300.
George IV., 77, 283.
Giant's Causeway, 211.
Gibbon, Edward, 67, 230, 293.
Gladstone, Right Hon. W. E., 81, n. 1,
  300, n. 1.
Glamis Castle, 173.
Glasgow, 94, 117, 123, 198, 262-66.
Glen, 157.
Glen Clunie, 156-57.
Glen Croe, 5, 13, 253-55.
Glen Elg, 10, 20, 163-67.
Glen Morison, 2, 19, 153.
Glen Shiel, 156-60.
Goat Island, 174.
Goldsmith, Oliver, 3, 32, 33, 49, 244,
  285-87.
Golf, 9, n. 1, 98.
Graham, Marquis of, 172.
Graham, Peter, R.A., 207.
Grant, Colonel, 136.
Grant, Rev. Mr., 136, 137.
Grants of Glenmorison, 155.
Gray, Thomas, 26, 28, 33, 45 n. 6, 47, 123,
  143, 173.

INDEX.

Green, Matthew, 103.
Gunning, Elizabeth. See ARGYLE, DUCHESS OF.
Gustavus Adolphus, 113.

Hackney-coaches, 65.
Haddington, 43, 68.
Hailes, Lord (Sir David Dalrymple), 8, 14, 80, 132, 292-97.
Hailes, Miss, 297.
Hallam, Arthur, 294.
Hallam, Dean, 294.
Hamilton, 290.
Hamilton, Duke of, 248.
Hamilton, Lady Betty, 251.
Hamilton, Patrick, 93.
Hamilton of Bangour, 269.
Hawthornden, 304.
Hebridean sailors, 21.
Hedges, 16, 109.
Henderson, Andrew, 144, 155, 171.
Hereditary Jurisdictions, 192, 228, 234-38.
Heronry, 200.
Hesiod, 95.
Highlands and Hebrides, air, 25; books, 168; chiefs, 228; dress, 171-73, 181-82, 203, 255; fidelity of Highlanders, 183; like Indians, 154, 161; "banditti," 165; unknown, 24.
Hill, Mr. Frederick, 265.
Hill, Sir Rowland, 170.
Holland, 272, 274.
Home, John, 10, 39, 63, 298-99.
Honest man, 169.
Hottentots, 15, *n.* 3, 288.
Houses, 15, 21, 32, 42, 45, 170, 177, 220, 229, 240, 296.
Hudibras, 138.
HUME, DAVID, ill-will to England, 7; benefits of the Union, 39; houses, 57, 66, 74-77; in the mire, 59; journey to London, 59; accent, 62, 67; copy-money, 63; Poker Club, 64; cookery, 66; "infidel writer," 66; conversation, 67; father's house, 68; no statue, 77; Advocates' Librarian, 80; dread of the sea, 87; Reynolds's picture, 123; Clow preferred to him, 263; Lord Hailes, 294; Select Society, 298; Mary, Queen of Scots, 299; Dalrymple's *Memoirs*, 303.
Humphry Clinker, 38.

Iceland, 23.
Inch Galbraith, 257.
Inch Keith, 85.
Inch Kenneth, 6, 218, 221-25.
Innes, Rev. Dr, 96, *n.* 2.
Inns, 49, 63, 89, 151, 165, 180, 219, 229, 245-46, 262, 304.
Inverary, 232, 245-53, 257.
Invermoriston, 152.
Inverness, 137, 142-48.
Iona, 214, 226-31.
Ireland, 64.
Irish people, 14.
Irvine, Robert, 115.
Irving, Edward, 86, 88, 291.
Irving, Mr Henry, 140.
Isa, 174, 199.
Isle of Muck, 199.

James IV., 120.
James V., 180.
James VI., 135.
James II. of England, 182, 250, 295.
Jardine, Rev. Dr, 65.
Jeffrey, Francis (Lord Jeffrey), 33, 62 *n*. 9, 256.
Johns of Scotland, The Four, 158.
Johnson Club, 160, 173.
Johnson, Michael, 23.
JOHNSON, SAMUEL, affection for Boswell, 272; altercation with Lord Auchinleck, 278-281; behaviour at Dunvegan, 188; broad-sword, 24; never complained, 20; complimented on his return, 22; cups of tea, 189, 204; dangers of his voyage, 21; delicate in his language, 196; *Dictionary*, 168; dominie, 278; dread of the Highlanders, 154, 161; dukes and lords, 270; Erse New Testament, 266; feared by professors, 122, 263; fresh air, 47; fretful, 164; harassed by invitations, 292; hatred of exaggeration, 22; hogshead of sense, 232; imitates the kangaroo, 137; "Island Isa," 174; laced clothes, 260; in a library, 295; love of life, 297; journey to

Edinburgh and return, 59, 304; *Journey to the Hebrides*, 17, 156, 259; lemonade, 71, 107; levee, 75; meals, 10; objects of his tour, 24; *Odes*, 1, 168; peats, 3; politeness, 257; projected monument, 288; retirement, 95; roving among the Hebrides, 23, 227; sacrilege, 132; Sassenach mohr, 1; scenery, 24-29, 86, 120, 245; Scotch feeling towards him, 7-16, 259, 300; his feeling towards them, 7, 16; sleep, 152; spurs, 173; tavern-life, 299; traditions of him, 1-7, 156, 164, 189, 191, 204, 296, 302; *Ursa Major*, 79; walking-stick, 2, 34, 173, 176, 220; wig, 3, 197; writing doggedly, 81; young English buck, 182.

Johnston, 2, 5, 12, 195, 234.
Jonson, Ben, 304.
Jopp, Provost, 116.
Jougs, 138.
Judges, on circuit, 115; their brutality, 293.

Kames, Lord (Henry Home), 34, 41, 43, 62, 66, 80, 274.
Kangaroos, 137.
Keith, —, 66.
Kerr, Lord Mark, 123.
Kerrera, 242.
Kilarow, 235.
Kilmarnock, 271.
Kilmarnock, Earl of, 126.
Kincardine, Countess of, 272.
Kinghorn, 86-7.
Kinnoul, Earl of, 228.
Kirkcaldy, 87-8.
Knives and forks, 43, 252.
Knox, John (the reformer), 16, 81, 94, 95-6.
Knox, John, the traveller, 9, 45, 148, 161, 165, 187, 189, 204, 209, 243, 263.

Lady, title of, 189.
Land, 74, *n*. 2.
Lauderdale, Earl of, 49.
Laurencekirk, 109.
Leach, —, 25.

Leechman, Principal, 266.
Leuchars, 103.
Leven, Earl of, 49.
Lewis, Island of, 182-3.
Libraries, 84, 100.
Lichfield, 91, 133, 220.
Linlithgow, 171.
Lismore, 11.
Loch Awe, 141, 245.
Loch Bracadale, 204, 206.
Loch Buie, 5, 233-242.
Loch Duich, 2, 163.
Loch Follart, 185.
Loch Fyne, 247, 254.
Loch Grishinish, 184.
Loch Harport, 211.
Loch Hourn, 144.
Lochiern, 21.
Loch Lomond, 6, 25, 30, 253, 255-61.
Loch Na Keal, 218.
Loch Ness, 27, 30, 149-52.
Loch Snizort, 181, 184.
Loch Uisk, 233.
Lochbuy, Laird of (John Macleane), 5, 233-42.
Lochbuy, Lady, 6, 189, 234.
Lochbuy, Macleane of, (the present Laird), 237, 240, 242.
Lodore, 151.
Loudoun, Countess of, 296.
Loudoun, Earl of, 270.
Lovat, Lord, 141.
Lugar, 280, 287.
Luss, 255, 258.
Lyttelton, Lord, 15 *n*. 3.

Macaulay, Lord, 11, 135, 137, 253, 285-87.
Macaulay, Rev. John, 11, 253.
Macaulay, Rev. Kenneth, 135-59.
Macaulay, Zachary, 253.
Macbeth, 147.
Macdonald, Sir Alexander, 6, 22, 167.
Macdonald, Flora, 19, 181-83.
Macdonald, Sir James, 180.
Macdonald of Kingsburgh, 182, 184.
Mackenzie, Henry, 63.
Mackenzie, Mrs. 145.
Mackenzies, clan of, 158.
Mackinnon, Lachlan, 170.

Mackinnon, Mrs., 168.
Mackinnon's Cave, 226.
Mackintosh, Sir James, 226.
Mackintoshes, clan of, 155.
Macleane, Sir Allan, 6, 218, 221-30 234.
Macleane of Col, 4, 21, 35, 211, 220, 226, 234.
Macleane of Drumnen, 25.
Macleane, Dr., 218.
Macleane of Lochbuy. *See* Lochbuy.
Macleane, Miss, 218.
Macleod of Macleod, Miss, 2, 191, 284.
Macleod, Lady, 189-90, 194.
Macleod, Laird of, 2, 29, 177 186-9, 209.
Macleod, the old Laird of, 187, 192.
Macleod, Major Alexander, 189.
Macleod, Colonel, 187, 207-9
Macleod, John, of Raasay, 19, 171, 174-79.
Macleod, Malcolm, 171-73, 179.
Macleod, Mrs., of Ulinish, 204.
Macleod, Rev. Neal, 231.
Macleod, Sir Roderick, 193
Macleod's Maidens, 194, 207.
Macleod's Tables, 197.
Macpherson, James, 10, 11, 63.
Macquarrie of Ulva, 220.
Macqueen, Rev Donald, 4, 18, 171, 177, 179.
Macsweyn, 3 *n.* 1, 35.
Magus Moor, 88.
Maine, Sir Henry, 177.
Mallet, David, 62.
Mam Rattachan, 2, 164, 241.
Man not naturally good, 189.
Mansfield, Earl of, 20, 124.
Martin, M., 23, 173, 175, 179, 198, 200, 206, 216.
Mary, Queen of Scots, 69, 106, 250, 299.
Mason, Rev. William, 28, 151.
Matheson, Rev. Alexander, 145 *n.* 1, 156, 162.
Matthews, Charles, 284.
McCraas, 144, 161.
Meals, 20, 41, 43-5, 165.
Medical men, 232.
Melville, Viscount, (Henry Dundas), 77, 80.
Merk, Scotch, 121.
Mile stones, 253.

Militia, 64.
Millar, Andrew, 14.
Milne, Walter, 93.
Ministers, 19.
M'Nicol, Rev. Donald, 11, 135 *n.* 1.
Moidart, 14.
Monboddo, Lord (James Burnet), 15, 18, 80, 110-15, 276, 300.
Monboddo House, 113.
Montgomery, Lord Chief Baron, 58.
Montrose, 104, 107.
Moray, Bishop of, 120.
Mordaunt, Brigadier, 298.
More, Hannah, 111.
Moy, 233.
Mull, 6, 218-20, 227, 231-42
Murdoch, William, 289.
Murray, Dr. James A. H., 118
Murison, Rev. Dr., 100.
Muthill, 119.

Nairn, 134.
Nairne, Colonel, 101.
Nairne, Lord, 101.
Nairne, William (Lord Dunsinan), 85.
Napkins, 252.
Neal, 45, 108, 291.
New Hailes, 2, 291-7.
Newcastle, first Duke of, 274.
Newcastle Fly, 59.
Nivernois, Duke de, 66.
Nonjurors, 119.
Northcote, James, 123.
Northumberland, 109.

Oats, 42, 242, 257.
Oban, 242-44.
Ochiltree, 288.
Ogden, Rev. Dr. Samuel, 75.
Oglethorpe, General, 49, *n.* 2.
Old Mortality, 289.
Omai, 112.
Ormond, Duke of, 158.
Ossian, 18, 20, 294.
Ostig, 213.
Otaheite, 261.
Oxford, 98, 100, 117. 266, 304.

Paoli, Pascal, 74, 278-80, 287.
Patriarchal life, 177.

Patronage, 90.
Paufer, Thomas, 130.
Paul, Sir G. O., 221.
Peasants, 33, 34, 40-43, 112.
Pembroke College, Oxford, 97.
Penance rings, 137.
Pennant, Thomas, 24, 28, 34, 82, 91, 98, 109, 117, 137, 149, 165, 195, 211, 229, 235, 246-47, 249, 253, 264, 304.
Percy, Dr. Thomas (Bishop of Dromore), 22.
Perth, 117, 172.
Philibeg, 171.
Pictish Forts, 167.
Pinkie, 69.
Pitcairne, Dr. Archibald, 109.
Pitfour, Lord, 146.
Pitt, William. *See* EARL OF CHATHAM.
Pius IX., 106.
Plaids, 147, 171.
Plane trees, 101, *n.* 2.
Plutarch, 111.
Poker Club, 64, 303.
Poland, 279.
Porteous Riots, 78.
Porter, Lucy, 220.
Portraits, 192.
Portree, 180, 184.
Post chaises, 68, 87, 148.
Posts, 123, 145, 170, 262, 292.
Potatoes, 35.
Presbyterians, 274.
Preston Pans, 69.
Prince Charlie's Caves, 206.
Pringle, Sir John, 74, 274, 281.
Prisons, 54, 146. *See* DUNGEON.
Pulteney, William (Earl of Bath), 232.

Querns, 211.
Quin, James, 280.

Raasay, 2, 19, 142, 171-79.
Raeburn, Sir Henry, 192.
Ramsay, Allan, 77, 267, 269, 298.
Ramsay, John, of Ochtertyre, 45, 56, 174, 189, 241, 272, 278, 294.
Ranelagh Gardens, 49.
Rattachan. *See* MAM RATTACHAN.
Ray, James, 129, 149.

Rebellion of 1745-46, 101, 119, 123, 127, 129, 134, 142-46, 149-52, 154-55, 171, 179, 181, 264-65, 296, 298.
Reformation, The, 16.
Reid, Rev. Dr. Thomas, 63, 120, 263.
Reynolds, Sir Joshua, 17, 123, 127, 249, 277, 283.
Ritter, Joseph, 86.
Rizzio, David, 85.
Roads, 87, 147-48, 184, 224, 245, 260.
Robert II., 267.
Robertson, Rev. Dr. William, 14, 22, 48, 63, 66, 77, 81-5, 123, 223, 298-99.
Robinson, " Peter," 79.
Rochester, Earl of, 91.
Rogers, Samuel, 59.
Roger, Professor Thorold, 237.
Rollo, Lord, 119.
Room-setters, 71, *n.* 4.
Rorie More, 186, 190, 193-96.
Rosedew, 257.
Rosslyn Chapel, 304.
Rosslyn, first Earl of, 287.
Rousseau, 5, 77, 111, 287.
Rowlandson, Thomas, 281.
Royal Charlotte, 192.
Ruddiman, Thomas, 80, 109.
Rum, Isle of, 213.
Ruskin, John, 57.
Russell, Lord William, 303.

Sacheverell, William, 162, 216, 219, 229.
Sacrament-Sunday, 201.
Saint-Fond, Faujas de, 29, 51, 84, 90, 92, 96-7, 243, 252-56.
Salters, 69, 236.
Saluting, 182.
Sandiland, 224.
Scalpa, 173.
Scarsdale, Lord, 168.
Scenery, 24-34, 87, 218.
Schools, 259.
Sconser, 211.
SCOTCH, boastful, 14 ; clannish, 14 ; combination, 14, 39 ; decencies of life neglected, 41-8 ; English abuse, 38 ; English ignorance of them, 24, 36 ; English imitated, 7, 60-3 ; historical nation, 63 ; hospitality, 65 ; ill-fed, 41 ; learning,

INDEX.   317

60, 290; neglect of the beautiful, 32;
outcry against Johnson, 8-15; road
to England, 38; sensitive to criticism,
7; vigour of character, 32, 38, 40
Scots Hunters, 49.
Scots Magazine, 7.
SCOTT, SIR WALTER, Lord Auchinleck,
274, 278; Sir A. Boswell, 283-84; Buchanan a favourite author, 91; colliers
and salters, 259; cruise in 1814, 124;
Duke of Cumberland, 142; death of
Col, 220; dominies, 279; a Dunvegan,
188, 191, 193, 195; Lord Elibank, 298;
Highland accommodation, 8; Highland
dress, 172; house in the College Wynd,
48, 78; Inch Kenneth, 221; inns, 151;
Iona, 229; Johnson and Adam Smith,
263; Johnson's *Ode*, 168; last quotation from Johnson, 83; *Johnston*, 234;
Lord Monboddo, 112, 114; *Old Mortality*, 291; *Peveril of the Peak*, 79;
his popularity, 286; Scotch learning,
61; Archbishop Sharpe, 88; at St.
Andrews, 96; in Skye, 1; Lord Stowell,
71; at Tobermory, 217; trees, 34;
Wizard of the North, 38.
Scott, William (Lord Stowell), 68, 71.
Seaforth, Lord, 161.
Sharpe, Archbishop, 88, 97.
Sheep-shearing, 163.
Shenstone, William, 72, 214
Sidney, Algernon, 303.
Sikes, Sir Charles, 285.
Silver fork, 252.
Singing, 173.
Singing-birds, 163.
Skinner, Rev. John, 119.
Skye, the verge of European life, 170; one
magistrate, 177.
Slains Castle, 124-29
Slaves, 292.
Sligachan, 211.
Smallest of Dumbarton, 217
SMITH, ADAM, praises Boswell, 272; conversation, 278; farming, 35; Kirkaldy,
66, 87-8; old town of Edinburgh, 59;
peasantry, 41; professor at Glasgow,
263; reported quarrel with Johnson,
263; room in Hume's house, 67, 74;
Select Society, 298; no statue to him,

77; tax on coal, 263; the Union, 39;
Wealth of Nations, 63.
Smith, ——, an architect 294.
Smoking, 92.
Smollet, Commissary, 260.
SMOLLETT, TOBIAS, ancestor, 217; beggars, 43; churches, 82; Edinburgh
High Street, 52; Lord Elibank, 297;
funerals, 227; Glasgow, 264; Hamilton,
291; Highland dress, 172; and meals,
44; *Humphry Clinker*, 37; inns, 50;
living, 41, 46; his pillar, 261; rebel
prisoners, 155; St. Andrews, 91; *Tears
of Scotland*, 142; turnips, 36; Union,
39.
Snuff, 161.
Society for Propagating Christian Knowledge, 266.
Soldiers, 154, 165.
Somerset, Duke of, 69.
South, Rev. Dr. Robert, 16 n. 6.
Southey, Robert, 105 n. 1.
Spanish Invasion, 158, 217.
Speke, Captain, 136.
Spey, 130.
Spouse, 107.
ST. ANDREWS, 16, 17, 88-103; Castle,
92; Cathedral, 94, 102; Cloisters, 95;
Glass's Inn, 89; nonjuring parson, 119;
professors' dinner, 97; St. Leonard's
College, 89; St. Mary's College, 100;
St. Salvator's College, 99; St Rule,
96; streets, 91; trees, 97; University,
98-9, 102.
St. Kilda, 198.
Stablers, 51, 69.
Staffa, 24, 226.
Stairs, Earl of, 296.
State of nature, 260.
Steamboats, 256.
Stewart, Lady Henrietta, 142.
Stockdale, Rev. Percival, 98.
Stone, Jerome, 101.
Strahan, George, 186.
Strahan, William, 14, 55.
Streatham, 176, 276.
Strolimus, 212.
Struan, 205.
Stuart, James, of Duncarn, 284.
Stuckgown, 256.

Sugar-tongs, 6.
Supper-parties, 65.
Swift, Jonathan, 82, 189, 191.

Tait, John, 264.
Talisker, 206-11.
Tarbet, 253, 255-57.
Tay Bridge, 240.
Taylor, Rev. Dr. 305.
Temple, Sir William, 61, 272.
Temple, Rev. W. J., 267.
Tennyson, Lord, 249, 294.
Thomson, James, 57, 63.
Thrale, Mrs., 1, 23, 168, 199, 292.
Thrale, Miss, 156, 224.
Tobermory, 216-18.
Toland, John, 175.
Toll-gates, 87.
Topham, Edward, 9, 42, 47, 50, 182, 261.
Towns, their oddness, 51.
Tranent, 69.
Transportation, 116.
Trapaud, Governor, 161.
Trees, 16, 32-4, 149, 190, 227, 232, 249, 275, 288, 296, 302.
Trevelyan, Sir George, 135, 253.
Turk's Head Coffee-house, 23, 292.
Turnips, 35.
Tytler, A. F., 277, 304.

Ulinish, 204.
Ulva, 4, 218-221.
Union, 15, 39, 236.
Universities, 83, 99, 120-22, 265.
Up streets, 53, *n.* 3.
Utensils, 176.

Vails, 48.
Vegetables, 35, 44.
Venice, 16.
Vested interests, 237.
Village communities, 177.
Vitrified forts, 148.
Voltaire, 22, 123, 280.

Wade, General, 147, 150.

Waggons, 87.
Wales, 85.
Walker, Rev. George, 289.
Wallace, Rev. Robert, D.D., 9.
Wallace, Sir William, 294.
Waller, Edmund, 121.
Walpole, Horace, 37, 64, 127, 132, 215, 248, 250, 296-97, 303.
Walpole, Sir Robert, 231.
Walton, Isaac, 102.
Washing, 137.
Washington, George, 188.
Watson, Professor Robert, 63, 89.
Watts, Mr., the painter, 229.
Wellington, Duke of, 301.
WESLEY, JOHN, Aberbrothick, 105; Aberdeen, 119; arrested, 56; Edinburgh dirt, 47; freeman of Perth, 117; funerals, 241; Glasgow, 264-65; Holy Rood House, 85; inns, 49; Inverness, 145, 149, 163; Johnson's *Tour*, 17; meals, 44; mountain scenery, 28; Nairn, 135; preaching to the Scotch, 40; reforming mobs, 94; Spey, 130; St. Andrews, 89, 99; towns, 51.
Wheaten bread, 44, 161, 257.
Whigs, 282.
Whisky, 245.
White Horse, 69.
Whitefield, Rev. George, 76.
Wia, 205.
Wilkes, John, 66.
William III., 274.
Wilkie, William, D.D., 10.
Wilson, John, 77.
Windows, 47.
Wishart, George, 93.
Witches, 90.
Wolfe, Major-General James, 25, 41, 47, 142-43, 145, 154, 171, 254.
Worcestershire Volunteers, 265.
Wordsworth, William, 28, 32, 135, 254.
Writers to the Signet, 222.

Yew Tree Island, 258.

Zoffany, John, 188, 195.

CHISWICK PRESS:—C. WHITTINGHAM AND CO.
TOOKS COURT, CHANCERY LANE.

www.ingramcontent.com/pod-product-compliance
Lightning Source LLC
Chambersburg PA
CBHW032031220426
43664CB00006B/440